The Life of
WILHELM CONRAD
RÖNTGEN

The Life of

by W. Robert Nitske

WILHELM CONRAD
RÖNTGEN
Discoverer of the X Ray

THE UNIVERSITY OF ARIZONA PRESS

TUCSON   ARIZONA

About the Author . . .

W. ROBERT NITSKE, professional writer and author, widely traveled in both the European and American continents, devoted personal research in Germany and its vicinity, gathering material in preparation for writing on the life of Wilhelm Conrad Röntgen. Born and educated in Germany, the young Nitske immigrated to the United States, where he obtained citizenship, worked in business enterprises and subsequently entered into service with the United States Army during World War II. On returning from military service, he turned to writing as a profession. He published many articles on travel, later specializing in writing about automobiles, especially those of European manufacture. In addition to articles and columns for magazines, Nitske's writings include books, among which are *The Complete Mercedes Story, The Amazing Porsche and Volkswagen Story,* and *Rudolf Diesel, Pioneer of the Age of Power.*

THE UNIVERSITY OF ARIZONA PRESS

I. S. B. N.–0–8165–0259–5
L. C. No. 79–125167

To my wife Betty,
loyal traveling companion
of more than a quarter of a century,
whose patience has made
this work possible,
this book is sincerely dedicated

Acknowledgments

SO THAT THE MEMORY of the life and work of Wilhelm Conrad Röntgen should not entirely disappear, this book has been written.

The author is indebted to many individuals and organizations for their assistance during the preparation of this chronicle.

Of inestimable value was the most generous help of Herrn Ernst Streller of the Deutsches Röntgen Museum at Remscheid-Lennep, where my wife and I saw many personal possessions of Wilhelm Conrad Röntgen, browsed in his extensive library, viewed hundreds of his photographic slides, and read his private correspondence. The long, taped recollections of housekeeper Käthe Fuchs offered many interesting sidelights into the character of our subject.

Frau Josephine Berta Donges-Röntgen at Würzburg, the adopted daughter of Röntgen, gave freely of her time and of personal recollections in the Röntgen home until her marriage. Frau Anna Saratz-Trippi, granddaughter of the naturalist Enderlin, recalled incidents of her childhood as guest and friend of Röntgen in the mountains around Pontresina. Dr. Margret A. Boveri of Berlin-Dahlem cleared up some questions.

Universities and libraries at Zürich, Giessen, Freiburg, Strassburg, Würzburg, Munich, and Frankfurt were consulted. All these and other sources proved most helpful in the compilation of material for this book. During a six-month stay in Europe, my wife and I visited the cities and areas where Röntgen was born, went to school, worked, and spent his vacations.

The title page photograph (by Nicola Perscheid, Hofphotograph, Berlin, 1906) is used by permission of the Deutsches Röntgen Museum at Remscheid-Lennep, Germany. All other text illustrations are used with permission of the publishers of Otto Glasser's *Wilhelm Conrad Röntgen und die Geschichte der Röntgenstrahlen,* with a chapter, "Persöhnliches über W. C. Röntgen," by Dr. M. Boveri; second edition, Berlin, Göttingen, Heidelberg: Springer Verlag, 1959.

Finally, I am greatly appreciative of the assistance of the University of Arizona Press — particularly of editor Elaine Nantkes — in bringing out this biography under its imprint.

W. R. N.

Contents

ILLUSTRATIONS

The Life of
WILHELM CONRAD
RÖNTGEN

THE PHYSICIST WHO DEVOTES HIMSELF to the task of carrying out exact measurements and of planning the necessary methods and apparatus for doing so must start with a certain resignation. He must consider the possibility, which usually amounts to certainty, that his work will be superseded by that of others within a relatively short time, that his methods will be improved and that the results will be more accurate, and that the memory of his life and his work will gradually disappear.

— Wilhelm Conrad Röntgen

CHAPTER 1

The Discovery — The Magnum Opus

IT WAS TIME FOR DINNER. When Wilhelm failed to appear, Bertha sent the maid down to remind the absorbed professor to come to dinner. After repeated trips downstairs to the laboratory, the maid reported that the "Herr Doktor" would come presently.

When Röntgen finally sat down to eat with his wife, he was silent, as if he had left his mind in the laboratory. Occasionally when working on difficult and deeply complex experiments he was uncommunicative at the table. Bertha understood the mood. She did nothing to distract him.

But this time her Wilhelm ate very little, she noticed. That was unlike him. He picked at his food without enjoyment. She began to worry about him. Perhaps it was a particularly bad mood. Perhaps he was ill. He said nothing. Research had been his very existence. She understood. Perhaps his work was more important than it had been before. For the first time she asked him what he was working on. He made no reply at all; he was not even polite to her.

Something must have gone gravely wrong downstairs. Whatever the experiment was, it must have failed miserably. And worse, instead of calming him as she intended, she apparently had angered him. When he was barely finished with the meal, he got up and left the table without a word. He disappeared through the open door, walked along the hallway, and entered his study. She heard the door of the room close quietly behind him. He would take the spiral stairway to his laboratory below.

Bertha sat down with a book and read for several hours. When Wilhelm did not come up at their regular late bedtime, she went to bed alone, leaving him in the laboratory engrossed in his experiment. That was Friday evening, November 8, 1895.

Professor Wilhelm Conrad Röntgen, of the University of Würzburg, had deliberately chosen for his personal experimental work two small laboratory rooms at the end of a long hallway on the first floor of the Physical Science Institute. He liked the relative seclusion of the rooms. Well out of the way of the daily student traffic on the floor, they were most suited to important and undisturbed observations. The rooms were easily accessible from the large comfortable quarters assigned to him and Bertha on the floor above.

In June, 1894, Professor Röntgen had begun a series of experiments with cathode rays. He was convinced that many still unsolved problems existed in relation to cathode rays, despite the valuable observations already made and published by other scientists. Röntgen would skillfully repeat these known experiments but would watch for new and previously undetected phenomena. To Ludwig Zehnder, on June 21, he wrote that he had "seen the cathode rays in air and in hydrogen of normal heaviness and was really enthused over the fine experiment."

In fact he was so enthusiastic over the work that he had dropped his studies on optics and on the influence of pressure on dielectric constants of various liquids, now devoting his time exclusively to the fascinating cathode ray experimentation.

As one of his colleagues later observed, "Röntgen was a genius of interpretation of phenomena, had a keen sense of observation, and an inexhaustible thoroughness of critical judgment, combined with brilliant experimental skill."

While experimenting, Röntgen was startled by a slight reflection of a greenish ray on a distant crystal. He thought at first that his impaired eyesight played tricks on him — he had a slight case of color-blindness that made green difficult to distinguish. Cathode rays had never been known to span anywhere near as great a distance as he now observed. He repeated the exact experiment. The precise effect that had startled him before appeared again. A thin ray obviously emanated from the cathode tube!

Röntgen recognized the behavior as strange. He could not explain the phenomenon. He became so absorbed in his work that he lost all track of time.

That weekend, and in the week to follow, Röntgen worked tirelessly in his laboratory, repeating the experiment and noting carefully the results of the strangely behaving tube.

He expanded the simple test, using other materials — a book, a playing card, metal objects. He was able to change the density of the peculiar ray upon a fluorescent screen. He found that a piece of lead stopped the rays completely, but he was horrified when he recognized the outline of the bones of his own fingers which held the lead in front of the screen.

Röntgen did not tell his wife nor his closest friends and colleagues at the university about the strange discovery. On Theodor Boveri's deeply concerned and insistent questions as to what the grave matter was that had changed his whole personal relationship with everyone, Röntgen evasively said, "I have discovered something interesting, but I don't know whether or not my observations are correct."

For more than a month Bertha went through "simply terrible days." Her husband came late for dinner and was generally in very bad humor. He ate sparingly, apparently without appetite, completely in silence. It was so unlike him. Immediately after the meal, he would return quickly to his laboratory. When she asked what was troubling him, he would not reply. Later, to Bertha's recollection of neglect and bad manners, Röntgen stated:

When at first I made the startling discovery of the penetrating rays, it was such an extraordinary astonishing phenomenon that I had to convince myself repeatedly by doing the same experiment over and over and over again to make absolutely certain that the rays actually existed. I was not aware of anything else but the strange phenomenon in the laboratory. Was it a fact or an illusion? I was torn between doubt and hope, and did not want to have any other thoughts interfere with my experiments. I tried to exclude everything not pertinent to the laboratory work from my thinking. Any interference could have caused me to fail in the creation of identical conditions to substantiate the discovery. I made the observations many, many times before I was able to accept the phenomenon myself. During those trying days I was as if in a state of shock.

One evening after dinner — it was December 22, 1895 — Röntgen asked Bertha to come downstairs to the laboratory with him. He explained the apparatus and its operation to her. Then he had her place her hand on a cassette loaded with an unexposed photographic plate and, assuring her that it would neither hurt nor damage her rings in any way, directed the rays from the tube on it for fifteen minutes. Then he developed the plate and showed her the results. It was an outline of the bones of her hand, which appeared light, with darker shadows of the surrounding flesh. The two rings on her finger had almost completely stopped the rays and were clearly visible. It was an excellent precise photograph. Bertha gasped and shuddered when he explained that this bony structure was actually her hand and that she saw indeed her own skeleton. To her, as to many others later, the grisly view of one's own bones was a vague premonition of an early death, and what he hoped to be a pleasant surprise to her, actually frightened her terribly.

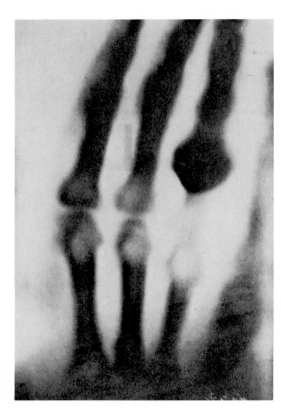

X ray photograph of the hand of Bertha Röntgen, made by her husband on December 22, 1895.

Röntgen was convinced that his strange observations were indeed based on sound experimentations. He also realized that he had to publish his findings as quickly as possible. Tediously but methodically he assembled his essential notes.

He sat down at his *Schreibtisch,* notes flat before him or tucked in the pigeonholes of the desk. The two framed pictures of his parents looked down on their fifty-year-old son as he wrote, "Not a single word not imposed by absolute necessity," beginning in his fine, precise handwriting.

Having finished his writing, Röntgen made but few corrections — there are two on the first page — took the manuscript on December 28, 1895, to Professor Karl Lehmann, president of the Physikalisch–Medizinischen Gesellschaft zu Würzburg, and requested that the paper be published in the next *Sitzungsberichte der Gesellschaft.* This was an unusual appeal, for only papers that had been presented at regular meetings of the society were published in the report. Röntgen, however, did not wish to waste time. That he recognized the full importance of the

Ueber eine neue Art von Strahlen.

von W. C. Röntgen.

(Vorläufige Mittheilung)

1. *Lässt man durch eine Hittorf'sche Vacuum-röhre, oder einen genügend evacuirten Lenard'schen, Crookes'schen oder ähnlichen Apparat die Entladungen eines grösseren Ruhmkorff'*

gehen und bedeckt die Röhre mit einem ziemlich eng anliegenden Mantel aus dünnem schwarzem Carton, so sieht man in dem vollständig verdunkelten Zimmer einen in die Nähe des Apparates gebrachten, mit Bariumplatincyanür angestrichenen Papierschirm bei jeder Entladung hell aufleuchten, fluoresciren, gleichgültig o angestrichene oder die andere Seite des Schi zum Entladungsapparat zugewendet ist.

Fluorescen ist noch in 2 m Entfernun

Appara die Ur

Ma

Flu

un

---

frühere Mitglieder der Gesellschaft lediglich deshalb nicht mehr im Personalverzeichnisse geführt würden, weil sie bei ihrem Weggange aus Würzburg vergessen hatten, den entsprechenden Antrag zu stellen. Herr von Kölliker stellt deshalb einen Antrag auf diesbezügliche Aenderung der Statuten. — Ueber denselben soll in der ersten Sitzung des nächsten Geschäftsjahres berathen werden.

Am 28. Dezember wurde als Beitrag eingereicht:

W. C. Röntgen: Ueber eine neue Art von Strahlen.

(Vorläufige Mittheilung.)

1. Lässt man durch eine *Hittorf*'sche Vacuumröhre, oder einen genügend evacuirten *Lenard*'schen, *Crookes*'schen oder ähnlichen Apparat die Entladungen eines grösseren *Ruhmkorff*'s gehen und bedeckt die Röhre mit einem ziemlich eng anliegenden Mantel aus dünnem, schwarzem Carton, so sieht man in dem vollständig verdunkelten Zimmer einen in die Nähe des Apparates gebrachten mit Bariumplatincyanür angestrichenen Papierschirm bei jeder Entladung hell aufleuchten, fluoresciren, gleichgültig ob die angestrichene oder die andere Seite des Schirmes dem Entladungsapparat zugewendet ist. Die Fluorescenz ist noch in 2 m Entfernung vom Apparat bemerkbar.

Man überzeugt sich leicht, dass die Ursache der Fluorescenz vom Entladungsapparat und von keiner anderen Stelle der Leitung ausgeht.

2. Das an dieser Erscheinung zunächst Auffallende ist, dass durch die schwarze Cartonhülse, welche keine sichtbaren oder ultravioletten Strahlen des Sonnen- oder des elektrischen Bogenlichtes durchlässt, ein Agens hindurchgeht, das im Stande ist, lebhafte Fluorescenz zu erzeugen, und man wird deshalb wohl zuerst untersuchen, ob auch andere Körper diese Eigenschaft besitzen.

Man findet bald, dass alle Körper für dasselbe durchlässig sind, aber in sehr verschiedenem Grade. Einige Beispiele führe ich an. Papier ist sehr durchlässig:[1]) hinter einem eingebun-

eines Körpers bezeichne ich das Verhältniss der m Körper gehaltenen Fluorescenzschirmes zu der s, welcher dieser unter denselben Verhältnissen aber örpers zeigt.

EINE NEUE ART

VON

STRAHLEN.

VON

DR. W. RÖNTGEN,

O. O. PROFESSOR AN DER K. UNIVERSITÄT WÜRZBURG.

WÜRZBURG.

VERLAG UND DRUCK DER STAHEL'SCHEN K. HOF- UND UNIVERSITÄTS-
BUCH- UND KUNSTHANDLUNG.
Ende 1895.

60 ₰.

Top left, Röntgen's original manuscript of the Preliminary Communication; *right*, page 132 of the report as published by the Physical-Medical Society; and, *lower*, cover of the first special printing of "A New Kind of Rays."

paper was evidenced by the fact that he did not keep it lying around for careful rechecking and possible correcting, as was his habit. Lehmann also realized that the work was indeed of great importance. He hurriedly contacted the three editors of the journal — the Professors Schultze and Reubold and Dr. Geigel. Röntgen's *Mitteilung* was rushed to the printers.

With copies of his "Preliminary Communication" in hand, Röntgen sat down at his writing desk to mail copies of it with several X ray photographs, to a select list of eminent colleagues, just as he had done with many other papers over the long years. The brief scientific report, describing the discovery of an unknown ray — an "X" ray — would startle the world. He also would include greetings for a Happy New Year.

In a mellow mood Röntgen reflected on the life he had lived so far. The full professorship in Würzburg, which had brought recognition of his diligent indefatigable work, enjoyable hours with his colleagues, stimulating discussions, and pleasant outings; the exciting work and dear friends in Giessen; the first real test of his capabilities in Hohenheim; the inspiring assistantship, or perhaps more accurately, apprenticeship, with August Kundt; the golden student years and wonderous unfolding love in Zurich; the harsh school years in Utrecht; and, yes, even the childhood time in Lennep. As Wilhelm Conrad Röntgen reflected upon his life of fifty years, he fully realized that he had indeed come a long way from Lennep.

CHAPTER 2

Antecedence and Early Environment

LENNEP WAS A SMALL TOWN in the Prussian Bergischen Rhein-Provinz. Although the Bergisches Land is a hilly country, the name does not indicate this topographical feature. That would be *bergiges*. Bergisches reflected the ownership of the entire territory between the Ruhr and the Sieg rivers by the Dukes of Berg, who had resided since 1348 in a castle *(Burg)* high above a bend of the Wupper river where it met with the Eschbach.

Thatch-roofed, half-timbered houses, and houses with shingled gray-slate sidings, slate roofs, and white painted eaves, crowded close together on the narrow, winding cobblestone streets. Occasional flower boxes in windows, framed with bright green shutters, added to the otherwise dull appearance.

In a house on the hilly Poststrasse 287 (later renamed Gänsemarkt 1, although it was never actually a market square but merely a street where geese were sold), a son was born on March 27, 1845, to Charlotte and Friedrich Conrad Röntgen. Dutifully, two days later, the father, accompanied by his brother and his father-in-law, reported the happy event of the birth of his son to the authorities.

The detailed birth certificate is a timely example of the thoroughness of the regulating bureaucracy in Germany at the time.

Geburt von Wilhelm Conrad Röntgen   *Evangelisch*
        Geburtsurkunde (Birth Certificate) *Nummer 86*
At Lennep, Lennep County, on the 29th of the month of March, 1845, at eleven o'clock in the forenoon, appeared before me, Bürgermeister Carl August

Theodor Wilhelm Wille, as official of the civil servants of the mayoralty of
Lennep, the merchant Friedrich Conrad Röntgen, 44 years old, residing in Lennep, who declared that his wife Charlotte Constanze, born Frowein, 37 years
old, residing at Lennep, gave birth to a male child on Thursday, the 27th of
this month and this year, at four o'clock in the afternoon, in their mutual
residence at Lennep, which child was given the Christian names of Wilhelm
Conrad.

This declaration is made before me in the presence of the two witnesses,
namely, (1) Richard Röntgen, 34 years old, merchant, residing in Lennep, and
(2) Heinrich Frowein, 48 years old, director, residing in Lennep.

This present record is therefore read to the attestors and witnesses,
agreed to by them, and signed: Friedrich Conrad Röntgen; Richard Röntgen;
Heinrich Frowein.

                                                                          Wille.

(The mayor signed the official paper quite correctly but rather
sparingly.)

The son, Wilhelm Conrad, was the couple's only child. He was
baptized on May 6 by Pastor Wissmann, most likely in the home, as was
the custom in that day (although some say that the sacrament was
administered in the Evangelical Church on the Marktplatz). The families,
the Röntgens and Froweins, for generations were of the Lutheran and
the Dutch Reformed faiths, respectively; but a much earlier influence of
English, Swiss, and Italian religious beliefs had come from the cosmo-
politan maternal ancestors who had lived in such far-away places as
London, Geneva, and Turin, and had emigrated from Italy to Holland
in the seventeenth century.

As frequently happened during those times, families in small villages
intermarried. Thus the textile merchant Friedrich Conrad Röntgen had
married his first cousin, the young Charlotte, born in Amsterdam on
February 28, 1806. Her grandparents had lived in Lennep, and the young
girl visited frequently with several other close relatives still living there.
Charlotte's father had married Susanne Maria Moyeth, a Dutch citizen
of an immigrated Italian family whose ancestors were generally merchants
and tradesmen. Not entirely satisfied with the opportunities in their small
Italian community, Charlotte's parents had emigrated to Holland and
established themselves as export merchants.

The earliest known ancestor of the paternal line was Engelberten
Röntgen, born in 1672 in Roelscheit, and died there. Prior to that, the
family name was sometimes spelled slightly differently. The Röntgens
had settled in the Wuppertal apparently soon after the Thirty Years' War,
which ended in 1648. Cloth manufacturer Mathias Röntgen, born on a
farm in this more agricultural area of Dabringhausen in 1697, was the
first to move into the Wuppertal to live. He died in Lennep in 1763. The

The house in Lennep where Wilhelm Conrad Röntgen was born.

boy Willi's great-grandfather, clothmaker and coppersmith Johann Heinrich (1732–1816), headed his community as a *Gemeindevorsteher,* an honorable equivalent of mayor, thus bringing considerable prestige to the family. The grandfather, also Johann Heinrich (1759–1842), in 1795 married Anna Louise Frowein (1773–1844); he also was a clothmaker and coppersmith. He became an elder of the Evangelical community. Anna Louise was the sister of Willi's grandfather on his mother's side.

When Willi was born, his father Friedrich Conrad Röntgen, born on January 11, 1801, had inherited the business and skills from his father and operated a profitable textile business, employing some twelve helpers who worked on looms with him in the workshop. In later years, with his reputation well established and demand for goods increased, his work force increased to twenty persons.

Contrary to published reports and generally accepted as historical fact, cabinetmakers Abraham Röntgen (1711–1793) and David Röntgen (1743–1807) were not close relatives of Willi Röntgen's immediate ancestors. They had gained a great measure of fame as superlative cabinet-makers, when some of the exquisitely executed marquetry (inlaid wood-work) found its way into the collections of such illustrious personages as Louis XVI, Marie Antoinette, Catherine the Great, and Friedrich Wilhelm II. At a visit around 1900 to the museum in Berlin where some items were exhibited, Röntgen told their housekeeper Käthe Fuchs that David was indeed a *Namensvetter,* but he probably used this term loosely. *"Ja, ja, das ist ein Vetter von mir,"* he had said. David actually was no *Vetter* (cousin), but merely a "kissing cousin" who had the same family name.

While most of the relatives of the Röntgens were craftsmen, there had been a musician, a surgeon, and an engineer who had been on the first steamboat to travel up the treacherous Rhine river.

In May, 1848, when their little Willi was only three years old, the Röntgen family moved to Holland, selling their house in Lennep to Gustav Kühne. Naturally they chose the town of Apeldoorn as their new home. It was only about a hundred miles from Lennep and was the home of the parents of mother Charlotte and of the Moll and Vincent families and many other close relatives. The change of residence apparently was made either because of better business prospects or to please Charlotte. During this time, unrest and revolutions swept many countries of Europe. Thus the possibility exists that the political turmoil also had something to do with the move of the Röntgen family.

Interestingly but perhaps merely coincidentally, the German National Assembly met on May 18, 1848, at Frankfurt am Main to draft a new constitution. At the instigation of the liberal elements, the meeting was made up of representatives chosen by popular vote in all of the states, and the goal was the formation of a new solid union and the creation of a real nation of all the Germans. The general and much more vociferous revolutionary movements in the separate Germanic countries were quite different from this organized attempt to reform the entire confederation, which the assembly tried but failed to accomplish.

Father Röntgen lost his Prussian citizenship, according to the law of the country, on May 23, 1848, the date he received his permit to move to Holland. He became a Dutch citizen several months later.

As befitting a well-to-do burgher, Friedrich Röntgen with his family lived in a pleasant house at Hoofdstraat 171. The home was comfortably furnished and richly decorated with fine paintings by old Dutch masters. One painting — of the Holy Family — was especially long remembered by their young son, who soon learned to appreciate true beauty and art. Splendid examples of Meissen and Wedgwood and old Chinese porcelain and china, beautiful silver, mahogany Empire furniture, and other art treasures had been brought by the Moyeth ancestors of the Froweins from the distant and mysterious Orient and the far-flung trading areas and colonies of the Netherlands. It was a rich atmosphere for the boy to grow up in.

Many of these family heirlooms were to find their way into the son's home thirty-five years later. After his death the items were sold at a public auction, along with other furniture from the Munich apartment and the Weilheim house.

For one Christmas, the father built for Willi a small wooden windmill, run by fine sand; at another an elaborate crèche, a stable scene, with figures of the Holy Family, kings, shepherds, and animals. The crèche was often recalled by Wilhelm Röntgen years later when he and his family celebrated their own *Weihnachten*. They retained the Rhenish custom of celebrating Christmas very early in the morning of the first holiday. Gifts were displayed under the tall beautiful candlelighted tree. After the presentation the family went to church.

At another time father Röntgen constructed a small replica of their house in Lennep, correct in every detail. It had a slate roof, slate tile sides, and two stone slab steps at the entrance — all of wood but painted properly to convey the right impression. This cleverly conceived and elaborately built model could be disassembled completely, part by part, and the various rooms exposed. Built in exact 1-to-50 scale, it was so highly treasured by Willi Röntgen that he kept it throughout his life. It is one of the pieces saved for the museum in Lennep. The work clearly shows where the future physicist inherited his ability to improvise laboratory equipment, which enabled him to make observations that less skilled men were unable to do.

Apeldoorn was a thriving community of about 3,000 inhabitants when the Röntgens moved there. A filthy evil seemed the several paper mills with their tall thin smokestacks emitting thick clouds of acrid smoke. The manufacturing plants fouled the air but also furnished work for many citizens, who accepted the situation gracefully. Local merchants exported the manufactured goods to the East Indies.

The town was surrounded by thick inviting forests with edges of heather. The area was ideal for a growing and extremely inquisitive boy who could roam in the countryside learning the secrets of nature. In the warm summer months Willi enjoyed the swimming holes in the cool waters of the picturesque Grift river; in the winter he enjoyed the considerably more invigorating activity of ice skating on the straight utilitarian Dieren Canal, when the long canal barges were berthed in secure winter shelters.

While Willi lived at home, his mother was devoted to him, and her son showed solicitously deep affection for her all his life.

Willi attended the primary public school in Apeldoorn. Then for some years and as a preparation for further schooling, he attended the expensive Kostschool, a private boarding school of Martinus Hermann van Doorn, located in a spacious country estate on "de Pasch" in the Middellaan, later known as Regentessalaan 8. Because his scholastic records for the period are not available, we do not know how well the youngster did academically.

On December 27, 1862, at the age of seventeen, Willi went to Utrecht and entered the Technical School, a small private institution. There was no *Gymnasium* or *Maschinenbauschule* in Utrecht. The Technical School, housed in some rooms of the House of Arts and Sciences, in two years of study prepared students of ages 14 to 18 years for entry into a technical college but not into a university. Private tutoring in Latin and Greek — subjects not taught at the Technical School — would be required prior to a student's acceptance into a university. Students could remain at the Technical School for a third year for practical studies. Models and equipment for classes in physics and chemistry were furnished by the university laboratories. Willi studied algebra, geometry, physics, chemistry, and technology, among other subjects. A few years later, in 1866, the Hoogere Burgerschool was opened; the Technical School, which had opened in 1850, was then suspended.

Willi Röntgen lived first at the home of Dr. Dompling. Many years later his mother recounted this first separation: "The lonesome boy hoped that evening, by the glow of a gas lantern, that his parents might return once again before they retired at the *Gasthaus*. Then, finally, while unpacking his small suitcase, he really understood that he had actually left his parents' home."

Soon a new home was found for the boy, with Professor Dr. Jan Willem Gunning, on the Nieuwegracht, corner of Schalkwijksteeg. At that time Jan Gunning taught at the high school, and in 1865 he became instructor of theoretical chemistry at the Technical School. When the professor wrote a textbook on chemistry, a short section written by the 20-year-old Röntgen was included in the text.

The teacher's wife, Elis, was like a mother to the boy; the daughter, Jo, just a bit older than Willi, tried to look after him, too. With Jo as a knowledgeable native and close companion, he explored the charming town. He found the city fascinating, his new life exciting. He admired his "foster father" greatly, and immensely valued his guidance and advice during his formative school years. Willi loved the attention of his "other mother." The family relationship was close and mutually most agreeable. In a reminiscent mood, mother Röntgen wrote to Frau Gunning, on May 28, 1880, recalling an incident about a sore throat:

Our excitement was so great, that immediately on that moon-bright night we took the wagon and hurried from Apeldoorn to Utretcht, always thinking, "How may he be?" And then, the anxious waiting in the middle of the night at your house. The light was on upstairs in Wilhelm's room and our indecision whether to ring the bell or not to disturb you. Finally the courage to ring, and Herr Gunning coming to the door. "Who is there?" he asked. "It it I," I answered. "Who is I?" he questioned. And then I told him. "But dear Frau Röntgen, what has scared you so?" he asked solicitously. We were assured by his tone of voice that it was not as serious as we had believed. Our Wilhelm was fast asleep. We went to our Gasthaus to rest. The next morning, Wilhelm met us on our way to your house, and all was well.

Utrecht was a provincial capital with some 100,000 inhabitants at that time. Willi learned that it was first called Trajectum ad Rhenum, or ford of the Rhine, by the ancient Romans, and later Wiltaburg by the Frisians and Franks. Utrecht was one of the earliest towns in the Netherlands. Twenty-six miles southwest of Amsterdam, it was dominated by the magnificent Dom, the oldest Gothic church in the country. As Willi knew, the church was built on the site of an ancient Roman fortress dating from 48 A.D. The fort was torn down during the seventh century to make room for St. Martin's Cathedral, which in turn was destroyed in 1253. During a fierce storm in 1674 the nave of the newer building collapsed, and the cathedral was reconstructed to become a large church with several small chapels and a number of fine stained-glass windows, and separated from its tower by a large square. The adventurous explorers Willi and Jo counted 465 steps of the tower, using a rest stop at the half-way mark in the fourteenth-century St. Michael chapel, and another in the Egmond chapel near the very top. On the way, the young student and his companion passed the seven great chiming Klokken, dating from 1506, and the 42-bell Klokkenspel, or carillon, installed in 1663.

Cloisters were now connected with the former Hall of the Chapter where the Union of Utrecht was signed in 1579 to lay the foundations of the later kingdom of the Netherlands. The Treaty of Utrecht, which ended the War of the Spanish Succession in 1713, was also signed here, changing the map of Europe as no previous treaty had ever done. Willi looked hopefully and expectantly toward the Universiteit, which had been founded in 1636 and was soon to earn a grandiose reputation as a center of higher learning. Originally thirty-seven professors instructed the 750 students in their care, but soon the facilities, originally part of the former archbishop's palace, proved inadequate and were considerably enlarged. The library of the university was grandly housed in the ornate palace built in 1807 expressly for King Louis Napoleon. It was heady fun for Willi to be close to the 110,000 volumes of books and 1,500 manuscripts, which included an invaluable and rare psalter of the ninth century and several priceless miniatures.

Various museums, crowded with many precious art objects, some old almshouses, fine medieval and Renaissance patrician houses and other interesting buildings, some even from 1432, afforded the youngsters great joy and a wonderful understanding of living history. Streets, swept clean, were lined with wild chestnut trees, heavy with brilliant white poker blossoms in the early summer giving the town a festive appearance.

The Stads Buiten Gracht, the widest canal, encircled the city, while smaller waterways dissected it. Willi and his friends often went to the old Vredenburg, the focus point on the site of the former ancient castles, for a superb view of the commercial traffic on the Gracht.

In the immediate vicinity of Utrecht itself were the elegant mansions with elaborate formal gardens and parks of the city's wealthy citizens; but the surrounding country offered many wonderful opportunities, only too eagerly grasped, for many joyous outings. A close school friend, Karel Reyter, completed a trio. They rode horses together, or just roamed the wide open spaces of fields, intersected by numerous still canals and watery fingers of the great Rhine itself. Here the young Willi was in his ecstasy, learning to appreciate nature and its invigorating atmosphere. He was never to lose this love of the out-of-doors throughout his entire life.

Winter days after school were spent ice skating. Then during the long evenings the entire family group would gather in the warm living room, playing games or reading aloud. Sometimes the young people would put on clever little skits of their own invention to the delight and entertainment of the adopted parents.

Some forty-five years later, Wilhelm Röntgen was to recall this carefree period of his school days when he wrote in a letter to Margret Boveri, the young daughter of a colleague:

The description of your activity, which changes from hard work to exciting enjoyment, reminded me of my own youth and especially of the time when I lived not with my parents in the small village, but in a friendly family circle in Utrecht. The father of this family was a fine scholar, a solid character, and really a splendid man who understood superbly the task of guiding a young person along the correct path in several areas in life. The mother was a loving, cultured, and kindly woman who provided the proper atmosphere for a full life, one of happiness and at the same time pleasant stimulation. There was no time for foolish and stupid things, but much for creative activities. Self-created pieces of happy fun were offered at community celebrations, but otherwise diligent work was demanded in serious learning. That was a happy and equally rewarding time! And thinking back to those years of my youth, I have to add that I also did a lot of riding and ice skating, and generally used my body in many wholesome outdoor activities.

Professor Gunning went to teach at his alma mater, the Athenaeum Illustre, and his family moved to Amsterdam. Willi Röntgen moved to live briefly at Maliebaan 192b. According to the Utrecht Inhabitants Register, he lived there from March 17 to May 23, then moved to the Schoutensteeg G122 (later No. 12).

Willi Röntgen was a happy youngster who had learned to enjoy life, particularly loving the outdoors and everything connected with nature. He had learned benevolent personal discipline, and he was a fair student. He also had developed a great sense of humor, not thinking at all that this beneficial trait would ever cause him difficulties or disappointments in life, but rather that a full appreciation of the gayer aspects of his existence would assist him immensely in the various vicissitudes that life in some measure was certain to bring him later.

As Röntgen himself told the story later to several of his best friends, he was once subjected to a *consilium abeundi,* a forced removal, from his school. One morning between classes one of Willi's fellow students with an artistic flair had drawn a most unflattering caricature of their unpopular head teacher on the blackboard. Many of the boys gathered around the hilarious crayon drawing, enjoying it loudly, but none more than Willi Röntgen, perhaps because he had absolutely no talent for drawing. He was so completely absorbed in the ridiculing likeness that he failed to heed the approaching footsteps of the teacher himself and the warning gestures of his schoolmates.

The teacher, red with rage, accused Röntgen, who stood alone now in front of the blackboard, of having drawn the infamous picture. This the youngster denied. "Then," stormed the instructor, "who did it?"

Willi refused to tell. He reasoned, rightly or wrongly, that he could not reveal the name of the culprit and still retain his own self-respect among his class comrades. A heated argument ensued, with the head teacher, of course, having the last word. The *Präzeptor,* Professor van Tweer, was called in, and the stern and strict director settled the dispute simply. Röntgen was ordered to identify the guilty youth. Again Willi refused. The recalcitrant student was dismissed from the Hoogere Burger-school forthwith.

At a meeting of the school teaching staff, the unpleasant matter was thoroughly discussed. Only one of the regular teachers of Willi's class, Hendrik Vondel, instructor of nature lore and history, spoke up for him. The dismissal remained. (The episode was later disputed by Gerrit Albert Evers, Conservator of the University Library. He could not substantiate it; there simply were no records available.)

It was an especially unpleasant blow to father Friedrich Röntgen, and it thoroughly disillusioned Willi. The lofty dream of a higher education seemed utterly shattered now. The sympathetic Vondel tried to console his former student, and suggested plans for the future. The local banker Speelmann, whose son had drawn the troublesome caricature, met with father Röntgen in the "Witte Societeit," a club for gentlemen, to discuss the problem and to find a solution to their predicament. But there seemed to be nothing left except to take Willi home and have him enter the family business in Apeldoorn to learn the trade and to carry on the work of his ancestors. Higher education and consequent fields of endeavor now seemed out of the question.

Willi's father was heartbroken. His dream was shattered. He had nourished hopes for his son to follow in the footsteps of the few ancestors who had attended a university and had become surgeons or attorneys. The extra expense of having sent the boy to the private preparatory school in Apeldoorn, then to one in Utrecht, all toward the goal of entering the stately university, had proven a bad investment. As a businessman, father Röntgen was willing to write the whole thing off and recoup his loss. Willi was to come home.

But Vondel came up with a last-chance idea. To salvage the already spent time of schooling, he suggested that Willi enter a different institute of learning in the next semester. Although his Utrecht school had refused to agree to any transfer in the approved manner, a privately tutored student could ask for a special examination and, if passed, would become eligible to enter another Hoogere School.

For almost a year Willi prepared for the examination that was to allow him to continue his studies. He worked hard, making up the studies of Latin and Greek, neither of which he cared for. Natural sciences were more to his liking. It had taken several months to get permission to receive private tests from the school which had expelled him, and Willi was determined to pass them with a satisfactory grade. But when the time for the examination came, the teacher who had been selected to administer the test became gravely ill and another who had been unfriendly in the dismissal proceedings was substituted. The good work of Hendrik Vondel had been in vain. Willi failed.

Some forty years later, as a professor in Munich, Röntgen was to write regarding examinations:

Student examinations generally give no clues whatever for the judgment of ability in a special field. They are entirely — and unfortunately — a necessary evil. Especially final examinations! They are necessary to keep one from a lifetime profession for which he is too lazy or otherwise unsuited, although that is not always the case. Otherwise they are a trial for both parties, and they cause repeatedly bad dreams! The real test of ability of any chosen profession or occupation comes actually much later in life.

Failure to pass the examination was discouraging, but when the blow of this fully unexpected result had somewhat abated, it was decided that the student without the graduation certificate of the high school would try to attend the university anyway.

Willi was allowed to audit several courses, and on January 18, 1865, he registered at the venerable institution as a student of mechanical engineering. The *Album Studiosorum Rheno-Traiectina,* Utrecht 1886, actually listed Wilhelm Röntgen as a student of philosophy at the Universiteit as of that date with the comment *"privata institutione uses est."*

At that time the Universiteit of Utrecht had such learned men on its faculty as the meteorologist Christoph Hendrik Didericus Buys-Ballot who lectured on analysis; and the renowned Professor van Rees on physics; other outstanding educators were the Professors Mulder, who headed the chemistry, Harding the zoology, and Miquel the botany departments — all of whom Röntgen regularly heard lecture.

The young student joined the famed society *Natura Dux Nobis et Auspex* — Nature is our Leader and Protector — founded in 1853 by Professor Harding; its "Communications" listed Röntgen as a member from May 9 to October 31, 1865. Wilhelm Röntgen was initiated into the society "in the midst of this *Urwald* [jungle]" on May 19 during a two-day outing to the Beekberger Wald.

University student Wilhelm Röntgen was well aware that he was not a fully accredited student as were the others but that he was merely being tolerated. Although he smarted under this stigma of exclusion, there seemed no easy way out of his dilemma.

CHAPTER 3

Student Days — Gaudeamus Igitur

A FORTUNATE EVENT was Willi Röntgen's acquaintanceship with the fellow student Carl Ludwig Wilhelm Thormann, whose father, Amandé L. Thormann, born in 1792 in Bern, had worked as engineer in a locomotive works in Switzerland but now lived in Utrecht. *Schulfreund* Thormann, a year older than Röntgen, believed that a student could enter the Polytechnikum at Zurich without the formal graduation certificate from a Gymnasium, but that he needed to pass a painfully stiff and complex entrance examination, even more difficult than the dreaded Abitur.

This indeed proved correct, and the "tolerated" student once again prepared himself diligently for the Matura and the entrance examination to become a de facto student of a college.

When applying for admission to the Eidgenössischen Technischen Schule (Federal Institute of Technology), or simply Polytechnikum, Willi Röntgen stated that he "was dissatisfied with his present courses offered at the university and that he preferred to devote himself to the studies of applied mathematics, at the Polytechnikum." He submitted a *Zeugnis,* a report card, with excellent grades in mathematics, which the student obviously preferred to other subjects. He was all set to leave for Zurich as soon as he received the official summons for the entrance examination. But, Willi contracted an eye infection, diagnosed as keratitis phlyctaenularis, and perhaps caused by some minor accident in his boyhood. He was unable to go to Zurich for the beginning of the semester 1865–66.

Willi Röntgen's letter of November 16, 1865, struck a kind responsive chord in Zurich. The director showed exceptional leniency toward the prospective student. For once, luck was with the anxious young man, now twenty years old.

Professor Gustav Zeuner, who had come to the school in 1855 and was made director of the institute ten years later, wrote to the *Schulrats-präsidenten* Karl Kappeler on November 24. Zeuner recommended that Willi Röntgen should be accepted as a regular student without further examinations, and enclosed the reports and a letter from a Utrecht physician who had treated the eye infection. The letter was marked "genehmigt K. Kappeler," that is, approved!

Zeuner granted Röntgen permission to enroll as a student in the *maschinenbautechnischen Abteilung*, the technical machine building division of the Polytechnikum. Because of his superior grades in mathematics, and perhaps because he was about two years older than other students in his class and showed extraordinary maturity, no examinations were required of him. The director was quite sympathetic to the young student's plight; he himself had experienced some difficulties during his professional career. Although born in Chemnitz in Saxony, he was refused employment in the state of his birth because he had participated in the *Aufstand,* the uprising of the radical liberals in 1849. He secured a position as professor for technical mechanics and theoretical machine studies at the Polytechnikum and lectured on those subjects. Zeuner also published many important observations. His best known papers were, *"Untersuchungen über Schiebesteuerungen," "Mechanische Wärmetheorien,"* and *"Grundlegende Beiträge zur Mathematischen Statistik."*

On a wintry day Willi Röntgen arrived in Zurich, the capital of the canton, the largest and most influential city of Switzerland. The attractive city was built on the north shore of the large crescent-shaped Zürich-See and into the gently sloping wooded hills. On both banks of the clear blue lake were villages, orchards, and vineyards climbing up the slopes of the highly cultivated land. The Limmat river divided the town into the newer *Grosse Stadt* on its right bank and the *Kleine Stadt* on its left, where the college was located and where student Röntgen would live.

One of the oldest cities of Europe, it was first occupied in prehistoric times. Later, the Romans' Turicum rose from older Celtic fortifications in 58 B.C. In A.D. 1292, the settlement joined Uri and Schwyz, and in 1351 it became a member of the Swiss Confederation. Soon Zurich became the intellectual capital of Switzerland, and during the time of the dedicated patriot and powerful preacher Huldreich (usually called Ulrich) Zwingli, it was also a center of the Reformation.

The Romanesque Gross-Münster, where the student irregularly attended Sunday worship services — and where the Swiss reformer had defied the Pope in Rome and the rest of the Confederation in Switzerland

The house in Zurich where
Röntgen lived as a student.

from 1519 until his death — was actually founded by the *römischen*
Kaiser Karl der Grosse, the Holy Roman Emperor Charlemagne. Student
Röntgen observed that the cathedral was shockingly austere and the
scholarly sermons equally cold. Zurich, with over 200,000 inhabitants,
was a busy manufacturing town, center of silk spinning and cotton weaving
mills, and had a number of iron foundries and large machine works.

The young German student from the Netherlands found a room not
far from the Polytechnikum, at the Frau Witwe Barbara Hägi residence
in the Seilergraben 7, a three-story gray-stucco house with green wooden
shutters on its fourteen windows. It was not the romantic extremely austere
corner room in an attic with the meanest necessities, as immortalized by
novels and operettas, but an airy, comfortable, and tastefully furnished
corner room in the middle-class household of the widow Hägi. Willi
Röntgen paid fifty-five francs per month rent, which included his breakfast. His other meals he usually ate in the company of some young

instructors and students from the college at the excellent and rather expensive but *bürgerliche Restaurant,* Zunft zur Waag.

Located on the fashionable side of the Limmat, on the Münsterhof 8, guests saw from the second-floor dining room the stately Frauenmünster on the square, the river, and older city rising beyond. Although a Zunft zur Waag suggested a guild of scale builders, Willi Röntgen quickly explained the rather inaccurate name of the fine restaurant. The patrician-style four-and-a-half-story building, restored in 1636, had actually housed the Weavers' and Hatmakers' Guilds for some five hundred years. A fancy wrought-iron emblem of a scale belonged to an apothecary shop which occupied the corner store in the building and gave it its name. "Cloth, or hats for that matter," the young student added in explanation, "were really never sold by weight in Zurich."

Willi Röntgen was a tall and handsome young man who, with penetrating brown eyes, looked soberly at the world. He had a well-shaped nose and a large mouth. He had thick, wavy black hair, was clean shaven, and always dressed well. His father supplied him with sufficient francs for dress and extravagant fun and good living. Usually he was attired in a modest dark coat, gray trousers, a soft wing collar with a large bow cravat, and a gold watch-chain dangling on his vest. He was conservative and modest. Although he disliked blatant conviviality, he was fun-loving, a popular young man in a city where students were not always as serious as its somber citizens.

On one occasion Willi and his close friend, E. L. Albert, bought new and expensive clothes and paraded on the crowded, fashionable Bahnhofstrasse on a Sunday afternoon. They attracted the *nota bene,* the good attention, they had hoped for. But after a while they began to feel too conspicuous, and sheepishly embarrassed took a carriage home. Their all-white suits were perhaps the only such sartorial attire ever seen in staid Zurich.

Zurich was not always sobriety personified. Every year, to release the pent-up explosive forces accumulated during the winters by the inhabitants, the entire population gathered in mid-April to celebrate the *Sechseläuten,* climaxing the riotous celebrations by the burning of Bögg, the traditional old man winter, in the spacious Bellevueplatz on the lake.

Röntgen liked horses. He often went riding with his student friend along the lake shore, but whenever the opportunity presented itself, or he found a justifying excuse, he hired a two-horse carriage, and basking in this luxurious splendor, rode stately and proudly through the city streets. Hiring a fancy carriage was his only expensive vice. For this extravagance he rationalized *"Dulce est desipere in loco"* — It is sweet to be foolish on occasion.

Röntgen was affectionately and identifyingly called "Apeldoorn" by his fellow students, especially when they gathered for a happy evening over a glass of beer and perhaps some serious conversation at their favorite Café Restaurant, the Wirtschaft zum grünen Glas. The owner of this pleasant establishment was a rather curious fellow, and a great favorite among his young clientele. Often the Wirt would abandon the place behind the counter and leave the dispensing of the foaming brew to one of his three daughters while he engaged in weighty conversations or profound arguments with the younger men.

Johann Gottfried Ludwig, the owner, was a highly educated man and a superior conversationalist. He had been forced to leave his home in Jena, the historic southern German university town, because of his suspected revolutionary activities there. Ludwig had first been barred from attending that university in the 1830s, then was expelled from his own country at the beginning of the actual revolution. He was less fortunate than other fellow revolutionists who had also found refuge in Switzerland or elsewhere. Because he could not find a suitable position, he finally decided to make a living by dispensing food and drink in a highly cultivated atmosphere. He bought the Green Glass Inn. While still actively searching for better or appropriate employment, Johann Ludwig married the young Swiss girl, Elisabeth Gschwend. They had four children, Lina Barbara, Anna Bertha, Hans Otto, and Maria Johanna. Only after the birth of their third daughter had the father reconciled himself to remaining a scholarly innkeeper.

Located just off the Hirschgraben, a major thoroughfare, on the Unteren Zäune street number 15, the Gaststätte zum grünen Glas occupied the entire ground floor of a narrow four-story apartment building with attic and dormer windows in its steep roof. A small, fancifully carved and gaily decorated enclosed balcony-like alcove graced the preferred second-floor apartment. The small garden in the rear, shaded by large leaf trees, set with tables and chairs, was a popular summer afternoon spot.

The row of similar houses — once even more fashionable than during Willi's stay — faced across the street the former cloister, now the Obergericht building, and a large theater where Richard Wagner himself at times directed his controversial musical works. The name of the street, Untere Zäune (Lower Fences), obviously referred to the lower fence line of the cloister. Each house on the street had a name painted on its facade, and neighboring number 15 one found in the local dialect with appropriate mural illustrating each of the titles: *Zum Meer Fräuli* (To the Mermaid), *Zum Gekrönten Fuchs* (To the Crowned Fox), *Zum Flie-*

The *Zum Grünen Glas*
inn of Johann Ludwig.

genden Fisch (To the Flying Fish), and *Zum Sunne blüemli* (sic) (To
the Sunflower).

Among the all-too-liberal-minded educators from Jena who had
been forced to leave also were a prominent chemist, Pompejus Alexander
Bolley; an author and philosopher, Friedrich Theodor Vischer; and an
art historian and poet, Gottfried Kinkel. All three had found good
positions at the Polytechnikum in Zurich.

Although Johann Gottfried Ludwig was not allowed officially into
the college, his "cousin," the poet Otto Ludwig (1813–65), an authority
on Shakespeare, and author of the dramas *Die Maccabäer* and *Der
Erbförster,* had had his works read in the school. Often considered by

writers as a close relative, Otto Ludwig actually was not related to Johann Ludwig at all. It was another case of a *Namensvetter,* or a "kissing cousin." While their supposedly mutual ancestors had been traced to Eisfeld, Thuringia, no relationship was ever proven by genealogists.

The fact that he was not a member of the faculty did not keep Johann Ludwig from utilizing his abilities. To students who felt that their important activity of parries was in need of improvement, he taught fencing so that these young men might acquire the highly valued proper cheek cuts from their friendly opponents' foils; thus the lay society by those very scars would forever recognize that the recipients thereof had attended a university and therefore indeed were learned men.

Student Röntgen was disinterested in fencing and excessive drinking, and no records show that he was ever a member of a *Burschenschaft,* a fraternity where fencing was the rule. He did belong, however, to a *hollandischen Verband,* a loose organization of students from the Netherlands, that met quite regularly for good conversation and fun over a meal or some wine. It was a purely social fraternity, with distinctive caps for the student members to be worn (under threat of a fine for failure to do so) at all of their meetings in their *Stammlokal.*

The "unofficial professor" Ludwig also privately tutored for coming examinations. He had an especially good knowledge of what was expected on these complicated exercises and whenever students found it beyond their own abilities to translate their theses into Latin — a compulsory requirement — scholar Ludwig would do it for them.

Student Röntgen, always behaving considerably older than his actual age, liked the stimulating company of the exiled Jena scholar. Perhaps some of the political opinions and the revolutionary vocabulary of Ludwig were reminiscent of the expressions the student had occasionally heard from his father at home. (Interestingly, years later Röntgen was to accuse his good friend Zehnder — wholly without a solid foundation — of using "despicable socialistic slogans" in an argument they had, although both insisted they were not Socialists.)

The young student and the older scholar found that they frequently agreed on many points of discussion, although some of their lively conversations eventually became heated controversies and ended in violent disagreements. Each respected the honesty and judgment of the other, and such intense talks seemed only to weld them closer together in mutual fondness rather than drive them apart in anger.

Occasionally an interested listener was Ludwig's second daughter Anna Bertha, usually standing a short distance from the table but listening eagerly to the provocative discussions. Six years older than Willi Röntgen, Bertha Ludwig was a tall, slender, charming girl with a twinkle in her eyes and a smile on her lips. She had acquired a healthy and wholesome philosophy of life listening to many of the intellectuals who came to visit her father.

Several years before, during the 1850s, when Bertha was a student at a boarding school in Neuchâtel, her father had written to her:

Dear Bertha: I do not yet want to lay aside the pen with which I have just written to your teacher without also writing you a few words. I am very happy to learn from Miss Grossmann that she is well satisfied with you in every respect. This shows that you appreciate the great sacrifice which your parents are happy to make for your education and that you are determined to contribute all you can to become what we would like you to be, sincere, orderly, and morally and scientifically well educated. These are the only treasures which you can acquire with the help of your efforts and those of your good teachers. Other treasures we can not give you, and even if we could, they truly would not be worth as much as these. I was happy to read that you continue to feel well. You seem to like the climate and mode of life, which makes you long less for your parents' home. You may easily forget the pleasures which you shared with us.

The weather continues to be bad and takes away all the summer pleasures. It probably is the same in Neuchâtel. And now, my dear daughter, continue to be industrious and good, so that we may always receive good news of you.

A very sincere good-bye from all of us. Your loving father.

Bertha loved the outdoors and was greatly interested in the natural sciences. She collected flowers and plant specimens, and carefully identified them with labels bearing their proper Latin identities before placing them to be pressed and retained for posterity.

It was natural that Willi Röntgen and Bertha Ludwig went on nature hikes together. She knew the surrounding area well and was a discerning guide for the enthusiastic student. The excellent Botanical Garden was amply stocked with Alpine and other native plants of the region. The *Alte Katz,* an old bastion, formed a lofty platform planted with fine trees, and provided an expressly inviting spot for the two serious naturalists.

Together they hiked up the steep footpath, called Leiterlei, to the Uetliberg (or Uto), 2,880 feet above sea level and northernmost of the Albis Range. The Uto was their favorite spot. A climb was an achievement, and the view from it, the nature lovers felt, while perhaps less grandiose than views from other summits nearer the Alps, surpassed all in sheer beauty. They could see the dark blue Lake Zürich and the green valley of the Limmat river, and behind it the snowy Alpine ranges from the Sentis to the Jungfrau, and the Stockhorn on Lake Thun with the

Left, W. C. Röntgen as a student; *right,* Bertha Ludwig as a young girl.

Rigi and Pilatus hovering in the foreground. To the west rose the Jura, to the north the Feldberg and Belchen in the Black Forest, and the volcanic peaks of the Högau. It was a vision of sheer ecstasy.

Both young people loved Zurich dearly. During the pleasant summer days they boated on the enchanting lake, often merely drifting with the light breeze. They lazed on the narrow deck of their small sailboat, admiring from afar the scenery unfolding majestically before them. Snowcapped Alps rose in the background of Zurich; to the left was the Glärnisch, then the perpendicular sides of the 9,200-foot Grieselstock, near it on the right the Pfannenstock, and further on the Drusberg, the ice-clad Bifertenstock and Tödi, the highest in the group, all fronted by the Clariden, with their westernmost point, the Kammlistock of 10,624-foot elevation. As if such an array were not enough, on the north side was the Schächental with the fantastic peaks of the Rossstock chain. Neither of the two young people could imagine greater beauty anywhere.

Willi enjoyed strenuous mountain climbing more than mere hiking up steep slopes. Often he went with his friend Albert to scale another challenging peak. Bertha was not well enough for the extravagantly demanding outings which constantly dared student Röntgen. One time he fell, injuring himself severely, and was treated by Dr. Ulrich T. Krönlein, but he never lost the love for scaling snowcapped mountains, gentle mountain climbing, or merely hiking in the mountainous outdoors.

In the winter he and his friend took hiking trips into the mountains in deep snow, the long-legged Röntgen leading the way and his shorter friend barely able to fit his shorter stride into the holes made by the taller pathfinder. This led to good-natured scolding and exasperation suffered by Albert, with Röntgen's sturdy laugh echoing in the wintry hills.

One time, however, the shorter student bested the tall one. Both students believed themselves fiercely in love with a popular actress, and having bought a huge bouquet of roses they called on her. When she herself opened the door to her apartment, both callers were so startled and embarrassed that they left the roses and departed speechlessly. Later that afternoon, the more courageous Albert actually made the acquaintance of the actress, thus clearly becoming the victor in this friendly rivalry.

All during his life Röntgen adored the Swiss mountains, visiting them with Bertha annually as long as they were able to do so. He benefited by their majesty and seemed miraculously invigorated by their proximity. He was quite convinced throughout his life that a sound mind could reside only in a sound body, and that it was his own responsibility to keep his body a suitable vessel for an alert mind. *"Mens sana in corpore sano,"* he quoted.

But the *Studentenleben* in Zurich was not all fun and frolic. The young student quickly adapted himself to the discipline of his new school work and seemingly enjoyed attending classes. Among the professors who were teaching mechanical engineering and the allied sciences at the Polytechnikum were some excellent scientists — Elwin Bruno Christoffel, Friedrich Erwin Prym, Gustav Zeuner, Kronauer, Ludewig, and Reye. Student Röntgen attended their lectures and took courses in mathematics, technical drawing, mechanical technology, engineering, metallurgy, hydrology, thermodynamics, and other branches of mechanical engineering, his major subject.

The Eidgenössische Schule, built in 1860–64, was barely completed when Willi Röntgen became its newest student. Already crowded with an eager student body of 1,300 who were being taught by 130 professors and docents, it became the Hochschule and was later merged with the adjoining university. The massive imposing building, with a huge cupola in its center, overlooked the city. The entrance rotunda opened into a large rectangular hall with Florentine columns all around and a three-story high ceiling in the accepted Roman architecture, with auditoriums in both wings of the ground floor. On the first floor was a permanent exhibition of a precious archeological collection of artifacts and Greek vases, a fine collection of some 60,000 examples of the art of engraving, and a gathering of illustrations on industrial hygiene. On the second floor under the center dome was the large reading room of the library and the huge Aula with its ceiling painted magnificently by the muralist Bin of Paris. From here, as well as from the open top terrace, one could enjoy a wonderful view of the Limmat city and its surroundings.

Willi Röntgen was a better-than-average student. He did quite well in the courses he took from Gustav Zeuner during the three semesters. For his work in the semester 1865–66 student Röntgen earned 4¾ and 5 points in technical mechanics; the first grade was for *Fleiss,* or diligence, and the second was for *Leistung,* or performance — 6 being the best possible grade and 1 the lowest.

The following semester, 1866–67, Röntgen received for performance 4½ points in technical mechanics, and 5½ and 5¾ in theoretical machine studies and in practical hydraulics.

During the 1867–68 semester he apparently settled down to serious work. He was awarded top grades of 6 points in mechanical heat theory and steam engines, and in turbines and ventilation.

In the ten subjects during the 1865–66 semester he received for performance one 5-1/6, four 5s, one 4¾, one 4⅔, and three 4½s, averaging slightly over 4¾.

In the eight subjects during the 1866–67 semester he had two 5¾s, one 5, one 4¾, one 4⅔, and three 4½s, averaging slightly over 4¾.

Of the four subjects during the 1867–68 semester, his last, Röntgen had the two 6s by Zeuner, and one 5½ and one 4 by Ludewig in machine building history and in machine construction, for an average of better than 5⅓ points.

As a condition of his final examination Willi Röntgen underwent an *Uebergangsdiplomprüfung,* a transition-diploma-examination, in February 1868, with these results: analytical geometry of the surface, analytical geometry of space, differential arithmetic, integral arithmetic, geostatics and hydrostatics, geodynamics and hydrodynamics, common physics and heat theory, electricity and optics, all with grade 6; in chemical technology of building materials and metallurgy, 5¾; in civil construction, 5½; and in demonstrative geometry, 4½.

The final examinations also were passed brilliantly by Willi Röntgen. In the oral portion, he received in theoretical machine history and in mechanical technology a 6, and in machine building history a 5½. The *Diplomarbeit-Schriftlicher Teil,* diploma work, written part, consisted of a project to equip a factory with new steam engines. He received a 5¾ and a 4½ for the thesis. Examining teachers commented, "The student showed an excellent interest in theoretical disciplines but less in actual construction problems." They recognized his "scientific and technical qualification for beginning the profession of a machine engineer."

Although he received his diploma as a mechanical engineer from the Eidgenössischen Polytechnischen Schule on August 6, 1868, student Willi Röntgen felt that his chosen field did not hold as much interest for him as he had believed earlier. Perhaps stimulated by the course in technical physics given by the famed Professor Rudolf Julius Emanuel Clausius, an excellent physicist in the field of kinetic gas theory and "the father of thermodynamics," the eager young student turned to this new field. Incredibly, Röntgen did not major in experimental physics while at college, the field in which he later made his name, although he took the fundamental courses in that subject.

While the Clausius lectures had stimulated the student from Apeldoorn and opened a new era of endeavor to him, the renowned scientist left Zurich for Würzburg the year Röntgen received his diploma. But this apparent dilemma was somewhat eased by the successor who was destined to have a deciding influence upon his student's life. Professor August Eduard Eberhard Kundt now occupied the chair of physics at the Eidgenössischen Technischen Schule and lectured on the intriguing theory of light. Röntgen also took some additional courses in higher mathematics, but was still quite undecided as to a career. He had no definite plans for his future.

When Zeuner, who had affectionately been called by his students "the soul of the mechanical-technical division," left Zurich, Röntgen was greatly disappointed, although he had then completed his work for the engineering diploma. But Zeuner's leaving had effected a shift of interest to Clausius and then to Kundt.

Befitting a young man with an engineering degree, Willi Röntgen now sported a short-cropped beard.

His friend Albert suggested that he discuss the important matter of his life's work with Professor Kundt, and Röntgen then asked the advice of the 29-year-old physics professor. Of this momentous personal interview with the short and elegantly dressed energetic man of science, Röntgen later wrote, "When he asked me, 'What do you really want to do in your life?' I answered him that I did not know. He replied that I should try physics. I had to confess that I had almost nothing at all to do with that particular branch of study. He suggested that I could catch up on that easily."

Years later, shortly before his death, Röntgen wrote to his old college friend Albert:

The memories of our very happy youth, which were awakened by your letter, struck a lovely chord in my own heart. A short time ago Besser came to see me, and we talked about our Zurich student years. You, he, and I can be satisfied with what life has brought us, especially remembering that at that time, to me at least, the future looked very problematical. Do you remember that it was through you that I met Kundt, who introduced me to physics, and thus removed the doubt and uncertainty regarding my future.

Thus, now with keener interest in experimental physics, the 24-year-old student spent more time in the laboratory in physical experiments on various properties of gases. This was fascinating, exciting, and challenging work for him; he enjoyed it immensely.

Bertha became ill and was hospitalized at the Dr. Vögeli Sanatorium on the Uetliberg. Willi then combined his love for hiking up the steep hill with visiting his girl friend. His visits to the inn became fewer and so did the discussions with Ludwig. Bertha became more and more depressed as her stay lagged on.

On April 22, mainly to cheer Bertha's sagging spirits on her thirtieth birthday, student Röntgen hired a carriage, drawn by four perfectly matched horses and ably driven by the top-hatted *Kutscher* in splendrous livery. Not only the elegant equipage but the huge bouquet of red roses, which just about filled the entire seat beside him, attracted the attention of the amazed ambulatory patients and the joy of his ailing Bertha. It was an extravagant performance but brought the expected therapeutic result.

Röntgen's work with gases resulted in his decision to submit these findings as his doctoral dissertation to the Universität, which then shared its facilities with the Technischen Schule. In the dissertation he mentioned in gratitude his *Gefühl der aufrichtigen Dankbarkeit,* or feeling of sincere thankfulness, for his *hochverehrten Lehrer,* or highly revered teacher, Professor Zeuner. The full title page of the thesis read:

Studien über Gase.
Inaugural-Dissertation/zur/Erlangung der Doktorwürde
vorgelegt
der hohen philosophischen Fakultät
der
Universität Zürich
von
Wilhelm Röntgen
von Apeldoorn (Holland).
Zürich,
Druck von Züricher und Furrer.
1869.

The experimental physicist, Professor Albert Mousson, on June 12, 1869, wrote the evaluation of this dissertation. The first thirteen pages dealt with the basic principles of theoretical heat theories, as propounded by Clausius. From there on the writer concerned himself with the consequences of an *ideal* gas, utilizing the thoughts of Régnault on this independence of heat with and without extensions of pressure and volume. The most important inference consisted of a modification of the Mariotte-Gay Lussac's law, having to do with the volume of gas at absolute zero (273 degrees below the point of freezing). The size had a definite concrete significance which Hirn had called *volume atomique*. The writer deduced that the coefficient of the pressure change through heating appeared greater than that of the change by volume in some gases, and the opposite seemed true in others. The evaluator concluded that Herr Röntgen's thesis contained more than the necessary proof "of solid knowledge and independent research talent" in the field of physics to recognize this work as an "entirely sufficient basis for promotion."

The astronomer Rudolf Wolf agreed with this judgment, and Wilhelm Röntgen was awarded the doctorate of philosophy at the faculty meeting on June 22, 1869. Attending were Mousson, Wolf, the stereochemist Johannes Wislicenus, the naturalist Oswald Heer, the geologist Escher von der Linth, the minerologist Kenngott, and the chemist Städeler.

After the official ceremony when he received his doctorate, Willi Röntgen immediately rushed to share his achievement and happiness with his Berteli, still at the Dr. Vögeli Sanatorium. He hurried along the footpath, usually a hike of an hour and a half, and after forty minutes from the Schützenhaus came to the Uto-Staffel, to pause only briefly for the striking view of the Rigi, Pilatus, and the Bernese Alps, as both had done so often on their mutual outings. He was anxious this evening to get to his beloved, and in another twenty minutes he was on top of the hill.

That happy evening, with two diplomas in hand — his doctorate of philosophy and master of engineering — the young couple made plans for their future. Although Professor Kundt had offered to take Röntgen on as his laboratory assistant, he had no assurance of a promising career. Bertha was in a sanatorium with a recurring illness that sapped her strength, seeming to defy definite diagnosis and consequent cure. Resolutely, the two made plans for an uncertain future.

The Röntgen parents in Apeldoorn had heard from their son about Bertha and his feelings for her, but when he wrote asking their permission for the marriage they were not at all certain they wanted to consent to having a Swiss girl in the family. They quickly planned for a convenient

Friedrich Conrad and Charlotte Constanze, parents of Wilhelm Conrad Röntgen.

visit to their old home town of Lennep for a short time, then went to see their son in Switzerland, and finally spent two weeks in a *Kurort* in the Schwarzwald on the Grosse Enz river. They welcomed the opportunity to go to Zurich, ostensibly to celebrate the earned doctorate; but actually the paramount purpose of their journey was to meet personally their possible future daughter-in-law.

In a letter dated October 3, 1869, the 63-year-old father wrote to his friend Herrn Buscher, in Lennep:

After we left Lennep, we continued our trip for three short days, and arrived by railroad in Zurich, where we were greeted by our son. We were very happy to be with him and met a Zurich girl about whom Wilhelm had already written to us. We had not given a definite answer to his letters, but when he insisted on having our opinion, we considered it our parental duty to look into the matter, and we were favorably impressed when we met her. Then we spent two weeks in Zurich and decided that, in order to get better acquainted with the girl, we would take her and Wilhelm to Baden-Baden for a few days and then go to Wildbad for two weeks. The result was that when we said *adieu* in Karlsruhe, for we were returning home and they to Zurich, we gave our consent to the **engagement. The** girl [Bertha Ludwig] is well educated, comes from a good family, is intelligent, of good character, and very agreeable. . . .

It had been a pleasant meeting all around. The elder Röntgens spent the two weeks in Zurich, met Bertha and her sisters and parents, saw the historic, interesting *Sehenswürdigkeiten* in the city, and made short excursions to several of the many places in the mountainous vicinity. The Alpine scenery impressed the folks from the lowlands greatly, but they expressed no preference for this stark beauty.

Dr. Wilhelm Conrad Röntgen became the first assistant of Professor August Eduard Eberhard Kundt and helped him reorganize the new experimental physics laboratory. It was not an elaborately equipped room, and most of the testing apparatus was merely adequate judged by the standards of that time, but it afforded the new assistant the rudiments to greater practical knowledge and further investigations in the realm of physical science. Röntgen himself had two younger men assisting him, Franz Exner and Heinrich Schneebeli, both advanced students — as he had been until the last semester. Both of these young men later became professors of physics, one at the Vienna University and the other at the Zurich Polytechnikum.

Professor Kundt liked his assistant and his precise work. From his superior, Röntgen learned to be exceedingly meticulous about the experiments he undertook. He handled the equipment with pride and responsibility. At one time he repeated a certain complicated examination eight times to check and recheck unpredicted results. He had to be

Professor August Kundt.

absolutely certain of the strange behavior of his investigated substance. He became an excellent laboratory technician. As much as Röntgen admired the knowledge and superior ability of the professor, he disliked the man's habit of working out difficult problems all by himself, without taking his assistant into confidence. At first Röntgen felt hurt by this obvious exclusion but eventually learned to live with it and, in fact, appreciated that Kundt also left him alone to pursue his own observations and conduct his own experiments.

Apparently only one serious disagreement occurred during the many years of association, and that right at the beginning of their affiliation. In one of the laboratory rooms Kundt kept some especially delicate instruments, which he solicitously guarded and expressly forbade his assistants ever to use or even touch during his absence. His characteristic fastidiousness extended to his laboratory and was reflected in his professional work. He tolerated no inexactitude. Professor Kundt was an ambitious experimenter, and one of his favorite sayings was, "What does not exist, must be created." Repeatedly, when a particular device was not available, or not yet invented, he would construct a practical contrivance which would suit the purpose and serve to complete the experiment.

Assistant Röntgen had acquired a habit of almost uninterrupted work whenever he found himself investigating an interesting or baffling phenomenon, and generally this work extended over the quiet week-end when the students and other assistants were not on the premises. He welcomed the greater solitude then; with no interruptions whatever, he could accomplish much more than during the regular week-day working hours.

On one such Sunday, while Röntgen was working in the laboratory, Kundt came into the room and found his assistant using some of the explicitly forbidden precision instruments. The professor became enraged and completely lost his temper. Röntgen defended his stand just as vehemently. His temper was equally fiery, and he had great pride. The argument finally subsided, with neither man quite gaining his point. However in due time Kundt forgave the infraction, and the unpleasant matter was forgotten and never referred to again. Both men worked together splendidly — in fact, so much so, that when in 1870 the chair of physics at the University of Würzburg was open and an offer was extended to August Kundt, who accepted the post, he asked Wilhelm Röntgen to join him as his first assistant.

CHAPTER 4

The Peripatetic Professor

DOKTOR DER PHILOSOPHIE UND DIPLOM INGENIEUR Wilhelm Conrad Röntgen disliked leaving Zurich and Bertha Ludwig. He had come to love the city and its surroundings nearly as much as he had come to love its fair daughter, whom he was anxious to marry as soon as his future appeared a little more secure. That time seemed to be now, but as he went with Professor August Kundt to Würzburg, Bavaria, Bertha went to Apeldoorn, Holland.

Röntgen's parents were greatly concerned about their future daughter-in-law. They had seen that she was an intelligent girl and had a good education, but they also recognized that she was not fully prepared to enter matrimony. Her faults, however, could quickly be corrected, and so it was mutually decided that Bertha should go to Apeldoorn to learn not only the rudiments of a German household but also how to cook certain German and Dutch style dishes that their son especially liked.

In Würzburg Röntgen found the laboratory at the institute terribly disappointing, as he was to find almost every laboratory at every institute where he was ever to work throughout his entire professional life. If anything, the deficient facilities were even older than those in Zurich. The old building was located, as if in jest, in the Neubaustrasse, and contradictorily was an *Altbau,* even by Würzburg's standards. The laboratory was so inadequate that Röntgen ruefully observed, *"Ein rechter Physiker muss mit Reagenzglas und Zigarrenkiste ein Laboratorium bauen"* — A real physicist must build a laboratory with test glass and a cigar box.

Kundt's critical remarks were more to the point. "This lends itself perfectly for the most ambitious expansion program ever undertaken at any laboratory in Germany," he suggested jokingly. "We will have to improvise, Röntgen, and therefore be the best men in the field! When the Education Ministerium in Munich provides unlimited funds for better laboratory equipment, then anyone can be a good physicist."

In this then so poorly outfitted laboratory Wilhelm Röntgen settled down to make further experiments on specific heat at constant pressure and constant volume, actually a continuation of the work done previously in Zurich. He hoped to make new discoveries on these problems first investigated by the two French scientists, father-in-law and son-in-law, Clement and Désormes, whose method was further improved by the renowned German physicist Friedrich Kohlrausch. Röntgen was especially intrigued by the experiments because he believed that he had actually discovered an error in the published observations and calculations. Thus he painstakingly repeated over and over again the very same experiment to ascertain absolutely that his new calculations, and not those published earlier by Kohlrausch, were correct. It was really audacious for the relatively inexperienced assistant physicist even to question the results of the eminent Kohlrausch, and the idea frightened Röntgen. Professor Friedrich Wilhelm Georg Kohlrausch was well known to the world of science in 1870, not only for his research of electric measurements and electrolysis but also as the author of the widely used textbook, the *Lehrbuch der praktischen Physik*. None had ever heard of Dr. Wilhelm Conrad Röntgen.

Nevertheless Röntgen pursued his work relentlessly, believing it almost impossible to be faultless in his observations, yet knowing decidedly that his findings were absolutely correct. Eventually this momentous work was completed, and he wrote down his observations meticulously in clearly understood terse sentences. Then he handed the paper to August Kundt asking that he permit its earliest publication. The professor accepted the paper without comment. This was not at all unusual for the "silent professor," who seldom commented on anything and offered a studied opinion only after seemingly endless periods of careful examination of all stated facts and conclusions.

Understandably Röntgen became impatient with the painfully long and unrevealing waiting period; he felt that perhaps after all he had made a mistake in his observations and consequent calculations which his superior had uncovered by his own experiments. The chafing assistant had about reached the limit of his anxiety when he found on his writing desk a copy of the *Annalen der Physik und Chemie* 141 (1870), opened to a red-lined article. It was his paper! Excitedly he read his familiar phrases in the printed article under the self-explanatory title, *"Ueber die Bestimmungen des Verhältnises der spezifischen Wärme der Luft"*— On the Determination of the Ratio of the Specific Heats of Air — *"von Dr. W. C. Röntgen."*

On the recommendation of Kundt the report was published in the official journal of the scientific society. Röntgen's findings were indeed correct and pointed to an error in the calculations of the mighty Kohlrausch!

That afternoon an extremely proud and happy Wilhelm Röntgen went to his room at Frau Troll's in Eckaert's Garten, a restaurant in the short street with the long name Veitshöchheimerstrasse. His thoughts were with his beloved Berteli in Apeldoorn, and *vinculum matrimonii,* the bond of marriage. The two young people were even more anxious to marry quickly now that they were separated by such a long distance.

The wedding was set for January 19, 1872, at the Röntgen family home in Apeldoorn. Röntgen's friend Carl Thormann was best man. It was Thormann who had been indirectly instrumental in bringing the couple together when he suggested to the auditing student Röntgen that he might be able to get into a university in Zurich without his Abitur. The festively decorated house was filled to overflowing with relatives and guests from near and far, but special favorites were his uncle Ferdinand and cousin Louise who were planning to emigrate to the United States of America, upholding the true tradition of the traveling Froweins and Röntgens. The brother of Louise, Johann Heinrich, had sent a Bible for a wedding present from Cleveland, Ohio.

A wedding was always a community celebration, and practically every inhabitant of the town, not merely the close neighbors, was welcomed to the bountiful reception. A sumptuous feast was held; the bride and groom, flanked by closest relatives, sat at the head table. Invited guests crowded every available space in several rooms of the home. A small group of local musicians played gay tunes while the joyful diners ate and drank and listened to short laudatory speeches. Then, furnishings moved aside, or even entirely out of the rooms, the untiring guests danced gaily until early dawn.

If the birth certificate was a wordy document, this marriage certificate was even lengthier, proving that the civil servants in the Netherlands were at least as deeply entrenched in paper work as were their bureaucratic colleagues in Germany.

The *"Huwelijks-Acte van Wilhelm Conrad Röntgen en Anna Bertha Ludwig"* was a long, detailed document, giving pertinent personal details of the two main subjects as well as biographical details of their parents, in 441 words, covering 67 lines and several pages. The paper was duly signed by the official, the esteemed Pieter Marius Tutein Nolthenius, Burgemeester van Apeldoorn, Province Gelderland. It was also attested to by the six witnesses, Fr. Conr. Röntgen, C. C. Röntgen-Frowein, Richard Röntgen, J. Boddens, W. Walter, and C. L. W. Thormann. And, of course, the principals signed as W. C. Röntgen and A. B. Ludwig.

The young married couple moved into a modest apartment on the Heidingsfelderstrasse, not too great a distance from the Würzburg university and the physics laboratory. As many newly marrieds, the Röntgens did not always manage too well, and the offered financial assistance from the elder Röntgens of Apeldoorn was readily accepted. Its addition to the hardly adequate salary of an assistant physicist made household managing at least a bearable chore for Bertha.

Wilhelm again worked long hours. He faithfully attended all of the lectures of Professor Kundt, usually assisting in the practical demonstrations before the students. In addition, he read many volumes of scientific expositions of learned scientists, concentrating mainly on the mysteries of electricity, which he considered the greatest gift of the nineteenth century. He spent many evenings alone in the laboratory investigating, exploring, testing, and observing new theories on heat and on light phenomena, while his bride Bertha sat alone at home.

Settling down to a pleasant routine of home life was not too easy for the new husband. As a young student, and later as a bachelor assistant physicist, he had enjoyed great independence and some laxity in his habits. The daily routine of married life, the give and take, and the consideration of another person, no matter how much loved, was not always a simple matter for Röntgen. Money for the household expenses was limited, and Bertha was surely disappointed in having to do practically all of her own work. The drudgery of washing, cooking, sewing, and mending sometimes overwhelmed her. Once, while the couple were on a leisurely walk on the Frankenwarte, a domestic argument reached a high pitch; to end it, Wilhelm hailed a carriage and sent Bertha home alone. When, somewhat later, he reached home on foot, they had both cooled off sufficiently to be their amiable selves again. Generally both were in good humor, and those few temporary minor differences presented no real barrier to their mutual happiness.

When their uncle Ferdinand and his daughter were ready to emigrate, Bertha wrote to her cousin in a letter:

Yes, my dear Louise, it is infinite happiness to share everything with the man one loves from the bottom of one's heart, happiness and pain, everything that the dear, all-wise God sends us. And then, dear Louise, to have one's own household, in which one can do whatever one likes! Unfortunately, I am unable to describe to you this happiness in words, but I shall pray to God that you also may enjoy the same thing.

And Wilhelm added in that letter:

I little expected that when we celebrated the wedding, so hale and so happy, that it would be the last time we would see each other for such an indefinitely long period. Had I known that, much of the joy that day would have been spoiled. I send you all of the best luck and ask God's blessing for you on the long voyage ahead. May German love, industry, faith, and custom have their beneficial influence upon you and your surroundings also in the far West. Then you will soon send us reassuring and happy news, tell us that you are well in your new field of activity. Think once in a while of those who hate to see you go, and always remember us kindly. A pleasant voyage, and all good wishes in your new home.

The newly married Röntgens undertook a wholly unexpected trip in March. Professor Kundt asked Röntgen to come with him, as assistant, to the newly reopened Kaiser-Wilhelms-Universität at Strassburg, where Kundt had accepted, for April 1, 1872, the chair of physics. Röntgen had never been quite satisfied with the arrangements at the University at Würzburg and he greatly welcomed the opportunity to leave.

At Würzburg, Röntgen had been disappointed in the poorly equipped laboratory, which did not allow him to conduct really outstanding experiments, the facilities being inadequate for precise observations. What hurt his pride most was that he was not permitted to become a member of the faculty because of his lack of the Abitur. That he had never finished the Gymnasium proved to the college board that he lacked the requisite training in the classical languages, as properly taught in a Humanistischem Gymnasium and certified by its final graduation document, the passing of the Abitur. Despite the efforts of Professor Kundt, who urged his colleagues on the faculty to vote for the *Habilitierung* of his assistant, they turned him down. The venerable institution had strict traditions to which it unerringly adhered, and so it was impossible for *Doktor der Philosophie und Diplom Ingenieur* Wilhelm Conrad Röntgen to receive his *venia legendi,* his initial academic teaching credentials. He could not even become a *Privat Dozent,* a lecturer not an official member of the teaching staff, with income dependent upon the fees of his students only. Röntgen hesitated at first to leave Würzburg, believing that he should stay and establish himself there despite the negative response by the authorities to his application for the *venia legendi.* But Kundt pointed out that the successor to the chair undoubtedly would bring his own first assistant, and then Röntgen would be relegated to a lesser post. This argument convinced him to leave, and he looked anxiously forward to the new position at Strassburg, which promised greater opportunity.

There were doubtless no traditions to hinder his progress there. The original institution of higher learning had been founded in 1567, and had a distinctive tradition of superior teaching. The old university, however, had been practically closed since the time of the French revolution, and now, after the Franco-Prussian war, it was being reopened in new and well-furnished buildings.

Many distinguished Germans had been educated there. Its best known alumnus was the great writer and philosopher, Johann Wolfgang von Goethe who, after extensive studies, was graduated with a Doctor of Laws degree. In his company were Herder, Stilling, and other talented students. The university had a great reputation for liberal philosophies, so much so that the *Assemblée Nationale* suppressed the université in 1794 as being a hotbed of the troublesome German element in Alsace. In 1803 it was converted into a French académie, which in turn was closed in 1870 when war became imminent.

The Röntgens liked Strassburg better than the rather provincial Würzburg. As capital of the once again German Provinz Elsass-Lothringen, created after the war of 1870–71 from the French provinces Alsace and parts of Lorraine, it was the seat of a Catholic bishopry. Its famed cathedral with its one pointed spire and one flat tower dominated the city. The elaborate Münster was actually begun in 1015 by Bishop Wernher von Habsburg and continued after his death by Bishop Wilhelm I. The Protestant Röntgens, however, attended worship services in the newer and much smaller Protestant St. Thomas Kirche, which consisted of a part of a Romanesque and Gothic former cathedral, built in 1200 to 1240, and finished during the latter part of the fourteenth century.

Although a metropolitan city, Strassburg reminded Röntgen somewhat of Utrecht during his boyhood. He enjoyed walking along the river and canal meadows and watching the heavy barge traffic on the Rhein-Marne Canal and the Ill River, which handled a large volume of iron ore and steel from Lorraine. As an inland port, with its ample waterways and harbor facilities to accommodate the vast traffic, Strassburg was an important water freight center.

The time Röntgen spent at the Strassburg Universität was in many ways profitable and the best of his academic life. The equipment in the new laboratory was the best he had ever worked with, and he threw himself avidly into the fascinating experiments and observations he had not yet fully completed. Often he worked with a colleague named Flexel, from the Gymnasium, developing a new application for the Bunse Gishalorimeters for the animation of the intensity of sun rays. Luckily, there was no traditional obstruction for Röntgen in conducting his own experiments, and the two researchers worked to their hearts' delight.

Ambitious plans were already definite for the spacious Universitäts-Kollegiengebäude to be erected in Renaissance style and to be adorned with thirty-six larger-than-life statues of men of learning. It was designed to dominate the entire complex of buildings, including the already existing Physical Science and Chemical Institute, the Geological and Mineralogical Institute, the Zoological Institute, and the Observatory, as well as the expansive Botanical Gardens with greenhouses.

During the year 1873 Wilhelm Röntgen published two papers on his experiments. The first was on the "Determination of the Ratio of the Specific Heats at Constant Pressure to Those for Constant Volume for Some Gases," and the other "On Soldering of Platinum-plated Glasses."

That year Röntgen's parents decided to give up their home in Holland and move to Strassburg to be with their son. The father was then 72 years old and the mother 67. Before leaving Holland, the elder Röntgens visited familiar places as well as relatives and friends. They stopped to visit the Gunnings in Amsterdam, but unfortunately that family was not at home. Frau C. C. Röntgen-Frowein wrote on September 6 a long letter to Frau Gunning, expressing her disappointment. She also wrote that they had stayed at the "Rondeel" for several days, hoping for a call from their friends. The move to Strassburg, she said, was in response to their own as well as their children's wish, but to leave their accustomed and dear place at their advanced age was indeed costly. Wilhelm and Bertha, vacationing since the beginning of August in St. Moritz (Bertha was also recuperating from a recent bout with dysentery) would come to assist in packing and looking after their affairs. Professor Kundt had recommended Wilhelm to a position in Rostock (Mecklenburg-Schwerin), but Wilhelm was uninterested in the professorship of physics in that city. Frau Röntgen, herself, hoped for a Dutch city for Wilhelm, but that perhaps was too much to hope for. Recalling a pleasant evening they had all spent together, with Wilhelm and the Gunnings, Frau Röntgen closed her letter with the thought that it was *"eine so herzliche und angenehmene Erinnerung an die früheren Jahre"* — so hearty and pleasant a remembrance of former years. The elder Röntgens moved to Strassburg on October 30, 1873. The move worked out to the mutual benefit of parents and children, and was never regretted.

When on March 13, 1874, Röntgen was appointed a Privat Dozent für Physik, his devotion to teaching and to experimentation began and no obstacles were to curtail his enthusiasm. Fired by his ardor, he constructed a number of simple devices to add interest and to demonstrate basic physical phenomena for his lecture courses.

During 1874 Röntgen published three more papers: "On Conducting Discharges of Electricity," "On a Variation of the Sénarmont Method for the Determination of the Isothermal Areas in Crystals," and, with the collaboration of Franz Exner, "On an Application of the Ice Calorimeter for the Determination of the Intensity of Sun Radiation." Much of the work with Exner, of course, had begun in Zurich, but it was brought to fruition at Strassburg.

Röntgen also made several important investigations and experiments with August Kundt, whose main field of research was optics and acoustics; but none of these observations were yet definite, and final results were not to be published for some years. The laboratory work was fascinating and pleasant. There was really no reason to be dissatisfied with anything in Strassburg. One of the colleagues was the chemist Adolf Bayer, who later discovered new methods of synthetic dyes and who had been greatly interested in bringing Kundt to the university.

The elder Röntgens lived close to their son and his wife. They visited frequently and spent short week-ends together, or merely went for a day's outing into the surrounding mountainous area. Excellent places were offered by the Vogesen (Vosges) Mountains, and the Rhine Valley; further away, the Schwarzwald with its heavy black forests was ever inviting. The younger folks explored many of these natural beauty spots, hardly missing their beloved and considerably more rugged Alpine regions.

In April 1875 Wilhelm was offered a full professorship in physics and mathematics by the Landwirtschaftlichen Akademie (Agricultural Academy) in Hohenheim, on the recommendation of Professor Heinrich Friedrich Weber, who was leaving that post for a similar position at Zurich. The prestige of having his own department, although in a rather insignificant institution, was a most welcome prospect, but to leave Strassburg and Professor Kundt seemed a greater loss. Röntgen met Weber at Heidelberg to discuss the position. It was not an easy decision to make, but after long deliberations, many discussions with colleagues, and particularly on the advice of the esteemed August Kundt, Röntgen decided to accept the position.

Hohenheim was located some six miles south of Stuttgart, the capital of Württemberg. Later it was to become part of the city. A royal palace with a magnificent view of the surroundings had been built at Hohenheim by Duke Carl, and the agricultural college had been established to assist farmers and landowners in this abundantly rich farm area. Several model farms were organized and operated at the nearby Klein-Hohenheim, Scharnhausen, and Weil. The state of Württemberg was mainly an agricultural state and, as the name suggests, Stuttgart was originally a stud garden. The scientific raising of horses, principally for the use of agriculture, was one of the main activities of the Hohenheim college, especially the branch at Weil.

Although Röntgen had visited the Hohenheim college prior to his acceptance of the professorship, he was greatly disillusioned after he arrived. The laboratory was ill equipped, and he thought it even worse than that at Würzburg. He made several requisitions for some badly needed equipment, but the authorities were reluctant to grant additional money for such expenditures. He found that his time to do experimental work in the laboratory was appreciably diminished with the regular teaching schedule of a professor, and he was not able to achieve anywhere as much as when an assistant at Strassburg. This was a disappointing revelation.

The provided living quarters near the small campus also left much to be desired. The proximity of the barns and grain and feed storage buildings brought with them an abundance of *Kleinviehzeug,* or small animals and vermin, so that life was not always as joyful as it should have been. The desire to be at the former post became ever greater. Recalling the housing situation years later, Röntgen wrote on July 14, 1922, from Weilheim:

In Hohenheim there were rats, but we were on friendly terms with them. They got their daily food from the garbage in the outside gutter. Aside from that they did not disturb us. In our apartment in Strassburg we had found bedbugs and cockroaches, but my wife soon exterminated them. We were young then and could endure many an inconvenience with some good humor.

The time spent at Hohenheim was not a cheerful one, although the citizens of the small town were friendly toward the Röntgens. The people, speaking with the strong dialect of the Swabians, were difficult to understand; at times the strange dialect was totally incomprehensible to the ears of the newcomers. Later, when asked about it, Röntgen hesitated to talk about that period. He said that they sorely missed the congenial company of the many young friends they had made at Strassburg university, and even more missed the enjoyable outings and get-togethers with that happy, carefree group. But more than the lack of social activities was the fact that Professor Röntgen made no appreciable progress with his experiments and made no new observations whatever while he was there — an unendurable situation to the zealous researcher.

Thoroughly disenchanted, Röntgen wrote a bitterly complaining letter to his old mentor August Kundt, who consequently invited him to return to Strassburg. A considerably better position than that formerly occupied could probably be arranged. Kundt wrote that he would try to see to it that Röntgen would receive the section of theoretical physics, which would allow him almost unlimited research opportunities. Kundt admitted in his letter that he had urged Röntgen to take the unpromising post at Hohenheim because he honestly felt that a period of independent activity in the classroom and laboratory was essential for Röntgen's development of his own teaching routine and unfettered experimental work technique. The "breaking-away from supervised activities was absolutely necessary to awaken the rich fullness of the brilliant capability of a great scientist," which Röntgen promised to become, in the eyes of his former teacher. The Hohenheim period was just another step in the process of reaching the top rung on the ladder of success. In a later letter, Kundt concluded:

First was Zurich, the start and the finding of a way without a definite goal; then Würzburg, a step up and deep disillusionment; next, Strassburg, a city and new university of yet routineless activities. Hohenheim was the last course in this study of greatness; and Strassburg, once again, could indeed promise to become the realized fulfillment of Röntgen's dreams of limitless laboratory research work.

When the definite offer came the following year to return to the Strassburg Universität as an *ausserordentlicher* (an *a.o.,* or associate) professor of theoretical physics *(der Experimentalphysik),* Röntgen accepted with alacrity and dispatch. The Röntgens moved back, and Wilhelm started the work on October 1, 1876. The Hohenheim professorship had lasted but a year and a half.

For the next two and a half years Röntgen often worked with August Kundt, although Röntgen now had a better position than previously, which gave him considerably more time to spend in experiments of his own. During these years (and to some extent during the time spent at Hohenheim) he was able to perfect his techniques in physical methods and to gain valuable teaching experience, but primarily he learned the necessity for absolute accuracy in his experimental results. He studied the ratio of the specific heat of gases; and eventually he was to write, with Kundt's collaboration, four important papers on the effect of the electromagnetic rotation of the plane of polarization in gases. The titles were, "Proof of the Electromagnetic Rotation of the Plane of Polarization of Light in Vapor of Carbon Disulphide" (1879), "Supplement to the Paper on the Rotation of the Plane of Polarization in Carbon Disulphide" (1879), "On the Electromagnetic Rotation of the Plane of Polarization of Light in Gases" (1879), and "On the Electromagnetic Rotation of the Plane of Polarization in Gases — Second Communication" (1880). In these four papers the authors proved the very existence of this rotation, and they measured it quantitatively — a phenomenon which their great predecessor, the English chemist and physicist Michael Faraday, had failed to demonstrate successfully.

During his second Strassburg activity Röntgen actually published fifteen scientific articles. He especially liked to work with crystals during this time, believing that they were the embodiment of natural laws. He showed unusual experimental resourcefulness when he attempted to find in nature physical facts leading to such laws. He investigated the study of heat in crystals and eventually extended his work into the properties of actinoelectricity and piezoelectricity. The wide range of the published reports indicate the scope of his technical skills. They were "On the Ratio of Cross Contraction to Longitudinal Dilation of Caoutchouc" (1876), "A Telephonic Alarm" (1877), "Communication on a Few Experiments in the Field of Capillarity" (1878), "On an Aneroid Barometer with a Mirror for Reading the Scale" (1878), "On a Method for the Production of Isothermals on Crystals" (1878), and "On Discharges of Electricity in Insulators" (1878).

Röntgen mailed copies of these publications of his findings to an ever-increasing number of colleagues at other universities, a practice he had inaugurated earlier and was to follow regularly.

His colleagues noted — in the words of Otto Glasser — that:

In each of these papers Röntgen proved himself to be a fine classical experimental physicist in the tradition of Professor August Kundt. He clearly conceived the problem before him, was skillful in the experimental investigation, and carefully carried out rigidly controlled tests of the results obtained before presenting his findings in a brief but precise and logical manner.

Wilhelm Ostwald in his book, *Grosse Männer,* wrote later, defining the work methods of a Romanticist and a Classicist:

The Romanticist produces quickly and quantitatively, and thus he needs surroundings which readily accept these efforts of his. The Classicist, as Röntgen was, generally has a tendency against extemporaneous procedure and all existing knowledge is suspect to him. While the Romanticist first concerns himself to finish quickly the present problem so as to be ready for the next one, the paramount concern of the Classicist is to exhaust the present problem so thoroughly that neither he nor any other scientist of his time could ever hope to improve the results of his investigations. The works of the Classicist win longer life because as fountainhead they retain their value, while the advances of the Romanticist have long lost their peculiarities and have entered into nameless continuance of general knowledge.

Mother Röntgen wrote to Frau Gunning in April 1879 that all the Röntgens now lived in a spacious, airy, and comfortable apartment on the Münsterplatz instead of their former simple residence. From their front room windows they saw the splendid venerable minster before them, with the lyceum, the palace, and the post office also on the large square. Living was very agreeable, and all food items including the fancy delicacies they loved were abundantly available. As to the sociability between the Germans and the French, and especially the Elsässern, she made no judgment, because as elderly folk they did not partake in outside social activities. The younger couple had no outside social contacts, either; their friends all were university colleagues. But the other apartment dwellers she found as friendly and amiable as those in Stuttgart.

Her Wilhelm had now become 34 years old, she wrote, and she recalled with thankfulness that he had advanced so rapidly. By the grace of the All-highest and by his own diligence and hard work, he had this achieved, for he had no intercession or aid from them or others. Not that this would have helped without the grace of God. Wilhelm's health was good, but he had occasional trouble with his eyes, and studying made him rather nervous at times. Bertha's health was fair, but she took it very hard when their doctor told her that she would be unable to bear any children.

She chatted on in her letter. Their health, considering their ages, was still good, although her 78-year-old husband suffered from shortness of breath. She, for all her 73 years, had recovered quickly from an operation on a swelling on her head, and her memory played tricks on her, forgetting if she had written to Frau Gunning of her sister's death. However, that the Gunning family had been so dear and good to her Wilhelm she would never forget! Nor could she forget the visit two years ago to Apeldoorn, and now she would spend six weeks with her sister Boddens.

With professorial prerogative, Wilhelm Röntgen forgot to mail the letter until May 10. He had told his mother not to send it off until he added some writing of his own. But the additional work, a second trip to Giessen, the concluding of affairs at Strassburg, and finally the packing and moving interfered with that good intention. He would write a separate, long letter later, he felt. All this was explained in a detailed one-page postscript by his mother.

Toward his last years at Strassburg, Wilhelm Röntgen had earned a name for himself as a thorough researcher, and other physicists were well aware of the work the physicist contributed to science. When the chair of physics at the University of Giessen became vacant, the professors Friedrich Hugo Wüllner, Röntgen, and Kundt were under consideration for the post, but such eminent scholars as Hermann von Helmholtz, Gustav Kirchhoff, and Lothar Meyer recommended Röntgen for it.

Cautiously, the 34-year-old Röntgen went to Giessen himself to check the existing facilities for research work and to discuss in detail the offered position. Apparently the interview and the personal inspection trip had fortunate results, for Wilhelm Röntgen accepted the post as *ordentlicher* Professor und Direktor des Physikalischen Instituts at the Grossherzoglichen Hessischen Landes-Universität, as of April 1, 1879. A still well-preserved letter of the Grandducal Minister of Interior and Justice confirmed the appointment.

As his assistants Röntgen had chosen the nine-years-younger Ludwig Zehnder and Johann Schneider who assisted Zehnder. This trio set out to improve the existing facilities, as promised by the state authorities as part of the Röntgen appointment as Professor of Physical Science.

The student lecture room and the laboratory were located together in a spacious private villa on the Frankfurterstrasse where Röntgen's predecessor, Professor Heinrich Buff, had lived forty years until his death on December 24. A larger lecture room had been built onto the main residential building, but several of the windows were blocked up because a shed had been constructed against them. Smaller universities often combined residence of the department head with student instruction rooms, and the Giessen situation was not at all an isolated occurrence. However these old and much too crowded quarters were to be replaced, and the new facilities were to be available for the 1880 fall semester. Money for the new building had been duly appropriated by the grand-duchy of Hesse.

Selection of equipment for the laboratory was left to the discretion of the newly appointed Ordinarius für Physik und Direktor des Instituts, and Wilhelm Röntgen immensely enjoyed this challenging task of furnishing the institute with the newest apparatus for delicate experimentation and physics demonstrations for the students. In fact, he even designed and built some demonstration apparatus himself. One piece of equipment was created especially for the lecture demonstration of Poiseuille's law. Röntgen described it in detail in a paper, "On an Apparatus for the Lecture Demonstration of Poiseuille's Law," which he later published (1883). An outstanding paper, it was widely praised by his colleagues.

During this fertile period Röntgen made a number of momentous experiments, some of which eventually were published. "On the New Relation Between Light and Electricity Found by Mr. Kerr" (1880) was the result of work begun in Strassburg, even before this effect was discovered and published by Kerr, but observations were continued and finally concluded in Giessen. Other papers were: "On the Changes in Form and Volume of Dielectric Bodies Caused by Electricity" (1880), "On Sounds Produced by Intermittent Irradiation of a Gas" (1881), and

"Tests of a New Method for the Absorption of Rays by Gases" (1881). The latter of these papers covered a unique process of measuring minute physical effects with extreme accuracy; it has remained unchallenged for nearly ninety years.

Work with Röntgen was indeed exciting for his assistants, but also very demanding. One complained, "The Chief demanded such precise readings of instruments that I could not achieve them with my eyes." Röntgen had 3.0 sight, that is, three times the normal sharpness, although his eyes reacted poorly to green and he could not distinguish the colors on the caps of the student fraternities. While the work at the new laboratory pleased Röntgen greatly, he was also enjoying life in the small town.

The elder Röntgens had moved with their son to Giessen. The annual letter from Röntgen's mother to Frau Gunning, in response to birthday greetings from their Dutch friends, told of the move. When the Röntgens first arrived on May 4 in Giessen, they moved into a large apartment in the Alicenstrasse. Living was pleasant and urban; all the houses in the area were spacious and nicely built, and the surroundings were truly beautiful. When after six months, however, a suitable *Wohnung,* or dwelling, became available, the younger couple moved away and the parents remained alone in the large apartment. The street-level location offered many advantages during the summer, but the terribly cold winter period was far less pleasant. "It was a wonder that we came through it fairly well." They looked for a more suitable place than this *Paterrewohnung,* where occasionally water collected in the basement to stand for several days, and where the "monsterously" spacious rooms with large shutterless windows were "in the new style of most houses now." No, it was not agreeable and one could not feel homey. Thus, since May they lived at Neue Anlage 37, in a *Hochpaterre,* or high ground-floor apartment with smaller but comfortable rooms. The main point was the close proximity of their home to that of Wilhelm and Bertha, who lived across a garden from them. For their thirty-eighth wedding anniversary the parents received as a gift an electric bell which was quickly installed between the houses. In both instances, the owner of the villa lived upstairs.

Rents were fairly high in this medium-sized city, Frau Röntgen-Frowein continued in her letter. Wilhelm paid 700 marks (about $170) for the seven rooms, kitchen, maid's room, and cellar. But there was the advantage that houses in Germany had a tile heater in every room and a stove in the kitchen, all usually quite attractive and most useful.

She observed that life and social affairs for many people were varied and lively. During the winter one heard of nothing but dinners, suppers, dances, coffees, and tea affairs. The various social groups did not intermingle, and all had their individual groups and activities; the learned gentlemen with their ladies, the military men with theirs, and the factory owners and upper class citizens with theirs — and all had the usual disagreements and *Klatsch,* or gossip.

Wilhelm was well satisfied with his position and was, his mother felt, well liked and respected. He had an abundant salary and had many guest listeners at his lectures. Frau Röntgen assured Frau Gunning that she would not recognize the former tall, thin, pale youth, who had become a strong, broad-shouldered man. He was a good son, but his mother wished that he would be a bit more talkative in his daily *Umgang,* his associations, which would also be much more pleasant for her husband. "But such is his way, and he means very well."

His mother also wrote that Wilhelm and Bertha were both well most of the time, but that Bertha had suffered for some time from stomach cramps, headaches, and pain in her legs. On some days, she complained of dizzy spells. "We hope and pray that she remains healthy. She is for Wilhelm a well-suited wife and for us also a cordial and caring daughter." She wrote that she "had never met anyone who had not received a favorable impression of her, despite the fact that youth and beauty were passed and she did not have advanced schooling or abilities. Yet, she can judge all situations and conditions of life with understanding and so is a companionable and pleasant housewife. Her temperament is *ein wenig aufbrausend* — a bit hot-tempered — and that is bad. But our Wilhelm has the tact to overcome this. He is good, yes, soul-good, but he asserts himself, and his eye looks critically at his surroundings. He likes order and customary habits in his laboratory, in his study, and in his house."

The letter-writer continued. For the Pentecost holidays that year they all had taken a short trip together. The parents had dreaded the exertion but, appreciating the offer, they had agreed to it. They spent nearly the whole week, from Monday to Friday, in Wiesbaden, and from there went by steamer to St. Goar. From that town on the Rhine they returned home by way of Frankfurt am Main. The younger folk took every opportunity to walk and the older ones went along sometimes, but usually were driven to the designated spot to meet the *Spaziergänger,* or they remained at home altogether.

The surroundings here at Giessen are very beautiful, and they offer a rich choice of minor and major outings. The Lahn valley is romantically nice, and our hearts are full of thankfulness when we are together with our children. To sit in a good carriage and be allowed to admire the wonderful nature of God's creation in its ever new beauty is and remains a treat for us which we can never value enough and which makes life for us old people here in Giessen so infinitely more pleasant than in a larger city.

Located some thirty miles north of Frankfurt, Giessen had an ancient *Rathaus,* or townhall, an old palace and a newer one, several museums,

Bertha and Wilhelm during the Giessen period.

and a library famous for its 24,000 volumes of books and manuscripts. The countryside was inviting for walks, being mostly meadows, farm lands, and leaf forests. Fulfilling a long cherished desire, Röntgen leased some hunting grounds nearby where he could roam at will and convenience. Activities of the Röntgens were pleasingly satisfying, and this small university town was much to their liking. However, Röntgen sharply disagreed with Karl Baedeker's description of Giessen as a *"Sitz einer Universität mit althergebrachten Instituten und Sammlungen,"* a seat of a university with old traditional institutes and collections. *"So liegt die Sache dann doch nicht!"* "It just isn't that way!" Röntgen wrote to a colleague. Röntgen was proud of the growing university.

Some members of the faculty were close friends and remained so for life. The ophthalmologist and head of the eye clinic Arthur von Hippel, the surgeon Rudolf Ulrich Krönlein, the gynecologist Max Hofmeier, and Ludwig Zehnder, Röntgen's assistant, became part of a rather intimate circle of colleagues who had weekly get-togethers. The ladies found pleasure in planning the dinners. The men of science held long conversations on academic subjects, often rather dryly expounded, as in textbook style, but in a congenial atmosphere.

On many evenings after dinner the couples enjoyed pleasurable companionship. The men played chess and the ladies a game of cards. When the last guest had departed after the carefree evenings at their apartment, Bertha Röntgen complained bitterly about the smoke-filled drapes in their living room. But since the host himself with his continuously smoking pipe was the principal offender, nothing was ever done about the complaints. Had he smoked fancy briar pipes, Bertha would have hidden them, or perhaps even thrown them out, but he had the nefarious habit of using cheap Dutch clay pipes which he bought and used by the dozen, leaving them everywhere in a most disorderly manner.

The inveterate smoker claimed that clay pipes imparted an especially fine taste to the tobacco if they were first fired to a red-hot glow and allowed to cool before using. A blue-and-gold Chinese container which his father had given him held his costly imported tobacco. He cherished this container and protectingly kept it in a dark blue flannel bag. A small meerschaum pipe with decorative claws on the bowl reposed in its fitted lined wooden box and was but seldom used. To confound his visitors he always called it, "my hydrous magnesium silicate pipe." He later acquired two long-stemmed *Grossvater* pipes, but they were kept at Weilheim, as befitting a *Landbesitzer,* a country squire.

During one of the summer vacations in Switzerland, Röntgen had met Ludwig Zehnder. Perhaps because neither had his Abitur, the men felt a mutual bond. Like Röntgen, Zehnder had a diploma as mechanical engineer from the Eidgenössischen Polytechnikum; in addition, each man had a wife from Zurich, which led to a close friendship between the two ladies. Once during a conversation Zehnder complained that his expected promotion at the University of Berlin had not come to him because of this defect in his formal education, although he had later earned his doctorate. Röntgen suggested that he might like to try physics and work in a laboratory instead. The idea appealed to Zehnder, who had worked as machine engineer for some fifteen years, and when in October of that year the position of assistant at Giessen materialized, the thirty-three-year-old Zuricher accepted gratefully.

Wilhelm Röntgen expected his assistants to be fully dedicated to their work, so that it was a part of their very life's blood. *"Es muss einem im Blut fliessen,"* he said. He was a stern and exacting taskmaster, to himself as to others; as a master of concentration on a given subject, he had no time for frivolities while at work on some laboratory experiment. But when he occasionally noticed something amusing, his eyes would light up momentarily and a quick grin would brighten his bearded face.

As previously, Röntgen devoted much time and effort to the always challenging studies of the properties of crystals. He was truly fascinated by the effects of heat on them, which led to investigations on the absorption of heat rays in water vapor. This subject had engendered lively arguments between John Tyndall and Gustav Magnus. Röntgen constructed a simple but sensitive air thermometer, and with this delicate instrument he proved that humid air is heated more quickly than dry air. He found that water vapor actually absorbs heat radiation.

Because of his broad knowledge of scientific literature, Röntgen made experiments in many unrelated branches of physics. He was a voracious reader of scientific publications, often reading long into the night, while Bertha read a novel or did some fine needlework. His devoted application to the study of physics, his superb workmanship in the research laboratory, and his tenacious perseverance produced excellent results. It was much easier for him to do the actual physical experiments and make his observations than to write them down for publication. Occasionally he would take an interest in another, quite different experiment before the previous one was entirely completed. When he involved himself in an especially promising new experiment, he became so quickly absorbed that the results of the older one were not written up for publication until a long time afterward.

When in 1888 Röntgen discovered electrodynamic power, proving that magnetic effects are produced in a dielectric, such as a glass plate, when it is moved between two electrically charged condenser plates, his international reputation as a first-class scientist was secured. The Faraday-Maxwell theory had reasoned this electromagnetic hypothesis correctly, but it was left to Röntgen to accomplish it. The findings brilliantly proved his ability to combine the broad view of the theorist and the work of the definite experimental genius.

Many years later Röntgen tried to explain to Margret Boveri the distinction between experimental and theoretical physics in a letter: "To my view there are two methods of research, the apparatus and the calculation. Whoever prefers the first method is an experimenter, the other is a mathematical physicist. Both of them set up theories and hypotheses."

The paper in which Röntgen described his proof, *"Ueber die durch Bewegung eines im homogenen elektrischen Felde befindlichen Dielektrikums hervorgerufene elektrodynamische Kraft,"* or " On the Electrodynamic Force Produced by Moving a Dielectric in a Homogeneous Electric Field," was published in the *Mathematische und Naturwissenschaftliche Mitteilung aus dem Sitzungsbericht der preussischen Akademie der Wissenschaft, Physikalisch-Mathematische Klasse 1888,* the official journal of the Royal Prussian Academy of Sciences in Berlin, on the recommendation of the influential Hermann Ludwig Ferdinand von Helmholtz, the leading German physiologist and anatomist.

Recognition of this most important discovery came from many German scientists. The Dutch physicist Hendrik Anton Lorentz proposed that the new discovery be called the "Röntgen current." The theoretical physicist Arnold Sommerfeld wrote:

The new Röntgen current, together with the Rowland effect, forms an indispensable foundation for the concept that the dielectric properties of matter depend upon the presence of charges (electrons), and in their later quantitative perfection, decide directly against the original Maxwell-Hertz theory. This work further has led indirectly to the Lorentz and the relativity theories, and its results constitute the foundation of the modern study of electricity. [Radioactivity is measured in "roentgens," and it takes an accumulated dose of only 400-500 roentgens to kill a man.]

The German physicist Heinrich Rudolph Hertz had sent copies of his own published paper on the startling discovery on electric oscillation to Röntgen, and on March 1, 1888, Röntgen wrote to him:

Along with my thanks for your reprints I send you my sincere congratulations on the excellent investigations that you have made. I think that they are among the best made in physical science during the last years. I sometimes become impatient with my own experiments and must begin all over again. I must postpone detailed publications of them, but have presented a brief report, which I enclose, on the electrical effects of moving dielectrics.

It was this work of Hertz which was eventually instrumental in leading Wilhelm Röntgen to his greatest discovery half a dozen years later.

Even though impatient with his work, Röntgen had published several papers during the past years. Six papers were of his own experiments and observations: "On the Changes in Double Refraction of Quartz Caused by Electric Forces" (1883); "On the Thermo-, Actino-, and Piezo-electrical Properties of Quartz" (1883); "Observation on the Communication of Mr. A. Kundt: On the Optical Properties of Quartz in the Electrical Field" (1883); "On the Influence of Pressure upon the Viscosity of Liquids, especially of Water" (1884); "New Experiments on the Absorption of Heat Through Water Vapor" (1884); and "Experiments on the Electromagnetic Effect of Dielectric Polarization" (1885).

In collaboration with Schneider, several papers were published: "On the Compressibility and Surface Tension of Liquids" (1886); "On the Compressibility of Diluted Salt Solutions and of Sodium Chloride" (1887); "On the Compressibility of Water" (1888); "On the Compressibility of Sylvin, Rock Salt, and Potassium Chloride Solutions" (1888); and with Zehnder as collaborator, "On the Influence of Pressure upon the Refraction Coefficients of Carbon Disulphide and Water" (1888). Röntgen might have been impatient with his laboratory work, but unproductive he was not. Two other papers, with the collaboration of Zehnder were about ready for publication, but some results needed more verification.

When Zehnder wanted to publish a paper of his own on some of his own observations and their assumptions on a particular matter, Röntgen advised strongly against it, counseling that publications of major items only and then of tested and proven results, not speculations, should be brought to the attention of the scientific reader. He suggested that other writings, especially those offering a hypothesis, were nothing but presumptuous theoretical guesses, no matter how informed, and did absolutely nothing to enhance a man's scholarly reputation!

On the other hand, when Zehnder in his work on deformation currents observed results contrasting to those found by the physicist Braun, and wrote a paper stating his opposing conclusions, Röntgen suggested publication of these findings. As Zehnder later related, he submitted the first draft to his mentor for checking of details and for approval. The teacher slowly and cautiously read through the article, then took several hours in making corrections to express the precise meaning of each detailed experiment. After each word and each sentence had been closely examined and satisfactorily corrected, Röntgen laid the paper aside and asked Zehnder to return in two days for further examination of the written report. Then the ritual was repeated, and several hours of detailed discussions of the manuscript and some corrections followed. The paper was put aside once more. Two days later the third and final close reading, with minor corrections, took place. By that time Zehnder felt that every word was crystal clear and understandable and there was absolutely no room for error in the final draft. It was a painstaking effort, but it surely ascertained the accuracy so necessary to an important document.

The paper was then published, and Zehnder's work was highly acclaimed by the scientific community.

Röntgen's parents were not well but perhaps as robust as could be expected for their years. Thus it was quite a shock when his mother died at the age of seventy-four years, on August 8, 1880, the year after they had moved to Giessen. She had had heart trouble for some time. When the ailment became so severely aggravated that a drastic cure seemed advisable, Röntgen took his mother to nearby Bad Nauheim; but the hoped for results did not come, and she died there. Her body was brought back to Giessen for burial in the newly purchased family plot at the *Friedhof*.

Although Röntgen and his parents had been close during his boyhood and his student years, during later years while living in the same city they became increasingly devoted to each other. It was a sad blow to him when his mother died, being with her "one heart and soul." He wrote to Zehnder years later at the death of his friend's own mother, "The question of how my mother would have reacted or spoken to me in this or that difficult situation has often led me to the right solution."

Nearly four years after the death of his mother, on June 12, 1884, Röntgen's eighty-three-year-old father died. He, too, was buried in the Giessen cemetery, next to his wife.

Three years later, the childless Röntgens, realizing that they would never have children of their own, decided to adopt the daughter of Bertha's brother Hans, their six-year-old niece Josephine Berta, born on December 21, 1881. Little Berteli was a rather frail child, given to troubling headaches and backaches, and so did not attend school regularly. Her aunt, whom she called affectionately *"Mutterle,"* pampered her solicitously, often to the consternation of stern Uncle Wilhelm who would then be too strict with the little girl in an effort to counteract the softness and seeming lack of discipline. He felt that pampering made the illness only more aggravated. But the "parents" agreed fully on the need and the quality of little Berteli's education. She must learn languages and must practice her music lessons diligently. Because of complicated laws of adoption, the niece was not officially adopted by the Röntgens until she was twenty-one years old, of legal age to make her own decision in that matter.

Officials of the University of Utrecht extended an invitation to Wilhelm Röntgen to fill the vacated chair of physics, formerly held by the eminent meteorologist Christoph Buys-Ballot. Its former student was quite tempted to go back to his old Utrecht school, but after considering the pros and cons of the position Röntgen turned it down. Just two years before he had been offered the chair of physics at the prestigious old Friedrich-Schiller-Universität at Jena, which he also declined. The Utrecht invitation was extended because Röntgen was "a brilliant teacher of great experimental skill," and because "of the quality of the publications, which show an exceptional intellect and profound knowledge, combined with originality of ideas."

It must have indeed amused Wilhelm Röntgen — who had a great sense of humor — to receive such flattering praise of his abilities from the university that years before had rejected him as a regular student. In declining the position he simply wrote, "To move into entirely new surroundings would require too much of my time, which I had rather devote to scientific investigations." He did not think he would ever leave Giessen.

Röntgen had now been at the Ludwigs-Universität for almost ten years, during which time he had published enough papers to secure his reputation. He was forty-three years old and a well-established authoritative researcher. As a practicing physicist he was expert and experienced. Seemingly he was a happy and satisfied professor at Giessen, but when in 1888 a small game of "physics chairs" was played at several universities, Wilhelm Röntgen became interested, as he always had been, in the changes that would take place. When the esteemed August Kundt left Strassburg, the great experimental physicist Friedrich Kohlrausch resigned from the University at Würzburg to take the position at Strassburg; the open Würzburg position was then offered to Röntgen. He was invited to become the new professor of physics and director of the recently built Physikalische Institut. University officials writing to Röntgen said that "the accuracy of the experimental methods of investigation have made you an ideal successor to the master of the technic of physical mensuration."

Röntgen could hardly resist the attractive offer. He went to Würzburg for an interview with the officials of the Julius-Maximilians-Universität, and to have a good look at the facilities that he himself had helped to inaugurate years before. The stately and massive Institute of Physical Science stood on the wide, tree-lined Pleicher-Ring. The impressive building had a half-basement for storage; the main floor was given over to several adequate class rooms, smaller laboratories, and a large lecture room. The top floor was the private apartment of the director, with an airy conservatory facing the large garden, which would especially delight Bertha. The heavy crowns of trees outside formed a continuing backdrop to the *Wintergarten*. Röntgen found that the entire atmosphere of the physics department had been changed with the splendid new building. He accepted the offered position.

When Heinrich Hertz, who was invited to follow Röntgen as professor at Giessen, asked about that position, Röntgen replied in great detail, setting forth his routine and experiences in Giessen. He wrote on September 27 in a four-page letter:

I lectured on experimental physics for five hours per week during both semesters and gave no other lecture courses. The practical exercises took two afternoons per week from two until five o'clock if the number of students was fewer than eight, otherwise they took four afternoons. The number of students attending the main lecture was around seventy, and usually was somewhat larger. During the last few years the number of students in the practical courses has decreased somewhat, probably because the outlook is gloomy for the future of natural scientists and mathematicians. The highest number was seventy-three and the lowest six during the last semester. On the whole the students are very industrious.

The associate professor lectures on theoretical physics. The employees of the Institute are a first assistant with a salary of 1,000 marks and a caretaker with a salary of 1,000 marks and free apartment in the building, with light and heat. The yearly budget for operating the Institute is 2,500 marks. Heat and light are paid from a special fund of the university. As a director of the Mathematical-Physical Cabinet and the Geodetic Society the associate professor has over 6,000 marks per year at his disposal.

Regarding income, the minimum salary is 4,000 marks, and I received 5,000 marks when I came here. During the last few years I have received a salary of 5,500 marks, and the income from lectures and examinations amounted to about 5,500 marks per year. An apartment of five or six large rooms costs from 900 to 1,000 marks, according to the location. I pay 1,700 marks for my apartment of nine rooms and in the best location with a beautiful garden. Living conditions are moderate, but Strassburg was decidedly more expensive.

So, he could have added, would be Würzburg. But at the height of his academic life with an excellent reputation as a serious research physicist and teacher, Würzburg would be another city altogether than it had been when he and Bertha as a young married couple had come there. Then, they had harbored high hopes for a future which had been sorely shattered when the university refused to give him an academic title. Wilhelm Röntgen could not help but reflect that his fortune had indeed changed.

In a letter dated August 31, 1888, and signed at Oberstdorf, the Prince Regent Luitpold appointed Dr. Wilhelm Conrad Röntgen "als Professor der Experimentalphysik an der philosophikalischen Fakultät der Königlichen Universität Würzburg und Direktor des Physikalischen Instituts" at an annual salary of 6,000 marks (about $1,500), a plenteous income indeed.

CHAPTER 5

Relaxation — Die grossen Ferien

FOR SEVERAL SEASONS NOW the Röntgens had gone to Switzerland to spend the *grossen Ferien,* the long summer vacations, and they were to continue to go there every year until the beginning of World War I.

In vacationing, as in practically all activities, Röntgen worked out an almost inflexible itinerary. First they went to Zurich for a week's visit with relatives and friends and to renew acquaintance with old memory-rich excursion spots. The yearly ritual was a climb of the steep Leiterlei to the Uetliberg with a rest stop at the Uto-Staffel to feast on the marvelous view that recalled courting days.

Then they went into the Engadin, their favorite vacation area. A sixty-mile-long valley descending from the Maloja Pass (5,961 feet) on the southwest to the Tyrolese frontier at Martinsbruck (3,400 feet) on the northeast, and abundantly watered by the Inn, the Engadin is bounded by lofty mountains partly covered with glaciers and snow during the entire year.

The ten thousand inhabitants of the valley speak a peculiar Romanic dialect. "We have nine months of winter," say the natives, "and then three months of cold weather." But the summer temperature rises generally to a comfortable 75 degrees, with winter colds hardly ever less than 40 degrees below zero. Rapid changes of climate often surprised the vacationing Röntgens, and white frosts with new snow appeared at times in August to dazzle them.

Occasionally the Röntgens stayed at Dorf St. Moritz (called San Murezzan by the Romans), a sheltered resort with mineral springs impregnated with carbonic acid and alkaline salts. The baths, extolled by Paracelsus in 1539, were not systematically used until 1853. The Dorf and Bad St. Moritz are on the Sankt Moritzer See. The highest part of the Engadin valley, just above the village, is the most beautiful portion, with its severe mountain scenery, numerous lakes, and picturesque villages.

For Röntgen and his companions, the easiest and most enjoyable walk was a leisurely one around the lake. Later this same lake often became the goal of a strenuous hike from Pontresina across the Stazer Alp and past the Stazersee, with a pause at the Meierei for afternoon *Kaffee und Torte*. For a long hike Röntgen would start out early in the morning to climb the steep slope of Piz da l'Ova Cotschna (9,311 feet), rest at the small lake there, and descend by way of the Hanensee (7,064 feet) to Champfer. The last half hour of the walk was on a level path back to St. Moritz.

Another favorite leisurely walk was on the Waterfall Promenade just above the resort town, with an extended half-hour hike up to Chantarella (5,678 feet). For Röntgen this also formed the first stage of a climb up the Corviglia (8,156 feet). Still, there was Piz Nair (10,029 feet) to conquer, and a hike along the very crest to the Suvretta Pass, along the Fuorcla Schlattain, with the Nair on one side and Piz Schlattain and Sass Corviglia on the other, and back to the hotel at St. Moritz by way of the Corviglia.

From Silvaplana, Röntgen often undertook the interesting hike toward the Julier Pass along the regular carriage road for a distance. He climbed the formidable Piz Julier (11,106 feet) and once its neighbor, the Piz Albana (10,111 feet), although a less strenuous ascent was by way of the Suvretta valley from Champfer. Crossing the narrows between the lakes, a pleasant hike was to the Surlej settlement, then to the small Lake Nair, and back past Lej Marsch and along the larger Lej da Champfer. The hired carriage would bring the ladies to the edge of the Champfer Lake, where a picnic lunch would be enjoyed by all, especially by the famished hikers, who claimed that mountain climbing used up 600 calories an hour.

The Silvaplaner See also offered many splendid picnic spots and easy hiking paths along its meadow-like shore, and a bit more difficult ones on the larch-forested mountain side, from where a trail led the climb to the dominating Corvatsch glacier (11,322 feet), and its neighboring Fuorcla Surlej (9,091 feet).

After the first few years the ultimate destination was Pontresina, but for gradual acclimating they usually spent a week or two at a lower altitude resort.

Röntgen and his wife Bertha in a landau on a leisurely outing in Switzerland.

A time or two the Röntgens spent their "acclimatization period" close to Zurich, between the Zuger and the Vierwaldstätter lakes at a slightly higher elevation. Rigi-Scheidegg, at an altitude of 5,413 feet, was well worth the exertion expanded in reaching its summit. From Arth on the southern point of the Zuger See, Röntgen reached the Kräbel after a thirty-minute walk. Then the trail rose to several view spots — the Rigi-Kulm, Rigi-Rotstock, and Rigi-Dosen, on the way to the Rigi-Scheidegg Hotel. An almost level road led to the Rigi-First, the Rigi-Kaltbad, and the Rigi-Känzeli with its romantic lake trail on the south edge and the distant view over the splendorous Vierwaldstätter See (actually Four-Forest-Spots lake, called Lake Lucerne). Another trail led over Alpine meadows along the north ridge to the Klösterli. Further trails went towards Gätterlipass and Lauerz, on to Gersau and the higher Hochfluh and the Vitznauerstock. A view of the several hundred peaks over the many lakes and valleys, or the dramatic fog banks hovering about on a bright sunny day, was an unforgettable sight for Röntgen and his companions.

In the earlier years the Röntgens usually stayed at Tiefencastel (2,854 feet elevation), situated on the left bank of the Albula and at its confluence with the Julia river. Peculiarly hanging at the immediate foot of a steep drop from the Lenzerheide valley, and at a relatively low elevation, Tiefencastel was the gateway to four valleys. The Albula river had cut a valley from east to west — the eastern part being the Filisur valley and the western part the Thusis — where it flowed into the Hinterrhein; from the south came the Julia river, originating high in the Julier Pass area near Piz Julier to form the Julia valley. Possibilities for either easy hiking or more demanding climbing were really plentiful to accomplish the desired adjustment to a higher altitude.

Lenzerheide, only an hour and a half distant, was another favorite spot. At an altitude of 4,921 feet, the very heart of the Graubünden area offered many easy hiking paths through the lush meadows and thick forests around the large Heidsee, or in the expansive valley from Chur to Tiefencastel. More strenuous trails led into the rising mountains, on one side the Piz Scalottas (7,625 feet), Piz Danis (8,189 feet), and the Stätzerhorn (8,593 feet), to which Röntgen hiked in about three hours across the Stätzer Alp. On the loftier eastern side of the valley was the more challenging five-hour hike through dense forest areas and eventual climbs of the higher mountains, the Parpaner Rothorn (8,730 feet) and Aroser Rothorn (9,950 feet). An equal distance was the still more fascinating Lenzerhorn (9,703 feet) with a spectacular view of the Albulatal to Filisur as well as the Lenzerheide valley to Chur below, and an incomparable vista of the icy snowscape of Alpine peaks all around. Most of the time the Röntgens enjoyed the simpler excursions to favorite spots on the charming Heidsee, either for a picnic or a visit to one of the many restaurants on its shore.

At Lenzerheide Röntgen hired the landaulet of Kutscher Emanuel Schmidt for longer excursions. The large carriage was elegant and meticulously kept, a polished vehicle with its top folded back to let the passengers enjoy the bracing mountain air, but the front and first side windows were raised to protect the occupants from the onrushing wind. Drawn by two sturdy horses in glossy harness, the equipage gave the impression of comfortable affluence and provided maximum enjoyment. (Röntgen himself had an aversion to train travel — although he always rode first class, which insured him a private compartment — and he preferred the hired carriage of Schmidt to take him to his destination, a time or two even all the way from Munich to Pontresina. But this was an extravagance not often indulged in.) Dressed in their comfortable vacation clothes, he in the dark green suit and loose hanging overcoat of the forester, and Bertha in a more formal but still rather casual suit, they made almost daily picnic trips into the valley to meet friends there. Then after the prescribed period of acclimatization, Schmidt would drive them to Pontresina.

At Pontresina the greater part of the summer vacation was spent. It was the ideal mountain paradise for the Röntgens. Situated at an altitude of 6,070 feet and with a population of about five hundred people, the summer resort suns itself along the right bank of the Berninabach. The town actually consisted of Lower Pontresina (the Romans called it Laret) with a parish church and the villages of Bellavita, Upper Pontresina, and Giarsum. Right out of Giarsum was the little chapel of Sainte Maria, its wooden roof dating from 1497, and the ruined tower of La Spaniola.

This side valley of the Engadin at Pontresina commanded a really magnificent view of the peaks of the Bernina group of mountains. In some parts of the Alps trees seldom grow over 6,200 feet above sea level, but here the slopes were heavily wooded up to some 7,200 feet altitude with the graceful larch trees, distinguished by their short fascicled deciduous leaves and tough durable wood, and the Swiss stone pines, sometimes called the Cedars of the Alps, whose close-grained white wood was esteemed for cabinet work. The kernels of the cones have an agreeable flavor, not unlike pineapple.

For many years during vacations the Röntgens stayed at the Weisses Kreuz Hotel, with its splendid view of the Roseg Valley. *Wirt* Leonhard Enderlin, genial host and occasional mountain guide, was an extraordinary type of hotelkeeper. Being especially fond of the high mountains and lovely Engadin area, he had taken a teaching position in Pontresina where the valley of the Upper Engadin, on a terrace at 6,000 to 6,500 feet above sea level, was protected from the icy winds that blew through the Sils and St. Moritz valleys. Here Alpine flowers afforded botanist Enderlin full expression.

Enderlin took his meals at the moderate *Gasthaus Weisses Kreuz,* quickly becoming a close friend of the family and especially of the eldest daughter, whom he soon married. On the death of her father, she took over the business. But Enderlin had been a reluctant *Wirt.* His wife attended to the business details while he was an expert mountain guide to climbers, led trail hikers through meadows and woods, and furnished correct botanical identifications. Daily he supplied the tables in the *Gasthaus* with exquisite wild flowers.

Staying at this moderate and unpretentious hotel was so out of character for the Röntgens, one can only assume that the strong feeling of personal loyalty that Röntgen held of Enderlin was responsible for the decision to spend vacations there. Pontresina had five or more first-class luxury hotels, all of which had greatly superior facilities and would normally have been chosen by the Röntgens. But Röntgen had met Enderlin on the first visit to Pontresina, and the great respect he held for the innkeeper was no doubt the determining factor.

Most of the colleagues from the university (at either Giessen or Würzburg) also stayed there. Over the years this was usually the same group of vacationers, either all or most of the following friends: the von Hippels, Zehnders, Krönleins, Ritzmann, Lüders, Hitzig, and Schönborn. Occasionally they were briefly joined by other friends, such as Fräulein Vögeli from Zurich and Fräulein Lotte Baur. Boveri, who disliked the bustling Pontresina area as too commercialized, was there only once or twice with the group.

On rainy days the vacationers remained indoors to play chess and cards, but on clear days, or even when slightly inclement weather prevailed, the nature seekers were outside on the trails. All of the outings, the hikes, climbing expeditions, and picnics of the large Röntgen party were meticulously planned by Röntgen and Enderlin and often involved the entire guest list of the small hotel. These included, at one time, a Grand Duke of Baden, at other times, big industrialists and businessmen, who then became daily companions throughout their entire summer vacations. Little Berteli found a playmate and friend in the granddaughter of the Enderlins, Anna Trippi.

Easy hikes went along the slope beyond the Chalet Sanssouci, or a little farther to the Roseg Glacier, to the Schafberg, and to the Muottas Muragl. At times the sturdier vacationers would hike to an appointed spot, while the ladies and weaker members of the stronger sex would arrive by hired carriage for the planned outing. A rich display of exquisite Alpine flowers greeted them on the higher pastures in the early summer.

As a mountaineer, Leonhard Enderlin had found here in the Engadin more challenging peaks to climb than anywhere else, and as botanist he had located more flower species in greater profusion than anywhere else.

Botanist Enderlin and Röntgen pointed out various species of wild flowers on their hikes, and Enderlin usually reached the one-hundred mark first in their annual friendly contest of identifying *Alpenblumen*. Röntgen knew most of the Alpine flowers not only by their common but also by their proper Latin names, having first learned them through his young bride in Zurich, but his eye weakness for green was a decided handicap. While to their companions the abundant yellow daisy-like flowers were *"Weidenblätteriges Rindsauge"* and *"Grossblütige Gens-wurz,"* to Enderlin and Röntgen they were *Buphthalum salicifolium* and *Doronicum grandiflorum*. The purple *"Tauben-Skabiose"* was a *Scabiosa*

Röntgen showing an Alpine flower, after a nature walk.

columbari, and the *"Gemeine Braunelle"* a *Prunella vulgaris.* The blue-
bell flower Röntgen clearly recognized as a *"Kleine Glockenblume"* and
Campanula cochleanifolia, and the more delicate *"Heilglöckel"* became
the *Cortusa Matthioli.* The orchid-like mountain cuckoo flower, the *"Berg-
Kuckucksblume,"* was actually a *Platanthera chlorantha,* Enderlin and
Röntgen insisted. But when Röntgen pointed out amusingly that the huge
dandelion here was only a much healthier variety of the *"Löwenzahn,"*
the common pest in his garden at home, Enderlin replied that to a real
Wissenschaftler, or scientist, it was the *"steinhaarige" Leontodon hispidus.*
And so the game went on.

On their more daring climbing expeditions, especially to the mighty
Morteratsch glacier, the Röntgen party was enthralled at the wide expanse
of the red carpets of Alpine roses; and not one of the party felt inferior
when Enderlin referred to the flowers as *Rhododendrum hirsutum.* In
the still higher elevations, the mountaineers carefully picked the delicate
Edelweiss, queen of all Alpine flowers (called *"Alv etern"* by the natives
and *Stail alpina* by botanists), one for each of the fellow vacationers who
had stayed behind at the hotel.

Other enjoyable outings were taken to the charming unspoiled villages of Sils-Baselgia on the right bank of the Inn, to Sils-Maria in the lovely sheltered larch-clad hills through which the Fex river had forced its winding way, and to the Sils on the alluvial plain at the east end of the Silser See, the largest of the Engadin lakes, into which the Chaste peninsula protruded.

From Sils-Maria a moderate climbing path led, after an hour hike, to the Marmorei (7,255 feet high) and onto the west side of the Fex valley, actually a rounded spur of the serrated Furtschellas, which adjoin the Corvatsch. It was one of the finest vantage points and a special favorite spot of Röntgen's, where he sat on a certain bench under a sturdy tree to gaze on the scene of green valley, blue lakes, wooded hillside, and snowy rocky mountain tops, the Piz Lagrev (10,380 feet), Piz Polashin (9,885 feet), and Piz Julier just across, or the snowy Bregalin area and usually very stormy Maloja Pass, with the multitude of resorts and their activities below. From the Marmorei Röntgen often climbed the trail to Lej Sgrischus to descend by way of the Fex-Curtins. Another rather easy path led to the Fex Crasta where a lovely chapel offered a pleasant rest and a nice valley trail led to the Fex Glacier Hotel and a meeting with the nonhikers of the Röntgen vacation party. A hillside path on the other side of the valley offered a different return route to the sturdy hikers, while the carriage took the others home by the same mountain road they had ascended.

The highspot of many outings was the climb to the Marmorei. Here, Röntgen and his companions would sit for hours, enjoying the magnificence of God's masterful creation, while renewing their own strength.

While Wilhelm Röntgen fully agreed with Friedrich Nietzsche, who found Sils to be "the landscape of silvery hues and one of the loveliest corners on earth," still to Röntgen, Pontresina had no peer.

One of the very favorite short hikes that Röntgen liked to take from Pontresina, and which took hardly any effort, was to a rock-strewn spot about five hundred feet above the town. At the old Sainte Maria church he turned right at the rough stone wall of the *Friedhof,* passed the ancient square Spaniola Tower, and walked for some five minutes through a steep meadow, brightly colored and scented with white, yellow, blue, and pink wild flowers in great profusion to a fork where he took the upper path. After climbing steeply for half an hour on a switchback trail through a forested area where trees were so thick he could not see the mountains across, he came to his loved resting place. The weathered bench seemed not to change over the years and neither did the majestic view that always awaited him.

Amidst the huge broken boulders, surrounded by tall needle trees, Röntgen saw the valley with the railroad track and road below, the whitish-green rushing river sending up the appropriate sounds of cascading waters, and an occasional high-pitched train whistle. Above the narrow valley immediately ahead was the forested Muottos Pontresina (6,820 feet), with the snowy top of Piz Chalchagn (9,465 feet) watching over it. On the right was the upper portion of the icy Roseg glacier, and on the left the entire Morteratsch glacier with the huge field of red Alpenrosen clearly visible through the powerful binoculars he always carried.

Seventy years later, two tired neophyte mountaineers who had closely followed nearly all of the Röntgen trails, rested on the same spot. A sign on the cemetery wall showed the path to this *Röntgen Weg,* and here on the *Röntgen Platz* a plaque on one of the large rocks reminded us of his love for it:

WILHELM CONRAD
RÖNTGEN
ZUM GEDÄCHTNIS
DIE DEUTSCHE RÖNTGEN-GESELLSCHAFT

But many times the robust Röntgen took other trails starting at the cemetery above the town. There was the one-hour hike to Alp Languard. From there he hiked across an open slope, climbing to Piz Languard, some 9,700 feet high, or to the little Languard lake, an Alpine gem. These hikes took about four hours. Lunches were carried from below, and the noon picnic was always an outstanding and most welcome event for the small group of hardy vacationers, who would feast on the available food no less than on the spectacular scenery spread before them. The two glaciers ahead appeared actually below them, with them higher Piz Palü (12,812 feet), Piz Bernina (13,284 feet), Piz Roseg (12,917 feet), and the dozen or more peaks of nearly equal elevation surrounding them. Lower, toward the Bernina Pass, were the barren slopes, rocky walls, and mountain lakes, the large Lej Alv with its smaller Lej Nair, and Lej Pitschen adjoining. Farther to their right were the Maloja lakes, the Silversee, Silvaplanersee, Champferersee, and St. Moritzersee (as Röntgen called them, using the German version instead of the Romanisch), with the range topped by the Piz Julier and Piz Nair behind them. It was indeed an inspirational view of grandiose Alpine mountains spread before them, and well worth the physical effort and even the aching muscles next day, as Röntgen liked to point out to his companions who did not always share his enthusiasm for the climbing expeditions.

Other excursions with crampons, ropes, and ice ax under the expert guidance of either Enderlin or neighbor Leonhard Caflisch were undertaken by Röntgen — his stout *Bergpickel* has been preserved — and over the years in the Engadin he successfully conquered the challenging Piz Bernina, Roseg, Palü, and others. The men sometimes would climb into dangerous situations. Once, when Röntgen had engaged the local guide Caflisch to accompany him on the seemingly harmless but tricky ascent of the Rosatsch, the couple became lost in a snow storm. *Wirt* Enderlin went out with a search party when they failed to return to the hotel that night. The two climbers were located, nearly exhausted, in a precarious position on some boulders, unable either to move forward or to retreat with safety. The descent was eventually successfully engineered for them. This story was told and retold, a hair-raising topic of conversation for the entire remaining vacation period.

Despite such encounters, Röntgen often quoted the appropriate Latin phrase, *"Montani semper liberi,"* that is, Mountaineers are always freemen. Then he would add with a grin, "Even when they are held temporarily immobile."

His consummate drive for scaling high mountains, Röntgen soberly explained, came from the normal desire of the physicist. Working in his laboratory with such mighty forces and masses, similar to the dynamics found in these Alpine ranges, a physicist felt the urge to master such *Kräfte und Massen* also in nature.

Dining was a cheerful time at the Weisses Kreuz. The Röntgens with their friends shared the Enderlin's family table. The dining room was nicely decorated, a wooden molding waist-high around the walls, a large gilt-framed mirror, a solid oak buffet, fine linen, and heavy silver napkin rings on flower-bedecked tables. A round iron stove in the alcove warmed diners. The guest rooms were spacious and comfortably furnished with wide German beds, a large wardrobe and dresser to match, marble-topped washstand, a chaise lounge, chairs, and a table. The large squared parquet floors were of expert workmanship. And from the window of their room the Röntgens enjoyed a wonderful view of the Roseg glacier and its adjoining mountains, especially in the early mornings when the rising sun cast its first rays upon this scene of splendor.

Röntgen enjoyed taking photographs — about two thousand of his large single plates and stereoscopic slides remain — and carefully posed his large groups before fixing his bulky box camera with an automatic shutter, so that he could also appear in the picture. Generally being reluctant to dominate the photographs, he is often found half hidden behind Berteli or Anna. Sometimes he stood in an obviously well rehearsed but seemingly nonchalant position, on the very edge of the assembled group. Throughout most of the vacation period, the garden of the Weisses Kreuz was cluttered with the filled frames; according to Anna Saratz-

Trippi years later, there were "hundreds" of developing pictures, placed to face the bright sun rays.

After Leonhard Enderlin died at age 76 in 1899, Pontresina did not seem the same to Wilhelm Röntgen. A new hostelry, the elegant seven-story Park Hotel, built immediately adjoining but above the Weisses Kreuz, now became the Röntgens' summer residence. With vastly larger guest rooms, each with a balcony and a wider view of the Roseg glacier, and spacious public writing, reading, card playing, and dining rooms, it was a tremendous contrast to the simple old two-story twenty-room place of former years. But the intimate feeling of the past was gone. The brilliant Würzburg era, too, had come to a close then, and the new *Jahrhundert,* the new century, was decidedly different.

CHAPTER 6

To Würzburg, Again

WILHELM CONRAD RÖNTGEN became *öffentlich ordentlicher, ö.o.*, publicly regular, or full Professor of Physics at the Julius-Maximilians-Universität at Würzburg on October 1, 1888.

There was still much to be done by the Röntgens in Giessen before they could leave for the new post at Würzburg. While professional movers packed the home furnishings, under Bertha's strict supervision, Röntgen cleaned out the small office he had kept for the writing of reports and preparation of experiments. He saw to it that his personally owned apparatus from the laboratory was carefully packed for shipment.

Among the items of laboratory equipment to be taken along was a one-kilogram weight that had been duly checked by the Berlin *Normaleichungsamt,* the official governmental department of weights and measures. A similar weight at Würzburg, which Röntgen had inspected, appeared unsatisfactory to him; hence he wanted to take this one along, and then return the Würzburg weight to Giessen as an even exchange. Before packing the Giessen weight, Röntgen checked it once more against normal 100-gram weights. Finding a 1.5-milligram discrepancy, he hastily wrote an irate letter to his vacationing assistant Ludwig Zehnder in Zurich, admonishing him severely for having done an inaccurate job of previously checking the weight.

Somewhat later, while vacationing in the Swiss mountains, Röntgen wrote to Zehnder that he had now received a letter from a department official advising that the weight in question was indeed *"nicht ganz korrekt,"* not entirely correct, as measured by their delicate instruments. The

The Physical Science Institute at Würzburg in 1896.

investigation showed that the weight had been inaccurate by 7.70 milligrams at the previous calibration check and now was inaccurate by 7.43 milligrams. Even in an absolutely "clean chamber" the difference would be minimal, but the 1,000-gram piece had officially weighed 999.99230 grams before and now weighed 999.99257 grams. Over the six intervening years the object obviously had gained exactly 0.27 milligrams.

The weight controversy eventually was settled, and Zehnder was exonerated by his superior. The whole question was of such minute proportions that it probably would not have caused concern to anyone else, but Röntgen was so meticulous in his work that even the slightest discrepancy upset him frightfully. Only by being so exasperatingly particular in his observations did he achieve indisputably accurate results.

As head of the Institute of Physical Science, Röntgen lived with his family in the spacious nine-room apartment provided by the authorities on the upper floor of the institute. Their own fine comfortable furniture had arrived, and Bertha immediately began plans for the large glass-enclosed wintergarden where she could keep pots with blooming flowers, lush plantings, and the *Zimmerlinde* all year, well protected from the icy winter weather. The wintergarden was her joy. Berteli later recalled that she and her mother spent many happy hours together there while Röntgen worked alone in the laboratory downstairs.

The situation was indeed quite different from that of eighteen years before, when they had previously lived in Würzburg. There was a new institute, with adequate laboratory and teaching facilities; and now, of course, Röntgen was head of the physics department instead of a mere assistant to the professor, as he had been in 1870. Under these changed conditions, the Röntgens really liked the city.

Würzburg was one of the more ancient and historically important cities of Germany, then the capitol of the Lower Franconia district but formerly the seat of a prince-bishop. Burcardus, the first bishop, had been consecrated by St. Boniface in 741, and from that early date down to 1803 when Würzburg was incorporated with Bavaria, an uninterrupted line of eighty-two bishops had ruled the diocese. The bishops, who retained great wealth and immense power, were consequently made dukes of Franconia in 1120. In the seventeenth and eighteenth centuries even the see of Bamberg was often subject to the bishop of Würzburg. From 1805 to 1813 Würzburg was the state capitol of the Rheinischen Confederation. Its major fortifications were removed during the peaceful years between 1869 and 1874. The city grew steadily, and by 1890 it had a population of 61,032, of which 3,575 were military personnel.

On his regular daily walks Röntgen often crossed the Alte Main-brücke, turned right, and ascended to the left by the Erste Schlossgasse toward the Festung Marienburg, which overlooked the whole city. This former fortress stood 426 feet above the river in a nearly impregnable position, on the site of a fort once occupied by the Romans. It later became an episcopal castle. In 1525, the insurgent folk groups lost valuable time and broke their own strength in a vain attempt to capture the fort, after which the episcopal troops entered the town and mercilessly executed sixty of the people's leaders. In 1631 the castle was captured by the marauding troops of the Swedish conquerer, King Gustavus Adolphus.

Close by was the battlefield where Archduke Karl, in 1796, defeated the French army under General Jean Baptiste Jourdan. On July 27, 1866, the campaign of the Prussian Army of the Main terminated at Würzburg, with the decisive bombardment of the fortress; an armistice was established on the following day.

From the mighty Marienburg, Röntgen had a splendid view of red tiled roofs and the many tall spires and domes of the city's churches, nestled in a green half-circle of the Glacis, a park area, formerly the city wall and moat around the ancient parts of Würzburg, all bordered by wooded hills. The wide Main river formed a slow-running bend below the fortress and disappeared down a valley in the distance. Röntgen readily agreed with Gottfried von Viterbo, who observed in 1180:

*"Herrlich ist diese Lage, wunderschön erschien sie mir; im Tal eingeschnit-
ten liegt die Stadt da wie ein irdisches Paradies"* — Magnificent is the
location, exceedingly beautiful it appeared to me; cut in a valley lies the
city there like an earthly paradise. Although then called Herbipolis and
bordered by the Moenus Fluvius, now seven hundred years later, Würzburg and the Main were no less magnificent.

Also rich in history was the university, founded in 1582 by Bishop
Echter von Mespelbrunn, whose statue was placed in the Julius Promenade. Although the university was chiefly a medical institution, it also
had zoological, geological, and physical science departments of learning.
The large Neubaukirche of the university actually dated from 1582–91
and was mainly a mixture of Gothic and Renaissance architecture, as
were most of the churches, which constantly were being rebuilt. The
Röntgens, however, attended the smaller protestant St. Stephen Kirche,
formerly a Benedictine Abbey, but restored — in rococo style — as an
attractive place of worship.

Wilhelm Röntgen's academic work soon again became a regular
routine. He was not only an excellent scientist but also an educator of
considerable ability. His guiding fundamentals were accuracy and intellectual honesty, open mindedness and suspended judgment, a search
for true cause and effect, and finally critical evaluation, which included
harsh self-criticism.

Professor Röntgen disliked to lecture, and he spoke in such a soft
voice that his listeners in the back rows could hardly hear him at times,
but he employed ready wit and subtle humor, presenting his lecture
demonstrations and lectures on experimental physics with the same thoroughness that characterized his own research methods. He used the same
meticulousness in his laboratory experiments and exercises, and he fully
expected similar standards from his advanced students, whom he carefully
selected by expert questioning. He took extreme care in choosing candidates for doctor's theses.

Röntgen admonished his assistants, "Don't pamper the students,
for it is useless. Let each find his own way out of difficulties." He emphasized self-reliance in his students; he was definitely opposed to "leading
them by the hand and spoon-feeding them." A number of his students
who majored in medicine could not follow his classic presentations,
thought that his lectures were too dull, and so stayed away. These students
of course, failed Röntgen's courses.

Röntgen's examinations were invariably difficult, never routine,
and always comprehensive; they were dreaded by all. Although he really
did not value examinations himself, he knew they were a necessary evil

and had to be given. His belief was that "the experience of life itself is the real test of capacity for any profession."

As a teacher Röntgen was not the least interested in the popularization of science in any form, and he severely criticized "popular" lectures, especially on physics. "Physics," he said, "is a science which must be proved with honest effort. One can, perhaps, present a subject in such a manner that an audience of laymen may be convinced erroneously that it has understood the lecture. This, however, means furthering a superficial knowledge, which is worse and more dangerous that none at all."

As director of the institute he was well aware of his duty to conserve and to watch over all property in a most conscientious manner and to handle with the greatest diligence the funds that the government agency had entrusted to him. He fully expected his subordinates to accept the same responsibilities, especially as pertaining to the collection of apparatus, its care, and respect for its value. The caretaker, Marstaller, soon found the "Herrn Professor" a scrupulous disciplinarian but an eminently fair employer.

Röntgen's contact with his subordinates was always formal and cordial but generally authoritative. When on January 14, 1892, he was told of the death of Weiss, his former caretaker at the Giessen Institute, he at once wrote a letter of condolence to the widow.

Today I heard from Dr. Balzar the sad news of the death of your husband. My wife and I are dismayed, for we did not know anything about his illness, and thought that your husband was as well and strong as when we used to know him. We can imagine how keenly you feel his loss, and I write you to say that we share your sorrow. Here in Würzburg I have often thought of your husband. Because of his faithfulness and readiness to help he was of great assistance to me in the Institute, and I liked him personally very much. Be convinced that I shall always retain his memory.

Wilhelm Röntgen was an impressive man with a bushy beard and distinguished features. He had a penetrating gaze and unassuming manner which gave him extraordinary character and dignity. His nature was amiable and he was always courteous, but his reticence and shyness at times amounted almost to diffidence when he received strangers. In later years this shyness acted as a wall; it protected him from selfish and curious persons but also kept many fine and sincere people away.

Occasionally Röntgen appeared distrustful, but actually he concealed deep sympathy and understanding. After he was convinced of the sincerity of his caller, he would extend a warm friendliness toward him. He had close friends among his colleagues at the university who remained close to him for his entire life.

Röntgen showed no patience with persons whose behavior was actuated by selfish personal motives or was noticeably shaded by personal prejudices. His was an intellectual honesty that characterized not only his work but also his attitudes. He believed that alien attitudes interfered with the progress of science and were actually detrimental to a person. Many times Röntgen was gruff to "people chiefly concerned with their own importance," and he was not apologetic for such behavior. He detested those who would try to cover up superficial academic knowledge with brilliant but utterly meaningless rhetoric.

The Röntgens' wide circle of acquaintances and friends in Würzburg consisted of many eminent colleagues at the university: biologist Theodor Boveri; father of histology Albert von Kölliker; physiologist Adolph Eugen Fick; botanist Julius von Sachs; pharmacologist Adam Kunkel; stomach specialist Wilhelm von Leube; surgeon Carl Schönborn; anatomist Philipp Stöhr; mathematician Friedrich Erwin Prym; chemist Julius Tafel; doctor Max Hofmeier; and his own assistant, Ludwig Zehnder. Because most of the faculty members lived in the Pleicherglacis section of the city, the Röntgens, when walking in the park, would usually meet some of their friends.

Social activities took on a certain routine. A close circle of colleagues, including many of those mentioned, was soon established. During the regular school semesters, four or five families of this group gathered weekly at one of their homes for a leisurely dinner. Then the men would go into the library for a brandy, and to smoke and play cards or chess, or to discuss some weighty subject; meanwhile the ladies entertained themselves with embroidery work, cards, or just visiting.

Formal dinners given by the Röntgens were always elegant. The lavish table setting often included six settings of crystal and lovely china. A florist would be called in to supply just the right floral arrangement. The superb dinners consisted of soup and full courses of fish, fowl, and meat — often a whole roasted loin — and the coffee was served in fine Meissen.

Selecting the proper wines was according to a certain ritual. Röntgen would go into the dank wine cellar, where he kept a stock of 300 to 400 bottles of white wines. He would carefully lift a bottle from a pile so as not to disturb it, blow off the dust or cobwebs, and study the label while Käthe, the housekeeper, held the lighted candle close for better illumination. Then he either handed the bottle to Käthe or replaced it gently to select one from another pile. After the selection of what he considered a sufficient supply for the dinner, he supervised the carrying of the wine upstairs to make sure that none of it was disturbed by undue shaking. Red wine — French Burgundy — was always drawn from a barrel that

held a two-year supply. This wine Röntgen also drank daily at noon —
usually one and a half glasses.

Throughout the year, though mainly during the social season, some
of the senior members of the faculty were invited occasionally to a sumptuous home of the nobility for formal dinner. As one of the leading professors of the university, Röntgen, with his wife, attended many such affairs.
At one event, as Wilhelm Röntgen escorted a countess into the dining
room, he noticed that the wives of the professors were rudely left without
male escorts, to shift for themselves. He abruptly and angrily left the
dumbfounded countess, went back into the salon to get his wife and
escorted her to her seat at the dinner table. Then he returned to the still
astonished noblewoman. This marked the last dinner invitation extended
to this polite yet rude professor, but Röntgen did not consider this slight
a serious social handicap at all.

One time, when he attended the annual Maximilianball, a *Hofball*
in the opulent baroque Kaisersaal in the Schönborn Residenz where the
nobility and scientists as well were expected, Röntgen bribed one of the
many lackeys to lead him, immediately after the official line-up, through
a back door to his waiting carriage. By ten o'clock he was already at home
again, Käthe Fuchs recalled, and was able to take off his formal attire, in
which, he said, *"Ich fühle mich wie ein Koffer verpackt und beklebt mit
Orden"* — I feel like a trunk packed up and decorated with medals.

To allow his love for the great outdoors a wider expression, Röntgen
bought a small, two-room log cabin in the steep hilly Rimparer Wald,
some five miles from Würzburg, bordering on the fine hunting grounds
of the larger Gramschatzer Wald. Here Bertha and little Berteli would
stay, while Röntgen went with a guide to tramp the dense leaf forests
with dark needle woods in search of game birds and animals. Berteli
later recalled that whenever the women went along, her father would be
careful not to go farther away than their voices would be able to recall
him in case of an emergency.

In a year-end letter to cousin Louise in the United States, Röntgen
wrote on December 30, 1890:

Starting with the news from our side, I can generally report only good things.
Bertha's health has not been the best for several years, only rarely does she
really feel completely healthy and fresh. However, we consider it a great
fortune that her spirits and humor do not suffer. I myself feel well always
and enjoy life, with the exception of times when I am somewhat nervous from
too intensive work. The position that I occupy now really makes me very
grateful and happy. Frequently I wish my dear parents were still here to enjoy
the results of their efforts and troubles! Who of us would have thought twenty-

five years ago that I would occupy a professorship in one of the larger universities of Germany? Indeed, I have had good luck in my life.

Our household has been somewhat enlarged. A young friend from Munich lives with us and will probably stay a year with us. We also have taken into our home a little niece of my wife's, a child now nine years old. It will depend upon the success of her education whether we shall keep her or not. As already stated, the change in our household made last fall is a temporary one.

We have celebrated Christmas in the usual way. The big tree was beautifully lighted. The Christ child had brought a number of presents. Do you still remember the windmill that was run by sand, the fountain, and the *crèche* that my father had made in Apeldoorn for Christmas? At that time according to the Rhenish custom Christmas was celebrated on the first Christmas day, very early in the morning. Then one went to church.

Would you please use the enclosed sum to make your children happy, and tell them about their far distant cousin in Germany. . . .

Röntgen's former assistant Zehnder had left for another position because the school authorities would not grant him a promotion without his Abitur. Years later, when Röntgen dismissed Zehnder's replacement, Joseph von Kowalski, Zehnder asked to return as assistant. He complained that his present superior, Hagenbach, insisted that he do experiments only for Hagenbach and none at all for himself. Zehnder, an eager independent researcher, found this a deplorable situation. Röntgen was much affected by the show of appreciation in Zehnder's asking to become his assistant again. While Röntgen wanted Zehnder to return, he was certain that the authorities would unquestionably make difficulties again in future promotion affairs for the well-known reason. He confided that when he told his wife about the possibility of the Zehnder's return she wept for joy in anticipation of a possible reunion with their close friends. However, at a meeting of Röntgen and his colleagues, the proposal was turned down.

In July, 1891, the Röntgens wrote suggesting that the Zehnders join them in Pontresina to spend part of their vacation together. They added, humorously, that perhaps Frau Zehnder could give yodeling lessons to the *königlichen Preussischen Geheimrat,* his colleague Arthur von Hippel, who had been awarded this title of royal councilor. As usual, the Röntgens would first go to Zurich for several days, and then by the middle of August would go to Pontresina for the remainder of the summer vacation period. Plans for a mutual vacation did not materialize, however.

The two couples met later to attend the *Elektrizitätsausstellung* at Frankfurt. The vast electric transmission lines then put in use between Laufen am Neckar and Frankfurt am Main had become world famous. At the exhibition Röntgen and Zehnder took a daring ride in a *Fessel-*

ballon. The balloon was aloft only a brief time, but the two scientists got a splendid bird perspective of the city and its environs. The thrilling experience left them considerably exhausted. It was several days before they told their wives of the escapade, emphasizing the unsurpassed panoramic view and minimizing the dangers involved in such daredeviltry.

When the mother of Ludwig Zehnder died in January, 1892, Wilhelm Röntgen offered his warmest sympathy to his friend. He said that by personal experience he knew that:

Trying to console is really impossible. But it is nevertheless well to know that others take part in our sorrow. I can put myself into your situation particularly well since I suffered a similar loss a few years ago. With me, too, it was the deepest loved one since early youth, highly esteemed and to me seemingly nearly indispensable, my mother, who was taken before my father. While she was alive I loved her and valued her highly. And then I mourned her death. What I lost with her I have only later realized and felt. How often I think of her and how far the motherly love reaches beyond the grave! And so it will also be with you, as I have every reason to believe. The question of how my mother would have reacted or spoken to me in this or that difficult to decide situation is answered by the motherly heart with its unlimited fullness of love. That always-willing disposition to forgiveness shows the correct way, even when the mother is no longer with the living. . . .

Two years later death took three of Wilhelm Röntgen's colleagues, all outstanding professors and friends. Heinrich Rudolph Hertz died in Bonn on January 1, 1894. Born in Hamburg in 1857, Hertz had studied in Berlin under Hermann von Helmholtz and had become (in 1885) a lecturer at Kiel and professor of physics at the Karlsruhe Polytechnische Hochschule (College) and later (in 1889) at the University at Bonn. His most important work consisted of experiments with electricity by which he transmitted electromagnetic waves with the same rapidity as light, these waves showing the same phenomena of refraction and polarization as light waves. His first paper describing his electrical discoveries appeared in 1887, and others followed for many years in *Wiedemann's Annalen.* Heinrich Hertz further developed and proved by actual experimentation Faraday's electromagnetic theory of light. Wireless telegraphy became possible because of the discovery of the Hertzian waves. Röntgen corresponded often with Hertz, discussing some of his own observations on further experiments originally conducted by the Bonn physicist. The untimely death of the thirty-seven-year-old scientist was a blow to Röntgen.

An infinitely greater personal loss to Röntgen was the death of August Eduard Kundt, on May 21, 1894. Kundt, professor of physics at the University of Berlin, was convalescing from an illness and vacationing at his summer home in Lübeck, when he died. Röntgen often referred to the help he had received from Kundt in the furthering of his own professional career. It was Professor Kundt who had suggested to student Röntgen that he "might try physics," and thus Kundt really was personally responsible for Röntgen's career. It was Kundt who had first given the young Röntgen his initial opportunity to work in the physics laboratory as assistant, and later it was Kundt again who worked with him in conducting experiments and making observations that resulted in three published papers by the two scientists.

On September 8, 1894, Hermann Ludwig Ferdinand von Helmholtz died. Born in Potsdam in 1821, von Helmholtz became professor of physiology at Königsberg in 1849, at Bonn University in 1855, and at Heidelberg in 1858. In 1871 he became professor of physics at Berlin. Also in 1871 he was appointed director of the Physikalisch-Technische Reichsanstalt at Charlottenburg. He continued to hold both of these latter positions at the time of his death. In 1847 von Helmholtz had read his paper on the conservation of force, *"Ueber die Erhaltung der Kraft,"* before the Physical Society of Berlin. It became one of the epoch-making papers of the century. In 1851 he invented the ophthalmoscope, an instrument for examining the interior of the eye, and contributed immensely to the science of optics. Important investigations occupied almost his whole life. Von Helmholtz was one of the giants of German science, and his outstanding contributions were in many fields — on the conservation of energy, on hydronomics, on electrodynamics and theories of electricity, on meteorological physics, on optics, on the abstract principles of dynamics, and more.

The deaths of these three eminent men of science caused much speculation among the leading professors at German universities. The vacated posts were among the highest ranking available to physicists.

An unofficial invitation was extended to Wilhelm Röntgen to come to Berlin. It was a unique honor to be asked to occupy the position with the highest prestige of any institution in the country. But Röntgen did not desire the Reichsanstalt post. It offered practically no opportunity for serious laboratory experimentation, and Röntgen was less interested in prestige than in a hope of doing more research and less lecturing. The Berlin position went eventually to Friedrich Kohlrausch of Strassburg, who now followed in the steps of August Kundt, who had accepted the Berlin post just before his fatal illness.

Röntgen was interested in an open professorship at Freiburg. Through Zehnder he let it be known that he considered the relatively small and unimportant post most seriously, mainly because he felt that the climate in this Black Forest city would be the healthiest for his ailing wife. Bertha had suffered almost continuously from coughing spells and was able to get relief from these attacks only during their vacations away from Würzburg. Both Röntgen and Bertha liked the attractive Freiburg location, having visited there frequently when in Strassburg, and they preferred the proximity to their favorite mountainous vacation areas in Switzerland.

Early in 1895 Röntgen traveled to Freiburg to discuss the proposition in detail with officials of the Albert-Ludwig-Universität and ministry representatives.

Freiburg im Breisgau was dominated by the tall, delicately perforated spire of its famed Münster, pointing boldly into the clear sky. The huge cathedral dated from before 1250, its structure one of the finest examples of Gothic architecture in Germany, and entirely of dark red sandstone. The university, too, was old, having been founded in 1456. The city was situated in the beautiful dark forests of the Schwarzwald, surrounded by picturesque hills and mountains white with snow during the long winter months. The territory was most inviting to the outdoor-loving Röntgens; the steep trails were a challenge to him, and the plains offered much walking pleasure to both. Together they could climb the gentle vine-clad hilly trail to the Kaiserstuhl or remain on the flat and lovely valley of the Dreisam and walk to an outdoor restaurant for their afternoon Kaffee und Schwarzwälder Kirschtorte. Freiburg to the Röntgens was more enticing than the other far more prestigious positions available.

The Baden Education Ministry offered Röntgen 7,600 marks annually, the highest salary paid to anyone in Freiburg, but still less by several thousand marks than he received in Würzburg. He would have taken the smaller salary, but there was also considerably less equipment in the institute than at Würzburg. Röntgen asked to be allowed the sum of 11,000 marks for additional equipment, a reasonable amount to him. He also wanted the lecture room enlarged and the physical appearance of other small laboratory rooms changed. Röntgen felt that these changes were in the interest of the institute, to ensure that a competent job of teaching and research could be done by the faculty. But the government officials turned down his request, suggesting instead that a committee inspect the various institutes in other *Länder,* or states, and then make a definite recommendation. This stratagem did not satisfy Röntgen at all. He knew bureaucracy well enough to recognize this proposal as an empty promise.

Dr. Röntgen as Rector
of the University
at Würzburg, 1894.

Several meetings between Röntgen and the Baden Education
Ministry officials did not resolve the differences, and negotiations consequently were broken off. Röntgen, disappointed, remained in Würzburg.

Professor F. Himstedt, who had succeeded Röntgen at Giessen,
eventually took the Freiburg position. Ludwig Zehnder then applied for
the vacated Giessen post, but three other candidates — O. Wiener, P. K.
L. Drude, and K. R. Koch — were given prior consideration.

The selection of a professor was always an elaborate procedure.
Usually a picked commission of the faculty — consisting of the mathematicians and chemists, the mineralogists, botanists, and zoologists, and
the philosophy professors — made lengthy written proposals of their
choice. These recommendations then went to the state senate committee
and were finally acted upon by the Minister of Education, who made the
final decision. Generally though, the voices of leading educators in a
particular field carried the decisive influence in the selection.

In 1894 Professor Wilhelm Röntgen was elected to the high office of Rektor der Julius-Maximilians-Universität, attesting that he was concerned not only with the parochial activities of his own institute but that he took a broad interest in the wider functions of the Würzburg university. In his acceptance speech lay the foundation of his philosophy:

The university is a nursery of scientific research and of mental education, a place for the cultivation of ideals for students as well as for teachers. Her significance as such is much greater than her practical usefulness, and for this reason one should make an effort when filling vacant places to choose men who have distinguished themselves not only as teachers but also as investigators and promoters of science. For every genuine scientist, whatever his field, who takes his task seriously, fundamentally follows purely ideal goals and is an idealist in the best sense of the word. Teachers and students of the university should consider it a great honor to be members of this organization. Pride in one's profession is demanded, but not professorial conceit, exclusiveness, or academic presumptuousness, all of which grow from false egotism. One should feel strongly of belonging to a favored profession, which gives many rights but also requires many duties. All our ambitions should be directed toward a faithful fulfillment of duties toward others as well as toward ourselves — only then will our university be esteemed, only then shall we prove worthy of the possession of academic freedom, and only then will this valuable and indispensable gift be retained.

Only gradually has the conviction gained importance that the experiment is the most powerful and most reliable lever enabling us to extract secrets from nature, and that the experiment must constitute the final judgment as to whether a hypothesis should be retained or discarded. It is almost always possible to compare the results of ratiocination with practical reality, and this gives the experimental research worker the required assurance his work demands. If the result does not agree with reality, it must necessarily be wrong, even though the speculations that led to it may have been highly ingenious. Perhaps one may see in this necessity a certain inexorability, when one considers the great mental effort and the great amount of time required in the accomplishment of the result and the many fond hopes that must be destroyed in the process. Yet the investigator in natural sciences is fortunate to have such a touchstone, even though it sometimes brings great disappointments.

To celebrate his fiftieth birthday on March 27, 1895, and to escape the unpleasant spring weather in Würzburg, the Röntgens went to southern Italy for a leisurely vacation. They had taken longer trips for several years now over the short two-week Easter vacations, in 1891 traveling as far as Cairo. The extremely hot and dusty sightseeing trip to the pyramids and the Sphinx had been too much for Bertha. She became ill from the exertion, and they were forced to return earlier than originally planned. The year before they had visited Rome, finding its ancient structures and impressive ruins fascinating. On the return trip they stopped briefly at Venice. They sat one afternoon in the huge San

Marco Piazza, admiring the splendid cathedral and palaces while protecting their coffee and pastry from carelessly low-flying pigeons. At night they rode in a gondola on the Grand Canal. In 1889 — during their first venture into Italy — they had enjoyed a most pleasant, invigorating, and leisurely time at the Grand Hotel Alfred Hauser in Naples, with a short side trip to Vesuvius and to Sicily. Now they hoped to recapture some of those pleasures. They visited Sorrento and the Hotel Victoria for a restful time.

Now, at the age of fifty years, Wilhelm Röntgen reflected on his life and knew that his work in Würzburg had been satisfying. He had made notable contributions to science, exploring many divergent fields and publishing many reports of those findings during the six years there. His name was well known in scientific circles, and the results of his observations were readily accepted by his colleagues. When a paper was published, he sent copies of the work to many of his colleagues at other universities. In 1890 the list of ninety-two names included all important scientists of the time. It read like a veritable Who's Who of science in the world.

The offers of splendid positions extended to him attested to the excellence of his reputation. He had definitely made his mark in his chosen field of activity, and he was quite satisfied.

Röntgen's work schedule during those years did not vary appreciably. His schedule for the summer semester of 1895 was typical of the Würzburg era. He taught *Experimentalphysik,* consisting of mechanics, acoustics, and optics, daily from 3 to 4 o'clock, Monday through Friday, for a weekly total of five hours. For ten hours, from 4 to 6 daily, he demonstrated and lectured on *Praktischen Uebungen* (practical exercises) in the physics laboratory. The professor was available daily for guidance in independent laboratory work for advanced students, and he attended the Thursday (5 to 7 o'clock) *Physikalische Kolloquium,* a regular class of discussion for advanced students.

When Röntgen came to Würzburg in 1888 he had chosen Adolf Heydweiller to be his first assistant, with Ludwig Zehnder second assistant. When Zehnder became *habilitiert* in 1890 through Professor Hagenbach-Bischoff of the Basel University, and took a position at Freiburg in 1891, Rudolph Eduard Cohen replaced him. Heydweiller had left the previous semester and was replaced by Joseph von Kowalski, who then took over the position of first assistant.

For the fall semester of 1891–92, Otto Stern was second assistant to Röntgen, and by the summer semester, Max Wien had joined Stern.

Each of the subordinates worked on a definite project in the laboratory. After an assistant had completed the observation or experiment,

Professor Röntgen on
his way to a lecture.

Röntgen would write down the results. Apparently he considered them
of limited worth, not warranting publication, for no observations were
published covering work done by any of his assistants, with the exception
of Zehnder.

   In collaboration with Ludwig Zehnder, Röntgen obtained important
results in studies on the influences of pressures on various physical
properties of solids and liquids. He and his assistant had already, in
Giessen, carefully investigated the compressibility of many liquids,
notably ether and alcohol, and they continued these studies of pressure
on the dielectric constant of water and ethyl alcohol. He examined the
refractive index of these liquids and the conductivity of various electrolytes. Two additional papers carried Ludwig Zehnder's name as collaborator on this work on pressures, "On the Compressibility of Carbon Disulphide, Benzol, Ethylic Ether, and Some Alcohols" (1891), and "On the
Influence of Pressure on the Refractive Index of Water, Carbon Disulphide, Benzol, Ethylic Ether, and Some Alcohols" (1891).

Röntgen's own studies initiated in Würzburg included the measurement of the thickness of coherent layers of oil on water, from which conclusions were drawn about the "radius of effective spheres" of the molecule and the range of diameter of molecules. Röntgen then coordinated his results and those of other previous investigators on the compressibility of water. From the abnormal action of water as compared with other liquids — that is, its decrease of internal friction through pressure, or through the increase of the thermal coefficient of expansion with pressure — he concluded that water consists of two types of molecules: ice molecules, which cause a larger volume, and molecules formed with an increase in temperature with a consequent decrease in volume. Publications were "On the Thickness of Coherent Oil Layers on the Surface of Water" (1890), "On the Constitution of Liquid Water" (1892), "Short Communication on Experiments on the Influence of Pressure on Some Physical Phenomena" (1892), "On the Influence of Compression Heat on the Determination of the Compressibility of Liquids" (1892), and "On the Influence of Pressure Upon the Dielectric Constant of Water and Ethyl Alcohol" (1894).

In addition to these important investigations Röntgen again proved himself a master of experimentation, and he demonstrated his mechanical skill in several descriptive papers, including a "Description of the Apparatus with Which the Experiments on the Electrodynamic Effect of Moving Dielectrics Were Made" (1890), "Some Lecture Demonstrations" (1890), "Methods of Producing Pure Surfaces of Water and Mercury" (1892), and "Note on the Method for Measuring Differences in Pressure by Means of a Mirror Reading Scale" (1894).

Other publications were "Electrical Properties of Quartz" (1889), "On the Influence of Pressure on the Galvanic Conductivity of Electrolytes" (1893), and "A Communication on Some Experiments with a Right Angle Glass Prism" (1894). He also found time to write a historical paper "On the History of Physics at the University of Würzburg" (1894). This marked the forty-eighth published paper in twenty-one years since his doctor's thesis in 1870.

CHAPTER 7

The Strange Phenomenon

THE BASIC KNOWLEDGE OF ELECTRICITY had had its origin some three centuries earlier when the Englishman William Gilbert had first published his studies of magnetism and static electricity. Later, simple demonstrations of electrical phenomena, especially those of the effects of static electricity on evacuated spaces and living organisms, had found wide public appeal. Finally the entire knowledge of electricity had been systematized largely through the efforts of such notable pioneering scientists as Benjamin Franklin, Luigi Galvani, Alessandro Volta, André Ampère, Georg Ohm, Michael Faraday, and Joseph Henry.

The baromatic vacuum had been discovered by the Italian scientist Evangelista Toricelli in 1643, and at about that time the German physicist Otto von Guericke (1602–86) had built an air pump with which he could slowly evacuate air from tightly enclosed vessels. Vacuum pumps and simple electrostatic machines had been further developed by the British scientists Robert Hooke and Robert Boyle in 1660 and by Francis Hauksbee in 1705.

In 1855 Heinrich Geissler, a glassblower at the University of Bonn who earned a doctorate for his outstanding work, had built a practical mercury vacuum pump with which he evacuated tubes of his own design and development. Since no suitable apparatus was available to do the work to his fullest satisfaction, Geissler had been forced to invent such a device, a not uncommon practice in many scientific laboratories.

Filled with various gases, these tubes produced strikingly beautiful colored lights when high tension discharges from the induction coil were passed through them. Even if the experiments had served no practical purpose, the mere beauty of the effects would have been gratifying. In collaboration with Physics Professor Julius Plücker of the University of Bonn, Geissler had refined the tubes. Their history-making observation of an outflow from the cathode end of the tubes, when a high tension discharge was passed through them, was among the first to be made of the so-called cathode rays.

William Crookes called these cathode rays a new "fourth state of matter," at the conclusion of his lecture before the Royal Society in December 1878. He said then that "the phenomena in these exhausted tubes reveal to physical science a new world — a world where matter may exist in a fourth state, where the corpuscular theory of light may be true, and where light does not always move in straight lines, but where we can never enter, and with which we must be content to observe and experiment from the outside."

Others who had done much research in exploring real properties of the cathode rays were the scientists Hittorf, Hertz, Goldstein, and Lenard. Hittorf, who had published his investigations in 1869, and later Lenard, who was stimulated by Crookes' paper and had published his first results in 1893, equipped ordinary glass cathode-ray tubes with extremely thin aluminum windows, through which the rays could penetrate to the outside, thus allowing better observation of the properties of these mysterious rays in the free air outside the tube. In a series of experiments Lenard also established that the rays made the air electrically conductive but that they were easily absorbed in only a few centimeters of free air. He discovered further that the rays produced luminescent effects on fluorescent salts and that they darkened photographic plates.

While his assistants worked on their assigned experiments, Wilhelm Röntgen made his own investigations on various substances in the privacy of his own laboratory. In June 1894, just before the long summer vacation, he began a series of experiments with cathode rays.

A Ruhmkorff (occasionally spelled Rühmkorff, after the German scientist who went to Paris and left off the umlaut for simplified spelling) induction coil, manufactured by Reiniger-Gebbert and Schall at Erlangen, was installed in the larger of the two rooms where Röntgen conducted most of his research work. The coil was equipped with a Deprez interrupter and produced sparks of four to six inches in length. Several Hittorf-Crookes vacuum tubes (*Entladungsapparat,* or discharge apparatus, as Röntgen preferred to call them) together with some Lenard tubes — including the one he had obtained the year before from Müller-Unkel of Braunschweig — rested on a shelf. Other equipment was a Raps vacuum pump, reassembled to evacuate additional Hittorf-Crookes and Lenard tubes.

Induction coil and Hittorf-Crookes tubes, of the
kind used by Röntgen to create the first X rays.

Röntgen intended to use a unique apparatus in his cathode ray experiments. These experiments were based not only on the production of high tension electrical charges but also on the conduction of these charges through highly evacuated tubes. Initially he experienced considerable difficulties in the evacuation of the tubes, finding that those available were not sufficiently evacuated for his purposes. When the tubes were being used, heat created slight gas formations which had to be entirely eliminated, and this could be achieved only by time-consuming precise work.

As Röntgen wrote to Zehnder, the Hertz and Lenard experiments demanded such highly evacuated tubes that they took "several days to evacuate, using an apparatus which I have placed beside a Raps pump."

Röntgen, the excellent mechanic and unexcelled improvisor, devised much of the ingenious apparatus himself, as he had done before for many of his experiments. Leaving the vacuum tube attached to the pumping device, he could constantly control the degree of evacuation, creating a higher evacuation should it become necessary during the actual experiments.

Röntgen then made the Hertz and Lenard tests, in which the cathode rays penetrated a thin layer of metal foil and could be proven in the outer air. Lenard had stated that several kinds of such rays existed, but Röntgen, with his impaired ability to distinguish colors clearly, felt himself somewhat handicapped in this delicate observation. To counteract his deficiency, he reasoned that he could possibly achieve weaker or stronger effects of cathode rays by using different type tubes with differing degrees of evacuation. If the current were higher, then the tubes became harder and the rays more penetrating and less diffusive. With an exceedingly highly evacuated tube he might be able to observe these rays quite auspiciously.

Röntgen damaged several tubes in the experiments. One of the tubes he used as a replacement was acquired after Zehnder had burned a disk into it. This Hittorf tube was used with a 50/20-centimeter coil and a 20-ampere current, precisely what Zehnder had used. With a thin aluminum window, and with sufficient evacuation and current, a fairly strong ray could be observed, brightly illuminating the screen. By covering the tube with black cardboard and not allowing any light to escape, one could prove whether or not the cathode rays would penetrate the glass wall or even the paper.

Röntgen repeated nearly all of the early classic experiments to satisfy himself of their absolute accuracy — a *modus operandi* he always followed, accepting nothing whatever as certain unless he observed it himself. He suspected that the purely theoretical speculations made by Maxwell and also by von Helmholtz on electric and magnetic disturbances within the "ether" might also be important in the interpretation of his observations.

After the summer vacations and at the beginning of the fall semester, Röntgen, fascinated by the cathode rays, continued his experiments. In his own laboratory he worked in the true classic manner. He approached the problem before him with tenacity, was patient in its execution, critical in evaluating the observed phenomena, and totally uncommunicative. He pursued his particular problem stubbornly and objectively until he solved it to his absolute satisfaction, always his own most merciless critic. None of his assistants, though they realized he was working with cathode rays, knew the finer details of Röntgen's observations.

In one of the significant experiments that Lenard had made earlier, and which Röntgen repeated, the glass tube was enclosed in a tightly fitting piece of cardboard. This was then covered carefully with tinfoil to protect the thin aluminum window of the tube from possible damage in the strong electrostatic field. The covering also prevented penetration of visible light from the tube to the outside. Again Röntgen observed, and so confirmed the previous observation, that invisible cathode rays emanated from the tube, and that they actually did produce a fluorescent effect on a *Leuchtschirm,* a small cardboard screen painted with barium platino-cyanide. The effect would occur only when the screen was placed fairly close to the window.

Now, in similar experiments with heavier walled Hittorf-Crookes tubes, Röntgen reasoned that fluorescence might also be caused by cathode rays but that it might possibly be obscured by the strong lumines-cence of the excited tube. He had discovered a phenomenon far more intriguing than the already known behavior of cathode rays.

Röntgen was fascinated by the new idea and was most eager to investigate it further as quickly as possible. He had already repeated the experiments many times during the past year. Working alone in the late afternoons, as he did this early November afternoon, while no others were in the laboratory with him — as he told his daughter Berteli, while *keine dienstbaren Geister,* no subservient ghosts, were present — he decided to make the experiment to test the ability of a heavier tube to produce fluorescence on the barium platinocyanide screen.

He took from the rack a pear-shaped all-glass Hittorf-Crookes tube, without the aluminum window, and covered it securely with pieces of black cardboard. He was extremely careful to cut and paste them together to make an absolutely light-tight jacket similar to the one he had previously used on the Lenard tube. He hooked the tube to the electrodes of the Ruhmkorff coil. He drew the window curtains to insure complete darkness of the room so that he could properly check the opacity of the black cardboard covering. Turning off the light, he waited momentarily to accustom his eyes to the total darkness.

Then Röntgen started the induction coil and passed a high-tension discharge through the tube. No light penetrated the cardboard cover, and he was satisfied that he had done good work on it. He was now ready to set up the screen for the crucial test, and he prepared to interrupt the current.

Suddenly he observed a weak light ray shimmering on some crystals lying on a little bench nearby and a greater reflection about a meter distant from the tube. It seemed to Röntgen as if the thin ray of light or faint spark from the induction coil had been reflected by a mirror.

At first he was startled by this unexpected phenomenon. Then he passed another series of discharges through the tube. The same reaction occurred; the same unexplained fluorescence appeared. This time he noticed a faint dark cloud moving in unison with the fluctuating discharges of the coil.

By now his excitement had risen immeasurably. Röntgen had made many experiments that resulted in unpredicted reactions, but this was something totally different from all other peculiar phenomena he had ever experienced in his many years of observing phenomena.

Röntgen struck a match in the dark room and discovered to his great surprise that the source of the mysterious light was actually the little barium platinocyanide screen which lay on the table nearby.

He tried the experiment again and yet again, each time moving the small *Leuchtschirm* slightly farther away from the tube. Each time he got the same results.

The only explanation for him was that evidently something unknown emanated from the Hittorf-Crookes tube — something other than cathode rays. This peculiar effect on the fluorescent screen was produced at a much greater distance than he had ever observed previously in his cathode ray experiments, even when he had used the lighter Lenard tubes with the thin aluminum windows. His conclusion was certainly in direct contradiction to the general knowledge of cathode rays. His own wide experience with those rays had been that they never penetrated more than a few centimeters of air, but the rays he was now observing were effective at distances of over a meter.

He attempted to explain this strange phenomenon. Concentrating on the discovery, he was completely unaware of the passage of time and

Röntgen's laboratory in the institute at
Würzburg, where he discovered the X rays.

even his own surroundings. The loud ticking clock, usually a constant
reminder, was now inaudible. He failed to jot down a single word of
notes. The afternoon went and evening came, and still Röntgen was
completely absorbed in the impact of his discovery.

His total absorption was not unusual; he often worked in quiet
solitude in the afternoons on a weekend, when not a soul would disturb
him. His researches were much loved. He considered them his very life.
His laboratory was truly his *sanctum sanctorum,* his *Allerheiligste,* his
holiest of the holies.

Wilhelm Röntgen used the entire weekend, undisturbed in his laboratory, to repeat his work. The institute was practically deserted. The
students had no classes. Painstakingly, he recreated the exact, precise
situations. Again he observed the emanation from the excited Hittorf-
Crookes tube.

The phenomenon was exactly as before.

Finally he made his systematic and detailed notes on the apparatus and on his observations. The delay in making notes on the newly discovered phenomenon was not typical of Röntgen, although he was never anxious to write his final reports. What he had observed was almost unbelievable to him. He needed to test the phenomenon again and again to prove to himself that his observations were valid.

During the weeks following Röntgen spent even less time in his apartment. He had his meals brought on a tray, neglected his long daily walks, even had a cot brought into the laboratory so that he could take a short nap when exhausted. He wanted to utilize maximum time in experimenting with and observing this startling discovery. Feverishly, he devoted himself to identifying the properties of the emanation.

Finding that the rays — if they were rays — could actually penetrate air to a previously unobserved degree, he reasoned that they might possibly penetrate other substances never before exposed to experimentation with the phenomenon. The thought came to him suddenly when he noticed a slight and peculiar shadow on the green fluorescent screen, made apparently by a thin wire which ran across the tube from the induction coil.

Röntgen then recalled that two years ago von Helmholtz had pointed out in a published paper that, on the basis of the Maxwell theory of electricity and light, a sufficiently short-wave light-ray should go straight through solid materials. To test this supposition, Röntgen now at first used a sheet of paper between the tube and the screen, then after noting the penetration carefully, he took a thicker object, a playing card, and finally a book. Every time after he closed the switch to the inductor, and simultaneously with the passage of the current through the tube, the small screen lit up, with the object used regulating the intensity of the shadow cast. The fluorescence for the book was not as bright as that for the playing card or sheet of paper, but it came through clearly visible.

Stimulated by this success, Röntgen collected other materials. He began experimenting with sheets of various metals of varying thicknesses. He found that a thin sheet of aluminum affected the fluorescence to approximately the same degree as did the book. But when he used a sheet of lead, it seemed to stop the rays completely. No shadow at all showed. Obviously there was no penetration whatever of the lead. Seemingly then, the type of material used, as well as its relative thickness, was of critical importance.

Röntgen thought now of the new agent he had discovered in definite terms of rays. The phenomenon unmistakenly showed properties in common with known radiation, such as traveling in a straight line from the focus point and throwing a regular shadow.

Intrigued by the peculiar ability of lead to stop the ray, he used again the small disk of lead, holding it carefully between his finger and thumb and positioning it exactly between the tube and the screen.

To his amazement, not only did the precise outline of the leaden disk show clearly, but also the very outline of his thumb and forefinger. Even more startling, he recognized the distinctive outline of the bones of his own hand in darker shadows.

Wilhelm Röntgen was shaken considerably. It was a horrible and grisly sight to him — his own skeleton still encased in live tissue, his fingers casting long ghostly black shadows. Grave doubts and a measure of honest wonder raced through his brain. Röntgen suddenly stopped the experiments. What had before seemed of great and wonderful promise could quite understandably turn into disastrous disrepute in the eyes of his learned colleagues. He could be ostracized and wholly ruined as a responsible physicist. The forty-eight scientific papers he had published — the last one more than a year before — could be totally discredited.

After a period of sound evaluation of his position regarding the experiments and their eventual publication, Röntgen decided to continue with the laboratory work in strictest privacy, keeping the entire series of new observations secret. Fortunately the Christmas vacations would begin in another month, and the institute would again become like a tomb. Not a single student would hurry along its corridors, and no one — except perhaps the factotum Kasper Marstaller — would come into the laboratory when Röntgen would be observing the strangely behaving new rays.

He eventually decided to turn over the results to other reputable scientists, to have them either confirm or refute the discovery, but this was only after he had indisputable proof of his own findings.

Toward the end of the year 1895, Wilhelm Röntgen worked tirelessly to prove to himself that this strange observation was indeed a fact and not merely a chance phenomenon. Knowing that cathode rays darkened a photographic plate — and convinced that while the human eye may be mistaken, the photographic plate is definitely not — he decided to find out if the ray he had observed from the Hittorf-Crookes tube would also cause the same effect; that is, if the peculiar radiation was possibly yet due to cathode rays. He placed a disk of platinum on a photographic plate and made an exposure. After developing the plate he noted that a light area appeared where the platinum had absorbed the rays. This naturally led him to expose other opaque materials to the rays and capture their shadow pictures on a photographic plate. The fact that photography was so greatly developed pleased Röntgen immensely. It was of great value to him.

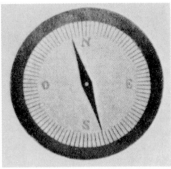

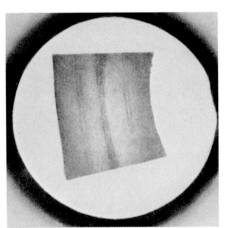

Some of the first X ray photographs made by Röntgen: box with weights, compass with needle, piece of inhomogeneous metal, double-barreled shotgun.

When he took his double-barreled shotgun to the laboratory, Bertha became most anxious, but he assured her that it was for a purely scientific purpose and solemnly promised with a sly grin that he would not fire it in anger at anyone, including himself.

Soon after the actual discovery of the mysterious rays had taken place, on Friday, November 8, 1895, Wilhelm Röntgen's assistants — Otto Stern was then first assistant, Julius Hanauer second — also detected a change in the attitude of their superior. He was more irritable and even less approachable than before. The orders for precise amounts of various metal disks, such as lead, zinc, aluminum, or tinfoil, attracted no particular attention; such materials were frequently used in laboratory experiments. The order for prints of certain peculiar photographic effects from plates furnished by the institute undoubtedly caused Siebenlist, the photographer, to wonder just how these mysterious lights and shadows had been achieved, but he was no scientist, and Professor Röntgen himself had brought the plates to the *Atelier* of the photographer and had asked of him absolute secrecy.

The secret of the discovery was well kept until the first preliminary report was written. Briefly and concisely, Röntgen set down his comprehensive investigations into the phenomenon.

The paper, "A New Kind of Ray," was submitted to the editor of the Physical-Medical Society, and was duly printed on pages 132 to 141, the last ten pages, of the 1895 volume of the *Sitzungsberichte der Physikalisch-Medizinischen Gesellschaft,* Würzburg. (See Appendix 3 for text of this Preliminary Communication.) Reprints of the communication became available immediately in a brochure, published and printed by the Stahel'schen K. [for Königlichen] Universitäts Buch– und Kunsthandlung in Würzburg. Bound in yellow wrappers it carried the inscription on its title page:

> *Eine Neue Art von Strahlen*
> *von Dr. W. Röntgen*
> *ö.o. Professor an der K. Universität Würzburg*
> *Ende 1895*
> *60 Pfennig*

Although Röntgen had, as always, included his middle initial in the signature when he submitted his manuscript, it was omitted on the printed form. Omitted also was the first word, "Ueber," or "On," of the title of his paper.

On New Year's Day, Röntgen mailed copies of the report to many recognized physicists, some of whom were his personal friends. The copies were imprinted *"Ueberreicht vom Verfasser"* — that is, presented by the author. It was probably a considerably smaller mailing than the ninety-two names he usually used for his scientific papers. He enclosed several prints of the X ray photographs of his wife's hand and of other subject matter to demonstrate the broad scope of the rays. He included personal greetings for the New Year.

As he walked with Bertha that Wednesday evening to the mail box on the Pleicherring, he remarked, *"Nun wird man dem Teufel zahlen müssen"* — Now the devil will have to be paid.

CHAPTER 8

Honors and Tributes

A VERITABLE FLOOD OF MESSAGES came to Wilhelm Röntgen from all over the world. Most offered congratulations on a wonderful discovery; some reflected envy, some criticized him, some condemned him and expressed dreadful fear over the "death rays which would surely destroy all mankind."

Among the earliest replies that Röntgen received was the letter from Emil Warburg, which pleased him greatly. The physicist wrote, on January 4, that he had taken the liberty of adding Röntgen's photographs to others to be shown at a temporary exhibit at the Institute of Physical Science of the Berlin University, to honor the Society on its fiftieth anniversary. The printed announcement of the event carried the acknowledgment that "a series of photographs is on exhibit which Professor Röntgen of Würzburg has taken with the X rays recently discovered by him." But Professor W. von Bezold, President of the Society, had written a footnote:

Unfortunately the speaker and other members of the society were so busy that evening that they did not know that among the exhibits were Röntgen's first photographs, hidden for many members in a secluded corner. If the speaker had heard but one word about these photographs, he would have closed his speech at the banquet quite differently and would have called attention to the rare honor given the occasion by a preliminary communication on a discovery so important that its significance could not fail to be appreciated, even at first glance.

On February 15, Professor Otto Lummer of Berlin wrote, "I could not refrain from thinking that I was reading a fairy tale when I read the

First Communication, but the name of the author and his sound proofs soon relieved me of any such delusion."

Ludwig Zehnder was one who congratulated Röntgen most heartily on the remarkable discovery. At the time, Zehnder's father was quite ill in Zurich and Ludwig spent a great deal of his time there with him, traveling frequently to and from his new Freiburg position during those trying months. He had been asked by a colleague to speak before the Freiburger *Naturforschenden Gesellschaft* and to demonstrate the X rays, perhaps because he had worked with the discoverer previously, but also because he himself had experimented with cathode rays. He wrote Röntgen and asked several questions about the physical aspects of the X rays.

On February 8, 1896, Röntgen replied:

Dear Zehnder! The good friends come last. That is the way it goes. But you are the first to receive an answer. Have many thanks for everything you wrote me. I can not as yet use your speculations on the nature of the X rays, since it does not seem permissible or advantageous to attempt to explain a phenomenon of unknown nature with a not entirely unobjectionable hypothesis. Of what nature the rays are is not entirely clear to me. And whether they are actually longitudinal light rays is to me of secondary importance. The facts are the important thing. In this respect my work has received recognition from many quarters. Boltzmann, Warburg, Kohlrausch, and (not least) Lord Kelvin, Stokes, Poincaré and others have expressed to me their joy over the discovery and their recognition. That is really worth a great deal to me, and I let the envious quietly chatter. I am not concerned about that at all!

I had not spoken to anyone about my work. To my wife I mentioned merely that I was doing something of which people, when they found out about it, would say, *"Der Röntgen ist wohl verrückt geworden."* [Röntgen has probably gone crazy.] On the first of January I mailed the reprints, and then the devil was to pay! The *Wiener Presse* was the first to blow *"die Reklametrompete"* [the advertising trumpet], and the others followed. In a few days I was disgusted with the whole thing. I could not recognize my own work in the reports any more. Photography was for me the means to the end, but it was made the most important thing. Gradually I became accustomed to the uproar, but the storm cost time. For exactly four full weeks I have been unable to make a single experiment! Other people could work, but not I. You have no idea how upset things were here.

Enclosed I send the promised photographs. If you wish to show them in lectures, that is all right with me. But I would recommend that you place them under glass and frame, otherwise they will be stolen. I think that with the aid of the explanations you will have no difficulty with them; otherwise write to me.

I use a large Ruhmkorff 50/20 centimeter with a Deprez interrupter, and about 20 amperes primary current. My apparatus, which remains on the Raps pump, requires several days for evacuation. The best results are obtained when the spark gap of a parallel connected discharger is about three centimeters.

In time all apparatus will be punctured (with the exception of one). Any method of producing cathode rays will be successful, also with incandescent lamps according to Tesla and with tubes without electrodes. For the photography I use three to ten minutes, depending on the conditions of the experiment.

For your lecture I send you the compass box, the wood roll, the weight set, and the zinc sheet, as well as a nicely preserved photograph of a hand by Pernet of Zurich. But please return these items as soon as possible, insured. Do you have a larger screen with platinocyanide? Best regards from home to home.   Your Röntgen

As he wrote to his friend, he was not able for four weeks to undertake a single experiment, and he strained to get back into his laboratory to follow up his own momentous discovery. He had completed only the preliminary work on it and intended to have the next part of his publication ready within a short time. There was still so much to learn about the new rays, yet the time to do that was not available to him, and he felt bitter about it. Other scientists were able to work on his early findings, but he wanted to publish his experiments in greater detail so that they could build on firmer foundations. He wondered how he could ever again return to the secrecy of his laboratory and do more testing, experimenting, searching, and observing the strange phenomenon of the rays.

Among the communications that Röntgen received soon after the first publication of his findings was an invitation to demonstrate his discovery at the Imperial Court at Berlin. Wilhelm I.R. telegraphed on January 9 to Röntgen saying that he read with deepest astonishment in the newspaper of the world-stirring discovery, and if the report proved correct, he sent his heartiest congratulations and praised God that this triumph of science was given to the German *Vaterland,* which hopefully would bring rich blessings for all mankind. "As soon as you have time, I would be thankful to you if you could give me a lecture on your discovery."

An invitation from his Kaiser was, of course, a summons, and naturally, Röntgen readily complied.

The *Flügeladjudant vom Dienst,* or imperial adjutant, von Arnim, telegraphed Röntgen the following day that the Kaiser would receive the *"Vortrag Eurer Hochwohlgeboren"* — lecture of your highborn — that Sunday at five o'clock in the Star hall, and the Berlin University would furnish laboratorium equipment should he need it. Professor Emil Warburg wrote the next day — on the back of his own visiting card — that he would expect Röntgen the following morning at his apartment for further arrangements.

Wilhelm Röntgen traveled to Berlin. On this extremely bitter winter Sunday, protected by a heavy fur coat, he walked from the Hotel Kaiserhof to the Kaiserlichen Schloss, and carried his bulky briefcase under his arm. He arrived slightly after the appointed time; then — as he enjoyed recalling later — with a wide smile on his face he apologized to the Kaiser: "I beg your Majesty's pardon for being late, but I am not accustomed to these long distances here in Berlin."

According to the *Neues Wiener Tageblatt* of January 14, 1896: "Last night at five o'clock Professor Röntgen set up his apparatus and demonstrated his X rays in the spacious Sternensaal of the Schloss before an august audience, which included the Kaiser, the Kaiserin Auguste Victoria, the ex-Kaiserin Friedrich, and many distinguished military men as well as scientists and statesmen, including the Minister of Culture Bosse and the Chief of the Imperial Civil Cabinet Lucanus." The dispatch was widely reprinted in European newspapers. The *Kieler Neuesten Nachrichten* of February 4 reported the affair in greater detail, as did many others.

Before Röntgen began his demonstration, he said, "I hope that I have *Kaiser-Glück* with this tube today, for these tubes are extremely sensitive and are often destroyed in the very first experiment, and it takes me about four days to properly evacuate a new one."

With a fluorescent screen Röntgen demonstrated how the rays penetrated wooden boards and cardboard boxes, and he photographed several lifeless objects, but because he had only that one tube available he did not offer to photograph a human hand. However, he had brought several X ray photographs, which created quite a sensation when passed among his attentive listeners.

Later, after a formal dinner, smoking cigars in the salon seated between the Kaiser and Graf von Moltke, Wilhelm Röntgen was continually kept busy answering questions regarding the future uses of his rays. The group, including the Surgeon General of the Army, Leuthold, speculated on the ultimate development of this startling discovery. Someone suggested even that the X rays might throw light on the secrets of gravitation or perhaps make possible the practical use of that force.

In recognition of his momentous findings, Röntgen was decorated by the Kaiser with the Prussian Order of the Crown, Second Class.

It was long after midnight when a proud Wilhelm Röntgen left the Schloss. This recognition of his achievement and the detailed intelligent questions and tremendous interest by the Kaiser had impressed him immensely, and he was in an elated mood as he walked along Unter den Linden back to his hotel, infinitely gratified with the singular honor shown him that evening by his sovereign.

Prominent scientists who dispatched congratulations to Röntgen (and whose letters were to be bundled together with thin wire into a

package to be saved and read by this author 45 years later) included
Emil Warburg of Berlin; Friedrich Kohlrausch, president of the Physical-
technical Reichsanstalt at Charlottenburg; Lord Kelvin of the University
of Glasgow; and George Gabriel Stokes. Henri Poincaré congratulated his
"très honoré collègue" in a long letter from Paris, as did the American
physicist Robert W. Wood, who studied then at a Berlin university and
lived in Charlottenburg and who asked permission to write an article
on the discovery for an American periodical. Walter König of Frankfurt
wrote several letters, asking for more information on the discovery for
the Physical Society of his city.

Röntgen replied — also in several long letters — in detail on the
equipment he had used for his experiments and regretted his inability to
lecture before the society. From his Lieden post, the Dutch physicist
Hendrik Antoon Lorentz wrote two letters congratulating Röntgen on
the fabulous discovery.

Professor Peter Lebedew of the Moscow University's Physical Science
Laboratory wrote on January 20 saying that he would give a detailed
report on X rays before a specially called meeting of the Scientific
Society. No record has been found indicating that Röntgen furnished
him any additional notes or photographs. But the *Münchener Medizinische Wochenschrift* of March 24, 1896, showed several X ray photographs made by Lebedew, among them one of a four-month-old fetal
skeleton inside the womb of its mother.

A telegram and letter reached Röntgen from St. Petersburg, sent by
Ivan Ivanowitch Borgmann, reporting on a demonstration lecture on
Röntgen-rays, held before the combined student body on January 22.
Professor Orest Dawidowitch Chwolson, who had published a four-
volume textbook on physics, also wrote from St. Petersburg that he had
given three lectures which resulted in receipt of 1,500 rubles, sufficient to
send seventeen poor sick children on a summer vacation to the island
of Oesel.

Among the letters Röntgen received, one of January 9, 1896, came
from a doctor of Breslau asking for a detailed description of the discovery
in the hope that it would prove practical to photograph the inner parts
of the eye, which would prove immensely beneficial to ophthalmology.

In another letter, dated January 17, a writer from Danzig suggested
in great detail a possible means of creating a "true picture" of a Röntgen
shadow photograph. Although the correspondent promised to be short,
his letter covered several pages of his process.

An owner of an apothecary shop in Sömmerda in Thuringia wrote
on January 23, offering a possible process to make veins visible in X ray
photographs. He proposed to bathe the hand in strongly white or colored

paraffin or stearintablet, or in real gold leaf, or a basin of anilin-violet colored water.

A physician wrote on January 25 from Reval, also suggesting a process of making real pictures of X ray photographs, using a thick *Knochenplatte* (bone-plate) in the manner of the Helmholtz eye-mirror to bring this about.

Crackpots also wrote letters. A self-styled author, Erhard Landmann of Rothebühlstrasse 49 B/4, Stuttgart, wrote in January 1896, that he needed the sum of precisely 200,000 marks to solve the social problems of the whole world. He would also solve, at no additional cost, the secrets of when rain and sunshine would prevail, and upon recognition of his genius by the population would repay the loan, interest, and interest on the interest!

From the Hotel Victoria, Sorrento, on April 1, 1896, where he had gone to escape the past-discovery tumult, Wilhelm Röntgen wrote to Jan W. Gunning. He thanked him for the congratulatory postal card of February 9, which had been "so valuable and so dear" of the many communiques of congratulations he had received during the last few months. Röntgen took the opportunity to ask forgiveness for his silence over the years and hoped that their friendship was still strong enough that he dared to write, *"Pater peccavi* [Father I have sinned], take me on again lovingly. I wanted to write to you that your place in my heart never became empty, and that I had never forgotten for how much good I was indebted to you both." In this letter of several pages, Röntgen deplored the fact that his dearly beloved parents — who were so proud of their son — could not live to see his success. *"Es ist mir ein grosser Schmerz"* — It is a great grief to me. But he rejoiced and was thankful that the two people who, after his own parents, had the greatest influence on his education and in whose house he lived as their very own child and who had the love and worry over him, could share in this happy event. As to a visit to them in Holland, Röntgen wrote that such a long absence would bring so many things about that he found it impossible to decide on such a trip. And especially now, with the discovery of the X rays, he needed the secret of making himself invisible!

Wilhelm Röntgen steadfastly refused all invitations for honors and personal appearances, including one before the British Association for the Advancement of Sciences later that year. Invited by Reichstags-präsident von Buol-Berenberg to speak before the German Reichstag, the German parliament, he declined the honor to appear. Many scientific societies asked him to lecture before them, but Röntgen felt that he "should better use his time to continue the experiments and search further." However, he could not refuse to hold an official lecture, scheduled for Thursday evening, January 23, 1896, before his own *Physikalisch-Medizinischen Gesellschaft,* the Würzburg Physical-Medical Society.

The lecture hall of the institute was not much different from the simple and functional auditoriums in other colleges or high schools. The rows of desks, rising toward the rear, provided an excellent view of the center where a plain table for demonstrations stood. The desks were old, carved with initials perhaps, as any desks in similar institutions of higher learning.

Invited guests included the scientists Adolph Eugen Fick, Wilhelm von Leube, Theodor Boveri, Carl Schönborn, Julius von Sachs, Albert von Kölliker, and Philipp Stöhr. The medical profession was equally well represented by their most gifted practitioners, as were the military and civil authorities by top officials. Students sat on the steps and on the radiators in front of the wide windows, filling all available spaces and crowding into the standing room at the extreme top and rear of the vast hall.

As Professor Wilhelm Conrad Röntgen entered the lecture hall from the side door which led to the laboratory, he hesitated momentarily, framed by the door, nearly reaching the top of the wood casing. His tall figure was dressed in the familiar long black cutaway coat, which he always wore for his lectures. It was in the accepted style of that period, making him look even taller than his 1.85 meters (about 6 feet, 1 inch), and adding appreciably to his regal bearing. An expression of disbelief crossed the face of this embarrassingly modest man as he beheld the crowded auditorium. To the students it was a signal to begin the tumultuous stamping of feet. First, the students trampled in wild disorder, then the noise took on a certain rhythm, and even the staid colleagues and officers were swept into this student manifestation of honoring the professor who had brought world-renown to their own institute and city.

Röntgen's face, surrounded by the full dark beard, with its high forehead, seemed to light up, and his piercing eyes reflected the elation he felt at this enthusiastic reception. He walked with deliberation the few steps to the table where the apparatus that had been used on that historic night was assembled for the demonstration which was to illustrate his lecture.

After minutes of standing ovation, the applause subsided and the audience sat down. Röntgen was visibly touched by this tremendous affectionate reception.

With deep emotion evident in his voice the professor began his lecture, but then his voice soon reached its steady rhythmic stride. In soft tones he told modestly about his research work, emphasizing that he considered it his duty to speak about it because of the general interest the work had aroused. But he cautioned his listeners that all of the experiments were still in the preliminary stage. He gave credit to scientists who had worked along the same lines, particularly such men as Hertz and Lenard. He himself had done only similar experiments, however, based on his own observations. Then Röntgen described the fluorescence of his small barium platinocyanide screen and told how he quickly had discovered that the tube was responsible for the strange phenomenon of the ray. "I found by accident," he said, "that the rays also penetrated black paper. I then used wood, paper, a book — but still believed that I was the victim of deception when I observed the phenomenon of the ray. Finally I used photography, and the experiment was then successfully culminated."

The lecturer demonstrated the actual power of the ray to penetrate paper, wood, tin, and then his own hand; he showed that lead foil stopped the rays completely. He used his expressive hands with the long thin, fingers emphatically when making a particular point in the discussion, the hands suggesting especially dexterous utility and great skill with instruments. He told about the early attempts to make photographs of X rays through the wooden door in his laboratory, which separated the room in which the induction coil and discharge tube were located from the room containing the photographic plate. After developing the plate, it had shown several light strips, which at first he was unable to explain. When this perplexed him, he decided to have the door dismantled, because the different shadows on the plate showed him that they were not caused by various thicknesses but by some other factor, perhaps by a surface peculiarity of the door. "I found that the door was covered with white lead, and since lead absorbs these rays considerably, it was easy to see that a layer of lead running in the direction of the rays absorbs more than does a layer through which the rays go perpendicularly."

Röntgen then showed several of his X ray photographs, pictures of the weights in the wooden case, a compass in which the magnetic needle was entirely surrounded by metal, a piece of wire wound around a spool of wood, and finally the picture of the human hand. All of these visual exhibits were critically inspected; they created enormous interest and brought forth much favorable comment.

To close his demonstration and lecture, Röntgen asked Professor Albert von Kölliker, the famous anatomist of the university, for permission to photograph his hand with the X rays. The scientist readily agreed, and a little later the audience was shown the developed photograph of the hand. The applause that greeted the showing of this excellent picture thundered in the hall for several minutes. Finally the aged Geheimrat von Kölliker was able to make some comments. He said that during his forty-eight years as a member of the Physikalisch-Medizinische Gesellschaft he

Above, door of Röntgen's laboratory; *right,* light area in X ray photograph of door panel, indicating lead in paint.

had never attended a meeting with a presentation of greater significance in the field of natural science or medical science. Leading the assembly in three *"Hochs"* for the professor, he proposed that the rays be called after their discoverer, "Röntgen rays." The audience heartily showed their approval by prolonged loud applause bordering on pandemonium. The meeting was concluded by its presiding officer, Professor K. B. Lehmann.

The speaker and a few of the top scientists retired to discuss several of the raised points in the relative seclusion of the Röntgens' private apartment. Here the conversation concerned itself mainly with the future applications of the X rays in the field of medicine. Von Kölliker was anxious to know in just what manner the X ray photography could be utilized in surgery and anatomy. He asked Röntgen, "Would it be possible to make photographs of other parts of the human body, so that diseased portions could be detected?" According to the experiments made, an apparent obstacle to this further development was the approximately equal density of the different human organs, nerves, muscles, and veins. These, unlike the bones, could probably not be differentiated on the photographs because the rays produced a definite shadow of bones only.

Surgeon Schönborn warned against too great optimism, doubting seriously that the X ray method would ever be of appreciable value in the diagnosis of internal conditions. Röntgen, however, pointed out that since it was not at all difficult for him to photograph a cat or a dog, it should not be more difficult to make satisfactory X ray pictures of larger parts of the human body. He suggested that while he himself did not have the time necessary to undertake experiments along that line, he would welcome other scientists, perhaps someone in a medical institution, to make experiments to determine just what could be expected in that field.

When Professor Lehmann was later asked to comment on the demonstration lecture, he said:

How did Röntgen speak? Quite simply and modestly. Without trying to enlarge the almost incredible news by elaborate additions, fancy hypotheses, or learned speculations and similar devices, he presented his discovery and demonstrated the most significant experiments to the crowded and highly attentive listeners. But especially by his modest greatness did the lecturer awaken the obviously warmhearted feeling of his audience.

No records exist to show that Wilhelm Röntgen ever gave another lecture on the discovery of his rays before any audience.

The medical profession had shown an immediate and immense interest in the X rays. In a letter of February 21, Röntgen mentioned a visit by two physicians at the institute to ask questions and to see the actual demonstrations of his rays. Taking them into his laboratory, he demonstrated his apparatus and made some photographs. The medical men urged him to work on further experiments along lines that would be of most advantage to their profession, and Röntgen intended to do so. But soon after that his equipment gave him some trouble — he ruined several expensive tubes. That particular phase of the work "had not been too fruitful," he wrote.

An interesting sidelight is furnished by Dr. Hermann Gocht, who related his experience at the time of the founding of the Chirurgisches Röntgen Institut at Hamburg-Eppendorf, the surgical X ray institute of the Eppendorf hospital. Later orthopedic surgeon at Berlin, the doctor told that during the first days of 1896, when he sat one evening at his desk filling out various forms for admitting patients to the hospital, a fellow intern burst into the room and told excitedly of the discovery by Professor Röntgen. He was very skeptical of this report himself, that photographs of opaque materials could be made, even without exposing the photographic plates, and consequently made fun of the whole thing. But his young colleague was highly resentful of this frivolity and finally became greatly angered.

Since it was time for supper, both interns went to the hospital dining room to eat. At the large table they found a rather lively debate going on on the same subject by members of the staff, all physicians of considerable years and experience.

The next morning the chief surgeon Dr. Kümmell called a staff meeting and announced to the assembled doctors that he had spent the whole night tossing about and thinking of nothing but these new X rays. Then he proceeded to evaluate the various reports on them, citing the limitless possibilities the use of X rays would offer to their hospital. His rapt listeners were startled when he concluded his talk stating that "such an *Apparat* we must have."

Then Dr. Gocht recounted the difficulties the hospital faced in getting such an apparatus. They searched frustratingly for it in the established supply houses and eventually contacted the owner of the C. H. F. Müller firm, makers of tubes and other electrical equipment. Herr Müller proved indeed most enthusiastic over the new discovery, had already made X ray photographs of hands, fingers, keys, and jewelry items, and was actually in the very process of assembling one of the first practical X ray machines for medical use. After much experimenting and testing of various types of equipment, a suitable apparatus was finally constructed and the hospital set up an X ray department, one of the earliest such facilities in the world. Dr. Gocht beamed with enthusiasm as he recalled this early incident to his festive audience.

On March 3, the University of Würzburg bestowed upon Wilhelm Röntgen the title of *Doktor der Medizin, honoris causa*. This amused him considerably, because his colleague Dr. Schönborn had expressed such definite pessimism on the medical value of the X rays only a few weeks before. Röntgen speculated that at least one vote must have been cast against the decision to award that doctorate to him.

Berteli was never to forget the high excitement of a certain night. One evening while Röntgen sat in his favorite chair reading and Bertha was doing some needlework, they heard the faint sounds of martial music. "Yes, it sounds as if the music comes nearer," Bertha said.

"So it seems," Röntgen replied. And laying the book aside, he refilled his clay pipe carefully.

Young Berteli jumped up from her school work and rushed to the window, but she saw nothing unusual outside. Bertha Röntgen also went to the window and pulled the drapes aside. Then they saw them.

"They are coming to the institute. Come, Willi," Bertha said, "come and see."

A colorful movement of caps and ribbons and humanity came toward them in the eerie glow of lighted, smoking torches.

At the onset of darkness, streets of the city were already crowded with spectators. And, yes, the youngsters had been allowed to stay up long after their regular bedtime, for a *Fackelzug,* a torchlight parade, even in this gay university town, was a rarity and a very, very special occasion.

The joyous participants lined up, according to the seniority of their *Korporationen,* their fraternities. The students marched in their respective groups, the *Landsmannschaft* first, then the *Burschenschaft* and *Turnerschaft,* each wearing proudly their brightly colored ribbons diagonally across their chests. Then came the seven Würzburger Corps, the Bavarians wearing blue caps, the Franconians green, and the Nassauers orange caps. The Westfalians wore their white *Stürmer,* the Mainländer marched with green and the Makaren with red headpieces, and the Rheinländer in splendid white. Seemingly, everyone carried a burning, fiercely smoking torch.

Several bands played marches, and the heavy bass drumbeats echoed and re-echoed off the houses along the wide Residenzplatz where they had assembled. Marching and gaily singing their beloved student songs, the group moved along the crowded Hauptstrasse, then the broad Juliuspromenade past the several institutes and finally to the Pleicherring where the Physical Science Institute and the object of their lusty torchlight parade, Professor Doktor Wilhelm Conrad Röntgen, lived and worked.

The students marched past the building, shouting jubilant greetings to the upstairs window where Röntgen and his family stood. Now each individual corps marched separately in circles, their smoking torches making fancy patterns in the darkness. The corpsman heading each group went upstairs to Röntgen's apartment to present his fraternity's compliments in a short speech, expressing the thanks and admiration of his *Bund*. Then, upon a signal, his group downstairs shouted a triple *"Hoch."* Another group leader took the place of the previous one. The routine was repeated many times. Then the student celebrants downstairs waited eagerly for the professor to speak to them from the opened window.

   With deep emotion choking his mellow voice, Röntgen spoke:

Kommilitonen! Fellow Students! When I was young I had many lofty and ambitious aspirations, but my dreams have never gone so high as to imagine that the students of a great German university would ever hold a torchlight parade in my honor to proclaim their recognition for a purely scientific achievement.

   I express my heartfelt and sincerest thanks to you for this rare distinction and the greater honor which I count among the highest given to me. And I would like to add a hope to my thanks that as students of this university you are especially selected to take part in the great future scientific progress of human knowledge which is constantly advancing.

   To wish that everyone of you might, once in his life, be honored by a torchlight parade in recognition of his work — it would fit the mood of a day like this — but this hope is probably quite beyond the realm of possibility. If it should happen that one or another of you should be so honored, I would be very happy indeed and would like to ask that one to remember that I was actually the first to congratulate him. But instead of this far-reaching wish, I should like to bring you another, the benefits of which I have tested myself:

   During the time when overwhelming congratulations and great honors were showered upon me from all sides, and unconsciously the new impressions erased the older ones, one thought has always remained lively and fresh, and that is the memory of the satisfaction that I felt when my work was developed and finally completed. This was the joy derived from successful effort and of achieved progress. All of you can enjoy this happiness in life, and each of you can and must reach this goal. That depends principally upon yourself. May this happiness, this inner satisfaction, come to each of you, and may the circumstances permit you to attain this end by a path that is not too difficult.

   That is the wish that I leave with you tonight. Now let me conclude by asking you to give loud cheers for our beloved Alma Mater, the University of Würzburg.

   The Pleicherring resounded three times, *"Hoch."*

CHAPTER 9

The News Media

In Vienna, Franz Exner was almost speechless when he first read the startling news from his colleague. Röntgen and Exner had worked together years before as assistants in the Zurich and Strassburg laboratories of August Kundt, and now Exner was a professor of physics and head of the Second Physical-Chemical Institute of the University in Vienna. He knew that Röntgen's discovery was indeed remarkable, and he was sad that Kundt could not have shared the tremendous joy; in his mind, he could hear Kundt exclaim, *"I, Donnerwetter!"*

In his enthusiasm Exner showed the article and the photographs to his brother Sigmund, Professor of Physiology, and a group of colleagues whom he invited to his home. One of those present was Ernst Lecher, a young assistant professor from Prague. The whole group was thrilled by the report and the pictorial evidence of the discovery. Young Lecher rushed to the office of his father, Z. K. Lecher, editor of the *Wiener Presse,* who at once recognized the news value of the discovery. Seeing the photographs, the experienced newspaperman realized at once the appeal that news of the rays would have for his lay readership, especially as it could apply in the study and diagnosis of disease. Ernst Lecher wrote a short article about the rays with that thought paramount and his father printed it in the Sunday edition of January 5, 1896.

In the *Wiener Medizinischen Wochenschrift,* issue 8, 1923, Professor Ernst Lecher stated that he was greatly astonished upon finding that his original short piece had grown tremendously into the lengthy article in the morning newspaper, in which his father "had quite correctly outlined the medical development possibilities of this new discovery with accurate foresight."

Other newspapers repeated the story. The representative of the *London Daily Chronicle* in Vienna wired it to his home office, and a similar article appeared in that paper on Monday, January 6. It read:

The noise of the war's alarm should not distract any attention from the marvelous triumph of science which is reported from Vienna. It is announced that Prof. Routgen [*sic*] of the Würzburg University has discovered a light which for the purpose of photography will penetrate wood, flesh, cloth, and most other organic substances. The professor has succeeded in photographing metal weights which were in a closed wooden case, also a man's hand which showed only the bones, the flesh being invisible.

An article, illustrated with striking photographs, appeared in the second morning edition of the *Frankfurter Zeitung* on Tuesday, January 7, 1896. It read:

A Sensational Discovery: In the scientific circles of Vienna the news of a discovery, made by Professor of Physics Wilhelm Conrad Röntgen of Würzburg, is being discussed enthusiastically. If this discovery fulfills its promise, it constitutes an epoch-making result of research in exact science, which is destined to have interesting consequences along medical as well as physical lines. The *Wiener Presse* reports as follows: Professor Röntgen takes a Crookes tube, a strongly evacuated glass tube, through which an induction current is passed — and takes photographs by means of rays, which are emitted by this tube into space, using ordinary photographic plates. These rays, the existence of which so far has been unknown, are entirely invisible to the eye. Contrary to ordinary rays they penetrate wood, organic and other nontransparent materials. Metals and bones, however, stop the rays. One can photograph in plain daylight with a "closed casette." This means not only that the light rays follow the ordinary path but also that they penetrate the wooden cover, which is placed in front of the light-sensitive plates and which ordinarily must be removed before a photograph is taken. They also penetrate a wooden cover in front of the object to be photographed. Professor Röntgen, for instance, took a photograph of a set of weights without opening the wooden box in which the weights were kept.

A few examples of this sensational discovery are being circulated in scientific circles in Vienna and deservedly are creating great amazement. The matter will be tested very carefully in the near future in the laboratories and probably will be developed further. The physicists must study this unknown radiation, which is capable of penetrating matter ordinarily opaque to light. The light rays from a Crookes tube penetrate dense objects as easily as sunlight penetrates a piece of glass. Biologists and physicians, especially surgeons, will be very much interested in the practical uses of these rays, because they offer prospects of constituting a new and very valuable aid in diagnosis.

At the present time, we wish only to call attention to the importance this discovery would have in the diagnosis of diseases and injuries of bones, provided that the process can be developed technically so that not only the human hand can be photographed but that details of other bones may be shown without the flesh. The surgeon then could determine the extent of a complicated bone fracture without the manual examination which is so painful to the patient. He could find the position of a foreign body, such as a bullet or a piece of shell, much more easily than has been possible heretofore and without any painful examinations with a probe. Such photographs also would be extremely valuable in diagnosing bone diseases which do not originate from an injury and would help to guide the way in therapy.

On the following evening, Wednesday, January 8, the *Frankfurter Zeitung* added to the earlier report:

There are nine photographs in Vienna which Professor Röntgen has sent to one of his colleagues. The most careful examinations of these photographs leave no doubt concerning the complete validity of Professor Röntgen's statements. The more strictly and carefully one examines them, the more convincing these pictures become. The Würzburg professor discovered these unknown rays by accident, as happens so often when sensational truths are disclosed. He had covered a Crookes tube with cloth, and, in making a certain experiment, he sent a strong electric current through this tube, which he had placed on his laboratory table. He noticed that a piece of sensitized paper, which was lying on the table, showed certain lines that were not there before. The perspicacious professor followed up this observation, and the familiar results of his discovery have just been reported.

The *Vossische Zeitung* of Berlin, which had also reprinted the original Viennese text, added in their Wednesday edition:

Dr. Jastrowitz of the Berlin Society of Internal Medicine reported last Monday on an interesting scientific discovery which was made by Professor Röntgen in Würzburg. Dr. Jastrowitz showed the photograph of the bones of the human hand, two of the fingers showing rings. This was made not on a skeleton, but on a living human being.

It was not until January 9 that the home-town newspaper of the now famous professor carried a story on the discovery. The *Würzburger Generalanzeiger* reported:

On a New Kind of Ray — Last month, Dr. W. C. Röntgen, a professor at the university, gave a lecture before the Würzburg Physical-Medical Society on a discovery that he made and that is termed epoch-making and sensational in long articles published in scientific publications. . . .

Besides being awfully late with such important news — twelve days had passed since Röntgen had delivered his first communication — this report was inaccurate in stating that the discovery had been reported by Röntgen in a lecture before the society. Certainly the editor did not hear it, for the group did not meet during the Christmas holidays. Röntgen had been able to get his paper inserted into the printed communication of the society, which generally printed only the lectures held before it.

Newspapers throughout the world reported on the discovery of the rays, generally adding their own speculation as to the value of the discovery. *Le Matin* of Paris printed the Viennese story in its January 13, 1896, edition; the *New York Times* translated the same article on January 16 for its readers.

Weekly periodicals were naturally slower in their reporting, but already on January 11 the *Saturday Review* of London carried an article on the "new photographic discovery." On January 25, *L'Illustration* of Paris added to a detailed description of the "new light" an illustration of the hand photograph made in the Hamburg State Institute.

The *Literary Digest* of January 25 reported on the "Photography of Non-transparent Bodies," but just to be on the safe side it also warned its readers that "this report, like other similar ones, is an exaggeration or distortion of experiments that admit of no such wide application." It was perhaps the only newspaper or periodical which was not at all enthusiastic over the possibilities of the discovery of this "all penetrating light."

The *Nation,* "a weekly journal devoted to Politics, Literature, Science and Art, and published by The Evening Post Publishing Company of New York," in its January 30 issue, carried in its "Notes" columns, on page 101, the following comprehensive report:

A recent discovery made by the distinguished physicist, Professor Wilhelm Conrad Röntgen of the University of Würzburg, is now exciting considerable interest in Germany, where it is being subjected to a thorough examination by scientific men. By means of the rays proceeding from a Crookes' radiometer, under the influence of electrical induction, Prof. Röntgen succeeded in photographing on ordinary photographic plates. These rays, which are wholly imperceptible to the eye, and the existence of which has been hitherto unsuspected, have the power of penetrating all kinds of wood and other organic substances and solid bodies, except metals and bones, which are alone capable of resisting them. Thus the photograph of a wooden box in which iron weights are enclosed, shows only the iron weights; the box leaves no impression whatever on the photographic plate, the electric rays passing through it just as the ordinary rays of light pass through the air or any perfectly transparent object. The same is true of flesh. A photograph of the hand or leg shows only the bones; the photograph of a man, whether clothed or naked, is merely a human skeleton with a watch or ring, if he happens to wear them. Neither his clothing nor his flesh offer the slightest resistance to the rays, which are also unaffected by sunlight, so that the photographic process can be carried on anywhere in the daytime. The importance of this discovery in its application to surgery as an aid to diagnosis in cases of disease or fracture of the bones is apparent. The photograph would reveal immediately and unmistakably the nature of the disorder without the long and often painful examination which the patient is now obliged to undergo. In a case of complicated fractures another photograph can be taken after the bones have been set, in order to ascertain whether the dislocation has been properly reduced or the broken parts have been rightfully replaced. The exact position of a bullet or the splinter of shell can also be easily found without the use of a surgeon's probe. In all probability the process can be perfected and modified so as to photograph the heart, lungs, liver, and other internal organs, and thus determine their precise condition; at present, however, these organs offer no resistance to the rays, and therefore leave no impression on the plate. Some months ago Prof. Röntgen read a paper on this subject entitled *"Ueber eine neue Art von Strahlen,"* and printed in the proceedings *(Sitzungsberichte)* of the Würzburg *Physikalisch-Medizinische Gesellschaft.* This report has now been issued in pamphlet form by the university publisher, Stahel, in Würzburg.

Scientific journals were quick to report on the new and startling discovery from Würzburg. (While the publication dates were not necessarily always the actual dates of the appearance of these various periodicals, they are the only available identifications for a preferential listing.)

The *Electrical Engineer,* of New York, in the issue dated January 8, 1896, led the scientific journals with the report, "Electric Photography Through Solid Bodies." On January 10, the London *Electrician* carried a report under the heading "Sensational Worded Story." The January *Il Nuovo Cimento,* of Pisa, had an article by the Italian scientists A. Batelli and A. Garbasso on "Röntgen Rays." The January 23 issue of *Elektrotechnische Zeitschrift,* of Berlin, published the report on "Röntgen Rays," and the February 8 issue of *L'Eclairage Electrique,* of Paris, told of "A New Kind of Light."

The medical journals also brought the news to their professional readership quite rapidly. The *Münchener Medizinische Wochenschrift* of January 14 reported on the January 6 meeting of the Berlin Society for Internal Medicine, where Dr. Jastrowitz had given a paper on the discovery of the X rays. The *New York Medical Record,* dated January 11, most enthusiastically told of "Illuminated Tissue." The *Journal of the American Medical Association* in its February 15 issue followed with a report on "A New Kind of Ray."

The English *Lancet,* of January 11, 1896, described the "Searchlight of Photography." The *British Medical Journal* of January 11 had an original article by the Manchester physicist A. Schuster on "Röntgen Rays." The *Wiener Klinische Wochenschrift* of January 16 published an article on the "X Rays" by Sigmund Exner, the brother of the man who had actually triggered all the publication rush. The *Settimana Medica,* of

Florence, in its January 25 issue, carried an article on the discovery of the rays. The *Comptes Rendus* (Paris) of January 20 reported on the first successful diagnosis using Röntgen's rays. In the *Sitzungsbericht der Akademischen Wissenschaften Wien* of January 23 appeared a report by L. Pfaundler on experiments with the rays.

General scientific publications also carried the story as soon as possible. *Nature,* of London, had an announcement in its January 16 issue. *Science,* of New York, for January 24 reported:

The Vienna *Presse,* the London *Standard,* and some other daily newspapers report what purports to be an extraordinary discovery by Professor Röntgen. It is claimed that he has found that the ultra-violet rays from a Crookes vacuum tube penetrate wood and other organic substances, whereas metal, bones, etc., are opaque to them. It is said that he has thus photographed the bones of a living body, which would be one of the most important advances that has ever been made in surgery.

Complete translations of Wilhelm Röntgen's Preliminary Communication appeared in *Nature* (London), January 23, 1896; *Electrician* (London), January 24; *L'Eclairage Electrique* (Paris), February 8; *Science* (New York), February 14; *Journal de Physique* (Paris), March 1896; and others at later dates.

Photography journals also found much of interest to report. The *British Journal of Photography* of January 10, 1896, described the discovery, speculating on the "wonder camera of the Würzburg professor." *Photogram* of London in its February special issue wrote of "The New Light and the New Photography." The editors had done a superb job apparently, for the fifth printing was not long in appearing in the kiosks. *Photographic Review* was able to reproduce several pictures by J. Hall-Edwards in its March issue.

While most of these articles were rather short and, for the greater part, obvious rewrites of not always accurate newspaper reports of the discovery of the rays, more detailed articles followed in short order. One of these was a comprehensive article on "The X Rays," written by Hugo Muensterberg, professor of philosophy of Harvard University who was at the Freiburg University at the time and who sent the contribution to the periodical *Science* of New York, which avidly published it in its January 31 issue.

By March, members of the French Academy of Science had heard twenty lectures on X rays, all of which were duly published by their own *Comptes Rendus.* Not limited by space or costs, it proved an excellent historical source to gauge the scientific interest created by the discovery of the X rays.

Toward the end of the year 1896, published articles were fewer than at the beginning of this important year, but their number was still immense. The German scientific societies had no such system as existed in France where every paper read before the society was published in its official publication. Thus, many reports of additional experiments and observations or unusual experiences with X rays during this pioneering period were never publicized. (A comprehensive bibliography of papers on Röntgen and his discovery was published in 1931 in the book *Wilhelm Conrad Röntgen,* by Otto Glasser, listing 994 such articles published during the year 1896.)

The *Münchener Medizinische Wochenschrift* summed up the development quite correctly when it printed the following article by the physicist Leo Graetz of Munich:

Since the beginning of the year — shortly before that time, the discovery of Röntgen became known — in no experimental field was perhaps as much work done as in that area opened by Röntgen with his X rays. Not only in the physical and in the medical institutes of the universities and the technical high schools, but also in all departments of the higher learning institutions, in a large number of photographic institutions, and further in large numbers of privately operated laboratories, the experiments of Röntgen are being recreated and the search goes on for the best solutions to the problems. This not only in Germany, but with the same or even greater zeal in France, Austria, England, Italy, Russia, and America. Consequently an extremely large number of publications — valuable and worthless — on this subject have appeared since January 1896. Regarding these scientific papers, Germany is actually far behind other countries, especially behind France. This is probably due to the fact that no official scientific publication exists in Germany which publishes such work immediately after its presentation by its author. The *Comptes Rendus* of the Académie Française, which appears every week, brings everything which has been presented by members to the academy. This has proven to be a most highly regarded situation in this particular case. Similar, if not quite as comprehensive, situations exist in England with its *Nature* and in Italy with their publications of the many academies. Indeed most of these appearances have been long observed by the *Physikalische Institut der Universität München*, before they were published in the foreign media, and they were perhaps also observed in a like manner by a number of other German institutions.

The tremendous interest in the discovery of these new rays was perhaps best illustrated by the great demand for reprints of the First Communication of Röntgen. The first edition, published at the end of 1895, was followed by a second edition appearing only a few days later, early in 1896. Here the author was listed as "Dr. Wilhelm Konrad Röntgen"; the publisher was unable to cope with the name, this time spelling the middle name in the modern style, but erroneously, with a

"K." The third edition came out with a light brown wrapper and had a separate title page with the same context as the wrapper. The fourth edition was identical with the third. But on the fifth edition, printed in February 1896, the statement was added, "The present booklet is also published in English, French, Italian, and Russian." Some of the later editions appeared with a wide bright red streamer across and the imprint "Contains the New Discovery of Professor Röntgen of Würzburg."

In three months five editions had been published, the words of the author himself testifying to the wide interest in the scientific details of the discovery.

Copies of the Second Communication "On a New Kind of Ray, Continued," had been forwarded by the publishers to Röntgen while he was in Baden-Baden. (See Appendix 4 for text of Second Communication.) Stahel again printed these but bound them in an orange-colored wrapper. As in one of the editions of the First Communication, this had a separate title page with the same context as the wrapper. The price was also 60 Pfennig. The text was printed on pages 3 to 9, and three additional pages carried advertisements of the publisher. One of them read: "X ray Picture of the Hand of Geheimrat von Kölliker. Price 50 Pfennig. This picture is of special interest since it was made by Professor Röntgen himself at that memorable meeting on January 23, 1896, in which he presented his discovery and also since this is the hand of the famous anatomist von Kölliker." Another advertisement read: "In its 5th edition appeared: Dr. Wilhelm Konrad [sic] Röntgen, *Eine Neue Art von Strahlen: I. Mitteilung. Preis 60 Pfennig.*"

But it was the imaginative writers of the popular weekly and monthly magazines who supplied readers with a wide scope of applications of the new rays.

Toward the end of the century the highly controversial question of vivisection had come in for much heated discussion in the United States and in Britain, and some of the articles on the discovery of the X rays speculated on the effects of the rays on that problem. *Life* of February 27, 1896, commented: "If the Röntgen method of seeing through things pans out anywhere near as well as its friends expect, we are entitled to hope that it will almost put an end to vivisection. There will be no need to put a knife into a live animal when a ray will make its inner workings visible."

A similar line was taken in the *New York Tribune* of February 27, in its "Public Opinion" column. In Britain, however, the *Saturday Review* of February 29, 1896, published an article "The New Photography and Vivisection," which expressed a much more skeptical view of the matter.

The proponents of the temperance movement in the United States also hoped that the X ray discovery would work for their particular cause. Miss Francis E. Willard, the militant protagonist of the movement, was quoted by the *Electrical Revue,* of June 5, 1896: "I believe that the X rays are going to do much for the temperance cause. By this means drunkards and cigarette smokers can be shown the steady deterioration of their systems, which follows the practice. And seeing is believing."

Believers in the Christian religion were startled to read that Röntgen's rays proved the very existence of a spiritual body in man. In the article "The Röntgen Rays and the Spiritual Body," the *Literary Digest* of July 4, 1896, quoted from an article of the *Herald and Presbyter:* "This discovery corroborates, so far as any material experiment can, Paul's doctrine of the spiritual body as now existing in man. It proves, as far as any experiment can prove, that a truer body, a body of which the phenomenal body is but the clothing, may now reside within us, and which awaits the moment of its unclothing, which we call death, to set it free."

This sort of reasoning seemed only rubbish to many professed believers in the doctrine expounded by the apostle Paul. The editor of *Appleton's Popular Science Monthly* spoke for them when he stated:

Röntgen's discovery does not point any more toward the direction of the spiritual body within our bodies than it does to a spiritual body within cats and dogs or sheep or trees or stones. Strictly speaking, Röntgen's discovery proves nothing about bodies in general that has not been known for centuries. That light can pass through solid bodies even of great thickness and density has been the common experience of mankind ever since the first transparent substance was discovered. Röntgen has merely discovered that substances which are not penetrable by ordinary light rays, are penetrable by other rays produced by electric discharges in a very attenuated gaseous medium. How we are to derive any confirmation of the existence of a spiritual body from the action of these rays, which could not equally have been drawn from the action of ordinary light rays in transversing such dense substances as glass and various crystals, is a question which would probably puzzle the *Herald and Presbyter* to answer.

We have no objection in the world to the theory, whether Paul's, or Homer's, or Plato's, of a spiritual body. But we do think it is a little hard that because a laborious experimenter like Röntgen has brought to light a new property of radiant energy — while like a well-trained man of science, he affirms only what he has been able to demonstrate — others should rush in and insist that without being aware of it, he has bolstered up some doctrine of theirs for which no scintilla of evidence can be given.

This sober evaluation should have made the extremists desist from their abusive evaluation of the discovery, but it did no such thing, of course. Worse was to come.

Another group which quickly recognized the value of X rays to further its cause was the spiritualists, believing that the mysterious fluorescent light of various materials under the influence of X rays offered them an opportunity to open the way to fantasy in their "sometimes sincerely motivated seances." (And the insincerely motivated ones, as well, the report could have added.)

According to *Science* of New York of March 3, 1896:

Shortly after the newspaper carried the report of the discovery of X rays, at the College of Physicians and Surgeons, the rays were used to reflect anatomic diagrams directly into the brains of advanced medical students, making a much more enduring impression than ordinary teaching methods of learning anatomic details.

The enduring result of this harebrained scheme would have been only baldness of the thus exposed students.

In Cedar Rapids, Iowa, a newspaper reported:

George Johnson, a young farmer from Jefferson County and a graduate of Columbia College, who has been experimenting with the X rays, thinks that he has made a discovery that will startle the world. By means of what he called the X rays he is enabled to change in three hours time a cheap piece of metal worth about 13 cents to $153 worth of gold. The metal so transformed has been tested and pronounced pure gold.

The newspaper did not report how many gullible and greedy readers believed the story.

The *Electrician* of London in its April 17, 1896, issue reported that according to a San Francisco newspaper, David Starr Jordan told the physicists of the impressionistic school:

Mr. Ingles Rogers and other physicists of the impressionistic school are now prominent in the news, perhaps on account of the supposed relation of their achievement to the discoveries of Professor Röntgen. Röntgen, and since him many others, have obtained shadow photographs from invisible light vibrations connected with the so-called cathode rays. These light rays passed through matter which is nearly impervious to the ordinary vibrations. Mr. Rogers has produced an impression on the photographic plate by simply gazing at it in the dark. Others claim to do the same by gazing only with the mind's eye, giving a photographic image of the subject of their thoughts. By this means they produce definite chemical action where no material basis for such action exists.

While most nonprofessional persons thought this blatant nonsense, a number of physicians, among them a Dr. Ottolenghi of Naples, firmly believed that the retinas of somnambulists, who pretended that they could look through opaque bodies, were sensitive to X rays. Others insisted that blind persons could be made to see by using "X ray eyes."

From France came the report of "sensational soul photography" by a Dr. Baraduc, who presented his theory before the august body of the Paris Medical Society. The French Dr. Albert Battanier gave a detailed description of these "wonderful possibilities," stating that Dr. Baraduc had studied a series of discharges of the human soul upon light sensitive plates and actually exhibited some 400 examples in Munich in 1896. He claimed to have made photographic exposures by transmission of thought with his friend Dr. Istrate over a distance of some 300 kilometers (about 186.3 miles). The public, however, gave little credence to these observations, and the *Daily Telegraph* correspondent suggested soberly, "These pictures of Dr. Baraduc are equally as unsafe as his theories."

Experiments were also conducted in Paris with various luminous insects, exposing them to X rays to test their reaction in the hope that the secret of their luminescence could thus be learned. A successful solution would also divulge the secret of the economics of the lighting method of the *Lampyris noctiluca.*

Perhaps the most bizarre doctrine with which X rays were to be associated was the phenomenon of "Od," which had received widespread notice during the middle of the nineteenth century in Germany. It was first introduced by Baron von Reichenbach of Stuttgart in 1846, who described it in detail in his "Odisch Magnetic Letters," published in 1852. The baron apparently believed he had found the combination of electricity, magnetism, and heat which was all-penetrating, and he called it "Od." According to the *Dublin Journal of Medical Science:*

In order to be certain that there was actually light given off in these cases, he made some very careful experiments with the daguerreotype, the result of which was that an iodized plate was acted upon when placed opposite the poles of a magnet. He also was able to concentrate the rays with a lens, but the focal length was found to be 54 inches, while for a candle it was only 12 inches. He could discover no action of heat with the utmost sensitive thermoscope. When the hand was laid before the poles, the light streamed through the fingers.

This doctrine had been discarded long before Röntgen made his discovery, but now it was quickly unearthed. In an article on "Röntgen's Rays and Reichenbach's Od Doctrine," Büchner described it in *Electrical Engineer* of New York, in the July 8, 1896, issue. The whole matter was expounded by L. Tormin later in a brochure, *"Magische Strahlen: Die Gewinnung photographischer Lichtbilder lediglich durch odisch-magnetische Ausstrahlungen des menschlichen Körpers"* — Magic Rays: The

Production of Photographic Pictures by the Odish Magnetic Radiation from the Human Body (Düsseldorf: Schmitz & Olbertz, 1896). The newly won disciples of the old Od doctrine now claimed that everything which was being done by X rays had actually been achieved some fifty years before by the mysterious Baron Reichenbach Od!

The outburst of this type of speculative future and application of the newly discovered rays by the lunatic fringe of pseudoscientists was perhaps, as Sir J. J. Thomson remarked in his Rede lecture on July 10, 1896, and as reported by the July 30 issue of *Nature* of London, "because Röntgen's discovery appeals to the strongest of all human attributes, namely curiosity."

The popular humor magazines had really found a subject suitable for inexhaustible exploitation. Cartoons, many rather macabre, yet still amusing, appeared in the British *Punch* of January 25 and March 7, and the American *Life* of February 27 and March 26. Preferred drawings were those of a fashionable party, with guests dressed in elegant attire, and then showing the same positioned persons as skeletons. Or this same device would be used merely in picturing a doting couple adoring each other. Another favorite subject was that of an eavesdropping housemaid, standing in front of a closed door, but instead of stooping to look through the keyhole, just holding a small apparatus and looking right through the door. The variations on this theme were bounded only by the ingenuity of the artists.

One editor quoted the "true discoverer of X rays":

> *Come, come, and sit you down; you shall not budge;*
> *You go not till I set you up a glass*
> *Where you may see the inmost part of you.*
>
> — William Shakespeare
> (*Hamlet* III. 4: 18-20)

Perhaps stimulated by the advertisement of "X ray proof under-clothing" by a London firm in February, when other suppliers offered "X ray opera glasses," *Life* magazine for March 12, 1896, carried these "Lines on an X ray Portrait of a Lady," by Lawrence K. Russel:

> She is so tall, so slender; and her bones —
> Those frail phosphates, those carbonates of lime —
> Are well produced by cathode rays sublime,
> By oscillations, amperes, and by ohms.
> Her dorsal vertebrae are not concealed
> By epidermis, but are well revealed.

> Around her ribs, those beauteous twenty-four,
> Her flesh a halo makes, misty in line,
> Her noseless, eyeless face looks into mine,
> And I but whisper, "Sweetheart, je t'adore."
> Her white and gleaming teeth at me do laugh.
> Ah! lovely, cruel, sweet cathodagraph!

In *Photography* magazine appeared the poem "X-actly So!" by Wilhelmina:

> The Roentgen Rays, the Roentgen Rays,
> What is this craze?
> The town's ablaze
> With the new phase
> Of X-rays' ways.
>
> I'm full of daze,
> Shock and amaze,
> For now-a-days
> I hear they'll gaze
> Thro' cloak and gown — and even stays,
> These naughty, naughty Roentgen Rays.

All of the reports and articles appearing in the newspapers and periodicals the world over were journalistic interpretations of scientific studies, often based on second-hand information, or even outright guesses and speculations on the effect of the great discovery. Wilhelm Röntgen was utterly disgusted by the many ridiculous stories and the wild conjectures that had been published in the press and in magazines. He had told the journalist Knut Hjörring that newspapers were not suitable media to explain scientific discoveries and that what they usually printed was *"ein Komplex von Irrtümern und Ungenauigkeiten,"* a combination of errors and inaccuracies.

Among the multitude of reporters who rushed to interview Röntgen was H. J. W. Dam, an Englishman who was also a correspondent for *McClure's Magazine.* To insure a hearing, the Royal Institution of Great Britain wrote on January 24, 1896, to "Professor Rontgen" [*sic*]:

Dear Sir:
Mr. H. J. W. Dam is a member of the Royal Institution of Great Britain. He is now leaving London to visit your country in the interest of Science.
> Yours truly,
> Henry Young
> Act. Secretary

Upon his arrival at Würzburg, Dam made the discovery that others had made before him. He was not allowed to see Röntgen. But unlike others before him, Dam had a few words to contribute. From the local Hotel Kronprinz he wrote a letter to the *"Cher Professeur Röntgen: J'espere que vous me permet de vous assurer que vous etes. . . ."* But now he told his dear professor that *"Vous etes trop difficile, beaucoup plus difficile que Berthlot, Pasteur, Dewar et toutes les autres hommes de science dont des decouvertes j'ai ecrit"* — You are very difficult, much more difficult than Berthlot, Pasteur, Dewar, and other men of science about whose discoveries I have written. Then he asked for an interview on a certain day and hour and suggested two o'clock for the interview. He wanted to bring a camera along to take photographs of the discoverer and the table where he took the first picture of a human hand.

Apparently taken aback by the audacity of this enterprising journalist, and perhaps wishing to have a sensible and responsible article written by a knowledgeable person, Wilhelm Röntgen allowed the almost always securely locked doors of the institute to be opened, and he granted Dam an exclusive interview.

CHAPTER 10

The New Marvel in Photography

A Visit to Professor Röntgen at His Laboratory in Würzburg
His Own Account of His Great Discovery
Interesting Experiments With the Cathode Rays
Practical Uses of the New Photography

By H. J. W. Dam

[This lead story in *McClure's Magazine,* April, 1896, resulted from Dam's exclusive personal interview with Röntgen.]

IN ALL THE HISTORY OF SCIENTIFIC DISCOVERY there has never been, perhaps, so general, rapid, and dramatic an effect wrought on the scientific centers of Europe as has followed, in the past four weeks, upon an announcement made to the Würzburg Physio-Medical Society, at their December meeting, by Professor William Konrad Röntgen, professor of physics at the Royal University of Würzburg. The first news which reached London was by telegraph from Vienna to the effect that a Professor Röntgen, until then the possessor of only a local fame in the town mentioned, had discovered a new kind of light, which penetrated and photographed through everything. This news was received with a mild interest, some amusement, and much incredulity; and a week passed. Then, by mail and telegraph, came daily clear indications of the stir which the discovery was making in all the great line of universities between Vienna and Berlin. Then Röntgen's own report arrived, so cool, so business-like, and so truly scientific in character, that it left no doubt either of the truth or of the great importance of the preceding reports.

To-day, four weeks after the announcement, Röntgen's name is apparently in every scientific publication issued of this week in Europe; and accounts of his experiments, of the experiments of others following his method, and of theories as to the strange new force which he has been the first to observe, fill pages of every scientific journal that comes to hand. And before the necessary time elapses for this article to attain publication in America, it is in all ways probable that the laboratories and lecture-rooms of the United States will also be giving full evidence of this contagious arousal of interest over a discovery so strange that its importance cannot yet be measured, its utility be even prophesied, or its ultimate beliefs be even vaguely foretold.

The Röntgen rays are certain invisible rays resembling, in many respects, rays of light, which are set free when a high pressure electric current is discharged through a vacuum tube. A vacuum tube is a glass tube from which all the air, down to one-millionth of an atmosphere, has been exhausted after the insertion of a platinum wire in either end of the tube for connection with the two poles of a battery or induction coil. When the discharge is sent through the tube, there proceeds from the anode — that is, the wire which is connected with the positive pole of the battery — certain bands of light, varying in color with the color of the glass. But these are insignificant in comparison with the brilliant glow which shoots from the cathode, or negative wire. This glow excites brilliant phosphorescence in glass and many substances, and these "cathode rays," as they are called, were observed and studied by Hertz, and more deeply by his assistant, Professor Lenard, Lenard having, in 1894, reported that the cathode rays would penetrate thin films of aluminum, wood, and other substances, and produce photographic results beyond. It was left, however, for Professor Röntgen to discover that during the discharge another kind of rays are set free, which differ greatly from those described by Lenard as cathode rays. The most marked difference between the two is the fact that Röntgen rays are not deflected by a magnet, indicating a very essential difference, while their range and penetrative power are incomparably greater. In fact, all those qualities which have lent a sensational character to the discovery of Röntgen's rays were mainly absent from those of Lenard, to the end that, although Röntgen has not been working in an entirely new field, he has by common accord been freely granted all the honors of a great discovery.

Exactly what kind of a force Professor Röntgen has discovered he does not know. As will be seen below, he declines to call it a new kind of light, or even a new form of electricity. He has given it the name of the X rays. Others speak of it as the Röntgen rays. Thus far its results only, and not its essence, are known. In the terminology of science it is generally called "a new mode of motion," or, in other words, a new force. As to whether it is or not actually a force new to science, or one of the known forces masquerading under strange conditions, weighty authorities are already arguing. More than one eminent scientist has already affected to see in it a key to the great mystery of the law of gravity. All who have expressed themselves in print have admitted, with more or less frankness, that, in view of Röntgen's discovery, science must forthwith revise, possibly to a revolutionary degree, the long accepted theories concerning the phenomena of light and sound. That the X rays, in their mode of action, combine a strange resemblance to both sound and light vibrations, and are destined to materially affect, if they do not greatly alter, our views of both phenomena, is already certain; and beyond this is the opening into a new and unknown field of physical knowledge, concerning which speculation is already eager, and experimental investigation already in hand, in London, Paris, Berlin, and, perhaps, to a greater or less extent, in every well-equipped physical laboratory in Europe.

This is the present scientific aspect of the discovery. But, unlike most epoch-making results from laboratories, this discovery is one which, to a very unusual degree, is within the grasp of the popular and non-technical imagination. Among the other kinds of matter which these rays penetrate with ease is the human flesh. That a new photography has suddenly arisen which can photograph the bones, and, before long, the organs of the human body; that a light has been found which can penetrate, so as to make a photographic record, through everything from a purse or a pocket to the walls of a room or a house, is news which cannot fail to startle everybody. That the eye of the physician or surgeon, long baffled by the skin, and vainly seeking to penetrate the unfortunate darkness of the human body, is now to be supplemented by a camera, making all the parts of the human body as visible, in a way, as the exterior, appears certainly to be a greater blessing to humanity than even the Listerian antiseptic system of surgery; and its benefits must inevitably be greater than those conferred by Lister, great as the latter have been. Already, in the few weeks since Röntgen's announcement, the results of surgical operations under the new system are growing voluminous. In Berlin, not only new bone fractures are being immediately photographed, but joined fractures, as well, in order to examine the results of recent surgical work. In Vienna, imbedded bullets are being photographed, instead of being probed for, and extracted with comparable ease. In London, a wounded sailor, completely paralyzed, whose injury was a mystery, has been saved by the photographing of an object imbedded in the spine, which, upon extraction, proved to be a small knife-blade. Operations for malformations, hitherto obscure, but now clearly revealed by the new photography, are already becoming common, and are being reported from all directions.

Professor Czermak of Graz has photographed the living skull, denuded of flesh and hair, and has begun the adaptation of the new photography to brain study. The relation of the new rays to thought rays is being eagerly discussed in what may be called the non-exact circles and journals; and all that numerous group of inquirers into the occult, the believers in clair-voyance, spiritualism, telepathy, and kindred orders of alleged phenomena, are confident of finding in the new force long-sought facts in proof of their claims. Professor Neusser in Vienna has photographed gall-stones in the liver of one patient (the stone showing snow-white in the negative), and a stone in the bladder of another patient. His results so far induce him to announce that all the organs of the human body can, and will, shortly, be photographed. Lannelongue of Paris has exhibited to the Academy of Science photographs of bones showing inherited tuberculosis which had not otherwise revealed itself. Berlin has already a society of forty for the immediate prosecution or researches into both the character of the new force and its physiological possibilities. In the next few weeks these strange announcements will be trebled or quadrupled, giving the best evidence from all quarters of the great future that awaits the Röntgen rays, and the startling impetus to the universal search for knowledge that has come at the close of the nineteenth century from the modest little laboratory in the Pleicher Ring at Würzburg.

On instruction by cable from the editor of this magazine, on the first announcement of the discovery, I set out for Würzburg to see the discoverer and his laboratory. I found a neat and thriving Bavarian city of forty-five thousand inhabitants, which, for some ten centuries, has made no salient claim upon the admiration of the world, except for the elaborateness of its mediaeval castle and the excellence of its local beer. Its streets were adorned with large numbers of students, all wearing either scarlet, green, or blue caps, and an extremely serious expression, suggest-ing much intensity either in the contemplation of Röntgen rays or of the beer aforesaid. All knew the residence of Professor Röntgen (pronuncia-tion: "Renken"), and directed me to the "Pleicher Ring." The various buildings of the university are scattered in different parts of Würzburg, the majority being in the Pleicher Ring, which is a fine avenue, with a park along one side of it, in the center of the town. The Physical Institute, Professor Röntgen's particular domain, is a modest building of two stories and basement, the upper story constituting his private residence, and the remainder of the building being given over to lecture rooms, laboratories, and their attendant offices. At the door I was met by an old serving-man of the idolatrous order, whose pain was apparent when I asked for "Professor" Röntgen, and he gently corrected me with "Herr Doctor Röntgen." As it was evident, however, that we referred to the same person, he conducted me along a wide, bare hall, running the length of the building, with blackboards and charts on the walls. At the end he showed me into a small room on the right. This contained a large table desk, and a small table by the window, covered with photographs, while the walls held rows of shelves laden with laboratory and other records. An open door led into a somewhat larger room, perhaps twenty feet by fifteen, and I found myself gazing into a laboratory which was the scene of the discovery — a laboratory which, though in all ways modest, is destined to be enduringly historical.

There was a wide table shelf running along the farther side, in front of the two windows, which were high, and gave plenty of light. In the center was a stove; on the left, a small cabinet, whose shelves held the small objects which the professor had been using. There was a table in the left-hand corner; and another small table — the one on which living bones were first photographed — was near the stove, and a Rhumkorff coil was on the right. The lesson of the laboratory was eloquent. Compared, for instance, with the elaborate, expensive, and complete apparatus of, say, the University of London, or of any of the great American universities, it was bare and unassuming to a degree. It mutely said that in the great march of science it is the genius of man, and not the perfection of appliances, that breaks new ground in the great territory of the unknown. It also caused one to wonder at and endeavor to imagine the great things which are to be done through elaborate appliances with the Röntgen rays — a field in which the United States, with its foremost genius in invention, will very possibly, if not probably, take the lead — when the discoverer himself had done so much with so little. Already, in a few weeks, a skilled London operator, Mr. A. A. C. Swinton, has reduced the necessary time of exposure for Röntgen photographs from fifteen minutes to four. He used, however, a Tesla oil coil, discharged by twelve half-gallon Leyden jars, with an alternating current of twenty thousand volts pressure. Here were no oil coils, Leyden jars, or specially elaborate and expensive machines. There were only a Rhumkorff coil and Crookes (vacuum) tube and the man himself.

Professor Röntgen entered hurriedly, something like an amiable gust of wind. He is a tall, slender, and loose-limbed man, whose whole appearance bespeaks enthusiasm and energy. He wore a dark blue sack suit, and his long, dark hair stood straight up from his forehead, as if he were permanently electrified by his own enthusiasm. His voice is full and deep, he speaks rapidly, and, altogether, he seems clearly a man who, once upon the track of a mystery which appeals to him, would pursue it with unremitting vigor. His eyes are kind, quick, and penetrating; and there is no doubt that he much prefers gazing at a Crookes tube to beholding a visitor, visitors at present robbing him of much valued time. The meeting was by appointment, however, and his greeting was cordial and hearty. In addition to his own language he speaks French well and English scientifically, which is different from speaking it popularly. These three tongues being more or less within the equipment of this visitor, the conversation proceeded on an international or polyglot basis, so to speak, varying at necessity's demand.

It transpired, in the course of inquiry, that the professor is a married man and fifty years of age, though his eyes have the enthusiasm of twenty-five. He was born near Zurich, and educated there, and completed his studies and took his degree at Utrecht. He has been at Würzburg about seven years, and had made no discoveries which he considered of great importance prior to the one under consideration. These details were given under good-natured protest, he failing to understand why his personality should interest the public. He declined to admire himself or his results in any degree, and laughed at the idea of being famous. The professor is too deeply interested in science to waste any time in thinking about himself. His emperor had feted, flattered, and decorated him, and he was loyally grateful. It was evident, however, that fame and applause had small attractions for him, compared to the mysteries still hidden in the vacuum tubes of the other room.

"Now, then," said he, smiling, and with some impatience, when the preliminary questions at which he chafed were over, "you have come to see the invisible rays?"

"Is the invisible visible?"

"Not to the eye; but its results are. Come in here."

He led the way to the other square room mentioned, and indicated the induction coil with which his researches were made, an ordinary Rhumkorff coil, with a spark of from four to six inches, charged by a current of twenty amperes. Two wires led from the coil, through an open door, into a smaller room on the right. In this room was a small table carrying a Crookes tube connected with the coil. The most striking object in the room, however, was a huge and mysterious tin box about seven feet high and four feet square. It stood on end, like a huge packing-case, its side being perhaps five inches from the Crookes tube.

The professor explained the mystery of the tin box, to the effect that it was a device of his own for obtaining a portable dark-room. When he began his investigations he used the whole room, as was shown by the heavy blinds and curtains so arranged as to exclude the entrance of all interfering light from the windows. In the side of the tin box, at the point immediately against the tube, was a circular sheet of aluminum one millimeter in thickness, and perhaps eighteen inches in diameter, soldered to the surrounding tin. To study his rays the professor had only to turn on the current, enter the box, close the door, and in perfect darkness inspect only such light or light effects as he had a right to consider his own, hiding his light, in fact, not under the Biblical bushel, but in a more commodious box.

"Step inside," he said, opening the door, which was on the side of the box farthest from the tube. I immediately did so, not altogether certain whether my skeleton was to be photographed for general inspection, or my secret thoughts held up to light on a glass plate.

"You will find a sheet of barium paper on the shelf," he added, and then went away to the coil. The door was closed, and the interior of the box became black darkness. The first thing I found was a wooden stool, on which I resolved to sit. Then I found the shelf on the side next to the tube, and then the sheet of paper prepared with barium platinocyanide. I was thus being shown the first phenomenon which attracted the discoverer's attention and led to the discovery, namely, the passage of rays, themselves wholly invisible, whose presence was only indicated by the effect they produced on a piece of sensitized photographic paper.

A moment later, the black darkness was penetrated by the rapid snapping sound of the high-pressure current in action, and I knew that the tube outside was glowing. I held the sheet vertically on the shelf, perhaps four inches from the plate. There was no change, however, and nothing was visible.

"Do you see anything?" he called.

"No."

"The tension is not high enough;" and he proceeded to increase the pressure by operating an apparatus of mercury in long vertical tubes acted upon automatically by a weight lever which stood near the coil. In a few minutes the sound of the discharge again began, and then I made my first acquaintance with the Röntgen rays.

The moment the current passed, the paper began to glow. A yellowish-green light spread all over its surface in clouds, waves, and flashes. The yellow-green luminescence, all the stranger and stronger in the darkness, trembled, wavered, and floated over the paper, in rhythm with the snapping of the discharge. Through the metal plate, the paper, myself, and the tin box, the invisible rays were flying, with an effect strange, interesting, and uncanny. The metal plate seemed to offer no appreciable resistance to the flying force, and the light was as rich and full as if nothing lay between the paper and the tube.

"Put the book up," said the professor.

I felt upon the shelf, in the darkness, a heavy book, two inches in thickness, and placed this against the plate. It made no difference. The rays flew through the metal and the book as if neither had been there, and the waves of light, rolling cloud-like over the paper, showed no change in brightness. It was a clear, material illustration of the ease with which paper and wood are penetrated. And then I laid book and paper down, and put my eyes against the rays. All was blackness, and I neither saw nor felt anything. The discharge was in full force, and the rays were flying through my head, and for all I knew, through the side of the box behind me. But they were invisible and impalpable. They gave no sensation whatever. Whatever the mysterious rays may be, they are not to be seen, and are to be judged only by their works.

I was loath to leave this historical tin box, but time pressed. I thanked the professor, who was happy in the reality of his discovery and the music of his sparks. Then I said: "Where did you first photograph living bones?"

"Here," he said, leading the way into the room where the coil stood. He pointed to a table on which stood another — the latter a small short-legged wooden one with more the shape and size of a wooden seat. It was two feet square and painted coal black. I viewed it with interest. I would have bought it, for the little table on which light was first sent through the human body will some day be a great historical curiosity; but it was *"nicht zu verkaufen."* A photograph of it would have been a consolation, but for several reasons one was not to be had at present. However, the historical table was there, and was duly inspected.

"How did you take the first hand photograph?" I asked.

The professor went over to a shelf by the window, where lay a number of prepared glass plates, closely wrapped in black paper. He put a Crookes tube underneath the table, a few inches from the under side of its top. Then he laid his hand flat on the top of the table, and placed the glass plate loosely on his hand.

"You ought to have your portrait painted in that attitude," I suggested.

"No, that is nonsense," said he, smiling.

"Or to be photographed." This suggestion was made with a deeply hidden purpose.

The rays from the Röntgen eyes instantly penetrated the deeply hidden purpose.

"Oh, no," said he; "I can't let you make pictures of me. I am too busy." Clearly the professor was entirely too modest to gratify the wishes of the curious world.

"Now, Professor," said I, "will you tell me the history of the discovery?"

"There is no history," he said. "I have been for a long time interested in the problem of the cathode rays from a vacuum tube as studied by Hertz and Lenard. I had followed theirs and other researches with great interest, and determined, as soon as I had the time, to make some researches of my own. This time I found at the close of last October. I had been at work for some days when I discovered something new."

"What was the date?"

"The eighth of November."

"And what was the discovery?"

"I was working with a Crookes tube covered by a shield of black cardboard. A piece of barium platinocyanide paper lay on the bench there. I had been passing a current through the tube, and I noticed a peculiar black line across the paper."

"What of that?"

"The effect was one which could only be produced, in ordinary parlance, by the passage of light. No light could come from the tube, because the shield which covered it was impervious to any light known, even that of an electric arc."

"And what did you think?"

"I did not think; I investigated. I assumed that the effect must have come from the tube, since its character indicated that it could come from nowhere else. I tested it. In a few minutes there was no doubt about it. Rays were coming from the tube which had a luminescent effect upon the paper. I tried it successfully at greater and greater distances, even at two meters. It seemed at first a new kind of invisible light. It was clearly something new, something unrecorded.

"Is it light?"

"No."

"Is it electricity?"

"Not in any known form."

"What is it?"

"I don't know."

And the discoverer of the X rays thus stated as calmly his ignorance of their essence as has everybody else who has written on the phenomena thus far.

"Having discovered the existence of a new kind of rays, I of course began to investigate what they would do."

He took up a series of cabinet-sized photographs. "It soon appeared from tests that the rays had penetrative power to a degree hitherto unknown. They penetrate paper, wood, and cloth with ease; and the thickness of the substance made no perceptible difference, within reasonable limits."

He showed photographs of a box of laboratory weights of platinum, aluminum, and brass, they and the brass hinges all having been photographed from a closed box, without any indication of the box. Also a photograph of a coil of fine wire, wound on a wooden spool, the wire having been photographed, and the wood omitted.

"The rays," he continued, "passed through all the metals tested, with a facility varying, roughly speaking, with the density of the metal.

These phenomena I have discussed carefully in my report to the Würzburg society, and you will find all the technical results therein stated."

He showed a photograph of a small sheet of zinc. This was composed of smaller plates soldered laterally with solders of different proportions. The differing lines of shadow, caused by the difference in solders, were visible evidence that a new means of detecting flaws and chemical variations in metals had been found. A photograph of a compass showed the needle and dial taken through the closed brass cover. The markings of the dial were in red metallic paint, and thus interfered with the rays, and were reproduced.

"Since the rays had this great penetrative power, it seemed natural that they should penetrate flesh, and so it proved in photographing the hand I showed you."

A detailed discussion of the characteristics of his rays the professor considered unprofitable and unnecessary. He believes, though, that these mysterious radiations are not light, because their behavior is essentially different from that of light rays, even those light rays which are themselves invisible. The Röntgen rays cannot be reflected by reflecting surfaces, concentrated by lenses, or refracted or diffracted. They produce photographic action on a sensitive film, but their action is weak as yet, and herein lies the first important field of their development. The professor's exposures were comparatively long — an average of fifteen minutes in easily penetrable media, and half an hour or more in photographing the bones of the hand. Concerning vacuum tubes, he said that he preferred the Hittorf, because it had the most perfect vacuum, the highest degree of air exhaustion being the consummation most desirable. In an answer to a question, "What of the future?" he said:

"I am not a prophet, and I am opposed to prophesying. I am pursuing my investigations, and as fast as my results are verified I shall make them public."

"Do you think the rays can be so modified as to photograph the organs of the human body?"

In answer he took up the photograph of the box of weights. "Here are already modifications," he said, indicating the various degrees of shadow produced by the aluminum, platinum, and brass weights, the brass hinges, and even the metallic stamped lettering on the cover of the box, which was faintly perceptible.

"But Professor Neusser has already announced that the photographing of the various organs is possible."

"We shall see what we shall see," he said. "We have the start now; the developments will follow in time."

"You know the apparatus for introducing the electric light into the stomach?"

"Yes."

"Do you think that this electric light will become a vacuum tube for photographing, from the stomach, any part of the abdomen or thorax?"

The idea of swallowing a Crookes tube, and sending a high frequency current down into one's stomach, seemed to him exceedingly funny.

"When I have done it, I will tell you," he said, smiling, resolute in abiding by results.

"There is much to do, and I am busy, very busy," he said in conclusion. He extended his hand in farewell, his eyes already wandering toward his work in the inside room. And his visitor promptly left him; the words, "I am busy," said in all sincerity, seemed to describe in a single phrase the essence of his character and the watchword of a very unusual man.

Returning by way of Berlin, I called upon Herr Spiess of the Urania, whose photographs after the Röntgen method were the first made public, and have been the best seen thus far. The Urania is a peculiar institution, and one which it seems might be profitably duplicated in other countries. It is a scientific theater. By means of the lantern and an admirable equipment of scientific appliances, all new discoveries, as well as ordinary interesting and picturesque phenomena, when new discoveries are lacking, are described and illustrated daily to the public, who pay for seats as in an ordinary theater, and keep the Urania profitably filled all the year round. Professor Spiess is a young man of great mental alertness and mechanical resource. It is the photograph of a hand, his wife's hand, which illustrates, perhaps better than any illustration in this article, the clear delineation of the bones which can be obtained by the Röntgen rays. In speaking of the discovery he said:

"I applied it, as soon as the penetration of flesh was apparent, to the photograph of a man's hand. Something in it had pained him for years, and the photograph at once exhibited a small foreign object, as you can see"; and he exhibited a copy of the photograph in question.

"The speck there is a small piece of glass, which was immediately extracted, and which, in all probability, would have otherwise remained in the man's hand to the end of his days."

All of which indicates that the needle which has pursued its travels in so many persons, through so many years, will be suppressed by the camera.

"My next object is to photograph the bones of the entire leg," continued Herr Spiess. "I anticipate no difficulty, though it requires some thought in manipulation."

It will be seen that the Röntgen rays and their marvelous practical possibilities are still in their infancy. The first successful modification of the action of the rays so that the varying densities of bodily organs will enable them to be photographed, will bring all such morbid growth as tumors and cancers into the photographic field, to say nothing of vital organs which may be abnormally developed or degenerate. How much this means to medical and surgical practice it requires little imagination to conceive. Diagnosis, long a painfully uncertain science, has received an unexpected and wonderful assistant; and how greatly the world will benefit thereby, how much pain will be saved, and how many lives saved, the future can only determine. In science a new door has been opened where none was known to exist, and a side-light on phenomena has appeared, of which the results may prove as penetrating and astonishing as the Röntgen rays themselves. The most agreeable feature of the discovery is the opportunity it gives for other hands to help; and the work of these hands will add many new words to the dictionaries, many new facts to science, and, in the years long ahead of us, fill many more volumes than there are paragraphs in this brief and imperfect account.

*   *   *

AUTHOR'S NOTE:
Aside from the inaccurate spelling of the name Conrad and the wrong facts as to birth and schooling of Röntgen, the observations appear to be quite correct.

The article was illustrated with a full page photograph of "Dr. Wilhelm Conrad Röntgen" and one of the Physical Institute of the University of Würzburg. A large number of decidedly clear and superbly reproduced X ray photographs were shown: (1) an aluminum cigar case, showing the darker shadow of two cigars inside; (2) a lady's hand, showing the bones and a wide ring on the third finger, and the outlines of the flesh; (3) the skeleton of a frog, showing the bones darkly, lungs and cerebral lobes in dimmer outline; (4) a razor and handle in a leather case; (5) the skeleton of a fish; (6) the bones of a human foot through the sole of a leather shoe, showing the pegs of the shoe sole darker and the dim traces of the foot; (7) the bones of a human foot and the flesh outlines; (8) a cork-screw, a key, a pencil with a metallic protector, and a piece of coin, all photographed through a calico pocket; and (9) several dark coins inside a purse, outlined. The photographs were credited to A. A. C. Swinton of London (1, 5, 7, 8, 9); P. Spiess of Berlin (2); Prof. Imbert and Bertin-Sans of Paris (3); and Dr. W. L. Robb of Hartford (4 and 6).

CHAPTER 11

Brief Interlude

WHEN WILHELM RÖNTGEN WAS URGED TO SIT for the sculptor Reinhold Felderhoff to create a monument to be placed on the Potsdamer Brücke in Berlin, he refused to pose. But when he was told that the plan was by "suggestion" of the Kaiser, and that if he would not sit his modeled likeness would probably look very unlike him and perhaps even quite uncomplimentary, he reluctantly consented. After seeing the finished bronze figure, Röntgen complained that the artist had placed an insect repellent gun into its hands instead of an X ray tube, and that he was now sentenced to hold this ridiculous contrivance on the bridge over the Landwehr-Kanal perhaps forever. This distress was, however, unwarranted. During the last years of World War II, the monument was melted down, by order of the Reichsminister for Armament, and the bronze was used for military purposes.

Röntgen was enormously vexed and angered at the many strangers who bothered him, looking on them with the same suspicion his ancestors did in the hilly Wuppertal country. He had hoped that the single interview given to a responsible writer would suffice to set the record straight, but apparently the publication of it served only as a stimulant for other news reporters to seek interviews.

The once pleasant life of quiet research and teaching work was changed into the busy irksome existence of a public personality. Röntgen had believed that the publication of his findings would stir scientists to further experiments along the lines he had so carefully outlined, to substantiate his startling discovery or to find his deductions and observations in error and discredit his experiments, but he had hardly expected such outbursts from scientists and laymen alike, who appeared most enthusiastic in endorsing his new discovery and disturbed his work routine most annoyingly.

Although she coped with the daily problems in her now rather turbulent household quite well, Bertha Röntgen wrote on March 4 to her husband's cousin Louise, who had married a minister, Julius Ferdinand Grauel, in Indianapolis, Indiana:

Willi has so much work that he does not know where to go. Yes, dear Louise, it is not a little matter to become a famous man, and the persons little realize how much work and unrest this carries with it. When Willi told me in November that he was working on an interesting problem, we had no idea how the thing would be received. But the work was barely published when our domestic peace was gone completely.

Every day I am astounded at the enormous working capacity of my husband. That he can keep his thoughts on his work despite the thousand little things with which he is bothered! But now it is high time that he should rest, and I am preparing everything for our trip south for a few weeks, in order to permit Willi to spend much of his time in the open air. Every day I am grateful to God that He made him so healthy and strong, but nevertheless I am fearful that some day the strain could become too much for him.

But now I talk only of the less pleasant part of our experience and have not said a word about our great happiness over the success of his work. Surely our hearts are full of gratitude that we are permitted to live through such a wonderful experience. How much recognition has my dear received for his indefatigable research. We are often almost dizzy with all the praise and honors bestowed on him. It would be alarming if the man who received all this were vain. But you know my brave, modest husband as scarcely anyone else does, and you can understand easily that he finds his highest reward in the knowledge that he was permitted to accomplish something valuable in serving pure science.

Berteli, however, thoroughly enjoyed the intensified activity in the Röntgen household. In her schoolgirlish enthusiasm and tremendous admiration for her father, she proudly let everyone know that she was the daughter of this great man. This caused definite displeasure to Röntgen, who did not like to be pointed out as an important person and considered any and all public adulation as an inexcusable invasion of his privacy. He complained that he was about to wear out a perfectly new hat from returning the greetings of people whom he did not know when taking his daily walks.

Completely disillusioned with the whole state of his affairs, and nearly exhausted, Wilhelm Röntgen was glad when the short Easter vacation period began. He wrote that the many honors caused him great concern, and he was most unhappy with all the attention he was getting. He felt too rushed by it all and "would like some *Beschimpfungen,* abuses, for a change of diet." He looked forward eagerly to the vacations and hoped to get away by March 10.

But first he had to complete the manuscript for his "Second Communication On a New Kind of Ray." Having enumerated seventeen points in his first communication, he began the second paper with point 18. Röntgen made four new points, describing the box he had built to achieve a fully controlled testing chamber, and explaining several experiments he had made to test the X rays. He promised that another, more explanatory paper would follow in due time.

Anxious to relax from the strain of the past months, he and Bertha again chose southern Italy for their short holiday. They packed their vacation wardrobe, including the Baedeker and the Italian language primer, and took a train to Naples, then planned to take a leisurely carriage to Sorrento.

But when their *Schnellzug* rolled into the domed station at Munich, the bearded professor was quickly recognized by reporters and representatives of the university. He dismissed the newsmen curtly and declined the invitation to lecture before a scientific group on the discovery of his rays. Even when their *rapidissimo* train arrived in Rome, the awaiting Italian physicists Salvioni and Righi easily recognized the black-coated Röntgen and asked him to lecture to their instructors and students at the university. Röntgen declined, then commented to Bertha that forthwith he would dispense with the black coat and would wear his brown suit instead! Bertha was happy that he had not lost his sense of humor. He had no brown suit!

The family finally arrived at Naples and hurried to the Hotel Victoria, relieved that news of their importance had not preceded them and that all was relatively quiet.

While enjoying the leisure and the salubrious climate of Sorrento, Röntgen remembered the words of Werner von Siemens, which he had quoted the previous year when he assumed the rectorship of the university:

If some natural law which has been long shrouded in obscurity suddenly emerges in the light of knowledge, when the key of a long-sought mechanical combination has been found, when the missing link of a chain of thought is fortuitously supplied, then this gives the discoverer the exultant feeling that comes with a mental victory which alone compensates him richly for all the struggle and effort and lifts him to a higher plane of existence.

Röntgen lived on that higher plane now. The momentous discovery had been made, but there was still much to find out before he could actually put this series of experiments aside and go on to another subject.

But first, he and Bertha wanted to enjoy fully the exquisite beauty of this fabulous bay. The favorite spot of mighty emperors and kings, great scientists and writers, talented musicians and painters, for more than 2,500 years, the Bay of Naples was indeed, as one writer put it, "a realm of compressed undiluted beauty."

From their hotel balcony atop a sheer cliff the Röntgens overlooked the clear blue waters of the serene bay and Naples gleaming distantly in the bright sun. To the left lay storied Capri, the pleasure ground of Roman imperators, and to the right smoking Vesuvius in the far background. At the foot of their cliff, the little harbor, Piccolo Sant'Angelo, was busy with sun-browned fishermen mending their nets and bathers bobbing about the salty waters and lazing on the shore. Nearby was the cave called the *Baths of Diana,* where wild pagan orgies had taken place. The tiny islands of the mermaids with their numerous grottoes cut into the sides of the cliffs were celebrated in mythology.

The Röntgens spent a day at the Isle of Capri, the ancients' island of the goats, where later the Phoenicians built a stairway to Anacapri, and then in the fourth century the Greeks came. Finally, Emperor Tiberius held his court and his revels there, but now most of the twelve villas were only ruins. Still, the magic of the island remained. From the Villa Jovis they again had a splendid look at Naples, but quite different from their view from Sorrento. The famed Blue Grotto was duly inspected. A boat took them to Ischia — of volcanic origin unlike Capri — which had not yet been invaded by tourists. Fishermen worked leisurely on their nets spread on the wide beaches and on colorful boats in the sheltered harbor. The tired but content Röntgens returned from their brief excursion to the hotel in Sorrento, and rest. In his well-thumbed Baedeker Röntgen noted that the round trip cost three lire.

After a week or two of relaxation in the balmy spring sun on the beautiful bay and the short excursions to Capri and Ischia, the Röntgens took a train north into the mountainous lake country. At Cadenabbia on Lake Como they felt nearly at home at Hotel Belle Vue, one of their favorite vacation spots. Here they met colleagues and enjoyed mutual outings. They took the lake steamer to Bellagio and to the Villa Arconati near Lenno to feast on the wonderful familiar view of the gorgeous lake, and cherry tarts with coffee, which Röntgen called no less wonderful.

To celebrate his fifty-first birthday, Röntgen secured from the Prince zu Meiningen the key to the private Villa Carlotta, the former Casa Sommariva of the Marchese Giorgio Clerici. Birthday guests walked through the graceful wrought-iron gate facing the lake. As had the French writer Stendahl, they admired the magnificent gardens with the tropical vegetation and overpowering scents, the majestic cedars, exquisite camellias, magnolias, and huge myrtles, and the vast areas of azaleas and rhododendrons. They paused in refreshing grottoes and groves, with glimpses of the shining placid lake. In the marble hall at the entrance to the villa, they admired the splendid collection of wonderful sculpture, with the works of Canova, especially the Cupid and Psyche group among the finest examples of this art. The exceedingly decorative frieze of the Triumphal Entry of Alexander into Babylon of Thorwaldsen, superbly placed against a background of rare plants and colorful flowers, encircled the entire wall of the spacious sculpture gallery. But they enjoyed the natural beauty of the luxurious grounds more than these priceless art objects, and rested on a well-placed bench in the park before returning to their hotel.

At a gala dinner with several of their friends that evening Röntgen received a sincere personal tribute from his older friend, Dr. Ulrich Krönlein, who as a younger doctor had cared for him after an injury sustained in mountain climbing. In proposing the toast, Dr. Krönlein enthusiastically endorsed the suggestion made by Geheimrat von Kölliker that the new rays be named after their discoverer. Wilhelm Röntgen merely frowned his disagreement.

In his earlier academic life, while at Giessen and Würzburg, the Röntgens' *Wanderlust* had taken them to distant places during their annual spring vacations. Röntgen and Bertha had visited Cairo, Corfu, Sicily, and other southern Mediterranean places of interest. Toward the beginning of the new century they began spending these spring Easter vacations at Santa Margherita on the Riviera, and more and more at Cadenabbia (in the Riviera delle Azalee) on the lovely Lake Como. Several times they went as far as Naples or Rome, but soon Cadenabbia at the Hotel Belle Vue became a routine matter.

For many of these observations and glimpses into the private lives of the Röntgens we are indebted to Margret Boveri, who published her *Persöhnliche Erinnerung* in 1931. As a child, Fräulein Dr. Boveri spent many days on outings with the Röntgens.

What later developed into a close and dear friendship began in a highly unpromising and even rather macabre manner. When Margret was about six years old, she attended, with her parents and other guests, a birthday party for Röntgen. There she was given a piece of *Croquant,* a crispy chocolate candy of which the Röntgens were especially fond and which was invariably a part of the celebration. But little Margret did not care for it and soon made a mess by getting most of it all over herself. When she had to be cleaned off, Käthe washed her. Liking the maid Kätchen very much, the little youngster told her that when the Röntgens died, she should come and live with the Boveris. After all, the Röntgens seemed to be awfully old people to her and she could not imagine that they would live much longer. Käthe laughingly told her Frau Doktor of this conversation, and since the health of Bertha was rather precarious, the innocent and well-meant compliment to the maid was not an amusing story at all. Consequently, the Röntgens did not take to little Margret.

Other "uncles" went shopping with Margret. Krönlein bought oranges and let her guess which ones were the preferred dark "blood oranges." Stöhr produced miniature chocolate bars during their hikes into the country. Reluctantly Röntgen occasionally took Margret on climbing expeditions into the mountainous country, but then only when his colleagues did not wish to accompany him. Usually ignoring the regular paths, they would take short cuts, climb steep grades and dangerously rocky terrain, and when they arrived at a given point long ahead of the rest of the outing party, they would sit down and secretly eat a piece of cheese and bread before the picnic really began. But theirs was a friendship only for convenience sake.

One time the two got lost coming down a hill by a shorter way, and to make up time they climbed down a steep cliff. Röntgen slipped, hitting his head on a rock. Frightened, Margret lost her bundled-up raincoat in the excitement. Röntgen roused, and the pair met the regular party in time for the excursion steamer across the lake. Röntgen did not say anything about his fall, and Margret did not justify the loss of her raincoat to her parents. Loyally she took the criticism in stubborn silence. This mutual secret created a firm bond between the two culprits, and from then on they became close hiking companions and good friends.

Röntgen, as usual, planned the outings most carefully, generally utilizing a full day for an event. There were steamer trips, long hikes, and carriage rides, culminating in the afternoon rest with *Kaffee und Kuchen*. A favorite hiking trip was to San Martino over rough terrain — no foot paths as yet — or to the Villa Arconti. Lenno, at the mouth of the Acquafredda, had an old church, Santo Stefano, with an interesting crypt and adjoining octagonal baptistry. On the shore was the site of Pliny's villa Comoedia. A more strenuous trip was the hour-long hike to the Madonna del Socorso by a road lined with fifteen chapels recalling the Sacro Monte at Varese.

On such long trips Bertha and some of the others of the party would take a carriage at noon to arrive at the appointed spot about the same time as the sturdy hikers who were making the event a whole day's affair. The robust members left their hotel early after a hearty breakfast. Stöhr suffered from gout and Krönlein had asthma, and neither man was as fond of long and arduous hikes as was Röntgen.

One evening Röntgen dressed hurriedly for dinner. The afternoon's outing had been a long and exhaustive one, and he was glad that he would not miss the bountiful meal. As he sat down, Bertha noticed that he wore only one black patent leather shoe; the other was the hobnailed hiking boot he had failed to change. The story of this hurried entry and the *lapsus memoriae* quickly spread among the guests and gave rise to much hilarity in Röntgen's circle of friends. On the following birthday Röntgen was presented with a fancy dried prune man, dressed in a formal dinner jacket and wearing one black and one brown shoe. Included was this formal letter:

> The British Colony of Cadenabbia, very much flattered to see that you have adopted their national evening dress, has decided to have your statue sculptured by the celebrated sculptor, Professor M. Klinger in Leipzig, in order to perpetrate [*sic*] the memory of Your First Appearance in this Dress. We have the pleasure of sending you a reduced model of the statue in honour of the sixty-second anniversary of your birthday, wishing you many happy returns of the day. Yours very respectfully, The very Reverend of Sheapshead.

Usually Röntgen planned his outings carefully, using his reliable Baedeker. But one day he excitedly revealed a rare find — with his sharp binoculars he had discovered a large white building, obviously a restaurant with a spacious terrace, just across the lake on the peninsula Bellagio. Röntgen announced an impromptu afternoon coffee hour. The party crossed the lake right after lunch, then set out on a rather narrow but well defined footpath along the lake. Soon, however, the path became narrower and less defined, eventually disappearing almost completely into what seemed a goat trail at most. But the building became visible on a promontory and appeared to be closer. So the party struggled on through the wild terrain, with the happy expectation of a refreshing repast before them. When they finally arrived, almost exhausted, the building turned out to be a private villa, boarded up for the season. There was no restaurant, and of course, nothing to eat or to drink, in fact not even a caretaker in attendance. With the afternoon already quite late and dusk rapidly approaching, it was decided to remain there, rather than to take a chance on the precarious and even dangerous path back to their hotel at Cadenabbia.

Eventually a fishing boat was alerted with blinking flashlights, but the man failed to understand any of the Italian words Röntgen believed would explain their situation. The lessons he had so diligently studied were utterly useless in this emergency. The *Wörterbuch* that Röntgen carried proved equally unproductive. He could not read the dictionary by the poor light beam. The fisherman took some of the stranded party — ladies and children only, because the boat had a small leak and was not too seaworthy for fine guests — across the lake and sent another boat which then picked up the remaining members of the ill-fated expedition. This total failure was a tremendous blow to the prestige of their *campione cicerone,* but since it was seldom that Röntgen was not an expert pathfinder, he was soon restored to his former position of authoritative *Führer.* But the debacle spoiled the remaining days of the vacation for him.

The vacationing group always split into two friendly rival factions, the Britannia Group and the Belle Vue Group. The desire leading to the amicable contention was to have the Röntgens live at the Britannia (110 beds, dinner 22 lire, full pension 40 lire — about $7.50) instead of the more affluent Belle Vue (160 beds, dinner 28 lire, full pension 55 lire — about $10.00).

At one lavish birthday dinner party for Röntgen, Stöhr read a lengthy poem written especially for the occasion; at the end of the dinner, after appropriate toasts had been drunk to the honored guest, Krönlein read several pages of his own rhymes, at least as clever. These witty verses extolled the creature comforts of the Britannia and compared them favorably with the aristocratic elegance of the Belle Vue. Röntgen felt uneasy — *in vino veritas?* — at this openly expressed lampoonery, but it was not more than at the satirical affair of the previous year when the *Geburtstagskind,* birthday child, was presented with an elaborately decorated, official scroll, ostensibly from the King of Italy himself. The fancy document, complete with ribbon and seal, was a reward for the "founding of a Swiss-German Colony at Cadenabbia which contributed so very generously through the consumption of rancid bacon and ancient salami sausage, thus assisting in a most commendable manner the prosperity of the struggling merchants of the small community, and thus elevating the state of health and well being of the resident population." This was prompted by the annual birthday gift of his favorite assorted food delicacies, the *Lieblingsleckerbissen,* presented in a large gift basket, beautifully decorated.

But Wilhelm Röntgen took their stay at the Belle Vue seriously and wrote to Boveri about that, explaining his reasons for the choice:

I have once again ordered the rooms at the Belle Vue. Please do not misunderstand this, because it is not of the luxury or of the well-dressed people there, but because the hotel offers so much more to my wife than does the Britannia. She can walk directly into the garden from her own room, and the large terrace gives her, who has to stay at home most of the time, a well-protected place and fresh air. Our beloved Tremezzo and its vicinity is so much closer, and the steamer landing is right at our door. The difficulty of climbing stairs is avoided, as there is an elevator in the house, and so on. As long as I can, I must give these conveniences to my wife.

And so it remained throughout the years.

At times, when his tired colleagues pleaded exhaustion, Röntgen felt well repaid for staying at another hotel. It widened the circle of chance acquaintances of sturdy hiking companions, and he would find a willing partner for a strenuous outing from either hotel's guests. Often, with such a companion, and fortified with food and drink in his *Rucksack* for a whole day's trip, Röntgen hiked the steep trails which ascended the Monte Crocione (5,368 feet), the Monte Calbiga (5,568 feet), and the Monte di Tremezzo (5,578 feet), which commanded an unexcelled view of the Valais Alps and no less than seven exquisite Alpine lakes.

On rainy days the Britannia guests would go over to the more comfortable and spacious Belle Vue and play cards in the expansive card rooms. The men were quite different temperamentally. When the dealt hands did not suit them, the real Bavarians Boveri and Stöhr would pound the table, the Swiss Krönlein would have a long melancholy face, and Röntgen would show his silent rage only in his eyes. In fact, he often became so angry at cards that he had some trouble finding willing partners who could stand his merciless criticism when, according to his reasoning, they played a bad hand. Frau Boveri, for one, would not play as his partner under any circumstances, but others were persuaded to do so, often to their later regret.

On their way home from Cadenabbia late that March of 1896, the Röntgens crossed the Saint Gotthard Pass to Lucerne to visit briefly in Zurich with relatives and old friends. Then they stopped in Baden-Baden, after a leisurely carriage trip through the Black Forest, to be greeted at the elegant Hotel de France by a vast amount of mail and telegrams that had accumulated awaiting their arrival. For all practical purposes their vacation was over and they were as good as home. The humdrum of activities had again begun. While they had been able to escape the harried life of a public personality for a time in Italy, here they entered again into the fast-moving fagging life of a celebrity.

From Munich Röntgen learned in a confidential note that he would receive another great honor on April 20, when Prince Regent Luitpold would bestow the Royal Order of Merit of the Bavarian Crown, carrying with it the mark of nobility. Again, Wilhelm Röntgen was pleased at this announcement from such a high source, but in the matter of nobility he had a definite contrary opinion. He insisted on remaining *sine nobilitate*. The "Lennep affair" illustrated this point.

When finally, on January 27, 1896, the *Lenneper Kreisblatt* had carried a story about the discovery, not even realizing that Wilhelm Röntgen was born in its community, some alert citizen — who remembered the Röntgen family from before their emigration to Holland — urged the Stadtverordnete-Kollegium to extend the *Ehrenbürgerrecht,* honorable citizenship, to its illustrious native son.

Thus, on February 27, Mayor Sauerbronn of Lennep wrote to Röntgen, asking if he was the one born in Lennep in 1845. Some doubt existed on that question, and the official asked for substantiation of the fact. Röntgen obviously replied in the affirmative, marking the letter merely *"erledigt* 2. April 96." Only a few days after that, on April 16, the mayor again wrote to inform Wilhelm Röntgen that the city council had decided to "honor one of her sons who was a discoverer of great significance to German science and to make him an honorary citizen of Lennep." On April 20, Röntgen replied briefly, "I accept with warmest thanks and with great joy the high honor of becoming an honorary citizen of the Town of Lennep."

An invitation to Lennep for the presentation followed. Röntgen wrote on June 13, that he could not come, but diplomatically invited the council to come to him instead. Then he continued:

With regard to the prefix "von," which you used in connection with my name in your letter of June 4, I should like to say the following: The paragraph of the rules of the Royal Bavarian Order of the Crown referring to this states, "The decoration of citizens with the Order of Merit of the Bavarian Crown includes the bestowal of personal nobility. The rights of nobility, including the prefix of nobility von, can be exercised only after matriculation has been accomplished. Failure to make application for matriculation means forfeiting the rights of nobility." Since to date I have not made such an application, and since I am not intending to do so, I am not entitled to the use of the prefix "von." Accept the expression of my sincere esteem. Dr. W. C. Röntgen.

An elaborately decorated *Ehrenbürgerurkunde,* dated June 15, 1896, was awarded "Herrn Professor Dr. Wilhelm Conrad von Röntgen zu Würzburg." The impressive document was signed by twenty citizens of his birthplace.

In the mail at Baden-Baden was a black-bordered letter with a *Todesanzeige* from his friend and colleague Ludwig Zehnder. His father had passed away at the age of seventy. Röntgen wrote to him:

Dear Zehnder! After a lengthy battle, death has at last released your father from his suffering. The life of a man is completed, who has been a help and comfort for very many of his fellow men, who could offer himself for them out of real love of mankind. He was a physician with head and heart. Shadow exists in every life, and we are not all by far without mistakes. We must accept the people as they are and not as we wish them to be. If we knew everything, we would surely forgive all. Both of us quite feel that these few lines should express to you that you, despite all you have thought earlier, have suffered a great loss when the two eyes closed. We hope to see you again within a short time. We will remain here until next week. That is, if nothing unexpected occurs.

Apparently Röntgen did not consider the letter from Theodor Boveri to be an unexpected occurrence. The professor wrote from Würzburg that a lot of work awaited Röntgen at the university on his return and that as rector he had many administrative duties to perform. "We beg you urgently to be back not later than April 19 if that is at all possible. Your influence as Rektor seems to us to demand absolutely your presence."

Perhaps Wilhelm Röntgen had a short pang of conscience when he read that letter of March 30. It was almost impossible to get back home by that date, for he had to attend the festivities at Munich for the presentation of the Order on the 20th.

CHAPTER 12

Priority Claims

WHEN RÖNTGEN RETURNED to Würzburg from his vacation, another rather unexpected development demanded his attention. Several priority claims to his discovery came from scientists who also had investigated cathode rays in their own laboratories and who had made certain observations.

Many such priority claims, made after the publication of Röntgen's Communications, were perhaps honest contentions, but the majority were pointless and warranted absolutely no consideration. Because the true character of the X rays was not definitely known for some years, several observations with Hertzian rays, with electrical brush discharges, with ultraviolet rays, with cathode rays, and other similar phenomena were then believed to have been due to the new X rays.

Undoubtedly several scientists had actually produced X rays during their experiments in related research work, as did Röntgen; but unlike him, these scientists failed to recognize the phenomenon, to observe it closely, and to isolate it for what it really was.

Hauksbee and Nollet already in 1700, and Morgan in 1780, and others in later years, observed unexplained effects of these rays. Francis Hauksbee had written that "the shape and figure of all parts of the hand could be distinctly seen," and these words were interpreted as meaning that he had indeed observed the phenomenon caused by X rays.

As Sylvanus P. Thompson said on November 5, 1897, "In the history of science, nothing is more true than that the discoverer, even the greatest discoverer, is but the descendant of his scientific forefathers. He is always essentially the product of the age in which he is born."

Röntgen was, of course, well aware of his significant predecessors in his field. Michael Faraday in 1838 had produced a discharge of electricity through space in a partially evacuated glass tube. These early observations of Faraday led Johann Wilhelm Hittorf in 1869 to further work in that area. Hittorf described cathode rays and referred to the passage of electricity in a vacuum tube as produced by an induction current.

William Crookes in 1861 had discovered a new element, thallium, and wanting to continue the search for still other unknown elements, he became interested in the production of glass tubes with more rarified gas content to use in his experiments. He was actually able to produce a vacuum of about 1/1,000,000 in a glass tube in 1877. This became known as a Crookes tube.

After much experimentation, Crookes concluded, in the words of I. W. D. Hackl, that "the cathode rays are a stream of particles, for they heat up bodies upon which they fall," and that "these particles carry negative electricity, for they could be deflected by an electromagnetic field," and that "these particles stream away from the cathode at right angles, for they could be focused by using a convex electrode, and with different velocities, for they are deflected at different angles." It seems evident that Crookes was actually producing X rays at the same time he made these observations, but failed completely to recognize the strange phenomenon.

As Alan R. Bleich pointed out, "When — as happened in November, 1895 — a new fact was demonstrated to him, Wilhelm Röntgen could recognize the departure from existing knowledge and pursue it until it became integrated into our scientific heritage. Röntgen had a special genius for a high achievement in laboratory work and for the application of these results in a very practical sense."

Dr. Monell wrote in 1896, "But a new door has been opened wide where none before was known to exist, and through it we may pass into a happier era, when uncertainty and empiricism shall give place to knowledge and definite therapeutics, and medicine shall take its rightful place among the sciences that are exact."

As often in the event of a notable discovery, voices of dissent and of envy made themselves heard, and some suggested that an obscure assistant or simple helper had actually made the momentous discovery. The voluminous publicity which almost at once brought the X rays before the entire reading public of the world also brought an unusually large number of persons who wished to ascribe the discovery to others or to proclaim it a mere accident.

Hugo Muensterberg of Harvard University once said, "Let us assume that accident actually played a role. Many galvanic effects existed in the world long before Galvani observed by chance the spasm of a frog's leg on an iron fence. The world is always full of such accidents, but there are only a few Luigi Galvanis and Wilhelm Röntgens."

Ludwig Zehnder wrote, "Röntgen seldom spoke of his discovery, and perhaps this reluctance, or even silence, to clarify idle gossip of other persons, contributed to feed the flames of maliciousness toward the scientist-professor." Röntgen had few close friends among his physicist colleagues. There had been, of course, August Kundt, who had taken such personal interest in him, first at Zurich when he urged Röntgen to try physics as his life's work, then when he invited him to Würzburg as his assistant, and two years later when they went to Strassburg. Both men had been closer to each other than to other laboratory colleagues, even Franz Exner and Zehnder.

The caretaker of the institute, Kasper Marstaller, claimed that he had seen the strange rays first, while Röntgen was busily engaged in adjusting some apparatus in the experiment. It could well have been that the helper was in the laboratory at the time of the first experiments, or when Röntgen set up his equipment for the experiments with cathode rays. It is highly doubtful that Marstaller first saw the actual phenomenon on the screen before Röntgen did, or that he was even in the darkened laboratory when the rays became visible. As Röntgen told his daughter Berteli, there were *keine dienstbaren Geister,* no subservient ghosts, present in the room at the time of the actual discovery, but the clever Marstaller surely reasoned that something highly unusual was taking place.

One of Wilhelm Röntgen's colleagues at the university, the physiologist Adolph Fick, claimed (according to his nephew R. Fick) that Röntgen told him of the discovery within an hour of its occurrence. Such action on the part of Röntgen appears entirely out of character, for he was too discreet and cautiously prudent. Indeed his close friends were never informed of any new observation until he had very carefully checked all facts and was uncontestably accurate in his statements regarding them. Not even Theodor Boveri, Röntgen's closest friend among the colleagues at Würzburg, was told the details of the work that seemed to be upsetting Röntgen greatly and which had changed him almost entirely. All Röntgen divulged to Boveri was that he had discovered something interesting but did not know if his observations were correct. It does seem obvious that Fick was mistaken in his recollection of those historic days.

Another version, also involving Marstaller, was suggested by Dr. F. Kanngiesser of Braunfels, who said that the servant told him that Professor Röntgen found one of the photographic plates, which lay on a table near the apparatus used for the experiments with the cathode rays, to be exposed. Röntgen admonished Marstaller for his negligence, but the caretaker insisted that he had not opened the metal container nor exposed the plate to any light. It was in this way that Röntgen then deduced that existing but invisible rays had penetrated the casette and spoiled the plate.

Still another version was contributed by A. Dyroff of Bonn, at the time a teacher at the Gymnasium at Würzburg (1894–99) and who had Marstaller's son in his class. Being interested in finding out some of the details of the discovery, he asked the youngster about it. The son told the teacher that his father had noticed a piece of photographic paper laying on a table. Between the experimental apparatus and this paper stood a small wooden box which contained Röntgen's wedding ring, and one morning Marstaller noted the outline of a ring on the sensitive paper. When he called Röntgen's attention to this image, the professor was momentarily startled and then seemed deep in thought. It was a fact that Röntgen always removed his ring when making experiments in his laboratory, especially when handling quicksilver, which could blacken the gold or under certain severe circumstances even dissolve it entirely. Then too, Röntgen was careful not to have any metal objects on his person which might cause diversion of delicate instruments or currents.

Teacher Dyroff also claimed that the Marstaller boy gave him the piece of photographic paper with the ring patterned on it, and that he placed it in his desk at the Gymnasium. He explained that the valuable paper was properly fixed with the developing solution because it maintained its clarity. When he accepted the position at Bonn, his personal things were hastily packed and the paper was apparently overlooked and most likely thrown away. At any rate it could not be located later on. Only because the interest in the discovery of X rays was again so keen at that particular time, Dyroff recalled the episode of the picture.

There was, of course, the admonition of Röntgen to Zehnder when he sent him several of his photographs for the lecture demonstration, "I recommend that you place the pictures under glass and frame, or they may be stolen." Perhaps those words were significant and suggest that Röntgen had suspicions of co-workers or helpers. Admittedly, he was a difficult and severe taskmaster and not at all easy to get along with, especially if one were not wholly dedicated to that work. Assistants soon realized the exceedingly high standards which he had set for them as well as for himself, and students quickly learned that he was a stern disciplinarian who expected much from them. They respected him as a superbly able and ingenious physicist, but they did not love him as a teacher as they did other professors who took a fatherly interest in their personal problems. Some of the students showed their dislike for Röntgen by referring to the X rays (or Röntgen-rays, as they were called there) as

Marstaller-rays. But it is highly unlikely that they were actually discrediting their professor or believed the lowly *Hausdiener* had discovered them.

Despite all of these claims, it appears quite evident that, based on his characteristic habits, Wilhelm Röntgen was alone in his laboratory on that Friday evening when he first detected the effects of the strange ray and further investigated the peculiar phenomenon.

These rumors, wild speculations, and sensational articles published by irresponsible editors annoyed Röntgen immensely, but he refused to dignify them by taking public notice of them. His attitude toward discussions on the subject was one of silence, and he believed that he could not add anything to clarify the whole question of the discovery. He had told all he knew about the event.

"Let the envious chatter in peace," he once said. "It is almost as if I had to apologize for discovering the rays," he complained.

In a letter in 1921 to Frau Boveri he wrote:

Zehnder has also heard the fable that I was not the first to notice the X rays, but that an assistant or servant discovered them. What miserable envious soul must have invented this story? I also learned recently that it is said that I had nothing to do with the medical application of the rays and that the first photograph of a hand was made at the suggestion of Schönborn! However, Schönborn was the very one who was reluctant and even unfriendly in accepting the news of the discovery. I must admit that these lies affect me a great deal more than they should. I should remember: Where there is much light, there is also much shadow.

At about the same time the preceding was written, Röntgen also wrote a long letter to Zehnder in which he mentioned the same subject, but rather briefly.

The infamous rumor that I did not personally discover the X rays has its origin presumably in Heidelberg from [G. H.] Quinke, on whose feet I stepped a few times. And Lenard probably cultivated it. I was surprised when going through my old letters to find some written by Lenard which showed a very friendly attitude toward me. However, this stopped completely at about the time Wien became my successor in Würzburg and I received the Nobel prize.

These two letters were written in Weilheim in May, 1921, when the controversy again was brought to the public's attention by an article in the newspapers.

When Richard Siebeck followed Lenard as professor of physics at the Heidelberg university he stated that the name of Wilhelm Conrad Röntgen had never been mentioned by his predecessor Lenard or the earlier Quinke in lectures at the institute. Lenard had become professor at Heidelberg in 1896, went to Kiel in 1898, and returned to Heidelberg in 1907. Two years later he was appointed director of the new radiological institute there.

Röntgen himself stated that he told no one about the discovery at the time, but in 1958 Frau Josephine Berta Donges-Röntgen recalled the eventful late evening quite differently when she told this version:

I remember that on the evening of November 8, father stormed up the stairs and knocked on the door. I was in the hallway practicing on the horizontal bars. I opened the door for him and asked, "What is the matter?" "Where is the aunt?" he asked. I told him, "In her room, writing, I believe. But what is the matter?" I asked again. "Nothing, nothing, keep on exercising!"

He went very hurriedly and excitedly and looked for Mother. What they said to each other, I could of course not know. But soon they both came out of the room, and I tugged at Mother's dress and asked her, "But what is the matter?" She replied, "Quiet, quiet. You'll find out. Keep on with your exercises." And both went downstairs to the Institute, which was below our apartment. We lived then in the Physical Science Institute.

After some time they came back upstairs, both very excited and so absorbed with one thing. I did not dare to ask any more. Then I was sent to bed — I was 14 years old and still a little girl — and the parents conversed probably longer about that which had happened downstairs. On that day I learned of nothing. That came only a few days later. The remembrance of that day is so alive, as if it were but yesterday. . . .

Perhaps meant to establish definitely the date and the facts of Röntgen's lone role in the discovery, this taped interview only added some confusion, rather than clarification, to the historic facts.

Lecturing, Röntgen told his students:

Only very slowly came the conviction that the experiment is the mightiest and trustworthiest lever through which we can overhear nature, and that the same must reflect the last resort for the decision of the question if a hypothesis should be retained or cast off. The nearly always existing possibility to compare the result of the theoretical work with the reality assures the experimental researcher the necessary security. If the result does not coincide with the reality, then it is wrong, even if the speculations which led to erroneous results were very gifted. One may recognize in this necessity perhaps a certain harshness, especially when one considers with how much effort of mental work and time the result occasionally sustains and how much high hope is ruined with it. The researcher in the field of the natural sciences considers himself really very fortunate to have such a reliable proof system, even if it sometimes brings him untold disillusions.

At the University of Pennsylvania, A. W. Goodspeed and his friend W. N. Jennings were making experiments with electric sparks and brush discharges and photographed such effects on February 22, 1890. After completing this experimental work Goodspeed demonstrated to Jennings some work with Crookes tubes. The following day Jennings developed plates which were left laying on a laboratory table littered with loaded photographic plate holders and other apparatus. On one of the plates he noticed two round disks superimposed on the spark tracings. Since neither he nor Goodspeed could explain this curious effect, the plates were put aside with other peculiar photographs to be forgotten eventually. After the discovery and publication of X ray photographs, Goodspeed located the early pictures and easily recognized the similarity between them and published X ray photographs.

In a student lecture on X rays, Goodspeed told his listeners, "We can claim no merit for the discovery, for no discovery was made. All we ask is that you remember, gentlemen, that six years ago to the very day, the first picture in the world by cathode rays was taken in the laboratory of physics of the University of Pennsylvania." Before the lecture, Professor Goodspeed had duplicated exactly the same photographs using the identical apparatus under precisely the same conditions and exposures as before, with the same results.

Other similar discoveries or experiences may have occurred, but they were never published in any scientific publications.

William Crookes had used, as early as 1879, a cathode ray tube with a concave cathode and platinum anode — the construction of the typical apparatus for X rays later — and often had found fogged photographic plates kept near the tubes ,which he promptly and angrily returned to the manufacturers as faulty goods. Apparently he never entertained the thought that experimenting with the unexposed plates near the discharge tubes may have affected them in any way and may actually have caused them to be darkened. Aside from complaining to the manufacturers Crookes had done no experimenting with the phenomenon, which in fact he had not recognized as a phenomenon at all. These incidents were later used as a foundation by Miller to credit Crookes with the discovery of X rays, albeit without his knowledge, for he was vacationing in Africa at the time.

Other scientists, notably the Englishman Herbert Jackson, and the Germans Johann Wilhelm Hittorf, Eugen Goldstein, and Philipp Lenard, had observed the fluorescence of certain materials when placed near a Hittorf-Crookes tube, but had not explained the phenomenon. Generally these men were absorbed with the definite study of a certain problem and thus excluded all observations which were irrelevant to the particular subject under investigation.

In his Nobel prize speech in 1905, an embittered priority claimant Lenard said, "In reality I had made several unexplainable observations which I carefully kept for future investigation, unfortunately not started

in time, which must have been the effects of traces of wave radiation."
But Lenard never mentioned these observations in his publications before
the actual discovery by Röntgen.

Yet Lenard had received great acclaim in England in 1896, and the
X rays were sometimes referred to as the "new Lenard and Röntgen
rays," as J. Jolly also called them in his demonstrations. In 1896 the
Rumford medal was awarded to both men with Lenard's name appearing
ahead of Röntgen's, thus clearly implying priority.

In his Preliminary Communication Röntgen mentioned indeed a
Lenard tube as being suitable for the production of X rays, but pointed
out that he actually had used a Hittorf-Crookes vacuum tube.

In 1929 the controversy over the discovery was again stirred up, and
Lenard intimated that perhaps more data regarding the discovery would
be forthcoming at a later date. He wrote on August 18, 1929, to Otto
Glasser:

There is no doubt that the road to the discovery led over my own researches.
At that time I was prevented by external circumstances from pursuing to my
satisfaction in every direction the great number of new phenomena that
appeared in my studies on cathode rays. But in my opinion, this is not yet
the proper time to express myself more thoroughly on the subject than I did
in my Nobel prize lecture. That would be only biographical anyway, and
what has already been said must suffice for the judicious. With this I believe
that I have done everything that the history of science can expect of me on this
point at this particular time.

Lenard maintained his enigmatic attitude. Again, in 1935 some of
his admirers made an effort to prove that actually a Lenard tube was used
by Röntgen when he made the discovery. Some historical material was
then made public, but there was not enough evidence presented to convince anyone that the discovery by Röntgen had taken place in any other
manner then stated by him earlier. Röntgen became rather bitter in his
attitude toward Lenard. To honor Röntgen in 1905 on his sixtieth birthday, a tablet was placed on the walls of the Physical Science Institute at
Würzburg by the important scientists of the time. Röntgen was painfully
disappointed not to find the name of Philipp Lenard among them.

Ludwig Zehnder, Röntgen's own assistant, told in 1933 in his personal reminiscences, "Röntgen's Time at Würzburg," of an episode that
happened to him there:

While a student, Zehnder asked permission of his professor to use
the apparatus and a Hittorf tube for experimenting with cathode rays.
Röntgen cautioned the young Zehnder to be extremely careful, since the
institute only had a single Hittorf tube on hand. Zehnder was particularly

attracted to this tube because it had a platinum plate positioned at a distance coinciding with the cathode rays which caused it to glow red hot. In his experiment, using 50/20-centimeter and 20-ampere current, Zehnder covered the tube with a black cloth to better observe the lighted square or plate. To his great surprise, a spot of light appeared on the small fluorescent screen. While he was contemplating this phenomenon of the strange light, the whole apparatus suddenly went dark. The valuable tube had burned out.

Zehnder told Röntgen of his misfortune, knowing that he had an especially appreciative attitude toward his laboratory equipment and took the most particular care of all apparatus, and so Zehnder suggested that a replacement tube be purchased and charged to him. He did not mention the strange light spot he had observed and which had undoubtedly caused his temporary laxity in watching the tube closer. Röntgen, however, did not blame Zehnder for the loss of the costly tube and turned down the offer of payment for a replacement. This episode had happened long before the November week-end when Röntgen himself observed a similar phenomenon. And it may well have been this similar strange sight which other scientists observed but also failed to recognize or further investigate as an important phenomenon.

As Otto Glasser pointed out in his book on Röntgen, investigations made by Lenard and other scientists were the foundation upon which Röntgen erected the structure of his X rays. Lenard, however, should then share credit with his teacher, Heinrich Hertz, and also with Hermann von Helmholtz, who not only deduced theoretically the existence of the X rays many years before they were discovered, but even correctly predicted some of their properties. Von Helmholtz had published his electromagnetic dispersion theory in volume 48 of the *Wiedemannschen Annalen* (1887), and called attention to the probability of the existence of electromagnetic oscillations of very high frequency that would follow certain laws of deflection and defraction.

As mentioned, for a time after the discovery by Röntgen, it was difficult to differentiate between cathode rays and X rays, and this led to much confusion and honest mistakes of opinions on priority. At a meeting of the German Natural Scientists and Physicians at Frankfurt during the summer of 1896, and soon after, at the Congress of the British Association for the Advancement of Science at Liverpool, Lenard himself promulgated his theory that Röntgen's X rays were cathode rays of infinite velocity. Lenard still considered the cathode rays to be an electromagnetic phenomenon, which was contrary to the British school of thought. Röntgen also had shown early in 1896 that X rays do not carry an electric charge, thus proving by these and other properties that they were fundamentally different from cathode rays, and clearly refuting the theory of the unhappy Lenard.

Röntgen himself was not certain just what the unknown, or X, rays were when he discovered this new phenomenon. He concluded that he was not dealing with transversal waves because he obtained negative results from repeated attempts to reflect or refract the rays, and he believed that the rays were longitudinal waves, similar in character to sound waves but of considerably higher pitch.

Many of the early investigating physicists shared his opinion, but the majority did not agree with his views. These scientists believed the rays to be exceedingly high velocity cathode rays, especially after J. J. Thomson had succeeded in explaining the real character of cathode rays. Lenard was also of this opinion; Röntgen certainly was not.

The theory that the rays were transversal electromagnetic waves gained more favor eventually, but it was not until 1912 — when Max von Laue had the brilliant idea of using crystals as grids to refract the rays and Walter Friedrich and Paul Knipping made the practical suggestion of using extremely long exposure times — that this important problem was solved. Physicist von Laue received the Nobel prize for that work in 1914. But during the first hectic year after the discovery, excellent scientists in laboratories the world over were occupied with that question, using the rather primitive apparatus available to them to solve the riddle.

The question was a most important one, and much was written on the subject, but the well-argued explanations of the character of the rays did not always convince skeptics. To some the situation was best summed up by A. A. C. Swinton, who was reported to have replied to a question on that matter, "It reminds me of the old definition of metaphysics: 'One fellow talking of what he does not understand to another one who does not understand him.'"

But the priority question and that of definition went relentlessly on, especially in periodicals. One report, in *Science* of June 26, 1896, credited the Greek physiologist Esseltja with having demonstrated before the Paris Royal Academy of Science his "Anthroposcope," with which he claimed to be able to see right through the human body to discover visceral diseases. This claim found some believers, but since it was not scientifically documented, nor was the mysterious apparatus used even described in detail, it failed to impress many scientists. In 1865, Sir James Simpson had predicted in an Edinburgh lecture that there would be a light which could penetrate opaque layers of matter which would be of immense significance in stomach surgery. Although he failed entirely to define this secret light in any way, the claim was made that he was the real discoverer of the X rays. And, according to *Lancet* of March, 1896, Dr. A. Blair of Dunfermline had dreamed twenty-two years earlier of a method of making the human body translucent. Unfortunately, when the doctor awoke he had forgotten the proscribed procedure.

The *Literary Digest* of October 31, 1896, reported that when Charles V. Zenger of the University of Prague showed pictures at the Paris Academy in 1884 and in 1892 which he had made from Geneva and called "Night Photographs of the Mont Blanc" by means of sensitized plates, these clear pictures created but little interest. Now these original reports were reviewed, and Zenger explained that the electric rays coming from the mountain had produced a certain fluorescence on the sensitized uranium plates, this fluorescence acting similar to the effects of the Becquerel radiations or to the effects of the X rays.

Writing in the *Electrical World* of February 8, 1896, A. E. Dolbear stated, "It is not new to photograph with electric waves through opaque screens. In April, 1894, I described this phenomenon precisely and there said that 'it is actually possible to take a photograph of an object in absolute darkness with the ether waves set up by working an electric machine.' There does not appear to be any evidence at all that the waves employed by Röntgen are different from other rays producible in many ways."

Other serious scientists believed that the X rays were identical with "dark heat rays," "lithonic rays," or ultra-violet rays, and then reminded the readers that they had made experiments with these rays actually years before Röntgen ever did. A certain Mr. Moore of Jersey City announced blatantly that he had made photographs with a vacuum tube for a long time. However, he had really been making quite ordinary photographs using Geisler tubes as source of light, but giving this method such imaginary names as the "Moore etheric light process," or "Phosphotography."

Another man, a Mr. Brooks, claimed to have made X ray pictures in 1877, using a magnet, the *British Journal of Photography* reported in its April 3, 1896, issue.

A college student in Munich, Hans Schmidt, stated that he had made successful X ray pictures, long before Röntgen did, with ordinary arc light. He described his process of 1895 in the *Elektrotechnische Zeitschrift* of February 20, 1896.

The method of making photographs with electric brush discharges, as was used by Goodspeed at Pennsylvania University, was brought up in connection with X rays. Sydney Rowland published a number of such inductograms in the *British Medical Journal* of February 15, 1896, explaining carefully that they were not made with X rays at all.

But the misunderstandings continued in spite of clarifications by authoritative scientists. In the unscientific *New York Daily Tribune* of January 19, 1896, readers had been told that "the Würzburg professor must share his credit with Professor Fernando Sanford of Leland Stanford University of California, who has made many pictures with electric brush discharges, long before Röntgen's discovery."

The physician, Dr. Draper, who had made pictures in 1840 and which were published in the *Philosophical Magazine,* was also called a predecessor of Röntgen, in an article in the *British Journal of Photography* of February 7, 1896.

Other claims were advanced by W. Holtz in "An old Analogue to Röntgen's Radiation Experiments," published in the *Annalen der Physik* of February 25, 1896, and another by H. W. Vogel, "Priority Claims in Connection with Cathode Light Photography," in the *Photographischen Mitteilung* (1896) and the *Wiedemannschen Annalen* of May, 1896.

And, of course, nearly every country stated its own case to advantage, at least before its own countrymen. The editor of the French *L'Eclairage Electrique* attempted to credit many French scientists in his February 15 issue, while the Englishman Lewis Wright made a case for his compatriots in his book, *The Induction Coil in Practical Work, including Röntgen's X Rays* (Macmillan, London, 1897).

However, no single correct interpretation of the phenomenon produced by X rays can be found in a thorough study of all early scientific literature as well as the many not as scientifically written instances, as roentgenologist Glasser pointed out. And thus, all claims of priority in the discovery of the X rays may be summarily dismissed.

To bring order out of this mass of confusion, a journal was founded by Sydney Rowland, devoted exclusively to articles and pictures of X rays. His first issue appeared in May 1896, called *Archives of Clinical Skiagraphy,* and published by the Rebman Publishing Company of London. On its plain title page the "Special Commissioner to the British Medical Journal for the Investigation of Application of the New Photography to Medicine and Surgery" offered "A Series of Collotype Illustrations with Descriptive Text, Illustrating Applications of the New Photography to Medicine and Surgery." Inside, his stated objective was to "put on record in permanent form some of the most striking applications of the discovery. Although Professor Röntgen's discovery is only a thing of yesterday, it has already taken its place among the approved and accepted aids to diagnosis. At the present time we are in a position to obtain a visible image of every bone and joint in the body." The claim that, "The greater part of the practical improvements that have led to the present stage of perfection of the process have been made in this country," was perhaps no more than nationalistic fervor, but quite incorrect. The successful journal was enlarged the following year, 1897, and its name changed to *Archives of the Roentgen Ray,* edited by W. S. Hedley and S. Rowland.

Similar publications were the German *Fortschritte auf dem Gebiete der Röntgenstrahlen,* founded by H. Albers-Schönberg of Hamburg, and the *American X Ray Journal,* by H. Robarts of St. Louis. Soon, many other scientific journals exclusively devoted to Röntgen's discovery entered the broad field in all parts of the world.

CHAPTER 13

By Any Name

WHEN WILHELM RÖNTGEN finished his lecture demonstration before the Physical-Medical Society at Würzburg on January 23, 1896, Geheimrat Albert von Kölliker suggested that the new rays really should be named "Röntgen rays." In fact, by then the rays already were being called by that term by several writers in various publications. Only four days after the Würzburg presentation, at a meeting of the Paris Academy of Sciences, a similar suggestion was made for France.

Although the designation "Röntgen rays" was soon adopted in Germany, there was some professional opposition, perhaps mainly because of the vague terminology of that appellation. In the book *The Technique and Practical Use of Röntgen's Rays in Medical Practice and Science,* the authors Büttner and Müller point out that "the term Röntgen rays, which has become so popular in Germany, honors more the reverence for famous men than for the mother tongue. They are not Röntgen's rays, but energy rays, or possible ether rays, and may properly be called Röntgen's energy rays."

In other countries the designation X rays was preferred, even though Sir Joseph Lister in Liverpool, September 1896, at the opening of the Sixty-sixth Congress of the British Association for the Advancement of Science, of which he then was president, spoke of the discovery of the Röntgen rays, so called after the man who first clearly revealed them to the world.

In the United States, on February 8, Michael I. Pupin of Columbia College said that "although Röntgen called the radiant energy the X rays, the rays will, and should, of course, be called Röntgen rays."

The Baltimore physicist H. A. Rowland agreed with that proposal saying, "The rays themselves should, according to my view, be simply called Röntgen rays or X rays, and the photographs by means of these rays should be known as Röntgen photographs, thus keeping the name of the discoverer of this wonderful phenomenon ever before the world, as it deserves to be."

Professor R. A. Fessenden of the Western University in Pennsylvania was of the same mind when he stated, "Since this valuable discovery has been generously presented to the public, it would seem only fit that the name of the discoverer should be used. This is the least return which we can make the man who has really given this great discovery to the world."

The editor of the *Electrical World* wrote in his periodical of February 29, 1896, "Owing to Professor Röntgen having in his paper applied the term X rays to his discovery, later writers have taken the modest savant at his word and continue the use of the term, though improperly. While the use of his designation may be accorded as a privilege to the discoverer himself, to others Röntgen rays is, according to the etiquette of science, the more appropriate name and, besides, should be employed as a tribute to the discoverer of one of the most startling phenomena with which man has ever been made acquainted."

Wilhelm Röntgen himself had felt immeasurably honored by the proposal of his friends in Würzburg, and later elsewhere, to have the rays named after him, but he had a personal strong objection to the identification of an individual's name with a natural phenomenon. He quickly stated his views on this matter and consistently refused to have his name attached to his discovery. He insisted vehemently that the rays be called X rays and that his name not be associated with their identification. Whenever his name was used without his knowledge or permission, he deeply resented this fact and made his wishes known without hesitation.

In scanning the voluminous bibliography available from 1896, one finds more use of the term Röntgen rays than X rays. In later years this ratio was reversed, and the shorter term, X rays, was preferred.

In March 1896, the *British Medical Journal* editorialized, "We should be glad if the discoverer's name could be thus [he had suggested the word Roentography] perpetuated in his intellectual offspring. But unhappily Professor Röntgen has not the good fortune on which Byron congratulated Goethe, of having a name sufficiently euphonious for the articulation of posterity."

In English-speaking countries, X rays is an easier word than is Röntgen rays, or Röntgen-ray photography. But in practically all English-speaking countries, roentgenology journals and societies use the discoverer's name in their title.

In an honest effort to bring some order into the question of proper identification of X ray photographs, the editor of the *Electrical World* sent questionnaires to all of the better known scientists in the United States who actually were working with X rays, asking for suggestions for a proper name for the rays. Answers were returned from such famed men as Thomas A. Edison, Michael I. Pupin, E. B. Frost, D. W. Hering, H. A. Rowland, A. W. Goodspeed, Elihu Thomson, Charles P. Steinmetz, and many others. But no name was chosen.

At about the same time similar questionnaires were mailed by other publications in other countries, such as the *British Medical Journal;* but this too resulted in a large variety of suggested names and not a definite one at all. It was almost as if each of those questioned had thought up a different term for the X ray pictures. Some suggestions were: skiagraphy, skiography, shadow print, roentography, new photography, electro-skiography, ixography, electrography, cathodography, fluorography, diagraphy, actinography, pyknoscopy, X ray photography, X ray picture (styles both with and without the hyphen were suggested), and dark light.

Finally the German scientists and writers almost exclusively used the term "Röntgen photography" while the English-speaking people used "X ray photography." Although the real character of the mysterious rays has since been discovered, and there is little reason any more to call them X rays, or unknown rays, the terminology meanwhile has become well instilled in the scientific community. Simplified usage, however, has begun to point forth a change in spelling from "X ray" to "x-ray" to "xray."

Wilhelm Röntgen did not realize that his X ray photographs would be responsible for the amazingly quick and excited public appeal of his discovery. With these graphic illustrations every reader could easily understand the phenomenon. And the indicated far-reaching possibilities of aiding medical diagnosis had a tremendous effect on the mind of the lay public.

This course of events displeased Röntgen greatly, for he never believed in making scientific matters a popular topic.

Most of the early X ray photographs for medical purposes were those of hands, the most famous ones being those of Bertha Röntgen and von Kölliker, both taken by Röntgen himself. A month or two later Röntgen made a photograph of a fractured forearm which he sent to the editor of the *British Medical Journal* on February 15, 1896, to illustrate the further diagnostic value of his discovery. The newspapers and periodicals had been most enthusiastic in their predictions of the use of X rays in this particular field. Undoubtedly that very fact contributed immensely to the universal acclaim.

When Dr. Franz König and Dr. M. Jastrowitz spoke on this subject before the Medical Society and the Society for Internal Medicine in Berlin on January 5 and 6, 1896, Dr. Jastrowitz said, "It is not necessary for me to add anything more to indicate what tremendous consequences may result from this method for diagnostic purposes." Showing a photograph of the hand of an assistant who had experienced continuous pain after an explosion of a small glass tank, the doctor emphasized that the small piece of glass easily identified in the X ray picture, was "by far the most interesting application of this new method which I have yet seen."

Similar pictures were made by Walter König of Frankfurt, showing the injured second metacarpal bone of the right hand of a boy. It was made at an exposure time of four minutes, with the photographic plate at 24 centimeters from the center of the tube. Another showed a needle embedded in a girl's hand. Pictures of a set of teeth were made by placing films, protected from light by a wrapper, into the mouth. This was done on February 2, 1896. On January 15 König had shown a picture, actually made by assistant Eugen Goldstein of the Berlin Observatory, of an amputated leg that "showed rather clearly a sarcomatous growth at the upper end of the tibia."

F. Kurlbaum and W. Wien of the Berliner Reichsanstalt made photographs illustrating cases of acute and chronic arthritis with large nodes and extensive destruction of the joints; these were shown at the Society for Internal Medicine, on February 17, 1896.

On March 26, W. Becher of Berlin published his investigations with X rays, having made successful photographs of the outlines of the stomach and intestines of a guinea pig, and suggesting several different solutions for use in human organs. This was done soon by J. C. Hemmeter of Baltimore, who published a paper on April 10, illustrated with clear X ray pictures of the human stomach and intestines. Dr. E. Neusser of Vienna observed that "kidney and bladder stones absorb the Röntgen rays like bones, and gallstones are less transparent to the rays than liver tissue, therefore the Röntgen method may well be used in the diagnosis of such diseases."

Also in Vienna, and working with Exner, E. Hascheck made photographs of the hand of a cadaver, showing "not only the bones of the hand and the rings on one finger but also the veins and, to a lesser degree, the muscles of the hand."

And Professor W. Peterson of Heidelberg wrote that "there seems to be no limit to the possibilities of this method. No doubt Röntgen's rays will be extremely important in all of our diagnostic procedures and very soon the famous words of a French astronomer, 'The photographic plate is the retina of science' will hold true also for medicine."

On March 6, 1896, at the University of Pennsylvania, Professor H. W. Cattel commented that "the manifold uses to which Röntgen's discovery may be applied in medicine are so obvious that it is even now questionable whether a surgeon would be morally justified in performing a certain class of operation without having first seen pictured by these rays the field of his work, a map, as it were, of the unknown country he is to explore."

X ray pictures were exhibited to scientific audiences or published in journals, showing abnormalities in the growth of bone in rachitis, of a hand with tuberculous bone destruction especially marked in the forefinger, of individuals at different ages to show the increase in ossification with advanced age, or gallstones which had been removed surgically, even of the backbone of an adult with the vertebrae and the spinal cord in full detail. Thus, by March of 1896, the medical profession in many countries had made full use of the possibilities offered by Wilhelm Röntgen's discovery.

In an article in the April issue, *McClure's Magazine* reported to its readers on the domestic development of X rays:

At the Sloane laboratory of Yale University, Professor Arthur W. Wright experimented with X rays and made photographs. He had worked constantly for years with vacuum tubes similar to the Crookes tubes used in producing cathode rays, and the new Röntgen development was an allied field of activity to him.

Using a nearly spherical Crookes tube of about 5 inch diameter, he took pictures with long exposures of one to one and a half hours. Wright was careful to place the objects as close to the sensitized plate as possible for best results. His sharpest pictures of metal objects, a hack saw with wooden handle, an awl, a pair of glasses in a leather case, all show clear outlines, with an exposure time of 55 minutes. A picture of a rabbit, placed on an ebonite plate, shows the bones and also the six grains of shot which killed the animal. The bones of the legs, the ribs, and even the cartilages of the ears are visible, and a lighter region in the center of the body marks the location of the heart. The professor has systematically photographed various metals, quartz and glass, showing the different characteristics of each substance.

At Trinity College, Hartford, Connecticut, the professor of physics Dr. W. L. Robb also conducted experiments with the new rays, having himself studied at the Würzburg University years before Röntgen was there. He made clear pictures, showing a foot through the leather shoe with the many pegs holding the sole strongly visible, a fish and its bone structure complete, and a man's hand showing that the bones were improperly set by the attending physician who lost the law suit brought by the patient.

Robb used a modified developing process and needed only 15 minutes to make a photograph through wood or leather. For a bicycle company he conducted tests to see if the carbon steel or nickel steel showed any radical differences in the crystalline structure.

At Columbia College, New York, experiments with X rays were made by Michael I. Pupin, resulting in at least one remarkable photograph which was published. A New York gentleman on a hunting trip to England, had his gun discharge accidentally and shooting him in his hand. Eventually the hand healed completely, but the professor urged him to have it photographed with the new discovery.

The distance from the tube to the plate was five inches and the hand was placed between them. After an exposure of fifty minutes, the developed picture showed not only the location of each of the 40 shots, but also showed clearly some of the lead in the bones, which were nearly transparent to the black lead.

Thomas A. Edison also had devoted himself and his well-organized force of scientists to experiments with X rays and announced confidently that in the very near future he will be able to photograph the human brain through the heavy bones of the skull, and perhaps even get a shadow picture showing the human skeleton through the tissues of the body.

One of the first private X ray photography laboratories was opened in London on March 11, 1896, when A. A. C. Swinton announced his new enterprise to the journals. Another photographer, W. E. Gray, opened a room for X ray work in Faraday House on the suggestion of several prominent surgeons, and the Photographic Association also announced that it would make photographs of a patient for a fee of two guineas.

The New York Post-Graduate Medical School and Hospital and the Hahnemann Hospital in Chicago inaugurated Röntgen departments, causing the *Electrical Engineer* to publish an article entitled "Doctors to become Cathodographers." Other individuals and hospitals soon were equipped to take "pictures of the interior human structure."

Early in January 1897 the Belgian government suggested that all hospitals be equipped for X ray photography. In Berlin, several laboratories for taking X ray pictures had been opened, and the city council of Munich, having decided in December 1896 to purchase such equipment for its *Krankenhaus,* voted to allow private physicians to use the apparatus for a certain low fee. The Army Medical Academy of St. Petersburg granted the sum of 5,000 rubles for further development of the discovery, the German government made a substantial grant, the British Animal Institute offered gold medals and other inducements for new improvements and developments, and several foundations and other governments underwrote further scientific research work.

Röntgen photographs of prominent people always created mild sensations, especially when they divulged abnormalities. So it was when the Chinese statesman Li Hung-chang, after attending the coronation of the Czar of the Russians and a visit to the German Kaiser, submitted to an X ray photograph of his head. This picture clearly showed the course and the location of the bullet fired by a would-be assassin in Shimonoseki at the signing of the treaty between China and Japan.

And the X ray photograph made of the Kaiser's left arm, useless because of a birth accident, created fascinating speculation. The *Literary Digest,* which — as in earlier-mentioned articles — was not always right, suggested that a simple operation would restore usefulness to the arm and hand.

X ray photographs of her court attendants, made on orders of Queen Amelia of Portugal, were to be used only to show them the damages to their internal organs caused by tight lacing of garments. However, styles were not soon to change noticeably, although most of the ladies who saw their "inside pictures" fainted dead away.

Reactions to the strange sight of one's own bones varied, but generally it created great shock to the subject. The editor of the *Grazer Tageblatt* had an X ray photograph taken of his head by a Graz physician, but after seeing the grisly picture himself, "absolutely refused to show it to anybody but a scientist." He had not closed an eye since he saw his own *Totenkopf,* his death's-head, a colleague reported in the paper!

Seeing the bones of other people did not usually have an unpleasant effect, however. Thus, an enterprising bootmaker in London used X ray photographs to illustrate the effects of badly fitting footwear on the wearer, and an explanatory skiagraph displayed prominently in his window attracted the attention of many passers-by.

Reports of successful X ray photography came from Munich, Frankfurt, Heidelberg, Paris, Montreal, Antwerp, Philadelphia, New York, Cleveland, Boston, St. Petersburg, Rome, Bern, Tokyo, Constantinople, and many other places where scientists or surgeons experimented with the rays.

Wilhelm Röntgen himself corresponded with many of his colleagues who were making experiments with his rays, and he received a large number of photographs made with X rays. This ultimate proof of a technique was made in the laboratories of scientists in various universities within a short time after the first communication of Röntgen had appeared in print.

Paul Spiess in Berlin, Walter König in Frankfurt, W. Becher in Berlin, and A. Voller in Hamburg, all produced excellent quality pictures. In Vienna the brothers Franz and Sigmund Exner and E. Hascheck already in February 1896 had reproduced, by a special process, a portfolio of X ray photographs of animals. This gave the appearance of delicate engravings and was brought out by J. M. Eder and E. Valenta of Vienna.

The scientist E. Hascheck made an X ray photograph of the hand of his colleague O. T. Lindenthal and sent it to Röntgen. This feat was remarkable because the veins were injected with a Teichmann mixture of lime, cinnabar, and petroleum, through the brachial artery, and they stood out in striking relief. This effect produced by injecting blood vessels with the liquid suggested that one could create a contrast on the X ray plates which would clearly show the organ and reveal its function. Perhaps one could equally utilize this process with other organs of the human body, such as the esophagus, stomach, intestines, lungs, gallbladder, and even the brain.

In England, X ray pictures were made in the earlier days by the scientists Arthur Schuster, J. C. M. Stanton, J. J. Thomson, Oliver Lodge, A. A. C. Swinton, Sydney Rowland, and Edwards.

In France, the early pioneers were A. Barthélemy, Paul Oudin, L. Benoist, Ch. E. Guillaume, G. Séguy in Le Roux's laboratory, and Odilon Marc Lannelongue and M. Albert Londe in the Salpêtrière Hospital.

From the United States Röntgen received photographs from D. C. Miller of the Case School in Ohio; Edwin B. Frost of Dartmouth College; A. W. Goodspeed; Arthur W. Wright; John Trowbridge of Harvard University; Thomas A. Edison; and C. L. Norton. Professor Michael I. Pupin of Columbia College sent a picture of a hand full of shot in which a remarkable detail had been obtained by placing the fluorescent screen behind the plate while making the X ray photograph — the precursor of the intensifying screen.

One of the pictures that Wilhelm Röntgen had made at the time of his early experiments and duly published was that of his shotgun. This, of course, suggested that the rays were also useful for close examination of metal objects for material faults. He made comments on the picture itself which was sent to Franz Exner in Vienna, pointing out the shells, small indentations in the metal, the serial number markings, the cardboard disks in the shell cases, and even showing a material defect in the barrel.

This photograph suggested to the German and Austrian War Ministries the importance of the Röntgen rays in detecting defects in guns and in armor plating. Arthur W. Wright of Yale University photographed a piece of welded metal and suggested that X rays were "of profound significance in the testing of armor for certain defects and discovering certain flaws in machinery."

The alert Carnegie Steel Works used this method for practical tests on some kinds of steel in February 1896. The Edison laboratory is believed to have found that use of X rays would increase the hardness of certain metals. In Paris, X rays were used in detecting the contents of parcels of explosive devices sent to members of the French Chamber of Deputies. Post office authorities used them also to detect coins mailed hidden in newspapers or in sealing wax, contrary to postal regulations.

Foodstuffs were tested for purity, and so was wine. Geologists hoped to be able to use the rays in locating coal and ore deposits underground, and J. W. Scott of Lloydsville, Pennsylvania, claimed to have achieved this.

In botany, zoology and paleontology, X rays were used with success. A mummy, which looked suspiciously unlike a human body, was found to be a wrapped ibis bird at the Vienna Museum of Natural History. The carcasses of sacred ibises, an Egyptian symbol of wisdom, were mummified and buried in the tombs of early pharaohs, especially Zoser, who reigned about 2980 B.C. In Frankfurt, Walter König was able to distinguish between real and artificial pearls by exposing them to X ray examination. This field of research was soon expanded by the scientist Dölter, who systematically investigated the reaction of gems and stones to X rays.

The nucleus of a pearl can be seen in much the same manner as a human bone can be observed. Tests between real and simulated gems indicated that some allowed the rays to pass through, while others absorbed them to some extent. Diamonds, amber, and jet were completely transparent when the rays were allowed to fall on them. By this means, diamonds could be distinguished from glass, pastes, and other white stones. Also, corundum (ruby and sapphire), being nearly transparent, could be distinguished from similarly colored stones. Opal and chrysoberyl were less transparent to the rays. All varieties of quartz, feldspar, topaz, and spodumene were found to be semi-transparent. Turquoise, tourmaline, peridot, and apatite were nearly opaque. Almandine garnet, beryl, zircon, and all forms of glass and pastes were opaque.

About a year after the first application of X rays to this new "detective work on ancient artifacts," curator Cushing of the Museum of the University of Pennsylvania used the method. He had conjectured that some pieces of turquoise, conceived to be the hearts of fetichistic birds, were concealed beneath the heavy wrapping of brown yarn that bound the finger loops of the prehistoric throwing stick in his collection. Because this object was too valuable and too fragile to permit physical examination, Röntgen rays were used instead, revealing the actual presence of four stone beads, presumably of turquoise.

CHAPTER 14

Pioneer Work —
Equipment and Utilization

THE HITTORF TUBE that Wilhelm Röntgen employed in his discovery of X rays was of pear-shaped design. Röntgen also used several different types of tubes, some of Crookes', some of Lenard's designs, all of which were standard equipment in physical science laboratories of the time. A multitude of different shaped tubes was developed in a short time by manufacturers to obtain better photographs and especially to make pictures of such parts of the body as the skull, thorax, and pelvis.

The exposure times with Hittorf-Crookes tubes were exceedingly long, because the size of the focal spot on the glass wall was rather diffuse, and lead diaphragms with small openings had to be placed in front of the tube so as to obtain clearer pictures.

To cut the exposure times, the distance between the tube and the photographic plate was shortened. Röntgen had stated that "the intensity of the rays is decreased with the square of the distance from the tube." He also suggested that the fluorescent screen be placed directly behind the photographic plate while making an exposure to shorten the time, believing that the fluorescent light of the screen would increase the direct photographic action of the rays. Max Levy of Berlin actually found that covering both sides of the photographic plate with sensitive photographic emulsion and placing it between two intensifying screens increased the photographic effect twelve- to fifteen-fold.

Many experimenters followed in the footsteps of Röntgen and did not protect their own improvements by patents. Very few patents were asked for and granted during the first year of feverish activity in all parts of the world. Of the twelve patents secured for improved apparatus, improvements in photography, and development in tubes, one was granted, on June 25, 1896, to Ludwig Zehnder for a "pressure regulator for evacuated tubes, especially for Röntgen tubes."

Other patents granted in 1896 were, in the United States and England, to T. A. Garrett and W. Lucas for films, to S. D. Rowland for photography, to C. F. Easton for apparatus, to J. von der Kammer for a bulb, to N. E. Johnson for apparatus, to Elihu Thomson for regulation of tubes, to E. Payne for apparatus, to C. H. Stearn and C. F. Topham for lamps, and to E. Bohm for vacuum tubes. In Germany patents were granted to Siemens & Halske for a tube, and to Max Levy for a tube. A patent in France went to A. and L. Lumière for a stroboscope. Many improvements in equipment were merely registered in a government office by their inventors, and no patents were issued on such requests.

Demand for all X ray equipment, but especially for tubes, rose enormously, and the better known suppliers had more orders than they could possibly fill. Glassblower Robert Goetze of Leipzig received seventy orders on one day alone, giving him enough to blow a whole year on the several hundred ordered tubes. Goetze was unyieldingly opposed to any further development of his tubes, and not to hamper their production by delays, did not take out a patent on them, although this could easily have been done since he and Walter König were the first to use a platinum mirror in a tube.

Firms in several countries advertised various apparatus for taking X ray pictures, and the industry developed new equipment almost as rapidly as the X ray photography developed.

The conical Hittorf tubes that Röntgen used for his early experiments were advertised, at that time, by the expert glassblowers of Gehlberg, Thuringia, for eight marks (about two dollars); improved tubes with a platinum anode were sold in May 1896 for less than four dollars. Even in those hectic days of new and improved tubes Röntgen could hardly have visualized that only fifty years later, tubes nine feet long would be available, powered by several million volts, producing X rays capable of penetrating steel a foot thick, and costing in the thousands of dollars.

Ferdinand Ernecke of Berlin advertised large Hittorf tubes for about six dollars, and a 4-by-8-inch barium platinocyanide screen for two dollars. A storage battery with current regulator, an instruction book on photography, and a large Ruhmkorff induction coil with a 6-inch spark gap cost less than 150 dollars. A completely equipped X ray room for doctors or educational institutions, "including a complete apparatus for successful photography with Röntgen rays," could be had for 590 marks, or less than 150 dollars.

In a pretentious advertisement the electrical firm of Siemens & Halske, in the *Zeitschrift für Elektrochemie* of March 1896, offered induction coils with 6-inch gap, mercury interrupter, and two glass spheres for about 800 marks, and suitable apparatus for about 600 to 700 marks. An Italian firm, Luigi Gorla of Milano asked from 230 to 600 lire (46 to 120 dollars) for a complete installation. A London firm advertised that 12 pounds 15 shillings (about 45 dollars) would buy an apparatus.

The F. J. Pearson Manufacturing Company of St. Louis, Missouri, advertised in June 1896, "a portable X ray apparatus for physicians, professors, photographers, and students, complete in handsome case, including coil, condenser, two sets of tubes, battery, etc., for the price of $15 net, delivered in the United States, with full guarantee."

For those interested in medical photographs, the American Technical Book Company offered in an advertisement: "Radiographs, life-size, good reproduced: Child, 9 weeks old (shows wonderfully the details of the bones of the skeleton, the situation of the liver, stomach, heart, etc.), $2.00. Head of grown person, with teeth roots, 60¢. Normal kidneys and kidneys with stone — on the same picture (shows the thickness of the stone), 50¢."

Strumper & Company of Hamburg-Uhlenhorst advertised in a book on X rays by E. Wunschmann, published in 1896, for sale at only 4 marks (about $1) a series of eight pictures by Professor Dr. A. Voller of the Hamburg State Laboratory, (1) a finger and middle of hand, (2) hand movement and middle of hand, (3) living hand, (4) drawing instruments *(Reisszeug)* in closed box, (5) thermometer in closed box, (6) broken arm, (7) white fish with visible fins, and (8) foot injured by horse's hoof at the battle of Langensalza.

Among the many firms which advertised equipment for X ray photography were Geissler of Berlin, Müller of Hamburg, Poeller of Munich, Goetze of Leipzig, and Greiner & Friedrichs of Stützerbach. In France it was Ch. Heller et Cie., and Chez Radigut and Compteir de Photographie of Paris. In England it was Thomas and Griffin, and G. Houghton & Sons (with the telegram code name Bromide) of London, and Reynolds & Branson of Leeds. In the United States there were the Edison Decorative and Miniature Lamp Department of Harrison, New Jersey, the Beacon Lamp Company, and Knott of Boston, the Sunbeam Lamp Company of Chicago, Willyoung of Philadelphia, and Greiner, and Eimer & Amend of New York.

That so many firms sold this equipment at rather reasonable prices was greatly due to the fact that Röntgen did not patent his discovery and that any firm capable of manufacturing this highly technical equipment was free to do so. The market was freely competitive. The technically complex machinery was developed openly, without hampering restrictions imposed by any private or governmental authority. Few patents on the various X ray apparatus were granted during the first year of development, and no evidence exists that the discovery was exploited commercially by any company to the exclusion of other competitors.

Soon after the discovery had been made public, several German companies had indeed interested themselves in acquiring the patents for the X ray process. They realized that Röntgen had published his original findings for all other scientists to read and to use as a basis for further developments, but they also felt that any further observations that Röntgen might make and later publish could be patented by him.

One of the visitors to the Würzburg Institute was Max Levy of Berlin, a consulting electrical engineer for the AEG *(Allgemeine Elektrizitäts Gesellschaft),* the major German electrical company. After giving a lecture on the newly discovered X rays before some company officials, Levy had been asked by directors to study their industrial value and their possible exploitation by the huge general electric company. Within a short time, Levy suggested that he get in touch with Professor Röntgen himself and discuss the possibility of having the discoverer turn over all further development processes to the AEG, under certain conditions to be agreed upon.

Röntgen received his visitor cordially enough at the institute, and was kind enough to listen to his suggestions and proposals. He then thanked him and said that he recognized that his company had already done considerable valuable work in further developing the X ray technique, and that he well realized the possible advantages of cooperation with such an important industrial concern. However, Röntgen unhesitatingly turned down the proposal, saying that "according to the good tradition of the German university professors, I am of the opinion that their discoveries and inventions belong to humanity and that they should not in any way be hampered by patents, licenses, contracts, or be controlled by any one group."

Röntgen recognized clearly that this attitude would not allow him to obtain any financial advantages from his discovery. Max Levy understood this fine spirit of the professor and left, "knowing that I had met a man not only of great accomplishments, but a scientist with the highest ideals."

Actually, as Röntgen himself stated, "Representatives of American companies were the first to attempt to buy my discovery by holding millions before my eyes."

Wilhelm Röntgen had received a communication from the American consul general Frank H. Mason at Frankfurt, who had a telegram from Richard A. Anthony, vice president of E. and H. T. Anthony & Company, New York, manufacturers of photographic materials and equipment. The consul was asked to contact Professor Röntgen forthwith and urge him to have the Anthony firm patent the process in the United States and offer him royalties.

Richard Anthony suggested "that perhaps already some other person has taken advantage of his generosity and has applied for an American patent to his invention," but further added that, "if the professor is one of those high-minded men who work for glory only, I hope that you will be able to induce him to see that if he can make some money out of this invention he will have the glory also and will be able to use the money for the benefit of mankind in some other direction, and not throw this whole thing open to the public without securing proper compensation for himself."

But Röntgen was an idealist. Immediately after his discovery of the X rays he stated that he was not at all interested in the material fruits of his great research work but that all of his knowledge on the subject should be made available to all interested scientists, to test and further develop and adopt this basic knowledge of the X rays to achieve the greatest possible use for the benefit of all mankind.

Having publicly expressed his attitude toward material gain, making his "invention" freely available to all serious scientists, Röntgen did not reply to the communication from Consul Mason, just as he ignored the many other similar proposals that followed.

In an editorial in the *Elektrotechnische Zeitschrift* of February 27, 1896, the matter was well expressed. "Professor Röntgen could have obtained a valuable patent on his discovery, but he preferred to give his discovery to humanity. He should be given the greatest recognition, for he has thus made it possible for numerous investigators to be unhampered in their work with the Röntgen rays."

Fellow scientists were also praising Röntgen for his unselfish stand. The *Science* article by Hugo S. Muensterberg suggested that the attitude of German scientists toward patenting and commercial exploitation was well established and wrote, "It is well known throughout the world that the physical science laboratories of Germany have no windows which look toward the patent office."

Naturally there were other opinions on this matter. Thomas A. Edison felt quite differently. The *Herald and Sun* quoted him as saying: "Professor Röntgen probably does not draw one dollar profit from his discovery. He belongs to those pure scientists who study for pleasure and love to delve into the secrets of nature. After they have discovered something wonderful someone else must come to look at it from a commercial point of view. This will also be the case with Röntgen's discovery. One must see how to use it and how to profit by it financially."

As a matter of fact, reporters had sped almost at once to interview the inventor-genius Edison at his Orange laboratories, for he was perhaps the best-fitted person in the United States to verify or to expose the whole X ray affair when news of the discovery flashed over the wires. The *Electrical World* wrote in its February 1896 number: "Edison himself has been having a severe attack of Röntgenmania. The newspapers having reporters in attendance at his laboratory do not suffer for copy, as the yards of sensational matter emanating from this source attest, and we learn that last week Mr. Edison and his staff worked through seventy hours without intermission, a hand organ being employed during the latter hours to assist in keeping the work force awake."

Edison had alerted his physicists two days after the first cabled news of Röntgen's discovery reached the New York newspapers. Undoubtedly Edison knew that his large complement of capable scientists could conceivably find a new angle on which valuable patents could be secured. His well-equipped laboratory and excellent staff was perhaps the best-suited single group of scientists employed by any private money-making organization to exploit the new discovery.

With his exhibit at the Electrical Exhibit in New York in May, 1896, Edison called public attention to the workings of the fluoroscope, which was daily demonstrated by an assistant, named Dolly (who died in 1904 from burns contracted by continuous exposure to X rays). In fact, the publicity of the Edison organization was so good that most of the people actually believed that the very process was discovered in the Orange laboratory. Of course Röntgen had mentioned the phenomenon in his published First Communication: "If the hand is held between the discharge tube and the screen, the darker shadow of the bones is seen within the lightly dark shadow-image of the hand itself."

The Italian scientist E. Salvioni demonstrated his "cryptoscope" to the Perugia Medical Surgical Society with great success; in Berlin the head of the physics department, Paul Spiess, used a fluoroscope to show the effects of X rays to his students at the university and to an audience at the Urania Society. Both of these physicists used the platinocyanide of potassium. Edison, however, having tested some 1,800 different substances — according to his own estimate — found that calcium tungstate properly crystallized gave much superior results.

Not all serious scientists were in agreement with Edison's exploitation of the X ray discovery as a crowd-pleasing novelty. Andrew Gray voiced a strong opinion on the matter, and Sir Oliver Lodge, the English physicist, said sternly, "It is somewhat disconcerting to have Professor Röntgen's original experiment treated as a novelty."

While making experiments with X rays, Wilhelm Röntgen was always quite careful to keep the discharge tube just outside a zinc box into which the rays were beamed. In later experiments he placed a lead plate between the exposed tube and himself, but still both outside the protective zinc. This was done not so much for his own protection against these unknown but suspected rays, but rather to achieve a more definite beam and to regulate the beam at will with diaphragms in the box, and also to prevent the annoying fogging of any photographic plates lying nearby. Throughout all the experiments that Röntgen conducted he was thus completely protected from extensive and harmful exposure.

Many of the early experimenters were equally cautious, but a great many failed to take any precautions whatever. Many experienced scientists reasoned, like F. H. Williams of Boston, that "rays having such power of penetrating matter as the X rays had, must have some effect upon the system, and therefore I protected myself." But a colleague of his, Walter J. Dodd, did not think it necessary to be careful and consequently suffered burned hands.

At Freiburg, Ludwig Zehnder intended to make a number of photographs which when assembled would be the entire skeleton. He used a healthy 14-year-old boy as a subject. After the first picture, that of his chest, the boy complained of chest burns where the rays from the closely positioned tube struck him most directly. But after a day or two in the hospital, mainly for observation, he was released as cured and suffered no further ill effects from that exposure. Zehnder brought him some chocolates and other small gifts, and the boy was perfectly all right. This was probably the first case of X ray burns experienced.

Zehnder went ahead to make pictures of other parts of the body, now using a soldier for the subject and being more careful. Then, when Zehnder needed a photograph of a head, his assistant Kempke volunteered to hold his head on the table for one hour. A small bullet was taped behind his ear to show such an object on the plate, and this turned out well.

The series of six separate photographs of head in profile, clear rib cage, and especially clear forearm and hands, were combined to form a whole skeleton (albeit of three different bodies actually) and were exhibited at the entrance of the *Tonehallesaal* at the occasion of the *Schweizerische Naturforscherversammlung*. Wilhelm Röntgen attended this meeting with Zehnder but made no comment at seeing the exhibit. Perhaps he thought it ostentatious or vulgar, Ludwig Zehnder felt.

There were other early reports of X ray burns suffered. At Vanderbilt University, J. Daniel, after having his skull photographed — this exposure also took an hour — three weeks later noticed an epilation (loss of hair by destruction of the roots) two inches in diameter on that part of his head which had been nearest the tube. "A plate holder with the plate toward the side of the skull was fastened and a coin placed between the plate and the head. The tube was fastened at the other side at a distance of one-half inch from the hair."

From England, L. G. Stevens reported that "those who work with X rays suffer from changes of the skin which are similar to effects from the sun burn." The Munich *Medical Journal* wrote of "dermatitis [inflammation of the derma or true skin] and alopecia [sudden loss of hair] after experiments with Röntgen rays." It was speculated that burns were caused by "an effect of the high tension currents which go from the tube to the body, and not due to the direct effect of radiation."

In the case reported at Vanderbilt, the epilation after a skull photograph had been observed to take place twenty-one days afterward. At the University of Minnesota a similar case occurred, according to Professor Jones, with the hair of William Levy falling out almost immediately after the exposure. Here, however, a high tension current of 100,000 volts was employed, perhaps higher than that used at Vanderbilt University and in other previously mentioned situations. The day after exposure Levy noticed a peculiar skin effect in the area that had been most exposed to the rays, and the hair on the right side of his face had come out. A few days later he was perfectly bald. His right ear had swollen to twice its normal size and appeared as if it had frozen. Sores were visible on his head. The mouth and throat were blistered so that he could eat no solid foods for three weeks, and his lip were swollen, cracked, and bleeding. Eventually Levy recovered from these effects, but the half-baldness of his head remained.

It was left to a clever Frenchman to interpret these startling effects as a beneficial beauty aid to distressed ladies and to translate them into a money-making scheme. The enterprising M. Gaudoin of Dijon was well aware that a considerable proportion of his countrywomen were endowed with a soft, silky mustache which was by no means appreciated by marriageable young girls and even long-married ladies. He conceived the idea to use the Röntgen rays as a *dépilatoire*. Having announced his intention, he was not long in securing a clientele, with the many eager customers crowding his laboratory-treatment rooms.

For a cheerfully paid fair fee, the Frenchman applied the X rays on the full-blown mustaches and incipient beards. But when these appendages made no sign of vanishing, and some ladies who had been under treatment asked to have their money refunded, M. Gaudoin appeased these infuriated graces hurriedly and retired from the business with the fees he had safely accumulated — vanishing much quicker than the hair he was supposed to have removed. The *Journal of Photography,* which published this story in its issue of July 31, 1896, made no final comment.

Demonstrators generally were the most severely burned victims of the unknown rays. For instance, H. D. Hawks of Columbia University, who gave demonstrations of Röntgen rays in Bloomingdale's department store in New York for several weeks, usually worked two or three hours daily, demonstrating the penetration of X rays through his hand and head on a fluoroscope. His apparatus, according to the *Electrical Engineer* of July 1896, consisted of "an eight-inch Splitdorf coil with the make and break circuit mounted on the shaft of a motor, the spark at the break being absorbed by condensers. The tube was of the focusing type, made by Greiner of New York. By proper manipulation he was able to make a very clear photograph of the hand with 20 to 30 seconds exposure and a picture of the ribs in about 10 to 15 minutes. A very essential thing in running tubes to the maximum effect was to keep the air around them dry."

Hawks first observed a slight dryness of his skin, which soon increased to resemble a strong sunburn. Then the fingernails stopped growing, his skin began to scale, his hair at the temples fell out, and his vision became impaired. His eyelashes and eyebrows fell out, and his chest showed effects similar to severe sunburn. Hawks required medical attention to relieve his intense pains. After taking some weeks off from his work, he returned to it, wearing gloves for protection and using petroleum jelly on his skin, at the suggestion of his dermatologist. However, the effects soon returned with even greater severity.

The difficulty of detecting damage caused by X ray exposure existed because the rays are extrasensory. One cannot see them, smell them, taste them, hear them, or feel them. They cause a burn, but there is absolutely no sensation of heat during exposure. To aggravate the problem, there was the common practice of exposing one's hand to the rays while adjusting the machine prior to the demonstration at the store, or before treatment of patients by physicians or examinations by surgeons; consequently demonstrators and physicians exposed themselves repeatedly to the inherently dangerous rays.

Because the X rays were not perceptible, they were generally believed to be entirely harmless; but the long list of casualties among the X ray pioneers testified to the fact that a great danger existed. It was not at all clear just what caused these harmful effects, and several schools of thought developed on the subject. Some investigators believed that the impact of minute platinum atoms from the target, or electrical induction current, or ozone generated in the skin, or that the ever-present violet rays were responsible, rather than the direct X ray exposures. Others, like the American physicist Elihu Thomson, made experiments on their own fingers by exposing them to direct rays for certain periods daily, and over a longer period increasing the exposure and observing its effect, thus definitely establishing the fact that the X rays were responsible for the inflammation. Thomson published his detailed observations on the process of the burns on a finger of his left hand in a periodical in April 1897, warning of the inherent danger of overexposure.

Sir Joseph Lister pointed out in his president's address at the opening of the Liverpool Congress in September, 1896, that "there is another way in which the Röntgen rays connect themselves with physiology and may possibly influence medicine. It is found that if the skin is long exposed to their action it becomes very much irritated, affected with a sort of aggravated sunburning. This suggests the idea that the transmission of the rays through the human body may not be altogether a matter of indifference to internal organs but may by long continued action produce, according to the condition of the part concerned, injurious irradiation or salutary stimulation."

In this acute observation, the eminent Lister pointed out the hazards of exposure to the rays, and also forecast the possibility of X ray therapy. This thought had also occurred to others.

The first salubrious effect of such treatment already had been achieved in Vienna when Dr. L. Freund suggested to Franz Exner, director of the Physical-Chemical Institute, that a little girl with a "tremendous hairy pigment birth mark" be treated with X rays. Exner considered the project absolutely unfeasible and flatly refused to let Dr. Freund use the apparatus, but Professor Eder disagreed with his elder colleague and allowed the use of his equipment for the Röntgenotherapy. After ten days of two hours daily exposure, a small circular bald spot appeared, the "first successful experimental proof of a biologic effect" and the first use of Röntgen rays for therapeutic purposes.

A plain square shaft of sandstone decorated with a victory wreath of laurel was erected in 1936 in the landscaped courtyard of the St. Georg Hospital in Hamburg. On its sides are carved 168 names of men and women of fifteen countries and of many nationalities — experimental physicists, medical doctors, laboratory technicians, hospital attendants, and clinical nurses. These men and women had one thing in common: all died of over-exposure to X rays. Every name represents a separate chapter in the history of further development of the then still unknown rays, and every one of these unfortunate victims had contributed, according to his respective calling, to greater knowledge and eventual safety of the rays.

At the dedication of the memorial column, presented by the *Deutsche Röntgengesellschaft* as a "token of thanks of the entire world," the eighty-one-year-old Röntgenologist of France, Antoine Béclère said:

Many names are here immortalized, some known and many others unknown, who earn equally our respect. Many of these names, as Albers-Schönberg, Bergonnié, Holzknecht, are names of renowned scientists whose research, discoveries, and reports, and whose teaching of the development of medical radiology has contributed exceedingly. Other names, less known, are those of outstanding practitioners, whose life work signified benevolent works. Others finally are unknown names of plain workers, modest nurses, or *Röntgenschwestern,* as they are here called. All of these victims have done their work, either modest or important, with equal eagerness, with equal devotion. All have earned a similar merit, and all have the same right to partake of this honor. These noble martyrs spoke not the same language, did not share the same native land, were of different races and differed in religious convictions. Excuse me for speaking so — it is not correct. They were all of the same race actually, of the race of brave people. They all were of the same religion, the religion of duty. They fought completely, with their very lives at stake, the same enemies, the illness and the pain, with the wonderful weapon which Röntgen presented to medical science. They were not afraid that this double-edged weapon, which was utilized without the currently employed safety measures, would hurt them one day so as to kill them.

The great name of Röntgen and his famous discovery constitute a part of your national property of which you are rightfully proud. You could have erected this monument only for the victims of German nationality without fear of any criticism whatever. You did not choose that. The names of those of all civilized countries who dedicated their lives to the same high ideal are here united brotherly in the same high idea.

By October 1959 the German Röntgen Society reported that 359 persons had lost their lives because of excessive X rays. During the early development years, the Hamburg (Albers-Schönberg) school advocated that heavy apparatus should be built and the technicians be protected, while the Vienna (Guido Holzknecht) school preferred smaller and more easily movable apparatus. Holzknecht himself became a victim of overexposure and died in 1931.

It was merely a matter of time before an ingenious barrister would use X ray photographs before a court of law to substantiate an injury suffered by his client.

This first case seemed of great historic interest indeed. Several scientific journals and general periodicals reprinted the story in its entirety, or rewrote it for their own particular readership. Accounts of the case

appeared in the *British Journal of Photography* of March 20, 1896, in
the June issue of the *British Medical Journal,* in the American *Electrical
Engineer* of June 10, and the *Literary Digest* of April 11 under the title
"The New Photography in Court."

According to the original account in *The Hospital* (of London) the
X ray evidence decided the case tried before Mr. Justice Hawkins and'
a special jury at Nottingham, England:

Miss Ffolliott, a burlesque and comedy actress, while carrying out an
engagement at a local theater early in September last, was the subject of an
accident. After the first act, having to go and change her dress, she fell on
the staircase leading to the dressing room, injuring her foot. Miss Ffolliott
was forced to remain in bed for nearly a month, and at the end of that time
was still unable to resume her vocation. Then, by the advice of Dr. Frankish,
she was sent to University College Hospital, where both her feet were photographed by the "X rays." The negatives taken were shown in court, and the
difference between the two was convincingly demonstrated to the judge and
the jury. There was a definite displacement of the cuboid bone of the left foot,
which showed at once both the nature and the measure of the injury. No
further argument on the point was needed on either side, and the only defense,
therefore, was a charge of contributory carelessness against Miss Ffolliott.
Those medical men who are accustomed to dealing with "accident claims"
— and such claims are now very numerous — will perceive how great a
service the new photography may render to truth and right in difficult and
doubtful cases. If the whole osseous system, including the spine, can be
portrayed distinctly on the negative, much shameful perjury on the part of
a certain class of claimants, and many discreditable contradictions among
medical experts, will be avoided. The case is a distinct triumph for science,
and shows how plain fact is now furnished with a novel and successful means
of vindicating itself with unerring certainty against opponents of every class.

A quite different episode was the admittance of X ray pictures as
evidence in a Western courtroom in the United States, as told by S.
Withers in "The Story of the First Röntgen Evidence":

James Smith was a rather poor boy who read law and did odd jobs
to meet his living expenses. While working he fell from a ladder injuring
his leg badly. He then consulted a physician who advised him to strengthen
his injured and weakened limb by diligent exercises. But when the sharp
pain persisted, Smith had an X ray photograph made, which showed that
he had indeed suffered a fracture of the femur in the region of the great
trochanter, with impaction of the fragments. Subsequently, Smith sued
for damages.

The trial began on December 2, 1896, before Judge Owen E.
LeFevre, of Denver, Colorado. When the X ray photographs were to be
offered in evidence, the expert photographer H. H. Buchhalter was ordered

to bring his equipment into the courtroom and to explain the method of X ray photography to the judge and the jury. Buchhalter duly demonstrated the procedure, but when — perhaps exceeding the explicit instructions of the honorable court — he offered to show individual members of the jury the actual bones of their hands, he caused such a vehement argument and resultant disturbance that additional bailiffs had to be called to restore order in the courtroom.

The attorney for the defense C. J. Hughes argued for three hours against the admission of the strange evidence, while the opposing attorney B. B. Lindsey argued as heatedly for it. The judge wisely took the matter under advisement. He contacted other judges in the critical question of admission, to help make up his own mind. One fellow judge replied that he strongly objected because it was "like submitting a photograph of a ghost, when there is no proof that there is such a thing as a ghost." Judge LeFevre ruled on the matter the following day. In a rather lengthy discourse he admitted that a regular photograph of an object unseen by the human eye was indeed inadmissible as evidence, but that this X ray picture was actually a photograph taken by means of a new scientific discovery, fully acknowledged in the arts and in science. "It knocks for admission at the temple of learning," the judge said, "What shall we say or do? Close fast the doors, or open wide the portals? The exhibits will be admitted in evidence." With these historic phrases a new precedent was established in a court of the United States.

Soon many court cases in many countries featured incontestable evidence presented by X ray pictures taken by competent scientific operators. These decisions also proved a great deterrent to extravagant claimants in injury cases, and quickly became of major importance in such judgments.

Undoubtedly this whole matter was carried too far occasionally, as indicated by a story in the September 8, 1896, issue of the *Electrical Engineer* of New York. A private detective named Slater used X rays to clear up divorce cases, the article claimed, but the details of this application are not further explained, leaving the reader to deduce just how this resourceful detective employed the rays. He may have seen the cartoon of the snooping maid, looking through the wooden door instead of the keyhole, or maybe he wanted to use the rays to take pictures in the dark. Or perhaps it was only to detect the proverbial skeleton in the closet.

Even legislative bodies were not immune to the development of X rays. Urged by his alarmed constituents or on his own initiative, assemblyman Reed of Somerset County, New Jersey, introduced a bill in the state legislature prohibiting the use of X ray opera glasses in theaters or elsewhere. The legislator undoubtedly had read in the *American Medi-*

cal Journal an article by Dr. S. H. Monell of New York, referring to the fluoroscope as "Röntgen's spectacles" and noting that they sold for from $5 to $20 each, depending on size. Such a device had, in turn, encouraged opportune merchants to advertise "X ray proof underclothing" to protect the decency of their customers.

Having located a half-penny in the intestines of a child, needles imbedded in girls' hands, glass slivers in soft flesh of a boy, and a bullet in a man's arm, X ray photography naturally attracted the interest of the military services of most countries. According to the *Reichsanzeiger,* and reported by the *Münchener Medizinischen Wochenschrift* of February 4, 1896, the Prussian Ministry of War started experiments at once to find out how X rays could be used by surgeons in warfare for the benefit of sick and wounded soldiers.

The Austrian Military Ministry was also intensely interested in the possibility of using the X ray techniques to aid their wounded men.

Already in May, 1896, the Italian army physician Colonel Alvaro used X ray equipment in his examinations of wounded soldiers on the battlefields of Adowa, Africa, where the Ethiopians under their King Menelik inflicted 7,600 casualties on the Italian legions. The Medical Department of the War Office of the British Government ordered two complete sets of Röntgen apparatus sent up for their Nile Expedition in 1896 "to be used by army surgeons in locating bullets in soldiers and in determining the extent of bone fractures."

Professor H. Kuttner of Tübingen, who was with the Greek armies in connection with the German Red Cross Society, as a result of his experience with Röntgen apparatus during the Turko-Greek War, stated, "The Röntgen rays are of great importance for medical aid in war, but only for fixed hospitals and those installed in fortresses, while for moving field hospitals their application is very limited."

This observation was also made by F. C. Abbott at the base hospital at Phalerum during the same war: "The use of Röntgen rays becomes an impossibility at the actual front. Fortunately it is not necessary there. We believe that the X ray in future wars will be of greatest use."

Surgeon General Jameson of the British Army also suggested that such installations be confined to base hospitals. "What the photography really determines is more the position of the bullet or the kind of fracture. But the urgency of operation is determined by other conditions."

The German army surgeon von Bergmann, however, did not share the opinions that the use of X rays had helped during war time. In his book *Die Resultate der Gelenkesectionen im Kriege* he argued that the ray "will prove a menace in military surgery in that its use will prove an incentive to unnecessary operative interference." He believed that "the consciousness of having some extra lead in one's body, especially when it causes no inconvenience whatever, does not in the least counterbalance the danger of an operation necessary for its removal."

Of particular interest is the experience of the Medical Department of the United States Army in the war with Spain in 1898. The surgeon general's report stated that Röntgen ray apparatus was supplied to the prominent general hospitals and three hospital ships, the U.S.S. *Relief, Missouri,* and *Bay State.* In all, seventeen such installations were made available during the war, of which five were static and twelve were coil machines. In the static apparatus the electric current was produced directly by the machine and carried directly to the tube, while in the coil machine the current was produced in the secondary portions or coils of a special apparatus, such as a Ruhmkorff coil. For base and general hospitals the coil apparatus was recommended, while in permanently established hospitals the static machines were preferred. During the Terah expedition an X ray apparatus was actually used so close to the fighting front that the operators were occasionally under gunfire. Such installations were definitely not recommended.

Bullet wounds were caused generally by the clean Mauser bullets of the Spanish regulars, or by the round, soft lead bullets having a bursting effect, and fired from Remington .41s by the Spanish irregular troops. "In locating lodged missiles, the superiority of Röntgen rays is so great that no other method should be used," Captain W. C. Borden reported to the surgeon general. "Because of its reliability of detection and precise location it makes disturbance of the wound unnecessary."

For cases of marked difficulty a clever method of crossed thread location was described, and special apparatus of several types was available for that particular purpose. In cases of gunshot fractures the Röntgen ray photography was extremely helpful in determination of the extent of the splintering or shattering of the bone. The differing effects depended upon the velocity of the projectile and the difference in the structure of the bones. Suggested exposure times were: for forearm and hand, one to two minutes; for shoulder and chest, ten minutes; for knee, nine minutes; and for hip joint, pelvis, and head, twenty minutes.

Only two cases of burns were reported during the Spanish-American War, caused either by faulty tubes or prolonged exposures. After three twenty-minute exposures with the coil machine, and still not a good diagnostic radiograph, a portion of the chest of a discharged soldier showed the effects of the prolonged exposure, causing a small ulcer that gradually spread. The greatest benefit was achieved by applications of a lead and opium lotion. However, after eleven months, the spot had not yet healed completely, although the intense pain had disappeared.

In another case a soldier was given exposures of twenty-five minutes on each of three days with a static machine to determine the presence of calculus in the pelvis of the kidney. Five days after the last exposure irritation occurred, which cleared up completely within ten days.

The surgeon concluded that four factors should be considered, the length of exposure, the nearness of the tube to the surface of the body, the physical condition of the patient, and individual idiosyncrasy. Exposures should not exceed thirty minutes under any circumstances, and a minimum distance of ten inches should be maintained.

The report emphasized that the use of the Röntgen ray marked a distinct advance in military surgery. In the American Civil War, where larger caliber rifles were used, the mortality rate was nearly double that of the Spanish-American War (12.96 to 6.64 per cent). The rate from wounds of the head, face, neck, spine, and abdomen did not materially differ, but chest wounds (27.8 to 11.4 per cent), wounds of the extremities, and flesh wounds of the back showed a marked difference in rate. The tremendous improvement in comparison loss was not due solely to the Röntgen ray usage the comprehensive report concluded, but to other medical advances as well.

Fatality rates of the wounded in later wars, of interest here for comparison purposes, were: World War I, 5.5 per cent; World War II, 3.3 per cent; the Korean conflict, 2.7 per cent; the Vietnam action, less than 2 per cent. This would indicate a constant improvement of techniques in treating wounded American soldiers.

CHAPTER 15

The Final Communication on X Rays

APPARENTLY THE SHORT VACATION did Wilhelm Röntgen immeasurable good. After his return to Würzburg he threw himself wholeheartedly into his work at the laboratory to complete the experiments on his X rays. It was almost like former times. Requests for lectures or appearances at various scientific gatherings had eased somewhat, perhaps because nearly everyone involved had by then definitely understood his wishes. He wondered how long the peaceful atmosphere would last.

In May Röntgen was advised that the *Preussische Akademie der Wissenschaften* in Berlin had elected him an Honorary Corresponding Member of their Academy of Science. It was the first recognition by any scientific society bestowed upon Röntgen for his discovery. The Berlin colleagues had — as had many other groups from other cities — tried unsuccessfully to persuade him to give them a lecture demonstration, after which they intended to present the discoverer personally with the *Ehrenmitglied* certificate. Röntgen, however, refused all such open or covert invitations. The Prussian Academy was merely the first to give in to the persistent physics professor from Würzburg.

Brief interruptions in his research work occurred when distinguished visitors kept coming to see Röntgen at the institute on the Pleicher Ring. Scientists came from afar to compare notes and to exchange with the discoverer himself some of their own experiences with the new rays. One of these visitors was Dayton C. Miller of Cleveland, who also brought hearty greetings from cousin Heinrich, who was pastor of the First Reformed Church in Cleveland and superintendent of the Bethesda German Hospital. Miller, who was at the Case School, had bought the entire exhibit of Crookes and Geissler tubes displayed by the Geissler Company at the Chicago Exposition of 1893, and thus was perhaps best equipped to experiment with X rays when Röntgen announced his discovery. He had mutually conducted revealing experiments with the surgeon George Crile and the dentist Weston A. Price, and Miller presented Röntgen with a picture of a whole human skeleton, fitted together cleverly in sections, which had been made in March of that year. In exchange Miller gratefully took with him several of the newly developed tubes of platinum targets.

Although there were really not too many interruptions in his work, Röntgen felt greatly relieved when the *grossen Ferien* came. He had become irritated at practically all of the published articles on X rays which were shown him. He maintained that the scientific matter should never have been widely discussed in lay circles by periodicals devoted to the general readership. And his temper quickly gave way when he read some of the correspondence with which he was inundated.

During the summer vacations the Röntgens again visited relatives in Zurich for about a week, and Röntgen attended some of the sessions of the Swiss Congress of Scientists there. With the Zehnders they went to Rigi-Scheidegg where, to their dismay, at the depot they discovered many tourists with cameras waiting to photograph Wilhelm and Bertha Röntgen as they walked from the railroad station to the hotel. This annoying activity did not persist however, and the Röntgens found leisure and seclusion in which to enjoy some walks along the Seeweg and even the closer-in Alpine garden near their hotel. Röntgen was occasionally recognized by other vacationers, a situation which embarrassed him acutely. But it was much preferable to Zurich, he acknowledged, where he could hardly appear on the street without constantly lifted hat in response to the greetings of totally strange persons.

At the Weisses Kreuz in Pontresina, under the roof of their friendly hosts, the Enderlins, they found sanctuary from the unpleasant intrusions into their privacy. Unfortunately the weather was not as good as usual, and excursions and even shorter hikes into the forested mountain areas — not to think of invigorating climbs in the more rugged terrain — could seldom be undertaken. But they had a pleasant vacation. Although much of the time was spent in playing cards with companions, there also were several outings of the genial small group of colleagues, organized by Röntgen.

A photograph, taken by the enthusiastic amateur photographer Röntgen himself, shows him in the center of the jovial group. He had carefully posed his fellow subjects, leaving a quick-to-reach spot for himself to attain after the camera had been set up and the automatic shutter ticked away. Besides Röntgen, Bertha, and the little Berteli, there were the von Hippels and the Zehnders, Baron and Baroness Haller von Hallerstein, and an industrialist named Beer, of Leipzig. The last named were slight acquaintances who stayed at the Weisses Kreuz. The group had been on a short hike that day and rested on a slope to pose for the historic photograph. None was dressed in hiking clothes; the ladies wore long and full-skirted dresses, the men wore their regular suit coats and hats and carried walking canes.

The Röntgens cut their stay short and left earlier than originally planned. After spending a few days in Weissbad, in the Swiss Alpenzell, they returned to Würzburg.

Anxious to complete his experiments with the X rays so that he could publish his *Dritte Mitteilung,* his Final Communication, Röntgen now concentrated his experimental work on increasing the penetration of the rays with increasingly higher voltage at the tube. But almost every time he increased the voltage to a certain level, the tubes were punctured. The failures were no small problem to him. The budget at the institute was limited, not allowing for the purchase of the larger number of tubes he needed in order to bring this series of experiments to a sound conclusion.

That fall semester of 1896 a veritable shower of honors fell on Wilhelm Röntgen from scientific societies of many countries. He was elected as Corresponding Member of the *Bayerischen Akademie der Wissenschaften* at Munich, the *Wissenschaftlichen Gesellschaft* at Göttingen, the Academy of Natural Sciences of Philadelphia, and the *Société Nationale des Sciences Naturelles et Mathématiques de Cherbourg.*

The Royal Society of London bestowed its Rumford Gold Medal on him and the Wiener Akademie honored him with its prestigious *Baumgärtner Preis.* Röntgen was also elected an Honorary Member of the *Naturforscher-Gesellschaft* of Freiburg im Breisgau, the *Physikalische Gesellschaft* of Frankfurt am Main, and the Chester Society of Natural Sciences. And, writing in French, the *Société Scientifique "Antonio Alzate" de México, Mexique,* made Monsieur le Dr. Guillaume C. Röntgen a Membre Honoraire on June 10, 1896.

With only a little time out to acknowledge these honors, Wilhelm Röntgen returned to his laboratory and his task. There were, of course, other matters that required attention. In a letter to Zehnder, Röntgen asked about the X ray picture of the human skeleton which Zehnder had made with Kempke. Obviously Röntgen had noticed it, after all, and was quite impressed by it. He would like to have two copies of it, one for the institute and, if this remarkable composite had not yet been shown publicly, one to send to the Kaiser, who had shown such knowledgeable interest in his discovery. If the assembled photograph had already been exhibited at other than a scientific meeting, it would not be suitable to present a copy to the Kaiser; however, Röntgen still would want one for the institute.

Zehnder took the pictures to the *Deutschen Naturforscher- und Aerzteversammlung* in Frankfurt, then visited briefly in Berlin and stopped at Würzburg to make some experiments with Röntgen, using a tube designed by Zehnder.

On Christmas Day Röntgen wrote letters. In one to Ludwig Zehnder he told of the *Weihnachten* they had celebrated. It was a nice Christmas. He and Bertha presented each other with furniture as gifts for the house, his wife having ordered a set of comfortable leather chairs to be made. There also was the long-desired dog — the first of several German shepherds — for additional company, and many other things, including a superb compass. The compass could have been meant as a subtle suggestion for improved planned hikes into the country! He had given his Bertha a traveling bag, a clock for her writing table, and a life-sized framed photograph of her latest favorite picture. And little Berteli had surprised them, making them happy and proud, with her accomplished piano rendition of *Nussbaum*. It was her own idea to study it secretly. They had songs and musical accompaniment, and a pleasant evening at their apartment in Würzburg. But he longed to hear again the sonorous bells ring out the old year in Zurich, and he was happy for the Zehnders that they were going there to see the new year in.

Röntgen also mentioned to Zehnder that he still had trouble with the tubes. He ordered two specially shaped ones through Zehnder, apologizing for taking so much time of his friend's busy work schedule with his problems, but there was just no manufacturer in his area who could supply the tubes he needed so badly. A usable tube had fallen over with the attached pump, as he experimented with it, and shattered completely. That was really his first *malheur,* but the next day he punctured the other of the two tubes he had. Now he worked with tubes from Reiniger, Gebbert & Schall, which were quite good, but too expensive. Since he had set in his head a certain goal, which endangered his tubes greatly, he had used up during that week no less than five tubes. That was expensive fun! But he had now reached the first part of his goal, and the second half should come along too, if his luck held out.

He wrote that for months he had asked the Greiner & Friedrichs people to get him some vacuum tubes, but they seemed too busy. They were good glassblowers but understood absolutely nothing of mechanics. So would Zehnder please send him two tubes from Zurich. Röntgen also asked that Zehnder please be extremely careful in packing and tying the package securely. When the other shipment was delivered to the institute, the mailman seemed to have several pieces — the outside carton, the excelsior, the paper, and also the two tubes, separately in hand. It was all there, but not in one parcel. He suggested that perhaps the good *Zollinspectoren* had difficulty in classifying the strange looking apparatus and so did not even bother to tie it up properly, to show their superiority in the face of adversity. Finally Röntgen mentioned that he hoped to write up some of his observations during the current Christmas vacations.

When Reiniger, Gebbert & Schall sent him tubes that stood up remarkably well, even under the most demanding requirements, Röntgen was prompted to write a letter asking for some special concessions on the price, a practice that was made most difficult because of his lofty professional pride. On November 27, 1896, he wrote to J. Rosenthal, the engineer of the firm:

Your tubes are really very good, but are too expensive for our means. I use these tubes not only for the usual experiments but also, as is apparent, for several other experiments in which the tubes must stand a much greater strain than normally, and the result is that they are destroyed more quickly. I would like to ask you whether you are able to let me have the tubes for twenty instead of thirty marks each.

The company accommodated him, and he paid them only twenty marks, about five dollars, for these highly useful vacuum tubes. They were still too costly to suit the expense-conscious Röntgen entirely; he still broke tubes, but the lowered cost made such misfortunes slightly less painful.

For the silver anniversary of their marriage, on January 19, 1897, the Röntgens stayed at home. A vast number of congratulations came to them from their friends and colleagues, but they decided not to make a great affair of the eventful day. An acquaintance, a Fräulein Baur, came to join them in the afternoon for a piece of *Schwarzwälder Kirschtorte* and fine coffee; the evening dinner they ate in solitude at home. Bertha had again her usual bad cold during these wintry days, and the coughing seemed even worse and of longer duration than during previous winters. They talked of plans to spend a few days at some place where the air was milder, but somehow the time was too short to get away. Besides, the Final Communication was not yet finished.

Röntgen worked on the various delicate investigations for the last communication under almost constant interruptive pressures from other physicists and scientists, others who were conducting individual experiments with X rays, developing them for specific purposes, and who then were contacting Röntgen to discuss their findings. Röntgen had at times angrily expressed the complaint — in understandable desperation — that he was hindered from completing his part of the work. Realizing that the X rays had many peculiarities that had not yet been explained nor properly observed by many experimenters, he believed that he was uniquely qualified to further investigate these perplexing and even confounding characteristics and that he alone was responsible to clear up any still undisclosed and unanswered questions about the X rays.

Röntgen intended to publish this final communication in the *Sitzungsberichte* of his own Würzburg society, as had been done with the first two reports. But when the prestigious — and all-powerful — Prussian Academy of Sciences in Berlin asked to publish that last communication, he felt that he had to give it to them. He sent to the editor his "Further Observations on the Properties of the X Rays — Third Communication," on March 10, 1897. It was duly published in the *Mathematischen und Naturwissenschaftlichen Mitteilungen aus den Sitzungsberichten der Preussischen Akademie der Wissenschaften, Physikalisch-Mathematische Klasse 392* (1897). (See Appendix 5 for text of Third Communication.)

This report contained a line drawing of a simple apparatus. It was the only one to have an illustration of any kind. None of the previous ones had X ray pictures or other illustrations. The report began with "point 1," and was not a continuation of the two previous reports. It described the behavior of the X rays and their characteristics, listed the transparencies of various substances to the perpendicularly impinging rays, and gave a comparison schedule of penetration of an aluminum plate. Experiments with either a soft or hard tube were described in detail, drawing as conclusion a comparison between the behavior of optical rays and X rays. Röntgen made eleven individual points in this last and longest of the Communications. Although he expressed the hope to report on the deflection experiments soon (in point 11), this *"Weitere Beobachtungen an den Eigenschaften von X Strahlen. Dritte Mitteilung,"* was actually the last published work pertaining to X rays from the pen of its discoverer.

With his part of the basic experimental work on the rays now conclusively finished, now that the *Dritte Mitteilung* was written and published, Röntgen was relieved and possibly more exhilarated than at any time since his first observations of his new rays almost one and a half years before.

CHAPTER 16

Why Munich?

Back in Würzburg, after a delightful restorative vacation at Cadenabbia, Wilhelm Röntgen again assumed his customary duties — lecturing to his students and experimenting in his own laboratory.

Although he had finished his investigations on the X rays, there was still an almost continuous flow of correspondence regarding them with other colleagues. Many scientists came on personal visits. Röntgen was now much more at ease on such occasions, showing his visitors his apparatus at leisure and conducting familiar experiments for their benefit. The pressure to finish the experiments and observations had ended, and his attitude was congenial.

Honors kept coming to Wilhelm Röntgen throughout the year. The Franklin Institute of Philadelphia awarded him their Elliot-Cresson medal, the *Académie des Sciences* of Paris gave him the *Prix Lacaze,* and the *Roma Societa* presented him with their *Mattencei medaglia.*

A number of scientific societies made Röntgen an honorary member: The *Schweizerische Naturforscher-Gesellschaft,* the *Physikalisch-Medizinische Gesellschaft* of Erlangen, the newly formed Roentgen Society of London, the *Société des Médecines Russes* of St. Petersburg, the *Société Imperiale de Médecine* of Constantinople, and the *Gesellschaft ehemaliger Studierender der Eidgenössischen Technischen Hochschule* in Zürich. The *Reale Academia di Geographici* of Firenze made him a corresponding member, and the American Philosophical Society of Philadelphia elected him a regular member, waiving the fee.

During summer vacation, the Röntgens visited relatives at Zurich, and then spent a week at Lucerne, where they met the von Hippels.

Together the vacationers enjoyed the area and the magnificent lake, the Vierwaldstätter See. Reservations at the Weisses Kreuz were made, and the Röntgens and von Hippels went to Pontresina for the remainder of their *Ferien*.

Back in school again, the old work routine at the institute was followed, with only a few minor interruptions. Honors continued to come from many societies. The Otto-Wahlbruch *Stiftung* of Hamburg awarded Röntgen a *Preis,* and the New York Medical Society elected him an honorary member. The *Reale Academia dei Lincei* of Roma presented Röntgen with a bronze plaque and made him a corresponding member, and the *Reale Instituto Veneto di Sienze* made him a corresponding member. He was voted a nonresident member of the *Société Hollandaise des Sciences* of Haarlem.

Varying the customary spring vacation at Cadenabbia, the Röntgens spent a day or two at the Hotel Bazzoni & Du Lac at nearby Tremezzo (or perhaps Bertha just needed a rest for a short while during an outing while Röntgen wrote a letter to a friend on the hotel stationery, postmarked in the area — this biographer's only clue).

For the summer the Röntgens went again to Switzerland. The Zehnders could not meet them there that year. Röntgen wrote afterward, "I was really sorry that we could not talk together during this summer and that we could not be together for a few days. I feel always the need, at least from time to time, to see old friends and to discuss everything with them. Although we were able to do that with the Hippels, we missed you sorely."

Before returning to Würzburg they went to Holland for two weeks to visit the Rembrandt Exhibition at Amsterdam and also to reminisce and relive some of the episodes of youthful pleasures. "At such a visit," Röntgen observed, "there remain many disappointments, but the overall experience was satisfying and enjoyable."

Regarding events and conditions at the institute, he mentioned, "Here everything goes along as usual. After long work I have finally begun with the building addition, but all other extras, such as the enlargement of the lecture room, etc., were not allowed. The Minister of Culture of Bavaria is a hardnecked bureaucrat, and in higher places there is absolutely no understanding or interest in scientific development." But then, Wilhelm Röntgen had seldom, if indeed ever, been able to see eye to eye with his superiors in the education ministries.

One of the assistants at the institute, Otto Stern, intended to go into a slightly different field of employment with a firm in Paris. This would leave a position of assistant open at Würzburg. Once again, Ludwig Zehnder asked to be considered for the job. Both men got along splendidly socially, but in the laboratory there was always a slight feeling of disagreement. The fact that Zehnder had received a patent for his pressure regulator for evacuated tubes had led to an extremely disagreeable discussion between the two men. Röntgen felt strongly that no member of the teaching profession should ever patent any of his scientific findings for personal gain, but should make all of such gathered knowledge public property for the general benefit of mankind and not limit the dissemination of such discoveries to a select group. And the close friendship of the two wives, both Zürichers and almost of like minds, was always an important matter to consider.

Röntgen wrote to Zehnder that the faculty had discussed the matter of the assistant but was not at all favorably inclined to recommend the applicant to the ministry. The lack of the Abitur, which lack Zehnder shared with Röntgen, both being physicists without the important document, was again mentioned as a stumbling block to further advancement, and might actually lead to a rather unpleasant relationship. However, Röntgen would try to persuade his colleagues to be at least neutral in the matter and leave it up to him to recommend Zehnder as his assistant. After all, it was Röntgen who would work with him, not the members of the faculty council. The rather low salary of 1,500 marks as assistant was somewhat counterbalanced by additional examination fees and the prestige of the position. Regarding the lectures to the students, while the Bavarian Ministry would not give Zehnder the title of professor, he would probably be allowed to use his title earned in the State of Baden, and the faculty would recommend that he be accepted as a bona fide teacher at the institute. All in all, Röntgen believed that he would be able to make it possible for Zehnder to come to Würzburg, but it would take some time and quite a bit of individual persuasion of certain persons. Yes, traditions were a solid part of *Universitatis Wirceburgensis!*

Toward the end of the year Stern accepted the offer of the firm in Paris and left the institute assistant's position open. But the first assistant Max Wien also left Würzburg, having been offered a better teaching position at the Aachen university. For the summer semester of 1897 Bernhard Wolff became assistant, and when Wolff left the following year, Julius Wallot took his place.

Ludwig Zehnder came to Würzburg as first assistant to Röntgen on March 1, 1899, with the privilege of teaching under his Baden professorship, the state not being willing to abdicate its rights of recognition of other states' educational, or all professional, titles. Zehnder was now "a.o. *(ausserordentlicher)* Professor Doktor," and "Cand. Phys." Julius Wallot became second assistant to Röntgen. For the fall semester of 1899–1900, another candidate of physics, Georg Nast, joined the laboratory force.

That year death took the aged physicist Gustav Wiedemann, who was well known for his outstanding work on magnetism and studies in electricity and who had occupied the chair of physics at the *Königlichen Sächsischen Universität* at Leipzig. The Saxon Minister of Culture sent his deputy, Wislicenus, to Würzburg with the purpose of persuading Wilhelm Röntgen to become head of the Leipzig institute of physical sciences. Should the discussions prove fruitful the official offer would be made by the ministry, but should the matter be futile, neither of the parties would be embarrassed. It was a good arrangement for all concerned.

Röntgen considered the offer quite seriously. But finally he decided to remain definitely in Würzburg — just as he at one time had decided that he would definitely never leave Giessen. The health of his wife was always of major importance when considering the various offers of a better position, and he believed that the air in Saxony was not preferable to that of Würzburg. Perhaps the winters would not be quite as severe as in lower Bavaria, but Saxony was considerably farther from their Swiss vacation places and friends and relatives there. His Bertha was ill much of the time now, especially with kidney stone problems — surgery was proscribed because of her weak heart — and the move to Leipzig would probably upset her excessively. Too, Röntgen was really quite satisfied with the existing facilities at the institute, although he hoped that his laboratory would be enlarged and better equipped. Their small circle of intimate colleagues was a most congenial group, meeting regularly for dinner parties in their respective homes, or going on the frequent outings they all enjoyed so much. No, Röntgen concluded, there was no reason at all ever to consider leaving the Würzburg post.

Perhaps in gratitude for his remaining in Bavaria, the government bestowed another great honor upon Wilhelm Röntgen by appointing him a *Königlichen Geheimen Rat*. This exalted distinction was not at all embarrassing to him, although he had often made fun of von Hippel's Prussian title. Röntgen considered it not as the offer of nobility, but accepted the title obediently with the aside comment that it practically brought him up even with his esteemed colleague, Geheimrat von Hippel!

Other honors came to Röntgen that year. The University of Zurich awarded him a special diploma; the *Cataafsch Genootschap* of Rotterdam made him a corresponding member; and the Royal Academy of Sciences of Stockholm elected him a nonresident member.

Having just stated the definite decision to remain in Würzburg, it came as a complete surprise to his colleagues when Röntgen announced only shortly afterward that he had accepted a post in Munich!

The Bavarian Minister of Culture had strongly urged Röntgen to accept this important position, the most prestigious post the Bavarian government could offer him, its best known scientist, after the sudden death of Professor Eugen Cornelius Joseph Lommel. To follow in the footsteps of Lommel was not difficult for Röntgen, but he abhorred the necessary administrative duties that the position required. He never spoke later of his strange reversal of his firm resolution, nor did he explain this move that was really so unlike him. He knew the city well and did not particularly care for its accelerated activities and social affairs. He knew the university and did not consider it to be the *ne plus ultra* of institutions, nor superior in any way to the achievements of much smaller universities in Germany. Perhaps he felt it his patriotic duty to go to the capital of the state when the highest authorities requested it; perhaps the pressure brought about was so great that he simply could not refuse the offer.

In a letter of December 7, 1899, Geheimer Rat Professor Doktor Wilhelm Conrad Röntgen was notified by the Ministerium that he was appointed as of April 1, 1900, *Im Namen Seiner Majestät des Königs, Luitpold, von Gottes Gnaden Königlicher Prinz von Bayern, Regent, ordentlicher Professor der Experimentalphysik und Vorstand des Physi-kalischen Institutes an der Philosophischen Fakultät der Königlichen Universität München, sowie zum Konservator des Physikalisch-Metro-nomischen Institutes des Staates daselbst,* at a combined salary of 8,100 and 900 marks.

Four or five (Käthe Fuchs did not remember exactly, 65 years later) large moving vans brought the furniture and household goods of the Rönt-gens from Würzburg to Munich. They had leased from the Wittelsbach prince Alfons the upper floor of the large villa on the Aeussere Prinz-regentenstrasse 1, at the corner of Mohlstrasse, overlooking the Isar river and the center of the city. The spacious apartment consisted of ten large rooms, with the kitchen and servants' rooms above. The main floor apartment of this elegant house — of large square stones in neoclassic style and a fenced garden — was occupied by a wealthy family named von Kauffmann. The tenants had absolute privacy. The rent was paid regularly to the bank, and whenever something needed repair, a call to the *Hof-marschall* brought immediate results.

The *Bayerische Königliche Haupt- und Residenzstadt* was a thriving metropolis of some 275,000 inhabitants. Its rather high elevation — 1,703 feet above sea level — caused the weather to be unpredictable, and its close proximity to the high Alpine mountain range rendered it liable to sudden changes of temperature, detrimental to the health of the fragile Bertha.

Munich was an ancient city, founded by Heinrich der Löwe (the Lion), who constructed a bridge across the Isar river and built a customs-house, a mint, and a salt depot on this site in 1158. The land was the property of the Monks of Schäftlarn, thus *Forum ad Monachos* in Latin, or München in German.

The Physical Science Institute building at the University at Munich.

Under the rule of the Wittelsbach princes, the town prospered enormously, and Otto der Berühmte (the Illustrious) transferred his residence there in about 1225. His son Ludwig der Ernste (the Severe) built the Alte Hof, initiating a fabulously ambitious building program for the city which was to make this Bavarian capital into the Athens of Germany. Duke Albert V founded the library; and Elector Maximilian I (1459–1519) erected the Arsenal, the Old Palace, the Kunst-Kammer, and the Mariensäule on the Rathausplatz. Maximilian III founded the Academie in 1757. The magnificent structures impressed Wilhelm Röntgen in 1900. (Many were restored after destruction during World War II.)

The elaborate monument of King Max Joseph on that square, the Royal Palace, the Old Residence, the Propyläen and the Glyptothek around the huge Königsplatz, the Alte Pinakothek nearby, the Royal Library built in 1832 in the Florentine style with colossal statues of Aristotle, Hippocrates, Homer, and Thucydides, and containing a million volumes and thirty thousand manuscripts, all contributed to make Munich truly a *Hauptstadt*.

The several buildings of the university formed a large square, the complex being intersected by the broad Ludwigstrasse. The Priest's Seminary, or Georgianum, stood opposite the Max-Joseph School; the imposing main university building, adorned with two fountains copied from those created by Bernini in the Piazza dei St. Pietro in Rome, made up the other side. Founded actually in Ingolstadt in 1478, the university was transferred to Landshut in 1800, and to its present site at Munich in 1826.

It was rather disappointing to Wilhelm Röntgen that the *Physikalische Institut* was located in an inner courtyard of the huge university complex. It was a three-story building, with a spacious *Aula* and several lecture rooms and laboratories as well as offices, but the structure was considerably less imposing than the solid building of the Würzburg university, stately placed on the broad Pleicher Ring.

Another annoyance to Röntgen was that the department of physics was the second section of the *Philosophische Fakultät,* and that with no less than five other *Geheimen Räte* in the department. The head of the philosophical faculty was the Königlicher Geheimer Rat Professor Doktor Karl Adolf Ritter von Cornelius, who did not lecture at all, of course, but merely administered the large department. Other notable members of the faculty were the Geheimen Räte Ritter von Zittel, Ritter von Müller, Ritter von Wölfflin, Ritter von Baeyer, Professor von Christ, Reichsrat Freiherr von Hertling, Hofrat Hilger, and twenty-one professors, thirteen a.o. (extraordinary) professors, three honorable professors, forty-one privat dozents, and two lecturers.

That first semester Wilhelm Röntgen, as head of the Experimentalphysik (II. Part) lectured daily from 11 to 12 o'clock, five times weekly, gave practical exercises in the physical science laboratory in private for twelve hours weekly, was responsible for the *Anleitung zu selbstständigen Arbeiten* — initiation and guide on independent work — in private, daily from 8 to 11 and 2 to 6 o'clock for 44 hours weekly, and led the physical science colloquium for two hours weekly in private and free of any fees.

As a lecturer, Röntgen was exceedingly dull, although occasionally a humorous sentence would brighten up the long dissertations. He did not believe that scientific subjects should be made popular — which to him meant nonacademic. Röntgen's students preferred the lectures of the a.o. Professor Leo Graetz, a tremendously popular teacher who came to Munich in 1901 and who lectured on introduction to theoretical physics, practical physics, and electromagnetic light theory. Graetz used ingenuity in cleverly dramatizing his demonstrations. Graetz and Zehnder assisted Röntgen in the practical experiments in the laboratory. Zehnder, as first assistant, had accompanied Röntgen from Würzburg to Munich; Röntgen engaged a Dr. Möller as second assistant.

Although Röntgen had satisfied himself by personal inspection of the physical facilities of the institute and had several discussions regarding the acquisition of some new equipment with his Excellency the Minister himself, he quickly found his working conditions less than ideal. The ministry's definition of "ideal" did not coincide with Röntgen's definition. Repeated requests for changes or improvements that had been promised were continually ignored.

Even before he had come to Munich, Röntgen's reputation for being difficult to work with had preceded him. This was, of course, quite true. His standards were exceedingly high, and when annoyed he was rather obstinate; he could be gruff and even rude. At the beginning of his Munich tenure, Röntgen appeared to be dissatisfied with nearly everything at the institute, and it seemed that the change was indeed a mistake. In due time, however, he came to realize that the move was an accomplished fact, and he soon worked himself quite well into the daily routine of the new position. Having turned down the offered nobility was also considered sufficient reason for being disliked by those professors who had been given a "von" because of some worthy endeavor. They felt that Röntgen had made their own acceptance of a title less than an honorable act. In fact, this refusal caused a considerable amount of unpleasantness several times, especially when dealing with ministers and other high government officials, most of whom were of the nobility, either inherited or newly created.

One of the duties (and an excellent source of additional income from the fees paid) of the head of the physics department was to administer examinations of pharmacists prior to the issuing of operating licenses. Röntgen, who utterly despised examinations of any type — for students and pharmacists alike — turned this rather lucrative work over to Zehnder. While on a bicycle tour on *Himmelfahrtstag* (Ascension Day), the traditional outing day, Zehnder, not too agile a rider, broke his leg when he jumped off his bicycle. Interestingly, the attending physician never ordered an X ray examination of the limb, but the leg healed properly, after having been placed into a heavy gypsum cast for a certain period. During the time of this incapacity one of the regularly scheduled examinations for pharmacists was held, and Röntgen, as he wrote in July 1900, was "forced to enjoy it."

At that time, a problem arose that illustrated the great concern with detail which Röntgen, as the responsible top official, felt for the institute. He watched closely over all purchases of equipment, replacements, and new apparatus alike. When a von Linde liquid air machine with an electric motor was to be installed, he had a great deal of trouble in finding out from the AEG, the general electric company, what happened to the "surplus" power of its motor. A 9.5-horsepower motor unit was furnished, and the Linde machine used only a fraction of that output. "Did the AEG know what went on?" Röntgen wondered in a letter to Zehnder. "If they do, let them give their answer in writing and get from Linde a written statement as to what his machine actually used in electric power." This minor detail seemed of immense importance to Röntgen. "Where was the extra power, and if there was a loss of power, where did it go?"

The year 1900 brought again many outstanding awards to Wilhelm Röntgen. The ruling house of Bavaria named him a *Ritter* of the *Verdienst Orden* (Order of Merit) of the Bavarian Crown and awarded him the Silver Medal of Prince Regent Luitpold. The State of Bavaria honored him with the *Grosskomturkreuz* of the *Verdienst Orden* of St. Michael, First Class, and gave him the *Pour le Merite* Order for Science and Art. The Prussian State government awarded Röntgen the Prussian *Kronenorden*, II Class, and the *Physikalisch-Technische Reichsanstalt* at Charlottenburg elected him to the Board of Governors of the institute. He also received a decoration and membership from the Maximilian Order for Sciences and was awarded a *Komtur* in the Order of the Italian Crown.

The Academy of Sciences, Columbia University in New York, suggested that he receive the Barnard Medal, presented every five years, having first been presented to Lord Rayleigh and Professor William Ramsay for their discovery in 1895 of argon, a gaseous element used for filling electric light bulbs. On the letter of June 13, 1900, received from the President's Room of Columbia University, Röntgen wrote, *"erhalten durch den Univ. Sekretär Nachier, 1. Oktob. 00. Röntgen"* — received through the university secretary Nachier, October 1, 1900.

Röntgen was also voted Honorary Member of the *Aerztlichen Vereins* of Munich, and of the *Erste Deutsche Akademie für Physikalisch-Diätetische Therapie* of Hamburg. The *Académie de Médicine* of Paris made him a Nonresident Member, and the *Akademie der Wissenschaften* of Munich made him a member of their society.

Röntgen received the Nobel Prize in 1901. When the Swedish Academy of Science had the task of distributing the prize money for the first time and making the choices of the recipients, it was natural that the selection for the Prize in Physics should fall on Wilhelm Conrad Röntgen. The award for medicine went to Emil A. von Behring of Marburg, and that for chemistry to Jacobus H. van't Hoff of Berlin.

Alfred Bernhard Nobel, the inventor of ballistite, a nitroglycerin powder, died on December 10, 1896, bequeathing his estate of nine million dollars to a fund of which the interest was to be distributed annually to those men who had contributed to the benefit of mankind during the previous year. The founder stipulated that an award be presented to "the person who has made the most important discovery or invention within the field of physics," and "the awards shall be made for the most recent achievements in the fields of culture referred to in the will and for older works only if their significance has not become apparent until recently," and "that no consideration whatever shall be paid to the nationality of the candidates — the most deserving being awarded the prize, whether of Scandinavian origin or not."

Although no minutes were ever kept or published of the meetings of the Academy, it was later established that twelve outstanding scientists had been proposed for the award, and that seventeen of the twenty-nine proposers — all prominent scientists from all over the world — had voted for Röntgen to receive the physics prize.

Wilhelm Röntgen himself suggested Lord Kelvin (formerly William Thompson), then perhaps the foremost physicist living. Of the eleven remaining candidates, eight subsequently received the Nobel Prize — the Professors Svante August Arrhenius of Stockholm (1903 prize winner), Henri Becquerel of Paris (1903), W. W. Campbell of the Lick Observatory, Gabriel Lippmann (1908), A. E. Nordenskjöld of Stockholm, Joseph John Thomson of Cambridge (1906), Johannes D. van der Waals of Amsterdam (1910), Pieter Zeeman of Amsterdam (1902), Philipp Lenard of Kiel (1905), and Guglielmo Marconi of London (1909).

A more worthy scientific achievement and one more in the spirit of the Nobel prize than Röntgen's can hardly be imagined. It was certainly a great satisfaction to the Swedish Academy of Science, which had actually undertaken its task with much hesitation and some reluctance, that such an eminent achievement could be rewarded at the first distribution. While his work had surely not been made "during the preceding year," as laid down in the will of the founder, it was still so new that it hardly had had time to be more than tested and fully accepted by international professional criticism, and it could be stated with assurance that it implied an immense contribution of lasting value to research.

Wilhelm Röntgen wrote, in typical Prussian submissiveness, on December 6, 1901, to the *Königlichen Bayerischen Staatsministerium für Kirchen- und Schulangelegenheiten* that the *ehrerbietigst, gehorsam Unterzeichnete,* the honorably solicitous obedient, undersigned, had been *vertraulich,* confidentially, notified that he was to be awarded the Nobel Prize, a *besonders wertvoller Preis von hoher Achtung,* an especially valuable prize of high esteem. He asked for a leave of absence for a week to accept the honor. The request was granted, and Röntgen traveled to Stockholm alone to accept this recognition. Bertha was too ill to make the trip with him and share the great honor. He wrote to her:

I just have received your message and read it with great pleasure. The letter arrived by the same train as I did, but I think that it probably was not as seasick as I was!

It was a bad day yesterday. We had steady rain with steady southerly winds from the time we left Berlin. The ferry boat in Sassnitz is good but not very large, and it was rocked up and down like a nutshell. The waves broke constantly over the boat so that it was impossible to be outside in the open air. I stood it for almost two hours, but then I had to give up and spend the other two hours in the customary manner. First I intended to stay in Malmö, but then decided to go right through to Stockholm. I stood the train trip quite well, but after having some breakfast I was glad to get to bed and slept for an hour. Professor Arrhenius had looked for me at the railroad station but missed me, so I met him later at the hotel. The formal celebration is tomorrow evening at seven o'clock, to be followed by a supper, and for the next day there are many invitations from professors. I probably shall decline them and return soon. Besides myself, van't Hoff and Behring of Marburg (discoverer of the serum for diphtheria) will receive the prize.

Sweden is totally covered with snow, and when the sun is not shining it is either raining or snowing. It must be very beautiful here in the summer time. Stockholm is a very peculiar city. More the next time, but I probably shall not write many letters any more and will return soon.

To his good friend and colleague, Theodor Boveri, professor of biology at Würzburg, Röntgen wrote, "I had been able to discuss you with van't Hoff, who has also given his explanation regarding some disagreement we had after a lecture of yours in Hamburg. Van't Hoff explained that the ovum enlarges in the direction of the approaching spermatozon and again contracts after its absorption, but I could not agree with this supposition, believing that this enlargement is due to a changed osmotic pressure and carefully explained my argument to him. We did not have time to come to a complete agreement, but I believe that he was not as thoroughly convinced that his opinion is right as he formerly was." This subject was, of course, not at all in Röntgen's scientific field, but he was interested in almost everything in science, especially if it pertained to nature.

"I went to Stockholm against my usual custom," he explained to Boveri, "but since the celebration included three or four persons and since I had to take part in it for only a day and a half, I could endure being feted. I must say," he added, "that the Swedes understand how to do that sort of thing in a simple, yet dignified manner."

Wilhelm Röntgen received the award the following evening, on December 10, the anniversary of the death of Alfred Nobel. The large hall of the Music Academy was filled with invited guests representing the governments of various nations and the elite of the professions of the

Scandinavian countries. The diploma, the gold medal, and the money prize were awarded in an elaborately staged ceremony by the Swedish Crown Prince, "in recognition of the extraordinary services you have rendered by the discovery of the remarkable rays which have been subsequently named after you."

Wilhelm Röntgen spoke a few words in response immediately after the opulent dinner that followed the impressive ceremony, saying in his quiet, soft voice, that he appreciated immensely the singular honor and that this recognition would certainly be an effective stimulant to him to greater unselfish activity in science, which he hoped would benefit all mankind.

Contrary to the custom which was then being initiated, Röntgen did not give an official Nobel lecture, as did the other recipients before the large selected audience. In his typical generous manner, Wilhelm Röntgen willed the prize money (150,800 Kroner, or $41,800 at the then prevailing rate of exchange) to the University of Würzburg for use in the interest of science. He valued highly the leather-bound richly decorated, gold-bordered parchment from the *Kongliga Svenska Vetenskaps–Akademien* in its fine brown leather folio. This Physical Society of Stockholm awarded Röntgen an Honorable Membership in their society, but he did not attend the meeting.

In Munich, the social life of the Röntgens in this *Königstadt* was quite different from the easier and rather carefree atmosphere of the smaller Würzburg circle of society. They had not made any close friends among the colleagues at the university, but the Zehnders spent many sociable hours with them. The friends from the Würzburg and the Giessen universities they saw now but seldom, except on vacations. These happy and gay times were spent, as in former years, in the regular places. In the spring the Röntgens vacationed on the Italian Riviera (in 1902, 1904, 1905, and 1906), staying at the Grand Hotel des Alps, Territet (1901), or at the Grand Hotel Miramare in Santa Margharita-Ligure, where they enjoyed the magic view of the lovely Gulf of Portofino. In 1902 they visited Florence during the Easter vacations, enjoying the expansive gardens at the Palazzo Pitti, and the unique collections of art in the galleries, under the expert guidance of Fräulein Sachs, a painter and daughter of a Würzburg professor.

The *grossen Ferien* during the summer were spent, as always, in their long-accustomed place, the Engadin, and the new Park Hotel, just above the older Weisses Kreuz. Here, all of their friends from Würzburg and Giessen would meet and the weeks would be crowded with picnics and

The Nobel Prize document and medal awarded to Röntgen in 1901.

hikes into the countryside, with mountain-climbing expeditions, or merely leisurely drives in the landaulet of Kutscher Schmidt. During inclement weather, the congenial group would gather around tables in the spacious card room of their hotel and play cards.

This was a tremendous contrast to the formal social life in Munich. The Prince Regent invited the Röntgens several times to state gala affairs, where his table partner was usually the Princess Therese, a well-educated young woman whose company Röntgen enjoyed. After the provocative conversation with the Princess had ended, Röntgen relished talking to the *Prinzregent,* as ardent a hunter as Röntgen himself. Those were delightful evenings. But members of the official court and higher government circle were not as gracious as their Regent. The nobility had, of course, never forgiven Wilhelm Röntgen for refusing the offered title when he was so honored by Luitpold. Eventually, the Röntgens refused all formal dinner invitations because of Bertha's poor health.

The bountiful cultural attractions of the city compensated for much of the dissatisfaction with their social life. There were more activities in art, especially in the field of music, than in any other city of Germany, including even the capital, Berlin. The Röntgens frequently attended the concerts of famous artists of the world. They attended an occasional opera, which they liked less than instrumental offerings.

Wilhelm Röntgen loved the proximity of their home to the fine Englischen Garten; the garden being situated between the home and the institute of the university, he walked through the garden twice daily. Occasionally he and Bertha chose it for their mutual afternoon walks. Covering an area of some six hundred acres, the park had a wonderful collection of old stately trees, wide expanses of grassy meadows and selected shrubs and fine flowerbeds, all abundantly watered by two convenient fast-flowing arms of the Isar river. The Röntgens would stop on their delightful walks, passing the Dianabad at the delicate Monopteros temple atop a hill, from where they could see the many towers of the various churches of the city, the cupolas of the Residenzpalast, and the uneven twin-helmeted towers of the historic *Frauenkirche* dominating the scene. The Dianabad, a unique Greek-style temple, had been erected by Ludwig I in 1837 to honor the Churfürsten Karl Theodor who created the huge park toward the end of the eighteenth century and to König Maximilian I who added to the project and dedicated it to the enjoyment of his subjects. The small lake, the Kleinhesseloher See, added to the pleasures with its majestic swans and frolicsome ducks. After watching the antics of the tame waterfowl, Bertha and Wilhelm eventually arrived at one of the *Waldgaststätten,* usually the restaurant at the foot of the five-tiered wooden Chinesischen Turm with pointed wooden roofs and golden bells on its corners, for their afternoon refreshments — *Bohnenkaffee* and a piece of favorite pastry,

Schwarzwälder Kirschtorte. From the Chinese tower they crossed the Isar on a wooden bridge to suburban Bogenhausen and their home. These extensive paths in the park also offered a splendid and quite magnificent view of the old city below with the distant Alpine mountains.

Sometimes the Röntgens would take an open carriage to distant Schloss Nymphenberg, patterned after Versailles and once the favorite palace residence of Max Joseph I. Here they walked through the extensive parks and well-kept formal gardens with marble statuary, and they visited the adjoining Botanical Gardens, where many exquisite plants and exotic flowers were being raised. It was a nature lover's paradise indeed, and the Röntgens visited it joyfully. They easily spent a whole afternoon, having fine *Kaffee und Torte* in the outdoor restaurant, or even in the smaller Cafe in one of the greenhouses where they sat near an open glass panel to escape the terrible humidity, before being driven through the city to their home on the opposite side of town.

Röntgen's singular liking for the rich *Schwarzwälder Kirschtorte* had come in for good-natured ribbing from his colleagues, especially Theodor Boveri, who suggested that Röntgen always ordered it because of his love of the two thick layers of whipped cream in the *Torte*. But Röntgen countered soberly that it was actually his curious fondness for cherries which made him prefer this rich pastry to others, such as *Nuss-, Mokka-,* or *Obsttorte*. "And since only one solitary solid cherry graces each portion of the *Torte,* I have to eat an exceedingly large number of pieces to satisfy the yearning for that particular and so beneficial fruit." He refused to consider at all the few crushed fruit found also in the thin layer. The *Torte* consisted of a white cake base, then a layer of crushed cherries, of whipped cream, of chocolate cake, all topped with white icing and chipped chocolate flakes, and a glacé cherry in a whipped cream rosette atop each piece.

The Röntgens enjoyed the walks in the large gardens, but Wilhelm actually preferred the wilder areas, the open fields, and the deep forests, untouched or merely cleared of accumulated dead vegetation by human hands. Nature fascinated Röntgen, and he often stopped during a walk to marvel at the beauty of a leaf on a bush or a rock in the path, becoming so absorbed in the miracle of creation that he was completely lost in thought, entirely oblivious to surroundings. There was so much hidden in every single created thing, and it was for men like him to find the mysteries of God's wonderful creations and to make them available for the good of all mankind. "What are the substances of this rock?" he might ask aloud, before realizing that he really addressed himself and not his companion; he then would sheepishly march on.

Always an enthusiastic hunter, Wilhelm Röntgen leased an area of the Gögerl hunting grounds for several years, and in 1904 found a villa in Weilheim which, slightly remodeled, became their cherished vacation home. A fairly large garden, with space for flowers and vegetables, was tended by Bertha to some extent, the spading and actual planting being done by the hired help, but all closely supervised by her. The house was unpretentiously furnished but comfortable, with an especially large and extensive library. The place gained in their favor from year to year, and they found it a pleasant spot to come to during the long periods of work at the institute when it was impossible to get away into the mountains of Switzerland. From the comfort of their own living room they could see the vast expanse of the incomparable valley with the strikingly beautiful Bavarian Alps, from the Allgäu to the Karwendel mountains as a backdrop.

In time the Röntgens kept ever more to themselves. They had but a limited acquaintance with other colleagues at Munich, with whom they socialized. One of the reasons was the occasional attacks of pain Bertha would suffer. This aggravated illness caused both of them much agitation, and only those friends and colleagues who knew about it were ever invited to their home. The Röntgens were most reluctant to accept invitations to other homes for fear that such appearances would have to be canceled embarrassingly at the last minute. Their intimate friends in Würzburg and Giessen understood that problem well, but in Munich the situation was quite different.

When Anna Trippi came to visit in Munich, Röntgen proudly showed this young "country girl" from Pontresina the great *Königstadt.* Anna was well educated and spoke fluently not only German but Italian, French, and English. This was her first visit to a metropolis, however. After every sightseeing trip, the 19-year-old Anna had to describe her impressions of what she had seen that day. Stimulated by her immense enthusiasm and intelligence, Röntgen showed her all of the *Sehenswürdigkeiten,* and they enjoyed these sights together. Anna noted that her host was liberal but very accurate with his money; he kept close track of all expenditures. When he was short ten marks, while writing down his expenses for the day at home, he would try his best to recall just how it was spent. And when he failed to account for the entire amount, he was very angry with himself.

During the full month of her stay, Anna had a good opportunity to observe the eminent Röntgens in their own home and contrast this behavior with that during their summer vacations at the Weisses Kreuz and the Park Hotel.

Years later Anna Saratz-Trippi recalled that she was amazed at the huge amounts of food they all ate. A few hours after the large breakfast, complete with fresh rolls just delivered by the baker's boy, came a second slightly smaller breakfast, then the main noon dinner, afternoon coffee and cake with whipped cream, and finally the evening meal, a full course supper.

Frau Röntgen did most of the shopping while Anna was there. Taking a *Droschke,* always with the same driver, she went to the large *Markthalle* where she habitually purchased more than the cook could possibly use. The food bought was the finest quality — potatoes and tomatoes from Holland, butter from East Prussia, and vegetables and fruit in season.

At dinner Röntgen himself cut the meat with a long-bladed knife of superb steel. With great aplomb he carved the roast into extremely thin slices and served the plates to everyone at the table. In the kitchen, the servants ate of the same food. One time, while cutting the meat, Röntgen sneezed. Bertha was almost beside herself. A rather heated exchange on sanitary conduct and contamination arose between the two and continued during the entire meal.

Frau Doktor Röntgen was *sehr penible,* very fussy, about almost everything and was usually difficult to please. Because of her primarily neurotic illness, Bertha demanded much solicitous attention from everyone around, Anna noted, especially from her husband, who lovingly pampered her and handled her like a child, catering to her every whim and wish.

The young girl from Pontresina recalled, however, that Frau Röntgen never interfered with her husband's work habits and made no special demands on his laboratory time. Usually, at night, when Röntgen worked late, Bertha sent Käthe downstairs to remind him to quit and to go to bed. Anna Trippi also gained the impression that Bertha was just the right wife for Wilhelm Röntgen, that he was able to work at his experiments just as he pleased, and that she really made no interfering claims on his work time. Anna once overheard Bertha tell Käthe, *"Ich wünschte, mein Kätchen, Sie hätten so einen guten Mann wie ich"* — I wish, Kätchen, that you had such a good man as I have.

During the late fall of 1901, the Röntgens visited briefly in Würzburg; soon after, it was decided that Bertha was too ill to accompany Röntgen to Stockholm for the Nobel Prize ceremonies. She then wrote to Frau Boveri, on November 2:

We followed our plan, after all, and went on to Würzburg for four days. The time was much too short, but it was better than to postpone the trip again. We also went to the garden of the institute and were happy to see that it was well kept. But how different it is from our old garden, which we miss so much. Though they are now building at the institute, and fall is coming, the garden should have looked better. Many of the roses were destroyed by frost and have not been replaced. Of course, it is none of my business, but I cared for this garden for so many years that I was actually irritated. But enough of that.

It was most gratifying to see how warmly everyone in Würzburg greeted us, and we felt as much at home as if we had never gone away. Unfortunately, the weather was not very good during the first three days. These were gray autumn days, and the Rimparer Wald did not look quite as good as it usually does in the fall. Still, we were as happy as children to be back at our little forest home and to take a good rest. We were rewarded for our patience by beautiful weather on the last day — the recollection of which we brought back here.

A year later, on December 27, 1902, Bertha wrote again in that same reminiscent and nostalgic mood:

If only my most sincere wish would come true — that we could live again in the same place with you. The times with our good friends in Würzburg were beautiful, we were always so congenial and could discuss things of common interest. Here, everything appears rather cold to me. I do not complain, for as long as one has no common understanding, one has nothing to lose.

CHAPTER 17

X Equals Electromagnetic

IN 1902 THE CARNEGIE INSTITUTE in Washington was established "to engage in research in the physical and biological sciences." This operating organization, which was to use its funds for the support of five research departments, invited Wilhelm Röntgen to Washington to use their superbly equipped laboratories to carry out any special investigation of his choice. He was enormously tempted to accept, but finally refused the opportunity at that time. From then on he had an ever-increasing desire to visit the United States. Ten years later he would make tentative plans to accept several New World invitations from a number of scientific societies to attend their meetings, and also to visit with the relatives in Ohio. Those plans, made in 1912, never materialized because of war threats.

That year, 1902, the *Instituto de Coimbra* of Portugal made Röntgen an honorary member, and the following year the Philosophical Society of Cambridge and the *Röntgen-Gesellschaft* of Berlin elected him to an honorary membership. *The Reale Accademia della Scienze* of Turin made him a corresponding member.

During the spring vacation of 1903, Bertha Röntgen contracted a persistent cough, and the stay at the Italian Riviera seemed to have little effect in abating the condition. They extended their stay there, and when the situation looked better they went to Lugano, on the orders of the doctor. After a pleasant week or two at the Hotel D'Europe, they reluctantly returned to the nasty climate of Munich and the household problems, both conditions which would greatly bother Bertha, Röntgen wrote. He had celebrated his fifty-eighth birthday that March, and Bertha was sixty-four years old that April.

That winter the Röntgens went briefly to Dorf Davos over the Christmas and the New Year's holidays, and from the Hotel Fuela he wrote that they had a wonderful sleigh ride with clear sunshine and skies.

But while again in Ligure in March, 1904, Bertha was once more quite ill, and he did not feel well enough to undertake any hikes into the surrounding areas. They rented a carriage instead for all of their outings.

While the routine of teaching and experimenting at the institute did not appreciably change during the school year, occasional situations arose which interrupted the usual regularity. During one of his closer inspection tours Röntgen noticed that some of the unused apparatus in a glass cabinet had gathered considerable dust, and he suggested to Zehnder that the two lesser assistants should certainly have kept this equipment clean. When Zehnder, in turn, admonished his colleagues, they objected, claiming that such cleaning work was really the responsibility of the *Institut-Diener* and not theirs. This argument eventually reached Röntgen, who then sided with the two younger men against Zehnder. Zehnder was humiliated by the whole affair, an argument arose, and finally Zehnder resigned his position in anger. He accepted a post at the newly created physics research department of the telegraph company in Berlin. Abraham Joffé, a Russian physicist, took his place.

The Prussian state government offered Wilhelm Röntgen the position of president of the *Physikalisch-Technischen Reichsanstalt* in Berlin-Charlottenburg. The eminent Friedrich Kohlrausch was ill, and the minister of culture wanted a worthy successor to him. It was a politically important post, and occasionally great political tact and clever diplomacy were needed to smoothly adjudge controversies so that each contestant believed himself emerging with a moral victory. This sort of expedient diplomacy definitely was not one of Röntgen's abilities, a fact he well recognized. In turning down the position, he stated that he could accomplish all he wanted to do "right here in Munich."

At the institute he was often called *der Unzugängliche,* or the Unapproachable, by his colleagues. He became more involved in his laboratory work than previously and showed increasingly less and less interest in social activities, mainly because of Bertha's continuous illness. The lectures before his large student audience — 430 registered students attended regularly — were extraordinarily well prepared, requiring much time and effort, as carefully thought through as his previous work. His attitude toward the students had not changed, and those who did not do their very best work felt his wrath. Those who worked diligently and tried hard found him a most willing listener, rather easily approachable, ready to assist or to clear up a perplexing problem by simple direct reasoning concerning any difficult question. He expected sharp observations and accurate measurements from those who conducted experiments under his tutelage.

One student, Franz Fuchs, thirty years later remembered that a small sign reading *Das Berühren der Apparate ist verboten* — The touching of the equipment is prohibited — was always prominently displayed on the demonstration table in the lecture hall. When a student touched something, Professor Röntgen would become most angry and berate him. But when the professor would show an X ray photograph in connection with the lecture on electricity, the entire student group would loudly trample their applause. Then the slightly embarrassed professor would say, *"Ich danke Ihnen, meine Herren"* — I thank you, my gentlemen. After the short pause, he would continue with the lecture.

The *Gesellschaft der Aerzte* of Vienna elected Wilhelm Röntgen an honorary member of their society, and the city council of Köln (Cologne) voted to name one of their streets the Röntgenstrasse, in 1904.

The year 1905 was the tenth anniversary of the discovery of the X rays, and March 27 marked the sixtieth birthday of their discoverer. To honor Röntgen in a special manner was suggested by Ludwig Zehnder to Friedrich Kohlrausch in Berlin, and at that meeting the plan was hatched to erect a commemorative tablet at the Würzburg Institute where the discovery had been made. Max Planck worked out the wording of the text, and Willy Wien, Röntgen's successor at Würzburg, arranged to have the plaque attached to the building. A number of scientists were contacted and invited to participate, but they were asked to be discreet about the matter so that it would come as a surprise to Röntgen. Zehnder wrote to Bertha Röntgen that a certain letter should be held until the birthday and then be opened in the presence of her husband, so that he would receive the enclosed envelope at the correct time. The plan went well, and on his birthday Röntgen read the letter:

Sehr verehrter Herr Kollege: This year marks the *dezennium* since you have presented mankind with the great discovery of your rays. You have opened a new path with it in our science and have pressed for great successes within a short time. Almost every year has brought new discoveries through follow-up of your discovery, and this has led to other fundamental events.

In the name of a commission of German scientists we would like to express this feeling of thanks, and we have attached a tablet at the place of your great discovery at the Physical Science Institute of Würzburg:

IN DIESEM HAUSE ENTDECKTE
W. C. RÖNTGEN IM JAHRE 1895
DIE NACH IHM BENANNTEN STRAHLEN
[In this house W. C. Röntgen discovered in the year
1895 the rays named after him.]
Signed: L. Boltzmann, F. Braun, P. Drude, H. Ebert, L. Graetz, F. Kohlrausch, H. A. Lorentz, M. Planck, E. Riecke, E. Warburg, W. Wien, O. Wiener, L. Zehnder.

The action by these friends came as a complete surprise to Röntgen. He was unaware that anything unusual had been planned for his honor on that day, and he felt most gratified and quite humble when he wrote a longer letter of appreciation to Zehnder, Kohlrausch, Planck, and Wien. He wrote shorter notes of thanks to the other signers of what he referred to as his "diploma," for their kind remembrance of the event. Röntgen also noted that Philipp Lenard had not participated in the greeting.

When this part of the institute was remodeled in 1937, the marble tablet was removed and the same inscription in enlarged letters was chiseled into the wall, actually the walled-in window of the laboratory where the phenomenal discovery was made.

During the closing period of World War II, on the night of March 16, 1945, some 240,000 incendiary bombs were dropped on Würzburg in twenty minutes of concentrated effort, and within three hours nearly the entire city was burning. The two-hundred high-explosive bombs which followed completed the destruction. Amazingly, only three direct hits were suffered by the institute itself, which resulted in only minor damage to the building. It was eventually completely restored.

About a month after the birthday honor, a group of outstanding Röntgenologists planned to hold a *Röntgen-Kongress* in Berlin to commemorate the tenth anniversary of the discovery of the X rays. An invitation to attend these festivities was sent to Wilhelm Röntgen, but he was most displeased by what he considered an usurpation of his rights and invasion of his privacy, despite the finest intentions of his admiring colleagues: Richard Eberlein, Max Immelmann, Walter Cowl, Hermann Gocht, Heinrich Albers-Schönberg, Hermann Rieder, B. Walter, Rudolf Grashey, and Alban Köhler, who planned the meeting which opened on April 30, under the auspices of the Berlin Röntgen Society, the *Deutsche Röntgen Gesellschaft,* a national organization, founded on May 2, 1905.

From Munich, the discoverer of the X rays had written angrily to Ludwig Zehnder, "Of course I shall not go to the Congress in Berlin which bears my name without my permission. I cannot understand how my friends could do such a thing to me!"

Yet, upon the founding of the society the group made Wilhelm Conrad Röntgen their first honorary member, and his anger apparently had subsided sufficiently to permit him to send the following congratulating telegram:

Please accept my most sincere thanks for the greetings sent to me by the executive committee in the name of the members of the Congress. Please let me assure you that I am filled with joy and admiration over the work which others, many of whom are now united in this Congress, have derived from the discovery of the X rays. Röntgen.

Two other honors came to Wilhelm Röntgen that year when the Society for the Encouragement of Arts at London and the Medico-Chirurgical Society of Edinburgh made him an honorable member of their societies. The following year the Royal Institution of Great Britain at London did likewise.

Röntgen, almost since his arrival in Munich, had been a member of the board of trustees of the Deutsches Museum in that city. He enjoyed the post and attended the meetings regularly. He took great pride in this remarkable institution, which quickly established itself as one of the finest in the world. But he could never forget the humiliating embarrassment he had once suffered because of this institution.

Wilhelm Röntgen was no public speaker. There is only this one instance known when he spoke at a formal occasion before a large audience. What was probably his greatest failure occurred at the *Grundsteinlegung,* the foundation stone laying, ceremonies for the Deutsches Museum at Munich in 1903. He was asked to give the *Festrede* before a prominent audience of the ruler and highest dignitaries of the state. He tried hard to be excused, but the founder, the illustrious Oskar von Miller insisted, and Röntgen was forced to agree to make the festive speech.

As Käthe Fuchs recalled, while Röntgen was being dressed in the prescribed gala dress suit, complete with wide ribbon across his chest and orders on his breast, his face turned white, he shook with much nervousness and could hardly talk coherently. When a newspaper reporter came to ask for a copy of his dedicatory speech, Röntgen brusquely told him that he should wait until he had actually made it. Then, before the huge audience of leaders in politics, in the military, and in education, Röntgen became so flustered that he merely stammered and fumbled and hardly got any words out. Few, if any at all, of his audience understood him and the local newspapers carried no text of the speech in their coverage of this significant event, so important in the history of their city. The reporters felt perhaps that this one time they were indeed cooperating with the reluctant Röntgen, but not for the same reason. As main speaker at the ceremonies he received the least publicity of all. This dismal performance was to be his last appearance at any open public function as a speaker, and the event was never referred to in his presence.

In 1906, when Röntgen retired from the board, the museum issued a commemorative folder in his honor.

Ten years had gone by since the momentous discovery, and Röntgen had published only one paper since that time, "Explanation" (1904). His own investigations, as far as they pertained to the X rays, concerned the physical character of the rays rather than the practical applications or even the technical improvements in the actual production of the rays. These other investigations generally were made by other scientists, often trained by Röntgen. Upon his urging, a separate department, closely affiliated with his own physics department, was established in 1906 at the institute of the Munich university. The department of theoretical physics was headed by Arnold Sommerfeld, and Wilhelm Röntgen followed with intense interest the studies and findings made by these other physicists. His own observations Röntgen published in a paper "On the Conductivity of Electricity in Calcium Spar and on the Influence of X rays on it" (1907).

Ever since he had come to the Ludwig-Maximilians-*Universität* in 1900, Röntgen had pressed for the establishment of the department of theoretical physics. Finally the professorship which he, as head of the entire department, could fill with any suitable person, was established. Röntgen "could not understand why Munich could not do as well as Leipzig, Berlin, or Göttingen," where, he felt, "the best conditions existed in most respects." The authorities did not agree with his viewpoint, however. The Minister of Culture, Wehner, in the eyes of Geheimrat Professor Wilhelm Conrad Röntgen, was merely a little bureaucrat. From his vacation spot at Santa Margherita, in a letter dated March 31, 1905, Röntgen commented on this situation to Theodor Boveri:

So many things could be so beautiful and good in Munich, if there were not some people who are chiefly convinced of their own importance — however, without sufficient reason. In addition to this, the Minister of Culture is a bureaucrat and has no real interest in the development and progress of the university, probably because he is not familiar with the conditions. It is really a miracle and a sign of great inner strength that science in Germany makes so much progress in spite of ministers and other impediments. You probably know that I am indebted particularly to the direct initiative of the Prince Regent, whom I esteem very highly, that a considerable amount of money was suddenly made available for the salary of Professor Lorentz of Leiden, who was to be called to Munich. Probably you know that I was sent by our ministry to Leiden, and that Lorentz finally declined their offer after due consideration because all of his demands had been met in Holland. This is a great pity. I believe that the two of us could have established physics on an excellent basis in Munich.

Two years later the situation in Munich had still not changed appreciably. The new department had been established headed by Sommerfeld, but Röntgen was less than totally satisfied with the developments. While he did not have close friends at the institute, with whom to discuss these matters, he usually unburdened himself to his old friends at Giessen and Würzburg, and he found that during the vacation times he had the best opportunity to write long letters to them. From Rigi he wrote on August 14, 1907, to Boveri:

I do not need to tell you with how very much pleasure I had looked forward to meeting you again. Disregarding all the other reasons you can realize how true this must be if you consider in what isolation I live in Munich and how I miss the mental stimulation which I received so often from you.

In commenting on some of the new ambitious development programs at the Würzburg university, Röntgen was "happy about the fresh breeze that comes from there," and then he suggests that "the air in Munich is so stagnant, you have no idea."

Significant observations were being published by several scientists. Among the more important ones were: "On the best Effect in the Process of Absorption of Röntgen Rays," by E. Angerer; another by E. Bassler on "The Polarization of Röntgen Rays"; and Walter Friedrich's "The Distribution of Intensity and Quality of Röntgen Rays around the Target." Röntgen encouraged his younger colleagues in these research projects and took a lively interest in them. As suggested by Friedrich:

The constantly growing significance of all these discoveries filled Röntgen with a certain pride in having given to humanity so great a blessing, and occasionally one could see a quiet gleam of happiness in his eyes when one overcame one's shyness and reported to him some new development in connection with the rays, especially if it lay outside his immediate field of interest.

The main research work at the Theoretical Physics Department was directed to the identification of the true nature of the X rays, and the answer to this so terribly perplexing question was finally found there, but not until six years later. In 1912 Friedrich and Paul Knipping worked on a theoretical suggestion made by Max von Laue, that X rays are electromagnetic waves, similar to visible light or radio waves; these men were able to obtain the first X ray diffraction patterns. After repeating the experiments several times to ascertain their correctness, Friedrich invited Wilhelm Röntgen to see the apparatus they used and to confirm the resultant pictures of this momentous observation.

Röntgen listened attentively to the explanations of the method used by the younger scientists, examined the evidence thoroughly and critically, and then declared that he could find no experimental error in the procedure. But he still hesitated to accept the pictures as uncontestable proof of the theory. Offering congratulations to Walter Friedrich for the splendid work done he added, "You know, I do not think that these are interference phenomena. They just look different to me."

Having himself worked on the problem for years and having failed in the attempt to discover the true character of the X rays, it was probably too difficult for the sixty-seven-year-old Röntgen to accept the fact that these younger scientists had actually been successful where he had not been able to penetrate the mystery. In his First Communication he had written, "I have often looked for interference phenomena of X rays, but unfortunately without success." Subsequent experiments brought no better results.

However, within a short time after the visit to the laboratory of Friedrich and Knipping, Röntgen became convinced that the pictures, which he had examined so carefully, actually demonstrated interference phenomena of X rays. This would then classify them with visible light, ultra-violet light, and all other related sections of the electromagnetic spectrum as transversal waves.

It was generally recognized that in the experiments made by Friedrich and Knipping, based on the theories of von Laue, the first fundamentally new contribution to the knowledge of the nature of X rays was made since the time when Röntgen had first published his papers some sixteen years before. Other valuable discoveries were that of secondary cathode rays made by Emil Dorn and that of the polarization of the X rays by Charles G. Barkla. These findings were confirmed by experiments made in the Munich Institute by Ernst Wagner and Robert Glocker, on the monochromatic character of the diffracted rays. And the father and son team of William Henry and William Laurence Bragg of England also made contributory studies on this matter.

While radio waves are about 10,000 centimeters in length, X rays are about 0.000,000,001 centimeters, and gamma rays — actually short-wave X rays created from radioactive material instead of X ray tubes — are about 0.000,000,000,1 centimeters. Electric tension is measured in volts, and X rays are measured in roentgens. One roentgen (1 r) releases in 1 cm^3 air at 0° and 760 mm baromatic pressure, one unit of electric tension.

In 1907 the *Societa Italiana delle Scienze* of Rome made Röntgen a nonresident member, and the Royal Academy of Sciences of Amsterdam gave him an honorary membership. The following year he received two honorary memberships from foreign countries when the Society of Physicians of Stockholm and the German Medical Society of New York bestowed honors. As a Christmas present the Prince Regent of Bavaria gave Wilhelm Röntgen the title of His Excellency. In 1909 the city fathers of Würzburg named a street after him, thus making that city the second in Germany to have a Röntgenstrasse; and the town of Weilheim named him an honorary citizen. The next year, the *Deutschen Nervenärzte* and the *Berliner Medizinische Gesellschaft* made Röntgen an honorary member of their groups.

The Saxon city of Halle an der Saale made one of its streets a Röntgenstrasse in 1911, the Society of Physicians of Smolensk made Röntgen an honorary member of its society, and he was awarded the order

Pour le Merite for Science and Art from his government. The following year he received a special Russian diploma from the Odessa Society, and the Deutsches Museum in Munich heard an address by him at the time of his election to a life membership of the museum — but delivered to a very small group of representatives of the board.

Emissaries from the Prussian *Akademie der Wissenschaften* at Berlin came to visit Röntgen in Munich in an effort to persuade him to accept the position held by Jacobus Hendricus van't Hoff, who had received a Nobel prize at the same time Röntgen did. But without giving the matter long consideration, he turned down the offer to head that institute.

Bertha was continually ailing, and Röntgen was in no mood at all to make another move, even to that highly desirable post. In fact, he had been seriously considering a visit to the United States of America, but the failing health of his wife made the mutual trip impossible, and he would not consider leaving Bertha at home while he undertook a long sea voyage.

When the unofficial inquiry was first made by representatives of the Berlin Academy — the Prussian ministry of culture had to obtain a formal release from the Bavarian ministry of culture before Röntgen could be offered the post — the Bavarian minister, Wehner, called the Geheimrat Röntgen into his office to discuss the matter. Röntgen, completely surprised, was silent at first. The minister, believing that Röntgen was giving the matter serious and favorable consideration, offered him a substantial salary increase to induce him to remain in Bavaria. This offer did not interest the Geheimrat at all, but it did give him an opportunity to present his request for more time to devote to his laboratory work and to suggest that he be named professor emeritus, so that he could arrange his own work schedule. At the age of sixty-seven he was too young to retire entirely, but if he could dispense with the burdensome administration and teaching schedule altogether, he would be perfectly happy to remain in Munich. Further negotiations on the question of the Academy position were not held, and the whole proposition was never officially pursued.

The vague promise by the minister of culture to arrange for an early emeritus professorship was the best Röntgen could achieve. The Berlin post he had not wanted at all, but it had served as a convenient vehicle to make his wishes known to the ministry. To became professor emeritus at the age of seventy would suit Röntgen perfectly.

CHAPTER 18

The Forest Haven in Weilheim

THE COMFORTABLE HOUSE on the southern edge of Weilheim's Krottenkopfstrasse was the one great pleasure of Röntgen's life. It made life in Munich bearable. In moments of ecstasy he referred to it as his *Jagdschloss,* but it was hardly the elegant and opulent hunting lodge suggested by that term. The white stucco villa had an upstairs wooden balcony extending half around the house, affording a splendid view of the spacious garden below, the Gögerl and the surrounding forests and meadows and the distant mountainous terrain rising toward the snowy-peaked Alps. The wooden covered gables of the four third-story servants' rooms gave the *Jagdhäusli* a rustic appearance. Originally meant to serve as a week-end home for hunting expeditions into the adjoining forests, it soon became the favorite summer and week-end vacation place where he and Bertha had an opportunity to relax completely.

On the walls of his own room Röntgen kept some of his trophies — a fine black grouse cock, a hawk with a prairie chicken in its talons, a small chicken hawk, and other birds. His hunting equipment, the shotguns, leather cases for the binoculars, small red bag for ammunition, larger woven hunting bag for game birds, and the walking cane with its triangular folding seat attachment, were all kept in a wardrobe with glass doors. He also kept the heavy alpine ax and ice pick there. On his desk he had an inkwell upon stag horns, and his round leather wastebasket had an embossed stag design.

The small parties with a few intimate friends — generally visitors from Würzburg and Giessen — were the high spots of the couple's limited social activities. Located some thirty-five miles from Munich, the Weilheim lodge served as a pleasant retreat where close friends would come out to hike or to hunt in season during the day, and after a fine day's invigorating outing in the field or forest would return to the *Häusli* for a hearty dinner. Then, after the meal when the men exchanged hunting stories, Röntgen would be the most convivial of hosts. In small groups he was at his genial best. Whenever he enjoyed a story — either his own or a friend's — he would fill the room with deep hearty ringing laughter, as he had done in his student days in Zurich.

When he was especially gay, Röntgen would entertain his guests with some ingeniously conceived laboratory equipment, to "demonstrate some of the very experiments made at the institute." One of these hilarious demonstrations was the "Simplified X Ray Experiment."

A small, cleverly constructed oblong wooden box contained four wooden blocks, each numbered from one to four. While Röntgen would be out of the room, his guests were free to rearrange these blocks in any way they wished. Then he returned and inspected the box most thoroughly, holding an obviously empty shell over the container, and looking into the shell he would name the proper sequence of the individual blocks correctly. It worked every time. There was absolutely nothing to see in the shell when shown to the amazed guests. The secret was that a minute compass was embedded in the bottom of the shell, and small magnets were fastened to the wooden blocks, arranged in differing order in each case. Number one had the magnet on the top, number two on the bottom, number three on the right side, and number four on the left side. The compass pointed to the north for the number one block, to the south for number two, to the west for number three and east for number four, enabling Röntgen to recognize quickly and easily the position of the hidden blocks in the box.

Röntgen's hunting lodge at Weilheim.

Another entertaining curiosity was an old barometer that he claimed to have discovered in an ancient cloister in the Bavarian mountains. This consisted of a rope fastened to a small board on which instructions for the correct weather observations were printed. A humid rope indicated bad weather, a dry and flexible one fair and warm weather conditions. This form of lay meteorology and physics amused Röntgen as much as it did his guests.

With warmth and affection he showed his guests the small model of his birth-house, which his father had given him years before in Holland. After taking it carefully apart and explaining the various rooms, he returned it to its place of honor in the guest room, atop a specially built stand.

But for as many years as possible, the Röntgens traveled to their favorite places to spend the vacations with their old friends. In 1906 Röntgen wrote from Weilheim that "because of the poor health of my wife, the doctor had allowed us to go to Rigi-Scheidegg for only two weeks and then over the Klausenpass to Pontresina by carriage for only a week, but we will meet the von Hippel, Krönlein, and perhaps the Boveri families there, and that will be a fine compensation for the limited time allotted to be away."

To celebrate Röntgen's birthday in 1907, he and Bertha were again in Cadenabbia and, as he wrote, "lived here surrounded by dear friends: Messling and his wife left yesterday. Hofmeier and wife and daughters, Boveri with wife and daughter, the Damen Vögeli, Krönlein, and Stöhr, and also the Gareis family, most of whom live in our hotel, others in the near vicinity." He did not comment on Bertha's health.

But when the following year they went to Cadenabbia for his birthday and the Easter vacations, Bertha suffered from advanced anemia. She showed some improvement soon, and Wilhelm also "felt greatly improved from the fresh air, believing that the climate actually was superior to that of the Riviera, especially for people who are in need of recuperation." However, he believed that the rapid change in temperatures was perhaps not the best for such complaints as coughs and roughness of the throat, as his wife had, and he hoped that the climate would not have a detrimental effect on her. After the short stay they were quite anxious to get back to their Weilheim place.

The Weilheim *Jagdhaus* was preferred as residence to their large apartment on the Aeussere Prinzregenten Strasse in Munich, and they spent ever longer periods of their time there. In May, 1908, Röntgen described a typical activity of his during the years when Bertha was constantly ailing.

On one particular day — during the game bird hunting season —
he had risen at two o'clock in the morning, rousted his dog, and after
a short carriage ride had hiked through the dense woods in thick morning
fog for nearly an hour to the hunting grounds. He carried a lantern to find
the way to the shooting blind of birch branches, to await the dawn and
the birds. He became so absorbed in watching the antics of the game
birds, pheasants, grouse, quail, snipe, that he failed to fire his gun at all
and returned a wiser bird watcher than a hunter. "I got only a *Schnupfen,*
a head cold," he said then, "but no *Schnepfen,* no snipes!"

Another time, however, he shot two fine grouse at about four o'clock,
and was exceedingly proud of his bag. "In time," he said, "the measure
of achievements change, and it is the act itself of which one is proud."
After such a brisk outing he would breakfast and take a train to Munich,
and in the afternoon would be back attending his duties at the institute.

The next year, when the physician suggested that Bertha take a daily
leisurely walk of two hours and spend as much time as possible outdoors,
the couple remained at Weilheim for several months. Röntgen took more
strenuous hikes into the deep forest and did some hunting during the fall;
meantime Bertha took her walks, usually accompanied by their trusted
Käthe, who had been with them since 1898, first as a maid and then as
cook and housekeeper. When Käthe and Frau Röntgen walked together
it was at a rather brisk pace, but Käthe noticed that when Herr Doktor
joined Bertha for the "daily dozen," Bertha had the appearance of an
invalid in need of much sympathy. Röntgen never failed to give the
desired sympathy in loving measure.

That year Röntgen spent much of his time writing reports on his
observations. His notes had accumulated, and the work might later be
published. For their Christmas vacations ever since 1903 they had preferred Dorf Davos to any other place. The invigorating atmosphere and
the mountainous scenery were so to the Röntgens' personal pleasure that
they had returned every Christmas since then, and would do so until 1912.
Wilhelm Röntgen especially enjoyed the surrounding area with its deep
snow-covered slopes glistening brightly in the daily sunshine. He was
fond of tobogganing and often raced wildly down the steep slopes of the
Schatzalp, to his utmost delight and to the expressed fear of his wife.
With her, he took the more sedate sleigh rides behind a team of horses with
tinkling bells. Relaxed in the comfortable seats of the vehicle, they were
warmed by the thick layers of several woolen blankets.

During the 1908 vacations the Röntgens went as frequently as possible on pleasurable outings in an effort to ease Bertha's nervous tension.
For some while now she had been absorbed with the plans of the forth-

coming marriage of their "little" Berteli, scheduled for the coming March. The Davos weeks, however, proved only temporary relief from those anxieties.

The wedding of Berteli and the young military doctor, Stabsarzt Rudolph Donges, was a small family affair. Bertha Röntgen was too ill to go out, so the ceremony was performed in their home. As the bride recalled the events to the biographer, fifty-six years later, she said that father Röntgen had a long talk with her several days before the marriage. He told her that she had been an exceedingly easy child to educate. She knew, though, that the Röntgens were quite disappointed when illness necessitated the discontinuance of her piano lessons.

Röntgen had always found Berteli very honest, and he suggested that one should always be certain that one could prove what was said. Upon this, the young bride's brown eyes sparkled and she felt forced to confess that she had indeed been untruthful to him on many occasions. After eating the fat of meat served at meals, she had become quite sick, so thereafter she would slip the cut-off fat from her fork into the napkin on her lap. Her father did not tolerate anything left over on the plates. When Berteli had first left the fat on the edge of the plate, he scolded her and insisted that she eat it. On this confession, Röntgen laughed heartily, finding it amusing that he had never noticed this long-practiced deception. "Even though he often wore one pair of glasses on top of another when he came to the table!" Josephine Berta Donges said. "He was an excellent father, stern but kind." As *pater familias,* he acted with the customary *gravitas,* the typical weighty authority.

Käthe Fuchs remembered that a box containing the jewelry items of Röntgen's mother was kept at the bank and that he refused to have Bertha give their daughter any of the pieces. Once, while Fräulein Vögeli was visiting, the jewelry was brought from the bank vault and the contents dumped onto the table. After all of the pins, bracelets, collars, and diamonds had been admired, they were replaced in the container and returned to the bank.

The following year, during the summer vacation in Pontresina, Bertha became quite ill with intestinal troubles. She had been ordered to bed by her physician when he discovered a fever, and their vacation plans were changed to accommodate her disability. They had stayed longer than anticipated at Rigi-Scheidegg before proceeding by carriage, with Kutscher Schmidt, to Lenzerheide and the next day to Pontresina. At the end of the vacation period Bertha seemed to have recuperated quite well, and they had some enjoyable days with their old friends.

When the next winter, at their Christmas vacation spot — Dorf Davos — Bertha was ill again, Röntgen became quite worried over her condition. Once again, after the situation had eased considerably within a week or two, they had a splendid time during some wonderfully sunny weather. They made acquaintance and enjoyed the company of a painter named Lehmann and his family; they discussed at great length Lehmann's plans to settle in Davos.

While the Röntgens were at Cadenabbia for the birthday and Easter time, the Boveris, the Krönleins, and the Zehnders visited them. However, Bertha was not well. The doctor suggested that they go south for awhile, and so they went to Florence for two weeks. By the time the Röntgens returned, the Boveris had left for Naples, Stöhr had to cancel his trip to Lake Como, and Krönlein was poor company — some disagreement with his assistant had caused him to be terribly annoyed and not inclined to discuss anything but the conflict and the tactless behavior of the man. Perhaps not altogether unexpectedly Bertha again suffered greatly from the intestinal disorder, for an entire month, running a fever. She had no appetite and lost much weight. Consequently her strength was nearly gone when the condition cleared up. Röntgen had planned to go to Berlin to attend a *Reichsanstalt Sitzung,* but the doctor believed such a trip too strenuous for Bertha. They went back to Munich instead.

The summer vacation promised to be most pleasant the next year. The Röntgens were at Rigi-Scheidegg that August, and plans were made for the carriage trip to Pontresina. The first day would take them to Chur, where Röntgen expected to have a talk with the Bishop of Chur, who was the brother of his coachman. The following night they would stay over in Lenzerheide, arriving in Pontresina on the night of the 18th. It was the customary way of travel, and they had adhered to this pattern for several years now.

Suddenly, on the day prior to their departure, Krönlein suffered a severe attack and fell critically ill at the hotel. The local physician called in a specialist from Zurich, who suggested that the sick man be returned to Zurich where he could be better attended.

The Röntgens were terribly saddened when their good friend and vacation companion Krönlein died on October 16, 1910. In a letter to Ernst Ritzmann, also a physician from Zurich and frequent fellow vacationer, Röntgen wrote, "The thought to lose him is terribly sad, because he was always full of life and of an alert mind, and he was beloved and valued by all of us."

Professor Hitzig and Dr. Ritzmann were named executors of the estate of Dr. Krönlein, and some small objects were sent to the Röntgens as a memento from the personal property of their friend. Röntgen wrote to Hitzig on February 5, 1911:

The items which shall be a reminder of our Krönlein for my wife and myself arrived safely and have already found their place in the daily used rooms that no day will pass when we are not reminded of our dear friend.

And now something different. Spring is expected and about the middle of March begin the vacations. A bit of recuperation we will need and so we are busy making vacation plans.

Cadenabbia, the magnificent resort without peer comes to mind again, and even though the thought of our friend who so liked to be there and now will be missed affects us painfully, a certain pull toward it definitely exists. The Boveris think likewise.

And now I want to ask if it would be possible that you will also seek your recuperation, which you surely need, in that place. We would be very happy if you did. It seems that we got along well together. The good wife should of course be included. I would like to say *"Auf baldiges Wiedersehen!"*

Usually after a faculty meeting or some other strenuous or controversial activity, Röntgen now suffered from vertigo, but his health generally was excellent. Once he suffered two slight hemorrhages from his lungs, greatly alarming his wife and his friends. In a letter to Boveri in 1910, he wrote concerning the vertigo: "I must admit that I was tortured by depressing thoughts during the first days of this illness. Fortunately the importance of it all was exaggerated and amounted only to a reminder that I had aged." After a few days of bedrest at home he returned to his lecturing and "rejoiced that I could work again and that I felt somewhat refreshed after the enforced rest." He realized that at age sixty-five he had to slow down on some of his work schedules.

In the summer of 1912, the hotel at Rigi-Scheidegg was unable to accommodate the Röntgens for the short stay there. They went to Parpan instead, then on to Pontresina by way of Lenzerheide, thus changing their customary routine slightly. Bertha suffered again from her chronic periods of nervousness and rheumatic pains during the vacation, but not as severely as she had prior to the Swiss trip.

That winter Röntgen himself fell ill with bronchitis, and an earache caused difficulties in his hearing. This was diagnosed as *Mittelohrentzündung* — inflammation of the middle ear. He refused to take any medication, but he permitted Käthe to give him hot compresses. After her home-cure had cleared up his difficulties, Röntgen gave the maid a gold bracelet for the successful nursing.

With the ear trouble apparently cleared up, Röntgen kept busy with "almost daily lectures and quite a bit more work than usual, which probably helps to get along better, since my mind is then occupied with scientific facts and I can get away from the unpleasantness of the severe illness of my wife."

They spent the Christmas holidays at Weilheim that year. The weather was disappointing during the entire time there, and the recuperation was less than they had hoped for.

The remaining winter weather in Munich was also abominable. Röntgen was happy when the first signs of spring became evident on his walks through the Englischen Garten, but even with the change in the weather he had little to be cheerful about. The earache recurred, and on March 24, 1913, he wrote:

For the past three or four weeks I have had a rather solid swelling behind the left ear. [This ear had become deaf.] The swelling was not large and at first did not cause any discomfort, but the otolaryngologist whom I consulted advised against leaving for the planned Easter vacation trip so that I could remain under his observation. I was discharged after the pain had practically disappeared but was told to return immediately in the event of severe pain or fever. There was only occasional pain and so nothing more was done for the ear.

Less than a month later, however, while at Badenweiler near Freiburg im Breisgau, where they met the Boveris briefly, his friend convinced Röntgen that he should have his colleague, Professor Krehl of Heidelberg, look at the infected ear. Quite reluctantly Röntgen agreed, and the otologist urged an immediate operation. This caused great concern, but the operation was successful. Röntgen even regained some of his lost hearing. He remained in a deeply depressed mood, however, for some time afterward. Bertha reported to the Boveris, writing:

My poor husband is still very nervous. Everything excites him terribly, and I hope that he will find new strength here in Weilheim so that he will soon be able to return to his work which will make him forget himself to some extent. He has to go to Munich two or three times a week to see Professor Heim to have his wound dressed. The wound is healing well and causes him no pain.

A month later she wrote:

The three weeks which my husband spent resting in Weilheim have done him a great deal of good, and on Thursday and Friday he was able to give his lectures. The first day this excited him somewhat, but on the second day everything went smoothly.

While Wilhelm Röntgen's health had improved remarkably after the summer vacations, the illness of Bertha had grown progressively worse. To Ritzmann in Zurich on May 19, 1913, he wrote:

Unfortunately I cannot report much good from here, and so will be brief. Only a little has changed in the condition of my wife. A few decent days come now and then, but the pain is otherwise very often and very strong. I myself have undergone a middle ear surgery, lasting three and a half hours, at the Heidelberg Ear Clinic when the colleagues told me that it should have been done long ago. From this operation I recover but slowly. The lectures I have not yet been able to begin again.

To the Boveris Röntgen wrote:

Bertha is continually growing worse. This despite the fact that there are occasional signs of improvement which are, however, becoming rarer and rarer. Narcotics must be used almost daily, but with few exceptions she is always very brave.

As for himself, he said:

It is perhaps a good thing that one becomes accustomed to bad as well as to happy conditions. The regularity of the lecturing before the students is becoming a beneficial event, and I have actually felt the need of working a little to get away from thinking constantly of the misery.

Somewhat later he wrote:

In addition to that comes the conviction that we are closely dependent on each other because of her severe illness, and really need special considerations in many ways which we cannot expect from the owner of a hotel or from the other guests who do not know us personally. Naturally, I want to help and console my poor wife as much as possible in her dark hours and therefore have become a poor companion for others. I need not tell you that it was difficult for us to give up our plans, but now we are content with our decision.

That decision was not to take a trip this Easter as they had done for so many years but to stay at Weilheim instead, except for a short meeting with the Boveris in the Black Forest.

By the end of that year, Bertha Röntgen was suffering ever greater pains from her renal colic. Wilhelm wrote:

I have been able to ease the pains by the use of alcohol, valerian, and hot compresses, in addition to the regular morphine injections. As a patient, she presents a most discouraging problem to the physicians, since they cannot help her, except to ease her condition by the use of morphine. One of the doctors told me not to spare any morphine, and another counseled to increase the dose very slowly, but neither could say how often and at what time the injections would be most beneficial. That I had to find out by myself. And because of the frequency of the attacks during the day, it is impossible to ascertain just how severe they are going to be and consequently how much to administer.

During the last years of her illness, Bertha received five injections daily, given with the greatest care by her husband. This gave him only short periods of time to absent himself from the house. He could never be certain just when the attacks would come and an additional injection become necessary. The illness and the treatment, the responsibility and the apparent uselessness of it all, caused him to be very depressed most of the time. However, when Bertha was without pain during brief periods, she was happy and joked with him; in pleasant weather she could go out into the garden, and her days were more endurable. She loved and enjoyed her flowers and would occasionally even sing to them as she used to do in better days.

Hunting played an important part in Röntgen's recreation. He wore the traditional *Jäger* costume of dark green, rather shabby from the years of wear, and such a contrast to the fastidious suit he wore in the city; the peaked feathered cap replaced the wide-brimmed black hat of the city. Because of his color-blindness he experienced difficulty in distinguishing the light red deer from their dark green background, but he often spotted a buck long before his companion did, whose eyesight was unimpaired.

Röntgen wrote to Boveri in June, 1911:

The splendid stag with the six points which you can shoot is now here. The gun with which you may shoot is here. The hunting license which gives you permission to hunt, only awaits your signature. Your quarters are here, and the happy anticipation of seeing you again is here. In short, everything that is necessary and pleasant is here, and now we hope only that your intention of coming to see us will bring you here!

In July, 1914, when all of Europe was ready to explode politically, he wrote to Boveri that he had shot four bucks so far that year, but had missed even more.

One large one has been hit, but not killed, and Lenz saw it run limping away. Searching for the buck was futile, he could not be located anywhere, disappearing without a trace! That is one of the dark sides of hunting! But usually it is a pleasurable sport. Two stately animals which we had observed eagerly and which we respectfully named the Geheimräte [privy councilors] must still be alive but cannot be located in these parts.

A year later:

Almost every day after a rain I have had the inclination and opportunity to go hunting, and I recall with certain pleasure last Sunday morning. The sun shone brightly after the rain, but there was a good breeze and no August heat.

I spent most of my time with the guide in the Feichtl, a rather large forest of tall young trees, in which several paths were cut a few years ago. The crowns of some of these trees are just thin enough to permit sunlight to penetrate, and the ground is covered with moss and mushrooms, and we collected many of the edible ones. There was not a sound and we had our breakfast of a piece of bread, an apple, and a cigarette, undisturbed by mosquitoes and flies so annoying at this season. We did no shooting, and thoughts of the war were completely thrust into the background.

Röntgen truly was in love with that area then.

My wife really had a most excellent idea when she suggested the creation of a home here and selected the little house in which we live now. Since it has become difficult to make long trips, we realize its value more than ever before. While I am writing these lines I enjoy the beautiful landscape in the evening sunset and the flowers that look into my windows from the balcony.

After a lengthy visit by the Boveri family, during which time the hunting proved rather poor, Röntgen wrote most happily that he had been successful on the day after they had left Weilheim:

I went at about six-thirty to the Gögerl, and fifteen minutes later a buck came out of the woods at shooting distance. I killed him with a shot into the shoulder, and you can imagine my happiness was great after so many failures over this young buck. Yesterday was an especially lucky day. At the opening of the rabbit and pheasant season, I went into the fields with my beloved old shotgun. In the morning I bagged one rabbit and two partridges, and in the afternoon a pheasant and a deer. The deer was in the Ammer forest near the Polling station, driven out by Lenz, who is certain that it is the same buck of the Schafbüchel that you and I were after that early morning and which we missed again the next day. You see that, after all, I have luck again.

Röntgen sometimes had disastrous and highly embarrassing failures in hunting. Margret Boveri told of a fox hunt at Weilheim where the fox was holed up in a hay-filled meadow shack where the dachshunds had cornered him, after having been bitten badly by the clever animal. The abused dogs came whimpering but still barking furiously at the wily fox, to seek comfort from their masters, who had positioned themselves to cover the shack from all possible angles. Even the ladies were present, sitting safely a good distance away in the meadow, in a field of lilies-of-the-valley. As *Jagdmeister,* Röntgen ordered absolute quiet so that the fox would think everyone had left the area; then he would carelessly leave his hiding place. Apparently the fox was deceived by this ruse and soon emerged nonchalantly from the hut, but only Bertha saw him. Excitedly

she called out, "Wilhelm, Wilhelm, the fox." But the badly frightened
animal, hearing this cry, did not pause even to hear the second "Wilhelm";
he disappeared before the hasty wild shots of the hunters could touch him.

Such failures made Röntgen exceedingly angry, so that he would be
most disagreeable and unsociable that day and the entire evening.

During the Pentecost vacations of 1913 Röntgen decided that Boveri
should have a shot at a splendid buck that he and his guide had seen earlier
in the area. On several occasions the buck failed to appear in the opening
at all. Once, while within rifle range, Boveri shot but missed, mainly
because of Röntgen's agitation. Then, later, twice the buck came again
within rifle range of Röntgen, who was by then stationed a good distance
away from Boveri, who did not even get to see the animal. Instead of the
usual cheerful banter with guide and hunting companion just a monosyl-
labic word was now spoken. This maddening pursuit of the buck continued
for five days, becoming ever more and more annoying to Röntgen. He
would sit at the table, absolutely silent and uncommunicative. No joy
whatever was left in him, not even a traditional *Waidmann's Heil.*

"Röntgen was a hunter through and through," Stacheter, a neighbor,
said. "He took good care of the game and was as interested as any disciple
of the biblical Nimrod in the condition of deer and birds. Even when
older, Röntgen was an excellent shot, especially when shooting birds
on the wing."

Generally the evenings at Weilheim were pleasant and congenial.
There was much talk of game, and Röntgen was an unexcelled teller of
hunting tales. A large round brass lamp hung low over a round table with
all of the guests seated cosily around it. There was reading aloud of parts
of a favorite novel, or an animal story, or of some other writing that had
caught Röntgen's fancy. With little Margret Boveri he often played a card
game, *Schmaussjass,* which he had taught her years before. But once,
during a heated game, an argument arose and the disagreement became so
violent that the game was not played for two years. Röntgen was not a
cheerful loser.

An especially amusing book, written in the rich Bavarian dialect that
Röntgen had learned to understand and to love, was the *Filser Briefe* by
Ludwig Thoma. On a long evening he enjoyed reading aloud to his guests
from the little book. Thoma was a clever satirist and knew his native region
well. Although he wrote novels, dramas, and poetry of enduring value,
his *Lausbubengeschichten — Tales of Rascals —* is his best-known work.
In fact, Röntgen became so enamored of these letters that Boveri wrote
him lengthy birthday letters annually in that same convulsive style.
Röntgen saved these hilarious letters carefully, reading them aloud to

friends as enthusiastically as he did the original letters from the fictional
rural Royal Bavarian representative to the Landstag. To one of these
birthday letters he replied to Boveri, "You have excelled the original!"

At Weilheim, Röntgen seemed to feel free to read lighter literary
works than at Munich where he usually pored over scientific theses, published either by other physicists or written by graduates who were working
on their doctorates. But at the country place he would sometimes read
aloud in the evenings to Bertha while she worked on some intricate pattern
of needlepoint for a pillow or chair cover.

Descriptive travel books were always of special interest to both, for
they were inveterate travelers themselves. But biographies seemed their
favorites. They read together *The Life of Robert Wilhelm Bunson,* the
Reminiscences of the Life of Werner von Siemens, Eduard Hanslick's *My
Life,* Clara Schumann's *Life and Letters,* the *Life of Jane Addams* of Hull
House, the *Letters* of Gottfried Keller, *Reminiscences of an Old Man* by
Kügelgen, and several biographies on the Iron Chancellor Bismarck.

In 1922 Röntgen wrote of reading "the autobiographies of Thomas
Platter and his son Felix Platter, and one of Agrippa d'Augigne, all of them
highly interesting personalities and beautiful characters whose descriptions
of contemporary conditions are well worth reading."

Röntgen also liked occasionally to read to his guests selected parts
from light novels, such works as the Swiss Jeremias Gotthelf's *Elsie the
Maid* and *How Joggeli Found a Wife,* and others, parts of which moved
him to tears as he read on. Theodor Storm and Gottfried Keller were other
favorite authors, best suited for reading aloud.

Usually on a Sunday forenoon, and especially so in later years,
Röntgen read aloud to Bertha excerpts from their Bible, a wedding present
from America. When Rudolph Cohen loaned him Stendahl's *La Char-
treuse de Parme,* Röntgen wrote:

... The best book [Marie Henri] Beyle ever wrote, although it was merely a
mixture of descriptive Italian stories, and of cynical court gossip without any
other interest. Then Kieland's *Poison,* then *Changed Times,* a well-written and
fascinating book by von Wartensleben, who traveled extensively in Japan and
China. *William Shakespeare's Life and Work* by Wolf, which I have glanced
through without finding much of interest. It is a typical product of the literary
historian, bombastic and full of hypotheses and theories. I enjoy rereading
Cervantes' *Don Quixote,* of which I own a very good edition. I learned again
to love the two men, the Don and the Sancho, and enjoyed reading about their
cleverness and their character attributes. I read a critique in the last Nobel
publication on [Carl] Spitteler's *Olympic Spring,* which I had not liked at all,
but whose author received the prize for literature.

Röntgen felt most sympathetic toward Gottfried Keller. Born in
Zurich, student Keller was unjustly expelled from school for an offense

which he did not commit. Then he tried painting, but soon found his proper milieu in writing verse, which earned him` a government scholarship, and he returned to finish his formal education. Keller's autobiographical novel, *Der grüne Heinrich,* was his great work and Röntgen's favorite.

After reading aloud *Bismarck's Letters to His Bride* and *Humboldt's Letters,* and other, similar revelatory books, Röntgen said to Bertha, *"Bei uns wird das nicht vorkommen"* — With us that will not happen. They wanted their personal letters destroyed and not used for publication later.

Some of the scientific periodicals found their way to Weilheim on occasion, but the large library of scientific and technical volumes remained in Munich. After thoroughly digesting the published monthlies in several langùages — Röntgen read texts in French, English, and Italian as well as German — he had them bound for permanent references. The vast library was partially acquired because universities had a practice of not maintaining books within a particular department. The director of a section generally purchased the books he needed from his personal income, and naturally kept them in his own office or home. Thus, Röntgen owned a large number of such books, which were later given to the University of Würzburg and were eventually placed in the Museum at Lennep.

There were fifty-four leather-bound volumes of *Nature,* a weekly illustrated journal of science by Macmillan & Co. of London and New York (1888–1913), forty-two bound *Journal de Physique* (1872–1913), seventeen *Deutsche Physikalische Gesellschaft* (1899–1915), thirty-one *Nachrichten von der K. Gesellschaft der Wissenschaften zu Göttingen* (1884–1914), twelve *Contributions* from the Jefferson Physical Laboratory of Harvard University (1903–1914), nine *Bulletin* of the Bureau of Standards, twelve *Leiden University Reports on Science* by the Physical Institute (1885–1913), and many volumes of scientific encyclopedias and textbooks in several languages, altogether well over five hundred such works.

The Röntgens enjoyed good music. They attended some opera performances and concerts in Munich, but at Weilheim with their merry guests they sang simple tunes for mutual enjoyment. In her earlier years Bertha had sung popular tunes occasionally. It was not until many years later when, because of the deteriorating health of Bertha and Röntgen's own inability to play the piano, they bought a player piano, a Welte-Mignon, which gave them a great deal of pleasure. He had given his wife flowers for Christmas of 1914, and to both of them Bach's *Variations* and Beethoven's *Opus 109.*

Both pieces were then given to the Mignon, and we listened to its lovely tones. The first one, although we have listened to it three times, is not entirely clear to us. This will probably take time for persons so little educated in music. The

Beethoven we could enjoy much more even though there are some parts in it which are difficult for us to interpret.

When the fourteen-year-old Margret Boveri played for them the *Pathetique Sonata* of Beethoven on the piano, Röntgen asked her whether the interpretation and expression of the piece was original with her or whether it reflected that of her teacher. This technicality soon put the actual music into the background and became the prime subject of discussion between the performer and the auditor.

Röntgen's mood was generally responsible either for his deep enjoyment of a musical offering or for a superficial impression of music barely heard. On this subject he said (in 1915):

Now I have been enjoying the Schwind, Spitzweg, Schleich, and other pictures, and Mozart's music. With me, whether or not I can enjoy it depends very much on the mood in which I may be at the moment. This mood cannot be forced, and its presence is usually entirely independent of my being happy or sad. The only thing is that I must not be tired, though fatigue occurs relatively soon when I see or hear a number of things within a short time.

While the player piano provided them with music, the Röntgens still preferred live performers. Years later Cohen came on Sunday afternoons to play for them for about an hour. Röntgen wrote about him to Margret Boveri in 1919:

This is a great pleasure for us, for we think that he plays beautifully, especially in regard to interpretation. He plays mainly Bach and Mozart, but also Beethoven, Brahms, and Schumann. His favorite musician is Mozart, and I must admit that because of not knowing him well enough I have hitherto somewhat underestimated Mozart. The *Sonata Number 2,* especially the *Adagio* movement, made a very deep impression on me the other day. Bach's violin concertos are sometimes extremely beautiful, and I only regret that I did not get acquainted with these lovely things earlier.

After an opera performance at Munich, in 1920, Röntgen wrote: "How I enjoyed the *Fidelio*. Both overtures were played, and Morena sang beautifully. I was quite enthusiastic and carried away by the music. It is wonderful how soothing and refreshing music can really be."

In yet another letter to Margret, Röntgen remarked:

I regret that I missed the opportunity to hear some music for which I have sometimes longed very much, and concerts do not take the place of a private recital. I have the most beautiful recollections of the Beethoven sonata *Opus 110*. [Margret Boveri was then practicing it for Zilcher.] My musical education is not sufficient to judge this, but just for this reason I do not miss perfection in the player and can enjoy the piece and its personal interpretation more tranquilly. According to my modest opinion, the main emphasis in the musical instruction of a talented pupil should be placed on the teaching of technique and less on implanting the interpretation of the teacher. It certainly may be of interest to learn several interpretations, but the essential interpretation and its reproduction, even though they may be teachable, should be the individual effort of the pupil. For self-sufficient personalities, this is bound to be the case. The same is, of course, true for painting, but there it is so self-evident that I could spare my remarks.

Röntgen's understanding and appreciation of music was certainly not as keen as that of his relative, Engelbert Röntgen (1829–97), who had been for nearly thirty years second concert master of the Leipzig *Gewandhausorchester,* nor Engelbert's son Julius (born in 1855) who was a fair composer.

There existed an extremely close friendship between the Röntgens and the Boveris. The men were very fond of each other, becoming good friends while colleagues at the Würzburg university. Frau Marcella Boveri had been a friend of the Röntgens even before her marriage to the biology professor. As the first university-educated woman in their circle of acquaintances, she was somewhat unusual. While studying, the American-born Marcella O'Grady had been a daily companion of the Röntgens, having been invited to afternoon coffee and cake at their apartment. She became known as *das zoologische Fräulein* — the zoological miss. Wilhelm Röntgen shared her enthusiasm for the natural sciences, and both he and Bertha were taken with the sheer exuberance of this American girl student. During her first year at Würzburg she was invited by the Röntgens to share their vacation trip to Cadenabbia and later to Baden-Baden. This friendship continued and grew in later years, after Marcella married her *zoologischen* Professor, Theodor Boveri, in Boston in 1897.

Regarding the higher education of girls, Wilhelm Röntgen believed that all women should be urged to use their abilities to better advantage than merely to keep house for their husbands. When on February 18, 1922, Margret Boveri decided to extend her studies further, Röntgen wrote to Marcella,

Let us hope that she will follow in her father's footsteps and that she tries to succeed at investigation and productivity in some definite scientific field, whatever it might be. I am convinced that she is capable, and hopes to do so. With her talents it would be a pity and would not lead to real happiness if she should become merely a *geistreiches* [witty] and socially prominent woman.

CHAPTER 19

The War Years

By March, 1914, the physical condition of Röntgen's wife made it practically impossible for him to keep up his correspondence. He now had to allot his time most carefully in order to accomplish anything at all. Bertha's health was so aggravated that he seriously doubted they would travel any more during the summer vacations, and probably not ever, he wrote in a deeply discouraged mood. On April 21, he wrote to Hitzig:

Now I must thank you heartily for a letter and a postcard. The remembrance of my birthday with the good wishes was greatly welcome, and the card from Cadenabbia brought much joy. We did not get away from Bavaria this spring and have spent a good five weeks here in Weilheim. The condition of my wife does not allow a stay in strange places. She likes very much to be here in the country where in good weather we can walk right into the garden from the room, where we can take a short ride now and again, and where it is primarily very restful and unusually quiet. Lastly, it was really wonderful because of the glorious sunshine. To observe the coming of spring is really a delight. I only wish that my wife had some company, but it is difficult to invite people when the housewife is sometimes for several days in such terrible pain that she does not come out, and is completely immobile. I feel reasonably well. In a week from tomorrow I begin again my lecturing. The preparatory work has helped me many times to overcome the sad thoughts during the winter.

A month later Röntgen wrote again congratulating Hitzig on his birthday and promising to be with him in spirit on that festive occasion. Then he continued:

We were unable to leave Weilheim for a vacation. The stay here is, especially for my wife, well suited. She can easily get into her garden and arrange the necessary work for spring and summer. That makes for a lot of diversity. Her condition was so bad that she could do nothing during the first several weeks. Only toward the end, when the weather became nicer, did she feel fairly well. We are greatly thankful that it remained so with only one daily injection of morphine, so that the pleasant visit with Frau Boveri, who had just returned from Naples, was most enjoyable.

Röntgen was stunned when the official *Mobilisierung* posters appeared everywhere heralding the imminent outbreak of war. He had corresponded with and had known personally most of the leading scientists in many countries, some of whom had come to see him and to discuss with him certain phases of his discovery of the X rays. It distressed him painfully to see that so quickly all educational institutions were affected by the conflict. These changed times brought with them the burden of increased responsibilities in teaching and in research work, as many of the younger scientists were now on the fighting fronts. It was not surprising that Röntgen was drained of his energy and in deep melancholy during these difficult war years.

When the war broke out the Röntgens moved back to Munich. He felt that he could be more useful in the capital than in the forest, although at his advanced age there was little to contribute, and the serious illness of his wife made long absences from home nearly impossible because of the constant care required and the need for repeated medication. He spent as much time as possible at the institute, having taken on added work schedules to fill wherever vacancies in teaching personnel existed.

A cheerful surprise was the visit of their Berteli, now happily married and known as Frau Doktor J. B. Donges. She and her children stayed with the Röntgens in their Munich apartment for three weeks. Berteli lived at the home of her in-laws, since her husband had gone into the war, attached to the medical corps. They were all greatly surprised to see the young Leutnant Donges at the railroad station when his troop train came through Munich on its way from the Serbian to the faster moving Western Front. The all too brief stay lasted an hour, but the *Wiedersehen* gave them all a lift despite the seriousness of the occasion.

Röntgen was terribly worried about the uncertainty facing his beloved country in the coming year, as he confided to Hitzig in a letter written on the next to the last day of the year. About their Christmas he wrote:

We were in Munich and had a small lighted tree. We admired it thankfully, because during the past few years one had often harbored the thought that this time may be the last time that we celebrated Christmas together. There were no gifts. I had bought a few music rolls for our Mignon, the sonata *Opus 109* by Beethoven and the *Variations* by Bach, which we put to work at once and which we enjoyed greatly. From Zurich we had the notice of the death of Fräulein Emma Vögeli. She was a devoted friend of my wife, and we valued her many-sided gifts and her good humor. We saw each other almost every year a few times and we will miss her sorely.

For quite some time now at Weilheim Röntgen had worked on his notes, getting them properly organized, so that several papers on his observations could subsequently be published. He also wrote a commemorative tribute on "Friedrich Kohlrausch" (1910). Two years later, "Determinations on the Thermal Linear Coefficient of Expansion of Cuprite and Diamond" (1912) was published, then later, "Pyro- and Piezo-electrical Investigations" (1914). Two other important observations on laboratory experiments made partly in cooperation with his assistant, Abraham Joffé, were completed. "On the Conductivity of Electricity in Some Crystals and on the Influence of Irradiation on Them" (1913), and another one with the same title followed in 1921. This made a total of fifty-eight scientific papers Wilhelm Conrad Röntgen published during his active scientific life.

Honors kept coming to him. In 1913 Röntgen was made an honorary member of the *Deutschen Gesellschaft für Chirurgie* and the Swiss Röntgen-*Gesellschaft*. The next year the New York Roentgen Society gave him an honorary membership.

When a group of German intellectuals circulated a document repudiating a well-publicized paper by leaders of the Allied Powers regarding the war guilt question, alleged atrocities, and wanton destruction committed by Germans, Wilhelm Röntgen added his signature to the list of signatures of ninety-two other scientific and academic leaders of Germany. This *"Aufruf der 93"* replied in detail to each specific accusation of the Allied propaganda device, beginning each lead paragraph, *"Es ist nicht wahr, dass. . . ."* — It is not true that. . . .

There is some evidence that Röntgen later considered this action unwise — as he wrote to Frau Boveri on December 8, 1920 — but he was as angry as any other patriotic German citizen at the venomous accusations at the beginning of the war. He did not believe that any soldiers of the Reich were any more barbarous or pillaging than were marauding and savage soldiers of other nations. Röntgen realized, of course, that the political situation of Germany, with nine foreign countries bordering on it, was unique in the world. He was aware that the problem of keeping the correct balance of power by various manipulations was staggering and not always successful.

In time, Röntgen also seemed to have regretted that he had given his gold and silver medals when the government asked for such precious metals for the war effort. When the slogan *Gold gab ich für Eisen* — Gold I gave for iron — suggested to all citizens that they donate their wedding rings and replace them with simple metal bands, most of the people brought all of their jewelry and gave these valuables to assist in the war. Röntgen, in this same spirit, readily contributed his English Rumford medal and all of the gold and silver objects of the household. Later, when he realized the utter uselessness of all this, he believed that he would perhaps have been justified in withholding some of his possessions.

When huge wooden monuments, each in the form of a cross, or merely a pilaster, were erected in public squares such as the Marienplatz, and the citizens were urged to contribute money for the war, Röntgen subscribed freely and most generously to these war bond drives. For every mark signed up, a simple black upholstery nail was driven into this receptacle; for five marks, a silvery one; for ten marks a gilded nail was awarded. The donor was allowed to drive the nail in a certain prearranged pattern into the wood. Röntgen did all he could to help his government in the war effort.

In his year-end letter of 1914 Röntgen wrote to Boveri:

We have known for months that in all foreign countries there is very little understanding of German ways and aims. We have to accept this fact. The conditions will become better only after a favorable but also a reasonable peace for us has been concluded, not one in the Pan-German sense as outlined by Ostwald.

When a bread shortage appeared in Germany, Wilhelm Röntgen thought that the *Kartoffelbrot* was quite satisfactory as *Ersatzbrot,* but Boveri disagreed vehemently and wrote:

Instead of bread we get here regular stones which lie heavily in the stomach. The bakers certainly do not seem to understand the proper use of the potatoes. It does not seem reasonable to me that one should make one vile thing from two such good things as bread and potatoes, unless the purpose is that one should become entirely weaned from food. Please excuse my grumbling, but it relieves me.

Three months later Theodor Boveri lay ill "with a lung inflammation in the sanatorium of Dr. Saathof in Oberstdorf in the Allgäu," as Röntgen wrote to Hitzig on March 17, 1915.

And we intend to be there by the 24th. Frau Boveri and Margret, who are of course greatly worried, have lived there already for about a week in the Pension Hubertushaus, a simpler house, and have reserved a room there for me and my wife for a certain period. You can imagine that I am worried about this trip with my wife because I do not know if I can ease her pain sufficiently for the entire journey. We hope for the best, however, and are joyful in our minds, that we can be together with our friends.

Ordinarily, a trip to Oberstdorf would have been a joyful experience for Röntgen, but the serious illness of his friend which necessitated the trip and the acute discomfort of his Bertha made it an unpleasant chore.

Located 843 meters (2,530 feet) above sea level in the southernmost corner of Germany at the very foot of the snowy Alps, Oberstdorf was a *heilklimatischer Kurort* of renown and a vacation spot of great Alpine charm. Theodor Boveri had, as had the many patients of the several sanatoriums on the hillside, come to seek renewed strength in this invigorating healing climate of the *Luftkurort*. Daily in the village a long lazy procession of cows, with gay tinkling cowbells in melodious confusion, was always one of the highspots of this *Allgäuer Ort,* snow, rain, or shine, and the vacationing guests happily stepped aside when the cows were driven, right along the one main street, to their Kuhberg pasture at sundown. Because of the prevailing heat of the sun and accompanying flies and gnats, the canny farmers found it advantageous to have their *Viehzeug* graze contentedly in the cool of the night and rest unmolested in their barns during the day.

Situated in a wide valley of fenced meadows, the spa was surrounded by several lower cone-shaped mountains, covered with black pine trees, the Rubihorn, Schattenberg, Riffenkopf, Kegelkopf, Furschiesser, and Himmelschroffen, which formed the *Tal* and continued into the snow-laden higher mountains. The Nebelhorn — when fog did not envelop the peak — formed the sentinel of the *Kurort.* Two wide valleys extended into the upper ranges. The Trettachtal, with the leisurely walk along the roaring Trettach river to the Oytal, was topped by the challenging snowy Hofats (7,450 feet), and the Grosser Krottenkopf (8,760 feet). The Stillachtal, with a trail along the equally wild Stillach, heavy with melting snows, was capped by the white Kratzer (8,000 feet), the Trettachspitze (8,560 feet) and the Mädelegabel (8,710 feet). A steeper hike led to the pleasing mountain lake, the Freiburg See, with a rustic but good *bürgerliches* restaurant on its tree-shaded shores. Youngsters ice-skated on the lake now, and during the summer months they would be swimming in its cold water.

A still longer hiking trail led to Einödsbach or the Spielmannsau or the Breitachklamm, the peculiar cut in the rock, where the river spilled and tumbled foaming into pools through the narrow gorge, and where the hiker, occasionally more clinging to the narrow path hewn into the rock than hiking in comfort and complete safety, would be thoroughly drenched if he should be without a protective raincoat and waterproof boots. Röntgen found it indeed a wet walk but a most fascinating work of nature. And the climb to the summit of the Nebelhorn, especially treacherous because of heavy snows in the bowl-like Alpsee area, was a particularly demanding excursion for the septuagenarian. For further exploration and only a short distance away was the Kleinwalsertal, another valley pocket near this resort area, but actually Austro-Hungarian territory with absolutely no access road to its own fatherland. The mountainous scenery culminating in the Bregenzer Alps was even more spectacular there. But Wilhelm Röntgen had only a mild interest for these inviting vistas; he kept mainly to his room at the Hubertushaus, a comfortable five-story Victorian hotel, when he was not visiting with his sick friend at Dr. Saathof's *Kuranstalt* Stillachhaus on the snowy slopes amid pine trees just above Oberstdorf, or administering pain-relieving drugs to his ailing wife. Bertha spent most of her time in the glass-enclosed veranda of the Hubertushaus which opened into the still wintry garden and overlooked the western mountains.

Wilhelm Röntgen spent his seventieth birthday there, at the bedside of Boveri, asking that no special preparations be made for the celebration of the rather eventful day. "I am not in the mood for them," he wrote, prior to his arrival at the spa, "but shall derive the greatest pleasure from the fact that our two families can spend the time together."

On the morning of March 27, he, Bertha, Frau Boveri, and Margret spent hours opening congratulatory telegrams and letters which had arrived for the discoverer of the X rays. He was overwhelmed by the multitude of greetings he received. While Röntgen enjoyed reading the messages, he was always embarrassed by such attention.

Again, great honors came to him on that day. Special Addresses came from the Würzburger *Medizinischen Fakultät,* the Röntgen-*Stiftung,* the Universität Giessen, the *Philosophischen Fakultät* der Universität Würzburg, the *Physikalisch-Technischen Reichsanstalt,* the Universität Strassburg, the *Annalen der Physik,* and others. The city council of Munich dedicated a Röntgenstrasse in their city. Röntgen was made happy with a personal letter and the Iron Cross, Second Class, award from the *Oberbefehlshaber der Deutschen Heeresmacht,* General Field Marshall Paul von Hindenburg, "in full recognition of the great value of your rays in restoring wounded soldiers." The Kaiser also sent congratulations from his *Grossen Hauptquartier.*

There was, of course, the annual *"Filser Brief."* Boveri, its author, had worked most diligently on it a long time, the task being indeed a strenuous one during his severe illness. Röntgen enjoyed it immensely, tears coming to his eyes as he read it; he would have been extremely sad if it had not come at all that year.

The day after his birthday was set for an audience with King Ludwig of Bavaria, and he had to leave Oberstdorf early by train for that state occasion. This caused some anxiety and earnest consultation, but the fact that the king might bestow the nobility on him worried him more than the concern for the proper formal dress suit. Röntgen had been successful in refusing the Prince Regent this honor before, but the new ruler was quite unpredictable. If he would insist on bestowing it, Röntgen felt that he was then not able to refuse the unwanted designation of nobility. He wished to remain just plain Röntgen, without the noble prefix "von."

The audience went well, and Wilhelm Röntgen returned to Oberstdorf that night. Having been able to attend the royal audience of his sovereign without having been ennobled, Röntgen was happy and with a group of close friends sat around a table and played the favorite game of cards. When the Poch game expressions of *"Schnipp, Schnapp, Schnurr,"* or even *"Schneppepper"* were called out, they got a resounding hearty laugh from Röntgen. This was the highspot of the game, and brought some gaiety to the Hubertushaus' card room. However, the players sorely missed the gay Bavarian Boveri.

On the suggestion of Boveri a sum of money had been collected to have a bust made of Röntgen, so that "posterity would have a form other than photographs to remember his likeness." The occasion of his seventieth birthday had been selected to have this idea carried out, but Röntgen was, as usual, vehemently opposed to such a concept. Eventually, however, he agreed to sit for the renowned sculptor Adolf Hildebrand. Boveri, anxious that the bust would be a true likeness of Röntgen, wrote asking if he had let his hair grow nicely, but not too long; he suggested that after the first sitting Röntgen should find out just how much hair the artist would want, so that his barber "could cut the superfluous hair according to the advice of the sculptor."

In July Röntgen replied that he had been sitting for Hildebrand for four mornings from nine to eleven and had no idea how long it would actually take for the sculptor to finish the bust. The hours really passed quite fast because Hildebrand knew how to entertain his subject of observation. Discussion never really stopped, and Röntgen suspected that this was a motive to be of advantage to the artist and the sculpture. He found the conversation most interesting and stimulating and regretted that he had come into close contact with such an artist only now when he was old and forgetful. "The man was full of problems and had a broad knowledge which surprised me greatly," Röntgen wrote.

As the sittings went on, Röntgen became aware of changes taking place in the actual work, and he regretted that his friend Boveri was unable to see the progress. He believed the bust to be very good, and Hildebrand seemed to find more and more pleasure in his creation. This promised a successful outcome. On a visit to the institute, the artist tried to find a suitable location for the bust, where it would get the benefit of the proper light, but so far had been unable to settle on a definite spot. Another point of concern was the availability of bronze during this wartime emergency. While Röntgen was concerned about the placing of the bust, he was also aware that "placing of sculpture in a public place smacked somewhat of ostentation."

When Boveri saw a photograph of the bust, he wrote that it looked at first a little strange to him because it was so narrow. Hildebrand had modeled the hair higher and reduced the beard at the sides more than his friend had ever seen Röntgen wear it. This was perhaps only an artistic modification, and Boveri would accept the likeness in due time. The expression was wonderful, and he believed the bust to be one of Hildebrand's best works.

"How beautiful the forehead is modeled! He also caught the tilt of your head and the look in the eye as well as anyone could have hoped," Boveri wrote. And then he suggested that "the halls of the Munich university are not good enough for this piece of art. It should be placed in the Glyptothek where many thousands can enjoy it."

Wilhelm Röntgen took to this suggestion with enthusiasm, and a day or so after he received the letter answered, "Your idea of placing it in the Glyptothek later where it could be enjoyed by many, as Hildebrand's work, has pleased me very much, and I went to him immediately to suggest it. He also felt that this was a good solution to the problem, provided a more suitable place could be found than the big hall in the Glyptothek where at present modern sculpture is so crowded together."

The Hildebrand bust was actually the first one of a series of similar sculptures. In 1928, Theodor Georgii of Munich, a son-in-law of Adolf Hildebrand, created a small replica and another larger than life size of Röntgen. Then, in 1935, Hermann Hahn, a student of Hildebrand, created a Röntgen bust for the Deutsche Museum at Munich. The sculptor Ernst Kunst donated one to the Röntgen Museum at Lennep in 1932, and Arno Breker created one which was placed on the Thüringer Allee in Lennep in 1930. The Russian artist Sinoisky made a bust for the Leningrad State Institute of Roentgenology in 1920, and Karl Kiesgen of Schleiden made one for the Madras Institute, a copy of which was exhibited in Cologne.

A few years earlier Röntgen had attended a meeting of the holders of the Maximilian Order, and he sat next to Adolf Hildebrand. Apparently the artist did not find the convocation all absorbing and took out a fairly good-sized sheet of drawing paper and made some sketches of the sculptured decorations on one of the Roman-Corinthian capitals in the large meeting hall. When he had filled the paper, Röntgen asked for it, and Hildebrand signed the sheet of drawings. Before having it framed, Röntgen wrote on the back, *"Von Ad. Hildebrand während einer Sitzung des Kapitels vom Maximiliianorden gezeichnet. München 1911."* It made a fine pencil study for the wall of a room in Weilheim.

On July 19, 1915, Wilhelm Röntgen wrote, "The condition of my wife is generally always the same. She has to suffer great pain, but not all of the days are the same. She receives now five injections daily: three times 0.02 morphine and two times 0.02 pantopon. She still remains very brave and can be quite satisfied and friendly at times." There seemed no cure for her renal colic — the severe pain produced by the passage of a calculus from the kidney through the ureter — other than the ease of the intense pain by the continuous administration of drugs.

But Bertha Röntgen felt well enough to supervise and arrange the planting of their garden at Weilheim. A portion of her beloved flower section was now replaced with vegetable beds to augment the dwindling, soon to be completely disappearing, supply of fresh farm produce from the market places.

Wilhelm Röntgen was preparing his work for the coming semester, and while the attendance at the institute was expected to be a rather small one, perhaps only twenty students, the work would take as much preparation as for two hundred. He was looking forward to the lecturing again, which he never really cared for, because it would take his mind off the worry over the poor health of his wife and his friend.

"With advanced age one does not make many new friends," he observed sadly, "and so have to value old ones even more greatly."

The Röntgens spent the entire summer at Weilheim, but they recalled the good times which they had in former years in Switzerland during the *langen Ferien* — the long vacations. After Arthur von Hippel, who had fairly well recovered from his illness, wrote from Pontresina, Röntgen wrote to Wölfflin:

Especially Pontresina! How many memories are tied to this place for my wife and myself. In the last letter I had from Hippel he announced an improvement in his condition. The nasty skin disease had substantially decreased, and his heart trouble also eased somewhat. For a while I was greatly worried over my friend, but now it appears as if he has torn himself away from the difficulties. Yesterday we also had a postcard from our former driver, Emanuel Schmidt, in which he asked if we would ride again together sometime. It warms our hearts when we think of these old times and the good people of yonder days. Especially of Switzerland! How much that is good and beautiful do I have to thank her for! Fräulein Vögeli has now also left us. If only again from somewhere pleasant news would come! My wife has progressively more to suffer from her terrible illness. She is still real brave and of a content disposition. Helmholtz is right when he said at the splendid banquet at his seventieth birthday, "The first seventy years are the nicest." I will be very thankful for everything good and pleasant of which my life was so full in overflowing measure.

His work at the institute kept Wilhelm Röntgen occupied and his mind away from the sad conditions of his personal friends and the state of his country. A situation arose when serious consideration was given to the calling of a new professor to fill the vacant chair of chemistry, and Röntgen strongly opposed the majority of the faculty who insisted that the work be divided. He wrote about this deep interest, "Sometimes I think, why do I, old fool, still worry about matters which irritate me and cause me many sleepless nights. But this does not keep me from doing so, for my interest is still too lively in all university matters and especially in the sciences related to mine."

When a *Siemens Preis* was inaugurated in 1916, Max Planck asked Röntgen for his suggestion, and he proposed the name of Albert Einstein as a worthy recipient of the honor. Einstein wrote to Röntgen, in his small handwriting, on November 29, thanking him for the proposal.

Ludwig Zehnder, then at the Kantonspital in Zurich, invented a metal-shielded Röntgen tube, and in the *Elektrotechnischen Zeitschrift* (Berlin) published the details of this device which would protect doctors and technicians who handled X ray machines and were constantly exposed to their cell-damaging rays. On his way to Berlin, Zehnder and his wife stopped over in Munich for a day and were the house guests of the Röntgens at their apartment. That noon, a representative came to see Zehnder to talk to him about the new tube invention. After the man left, Wilhelm Röntgen criticized Zehnder severely for having published the details of this device, because it had not yet been thoroughly tested, but Zehnder felt that such work should be carried out by interested manufacturers, since he had not patented the tube. However, because no patent protected the tube, no firm was interested in spending money on testing and fully developing the device. Eventually, Philips of the Netherlands developed such a tube, called the Metallix-tube, which proved quite effective.

Margret Boveri wrote:

During the long illness of my father, Röntgen remained steadily by his side and ours, inquiring of the attending physicians what was best to comfort the patient. He sent books to my father, had costly fruit delivered to his sanatorium, and wrote optimistic letters, which was not at all easy for him to do. He made perhaps the greatest sacrifice when three times he turned over the care of his wife to doctors and made one-day trips to Oberstdorf and to Würzburg to visit my father.

Of the Würzburg visit Röntgen wrote:

I was in Würzburg for a few hours, because the news from there seemed to suggest nothing good. I found him seriously ill. But the doctor did not want to give up all hope. His had become finally a most infirm body.

But the hopeless condition of Boveri gave Röntgen most concern. On October 9 he wrote:

My dear Friend: In my cellar I found a bottle of sherry whose contents are as old as I am. I bought it years ago in Würzburg, and the wine was supposed to be, according to the label, already fifty years old. This contemporary of mine I have sent to you today. May it contribute to your strength! Should it do that, then this old settler has been able to achieve something worth while.

Margret Boveri commented on Röntgen's demeanor:

It was most amazing to watch how this vigorous, happy, and reserved man reacted to the suffering of others, and how in times of stress, illness, and even death, he almost miraculously shed his reticence and acknowledged with dearest concern and deepest feeling the problems of his friends. His friendship was thus two-sided. On the one hand, the often hilarious, fun-loving happiness, and on the other, the deepest earnestness toward all difficulties in life.

Just a few years before, while Röntgen had been suffering with a fever of over 103°, having had a 100° temperature for a week which left him very weak so that he could hardly read, he had written a lengthy, detailed letter to Boveri, who was then considering the offered directorate of the newly founded Kaiser Wilhelm Institute for Biology at Berlin-Dahlem. Röntgen showed a deep personal interest and intense concern in this important matter and offered several pertinent points, both in favor of accepting the post and in rejecting the offered position, which Theodor Boveri then turned down.

It was a terrible blow to Wilhelm Röntgen when Geheimrat Boveri died of tuberculosis that October. It was never easy for Röntgen to talk publicly, and the words he spoke at the cremation of his dear friend on October 19, 1915, were exceedingly difficult for him to articulate. He eulogized:

A great man in the realm of genius has gone home. But it is not my task here to recount the importance of the scientist and research worker. It is about Boveri, the man and the friend, that I wish to say a few words. Boveri was a truly noble and distinguished man, full of unfathomable goodness of the heart. Kind and strong at the same time. As a friend true as gold. As an adviser absolutely reliable. Always seeing through situations clearly and judging them objectively. In happiness and sorrow a companion who always entered into the spirit of things and always was willing to lend a helping hand. He was an unusually versatile and gifted man, and gave of this rich store of gifts with generosity. Yet he was always modest and free of conceit and vanity. Always responsive and appreciative, even though he received but little in return. To live with him meant great pleasure and gain. Now he has left us. We stand at his bier, deeply grieved. It will be difficult for many to live without him. But we shall be grateful that we have had him and that his influence upon us was great enough not to cease with his death. On our future pathways we shall often remember him and in our thoughts we shall question him: How would you act now, how would you judge? We thank you, you faithful man, for all you have given us. At the height of your achievement you have left us. Only in the last days have you become tired. Rest in peace.

After Boveri's death, Röntgen had a bust made of him by Hildebrand, despite the shortages of material caused by the war, and had a small booklet published in commemoration of his departed friend and colleague. Although rather critical of his own writing abilities, he later regretted that his printed contribution was only a short one.

In December Röntgen wrote to Hitzig:

During the past few days my wife has been terribly upset, and I was also very grieved by the sudden death of the so sympathetic Frau Doktor Goedecke. The dear young person, so full of hope, had to go to ruin after a three-day illness of Landy's paralysis [*Rückenmarkentzündung* — inflammation of the spinal cord]. We feel so sorry for the poor man and the little child.

Frau Boveri and Margret had visited recently with the Röntgens for a week to rest and talk, and Röntgen thought that they were very brave under the difficult circumstances. So much had been destroyed. Their Christmas would be a sad one. "But," he wrote, "we will have again a small lighted tree, in deep thankfulness that we both are allowed to celebrate the feast together. How often had we thought that it would be the last one."

In addition to Boveri and Frau Goedecke, the colleagues Prym and Külpe also died that year, decimating the circle of friends still further.

Friend Hitzig underwent a prostate operation in March 1916, and when complications set in, Röntgen wrote him expressing deep concern. He would like to visit him in Zurich but found it impossible to leave his ill wife, besides the current travel situation made such a trip virtually impossible. His wife suffered actually less pain than a year ago, but there occurred from time to time certain conditions when his presence was absolutely essential, because of the critical shortage of physicians.

Röntgen recounted the activities of the previous day, his seventy-first birthday. He reread all of the telegrams and letters that had come during the whole year and so relived all of these enjoyable hours which the welcome correspondence had brought then. He told how he recalled with utmost pleasure the visit of his friend during the past year.

During the year, while the war raged on relentlessly, and shortages became ever more serious, another old friend, Arthur von Hippel, died.

That year Christmas was a lonelier time than ever before for the Röntgens. Their small circle of friends was quickly diminishing, and they felt this deeply. On January 28, 1917, Röntgen wrote in a long letter to Ernst Ritzmann:

A *Weihnachtsfeier* with children, and especially grandchildren present, can bring great happiness and joy, but our friends are being missed expressly at this time. But old folks have to search their memories to find gladness. We both went, with nice weather, to Weilheim and celebrated the Christmas Eve together there in our little hunting lodge with lighted tree. The tree was in a way a thank offering for letting us share once again the evening together. The death of friend Hippel affected us deeply. A warm friendship tied us together for nearly forty years, and the two ladies have also been very close.

Then Röntgen told about the last visit, how bad his colleague had looked, and that the death, while not fully unexpected, came quite suddenly. Shortly thereafter, a young Munich friend died, following his wife by half a year. Those left were now dearer than ever before.

The war conditions caused many changes in the institute. Koch went as an officer in wireless telegraphy, Du Prel as officer in a bureau, and Wagner as a laboratory technician at a military hospital in charge of X rays. Röntgen himself still served as full professor.

... but the laboratory is completely deserted, and there is no independent research work being done at all. About thirty students attend the physical science demonstrations and ninety the lectures, but most of them are medical students, with young women in the far greater majority. Talk is that the whole university may be closed down altogether next year, but I do not think that this rumor could be correct.

The war had affected nearly everyone, Röntgen stated, and he was — as was every citizen — deeply concerned about the terrific toll it had taken so far.

At home, Röntgen usually read aloud to Bertha. "Right now a book by Ermattinger on Gottfried Keller, the German poet of the nineteenth century, which we both enjoy. The book contains much which the biography by Bächthold omitted. In fact, we have read considerable of Keller's works and admire him and like him increasingly better."

Röntgen tried to be outside for at least three hours daily, hunting whenever possible, because walking in the forest got his mind off the unpleasant things of illness and war. The unspoiled beauty of nature and the fresh air seemed a stimulating treatment.

Because of the death of von Hippel and the move by Zehnder into his native Switzerland, Röntgen changed the executors of his will. He appointed Frau Boveri and Rudolph Cohen, who had worked with him in Würzburg and who often entertained the Röntgens with his superb piano playing in their home. But since neither was a lawyer, the attorney Dünkelsbühler of Munich was added to the group.

Wilhelm Röntgen also took a lively interest in the school activities of young Margret Boveri. He shared with her the anxieties at the time of her *Abitur,* the tough and crucial final examinations at the end of her *Gymnasium* period. The two had many serious academic discussions on various subjects, and one episode particularly stood out.

In December 1917, Margret wrote to Röntgen that she was working on her "nasty" theme. "With what right has Karl, the son of Pippin, received the surname *Der Grosse* [The Great]?" She had written eleven pages as her thesis on the Holy Roman Emperor, known in English history as Charlemagne. Röntgen wrote that he was curious to know just what she had written in these eleven pages on that theme, and asked if she would send him a copy of her work. "I assure you complete discretion and safeguard of all your author's rights," he added.

After the thesis was read by him, Röntgen wrote a long letter to Margret, asking under what conditions she had written her theme. Where had she found the facts contained in her work? He did not intend to criticize the work but had several questions to ask regarding the *Aufsatz.* How had she used her references, and were the books used in a library or at home? How much was her own observation, after having evaluated the already published material on Karl? Had she, on her own initiative, explained the meaning and the significance of the name *Der Grosse*? And so on.

In her responsive letter, Margret explained that the students were allowed one week at home to write the thesis. They were told to discuss Karl as field marshall, then as statesman, then as a personality, and finally analyse the effect of his reign on the period immediately following. They had a school history book as reference and had heard a lecture or two on the subject, but she also studied other sources and read a novel on the ruler and remembered things she had learned about him earlier.

This letter stimulated Röntgen to go to the *Staatsbibliothek* and get the textbook by Stich and the world history by Weber and read the parts on Karl dem Grossen. Only by this method could he evaluate properly just how much the student had relied on others and how much she had contributed herself. Apparently both correspondents benefited from this exercise.

Another quite similar episode occurred when both discussed Margret's studies of physics. On this subject, Röntgen wrote a letter from Weilheim in January 1918 to Margret, discussing in detail the monstrous word *Metersekundenkilogramm,* which is seldom, if at all, used in practice, being replaced by the simpler "Watt" or "Watt-hours," or if need be, "Meter-kilogram per hour." Then he asked about the instructions given, and offered his opinion that "memorizing by rote of countless formulas is not nearly as beneficial in later work as is the practical application of what is being taught in physical experimentation and the value of precise observation." One had to *"beobachten und daraus richtige Folgerungen zieher"* — observe and from it draw correct deductions — he insisted.

On subsequent visits to his laboratory at the institute, Röntgen and Margret made several experiments, and he asked her some rather difficult questions. Apparently she did well, for the professor who was so feared because of his severity at examination time told her that he would be happy to give her a *Zwei* — a *two,* or *B* — had she been one of his Physikum candidates. In a lengthy visit to the Deutschen Museum, he explained to her in great detail the functions of the various apparatus he had used during the early discovery periods, and now exhibited there.

All evidence indicates that Wilhelm Röntgen took a much keener interest in the school activities of Margret Boveri than he had in those of his adopted daughter Josephine Berta years before. When Berteli went to school, Röntgen was still deeply involved in his own scientific investigations and strenuously engaged in the so demanding professorship. By the time Margret reached her school period, he was already well established and found more leisure time for extra-curricular academic fields. Then too, the girls were entirely different types; Berteli was the good-natured, passive homebody, while Margret was the intellectual, agile, and discerning scholar, who later would earn a doctor's degree and make a name for herself as author of several literary works of consequence.

During the spring of 1918, when the German armies made their last big offensive to decide the stalemated war in France, Röntgen wrote to Frau Boveri (April 27):

The thoughts of every real German in these days are mostly occupied — and his emotions are moved the strongest — with the war effort and the question of Germany's future. I make an effort — usually successful — to have full confidence in our Highest Command and in our brave soldiers, believing that they will bring about a favorable peace which will endure and insure us rest for a long period to come. If this hope is fulfilled, I shall consider the war as a wholesome healing agent which was necessary to lead us from a downward slanting course. Consequential circles have been aware of the many prejudices and shortcomings that had manifested themselves in our society, politics, diplomacy, and the army. Even before the war I have thought and also stated that hard times were necessary to free us from these influences. I hope that we can free ourselves of the clinkers which this so fiery ordeal will leave us, and that a real purification may be accomplished.

But when the sudden collapse of the armies came, it surprised Röntgen as completely as it did many other Germans. Yet, instead of showing great bewilderment he felt that it would bring about changes for the good, and he prayed that a peaceful evolution would take place. In Munich he noted that the new government had taken steps to insure a broad representation of all parties, not only the social democrats who urged open revolution to change the course of leadership.

However, the brash proclamation of a Communist Council in Munich startled and upset him considerably. Still he sincerely felt, "Good things can be expected to come from the new government. But it is a question if it can hold its own in the future, at least during the most difficult period of transition, or whether ultra-radical influences of Bolshevism may gain the upper hand." Yet, he actually resented the Bolsheviks' duplicity. Brazenly calling themselves a majority *(Bolsheviks)* when actually this rabble was but a most vociferous minority *(Mensheviks)* was to Röntgen the height of impudent deception.

While returning from the institute one afternoon, Wilhelm Röntgen passed the Schack Gallery, where a demonstration was in progress. It had looked quite harmless to him, but when shooting started, he realized that it was not an entirely peaceful demonstration at all. Still, the harsh acts were probably caused by young hoodlums and excited persons, he rationalized, and were not organized incidents. Talks of unruly soldiers causing disturbances were going around, but such cases were usually only isolated ones and probably not of serious concern. At one time, rumors indicated that Prince Rupprecht was indeed approaching the city with a company of faithful soldiers to quell the unruliness of the revolutionary elements, but this did not happen. The demonstrations were taking place with some regularity in the area where Röntgen walked to the institute, and occasionally he was forced to go in a roundabout way to reach his destination without incident. There was talk of ransacking some houses in the well-to-do sectors of the city, and this worried him greatly for several weeks, but eventually the troublesome elements were suppressed by the authorities, and there was only minor street fighting by police and revolutionary Bolsheviks.

To Hitzig, Wilhelm Röntgen wrote that April that he had been badly remiss in acknowledging correspondence, especially from his ever-decreasing circle of intimate friends. He apologized for this shortcoming. He thanked Hitzig for remembering his birthday, which was spent at Weilheim. There were none of the exhilarating surprises of bygone years — he and Bertha spent the day quietly in each other's company. He continued:

The time from January 1st did not pass very well here. At first my wife suffered periods of extreme weakness for weeks and then suddenly came down with a 104° temperature and bronchitis which caused terrible anxiety. The danger subsided after one critical week, but the weakness remained and still exists. Then the continuous kidney pains, which have increased tremendously during the past months, caused great difficulties. Her heart has been affected and developed a weakness (*Angina Pectoris:* a peculiarly painful disease giving the patient a sense of suffocation contraction within the chest) which is being treated with digitalis. I fear what this eventually might lead to. That her morale is often rather low is understandable, but generally she carries her fate quite bravely and enjoys the visible coming of spring.

Then he wrote about the deteriorating economic situation and the war effort and ended on a cheerier note, stating that he was happy that the Hitzig home had "two charming daughters in attendance to his sick wife, and a small grandchild sometimes brings sunshine into the home." It was to be his last letter to his friend.

In August Wilhelm Röntgen wrote to Ritzmann that "the circle of friends is slowly melted down." He was deeply affected by the recent death of Hitzig and recounted some of the other friendships, now *nur Erinnerungen,* only memories. His wife seemed actually to show improvement, although the morphine injections continued unchanged in dosage. "Age is noticeable in both," he wrote, "and I recognize that my mental alertness has suffered along with the physical condition." Most of their time now was spent at Weilheim where they enjoyed Bertha's garden, although tremendously diminished from former years, and nature's bountiful forests, as inviting as ever, surrounding them.

Wilhelm Röntgen deeply felt the total collapse of his *Vaterland,* and when the new republic was proclaimed in November he wrote:

Already, long before the war, I have often spoken out on the fact that we in Germany have strayed off the right road in our social life, that instead of having a true love for our native land we had become too materialistic. I had proposed some remedies. But I had never thought, and far less hoped, that the remedy would be so terrible and that we have to suffer so heavily for our mistakes. The armistice demands and the proposed peace conditions are so depressing that it seems difficult to maintain the needed will to create a decent existence under these new circumstances. Perhaps age sees things too black, and I hope that youth has other views in this respect. Against this main worry, all others seem unimportant, or at least, should be. The loss of Elsass [Alsace], especially of Strassburg, is particularly hard for me. There I had lived at the reopening of the university with such unusually great enthusiasm, and there I spent some of the most pleasant and productive periods of my entire life. I often look at the picture of Strassburg on the wall of my study and hum the old ballad, *O Strassburg, O Strassburg, du wunderschöne Stadt.* . . . There are still many matters which will have to be overcome. Fortunately, my wife is fairly well right now. She has pains, but for her age [79] and despite all hardships she had to endure, is still quite active physically and mentally, and she is almost always in good humor. We are trying to decide what we can do with our large apartment in the city, how to arrange it so that we could accommodate other tenants, but have not come to a decision, missing good counsel.

To others Röntgen expressed grave doubts that a republican constitution would be better than a monarchial parliamentary government. Being ruled, he reasoned, was easier than choosing those to govern the country.

I am not convinced that the German people, who are politically uneducated, can live under this form of government as well as do the Swiss people. Poor, poor Germany, what will become of you?

To his old school friend Albert he wrote:

Then there are these depressing conditions under which we Germans have to suffer innocently. Not only that we have grown poor, for this could be endured, but our deepest sorrow is the question of what the future will hold in store for us, and of how the horribly distressed people can ever regain their composure. It requires much courage and confidence to keep up one's spirits.

To cousin Louise in Indianapolis he had written at about the same time:

The mistreatment and distrust that our fatherland has to suffer constantly from its revengeful enemies, especially from France and England, and which have led us close to the abyss — if not already into it — can hardly be borne. The future is very dark and the present is desolate and dangerous. I hope that in America the spirit of reason and truth which has been dissipated to a great extent by English and French propaganda, will be restored before it is entirely too late.

But to counteract these depressions, there was his work. Röntgen still worked regularly that winter at the Physical Science Institute. For the 1918–19 winter semester he lectured on experimental physics, part I:

mechanics, acoustics, optics, for five hours weekly; and the *Anleitung zur selbst. Arbeiten,* or guidance for independent works, for forty-eight hours. Practical demonstrations, for four hours, was under his direction, with the assistance of Professor Peter Paul Koch and Ernst Wagner. It was a heavy load for a man of 73 years of age, but it brightened his days.

Some brightness appeared too in the further development of X ray techniques. Röntgen followed eagerly all publications he was able to secure during the war years. Great strides had been made in the direction of the systematic application of X ray radiation in the treatment of disease. The famed gynecologist Dr. Bernhard Krönig of the recently founded Radiologic Institute of the *Frauenklinik* at the Freiburg University had, in collaboration with Walter Friedrich, published a paper in 1918 on the physical and biological foundations of radiation therapy. Röntgen followed this development with keenest interest and studied it as well as subsequent reports by Friedrich on the great value of X ray treatment of various diseases with special emphasis on cancers.

X ray treatments had, of course, been given many years earlier, initially by Dr. Leopold Freund in Vienna, who soon after the discovery inaugurated an X ray surface therapy to treat cancer patients. Friedrich Dessauer systematically investigated the possibilities of depth therapy in 1905, then using radioactive substances in treatments. Other pioneers included Dr. Francis Henry Williams and Dr. Emil H. Grubbe in the United States.

These reports actually represented the first systematic determination of correct radiation quantities and qualities by new and accurate physical methods for controlled therapeutic results. Otto Glasser, a pupil of Friedrich's, extended this method of treatment with gamma rays of radium and thereby opened an entirely new era in radiation therapy. Scientists from all over the world came to Friedrich's laboratory soon after the war to study his methods of accurately measuring radiation dosages. Among the distinguished visitors were Andrew Gray and F. L. Hopwood from London, Puga from Lisbon, H. C. Nauta from Batavia, J. F. Maisterra from Madrid, K. Fujinami from Tokyo, and G. E. Richards from Toronto. The United States was well represented by P. M. Hickey of Detroit, J. T. Case of Chicago, A. W. Crane of Kalamazoo, H. Schmitz of Chicago, and W. D. Coolidge of Schenectady.

However, the eventual development of a hot filament cathode tube, which was remarkably stable and permitted regulation of voltage and of current at the tube, greatly advanced the standardization of diagnostic and therapeutic X ray exposures. This tube had been developed by the General Electric Company in the Schenectady laboratories headed by William D. Coolidge, who had discovered a process for producing ductile tungsten which he used in the manufacture of targets for the tubes, giving them improved stability.

Wilhelm Röntgen was immensely gratified to know that his discovery had indeed contributed greatly to the amelioration of pain and that it had saved innumerable lives during the terrible war. It was a small counter-agent to the ravages of the conflict, and in a small measure it was beneficial to mankind as a whole. It also held the tremendously challenging promise to aid all people in the future.

Years later Röntgen received a letter that quoted the American physician, Dr. R. C. Beeler of Indianapolis. It read in part:

We were in the trenches near Toul when we heard that the roentgenologists in the German hospitals were celebrating Professor Röntgen's birthday. The American radiologists appreciate the discovery of the professor as much as the Germans do. We drank with French cognac to the health of the old professor. They shall not say that we were narrow-minded or prejudiced. We recognize the celebrity of this man and only wished that old Professor Röntgen could have heard us.

This letter made the old professor very happy indeed, and he liked to read it to his few friends often.

CHAPTER 20

After the War

ON MARCH 20, 1919, Wilhelm Röntgen wrote to Ernst Ritzmann, recalling the times when they had journeyed happily to the south at this time of year for the Easter vacations and reveled in the gay company of the Hitzigs, the Boveris, the Ritzmanns, and others to celebrate his birthday.

But those times are definitely gone now. Not only did the terrible war leave scars that will never heal, but most of the former celebrants have gone on, including Frau Hitzig. Still, the pleasant memories of those carefree days remain to lighten up the present dark days.

There was little change in the condition of his wife. She passed her eightieth birthday on April 22, though her age was never, never mentioned to any of their friends. "Now and then," Röntgen wrote, "I worry deeply that I might become immune to the situation and thus not have enough consideration for my wife." He faithfully administered the daily morphine injections and tried to make her as comfortable as humanly possible. Bertha was ever grateful for his constant protection and always let him know of her deep appreciation with a *"Gott schütz' dich!"* — God protect you!

June 22 was actually just another day to Wilhelm Röntgen, but a most pleasing occurrence was the receipt of a Special Address from the *Preussischen Akademie* at his fiftieth anniversary of the degree of Doktor der Philosophie. There was no celebration for the *Jubiläum* — the times and conditions were not suitable for any kind of celebration — and he and his wife were at Weilheim when the mailman brought the congratulatory messages.

The *Technische Hochschule* of Munich had given him a Doctor of Engineering degree, *honoris causa,* the previous year, and now the Züricher Universität presented him with a special doctorate diploma. He was also awarded two Helmholtz medals, one in bronze and one in gold. The *Deutsche Physikalische Gesellschaft* elected him an honorary member with a certificate signed by the leading scientists. The recognition from the *Preussischen Akademie,* however, pleased him most.

Röntgen wished to share this fine tribute with his closest friends, and wrote to Margret Boveri:

According to my thinking, it is perfectly beautiful, and you will probably like it too. Also, because you are among my closest friends with whom I should like to share sorrow and happiness I send it to you.

In a reminiscent mood, he wrote:

When fifty years ago I was handed my doctor's diploma I ran with it up the Uetliberg — near Zürich — where, at that time, my beloved stayed taking a cure. We were extremely happy and proud, although the affair really did not mean much, and I had good reason to worry about my still uncertain future. I had actually two diplomas — one as engineer and the other as doctor of philosophy — but could not definitely decide to enter the technical field, as I had originally planned to do. During this critical time I became acquainted with a young professor of physics who asked me one day "What do you really want to do in your life?" On my answer that I did not know, he replied that I should try physics. I had to confess that I had almost nothing at all to do with that particular branch of studies, but he suggested that I could catch up on it easily. So, at the age of twenty-four and practically engaged to be married, I began to study physics and to practice it. I remained true to it. Who — and most of all, myself — had the faintest idea that fifty years later I would receive such a certificate as that of the Berliner Akademie which I just received.

The *Preussische Akademie der Wissenschaften,* Berlin, wrote:

Esteemed Colleague: The fiftieth anniversary of the happy day on which you began your scientific career also is a day for festive remembrance for your academy. We cannot let it pass by without giving expression to the joyful pride that we can count you among our members, whose brilliant name is thankfully praised by all mankind.

A kind fate led you in your youth into Kundt's laboratory and permitted you to complete your education under the surveillance of this master of the experimental art.

Your first major investigation on the ratio of specific heats of gases is a fine example for your keen and critical precision workmanship. Still under the influence of your teacher, you soon entered other fields of investigation, which allowed the individuality of your scientific personality to emerge quite clearly.

Your great gift of discovering new methods was shown in the simple and ingenious method of measuring the conductivity of heat in crystals by defining the breath diagram.

Your astounding talent for construction manifested itself to its fullest extent in the investigations, made in collaboration with August Kundt, on the electromagnetic rotation of the plane of polarization in gases. In this classical work you succeeded in observing and measuring quantitatively in several gases the effect which had been sought fruitlessly by Faraday.

Again you showed the same skill in overcoming experimental difficulties in the numerous investigations made with your pupils on the influence of pressure on compressibility, capillarity, viscosity, and the refraction of light of various bodies. As a result of this valuable work, one should also consider your theory on the constitution of liquid water which has proved to be so extremely fruitful.

By employing a new unusual method, you brought the old controversy between John Tyndall and Gustav Magnus on the absorption of heat rays by water vapor to a final decisive solution.

You treated a question of fundamental significance in your investigations of the electrodynamic effect of a dielectric moved through a homogeneous electrical field. That you succeeded in observing with certainty the exceedingly small effect predicted by the Maxwell theory is again an indication of your keenly developed art of experimentation.

All of these investigations, among which must also be mentioned your comprehensive systematic examinations of the pyro- and piezo-electricity of crystals, are worthy of securing you an honored place among the leading physicists of Germany. However, these prominent scientific accomplishments fade as the stars before the sun when compared with your greatest discovery of 1895. Probably never has a new truth from the quiet laboratory of a scientist made its triumphal progress so quickly over the whole world as has your epoch-making discovery of these wonderful rays. The expectations of the theoretical and practical value of the new discovery were tremendous, but even these have been far surpassed by reality.

The history of science teaches that in every discovery there is chained in a peculiar manner, merit and luck, and many a man not entirely familiar with the facts may be inclined to ascribe in this particular case a preponderant part to luck. But whoever has penetrated into the individuality of your scientific personality understands that this great discovery was destined to success only by you, the investigator free from all prejudices, who combined perfected experimental art with the greatest scrupulousness and carefulness.

The three treatises in which you described the wonderful properties of the new rays belong because of their modest form, their essential brevity, and their masterful presentation, to the classical works of physical science. The value of discernment contained in your discovery has inaugurated a new era in our science, which constantly arrives at more gratifying results and reaches out to higher goals.

The eminent practical significance of the new rays, which you recognized immediately but which you, in your noble unselfishness, have left to others to develop practically, was revealed in a most striking manner during the World War. One can say with complete authority that the fruits of your scientific investigations have spared the life or the use of limb of hundreds of thousands of poor wounded, friend and foe. Thus you are not only esteemed by physical science as its immortal master but also by the whole world as its benefactor.

May the rapturous feeling of having contributed so greatly to the further-ance of our knowledge and to the benefaction of suffering mankind help you on this day of honor to overcome the distress which we all feel over the collapse of our beloved fatherland. May it be granted you to see the dawn of better times. This is our sincere wish.

Many years later, on May 18, 1959, Professor Arthur H. Compton stated, "We can show that the number of lives that have been saved by X rays since their discovery by Röntgen is as great as the number of lives that have been taken in all of the wars that have been fought since that time."

The physical condition of Bertha Röntgen deteriorated rapidly that summer of 1919 and she hardly ever left her bed. With the help of Kätchen, Röntgen would carry her onto the balcony. From there she could see and enjoy the small, colorful patch of flowers which had not been given over to the vegetables, as prudence would have indicated. It was a luxury nobody could really afford during those days of shortages, but it was the only pleasure left to her that summer and fall, before they returned to their Munich home.

In October, Wilhelm Röntgen wrote:

What I know from my talk with Dr. Quenstedt and from my own observations, about our dear patient: The illness is not curable and the cardiac and renal insufficiency increases from day to day and along with it the weakness of the body and spirit. The medicaments which we use can merely make Bertha's life easier. The great amount of swelling of her legs and abdomen will not decrease. There is a decided dropsy. It is hard to say how long Bertha is going to survive; it may be only a few days, or it may be several weeks. It is difficult for her to talk or to think, and we are grateful when she can sleep most of the day and night, and if, between times, I can talk to her for short periods. We frequently speak about death, which is not too difficult for either of us. I try, of course, to avoid telling her my opinion and try to encourage and reassure her. Her own idea on imminent death vacillates, but she has an exemplary patience and always is grateful for whatever one is able to do for her.

The day after he had written this letter, on October 24, the doctors Quenstedt and Müller assured him that Bertha's condition was not that serious. Her vitality and heart action were sufficient to permit them the hope that she would recover enough to spend a few hours out of bed every morning and afternoon. They decided that the dropsy was due to her age and would not improve, but really did not cause too much discomfort. Röntgen did not share that opinion.

To add to this deep anxiety, Röntgen also had to be concerned with moving during that very week. Their landlord, Prince Alfons, had been forced out of his residence and wanted to move into the apartment which the Röntgens had occupied for these nineteen years. Fortunately, Röntgen had located a satisfactory *Wohnung* in the immediate vicinity of the old one — situated some 600 feet away, at the Maria-Theresia-Strasse 11, in a fashionable two-and-a-half-story villa of light brown brick trimmed with red stone, and surrounded by a spacious garden, formal in the front and an expansive lawn with large trees in the rear, all enclosed by a tall iron fence. A preferred first-story apartment was not available, but with the privacy of the fenced-in garden on this exclusive street of fine villas on one side and the steeply sloping park on the other side, Röntgen was satisfied to live in this *Hochpaterre* apartment.

Käthe Fuchs remembered that the moving was a major task. Some fifty to sixty boxes were used to hold the furnishings and books. Bertha was disquieted by the noise of the packing. "Wait until I am dead," she pleaded. But there was no possibility of postponing the move. The furnishings of her bedroom were moved first, and then she was taken into the new room in their new home, but she showed no interest at all in it. The noise of all of the activity annoyed her greatly, although the workmen were constantly urged to be quiet. Arranging furniture in the various rooms was left entirely to Käthe. Bertha was Röntgen's chief solicitude.

Bertha died on October 31, 1919. A severe attack was fatal to her. The wonderful companionship of the couple was ended.

Wilhelm Röntgen was desolate to lose his love of more than fifty years, and his grief was deep. She was buried in Giessen with his parents. Röntgen could not visit her grave often, but Käthe later told how he brought flowers from the garden and decorated her bed daily for the three years after her death. In his loneliness, he often sat in his favorite easy chair in front of a photograph of Bertha in silent contemplation with her. Sometimes he read aloud from the newspaper or a novel they had liked, or mail received, pretending that she still shared her thoughts with him.

Among the many letters that he received, and that he felt would have been of interest to Bertha, was one from Count von Moltke. Röntgen was deeply touched by the letter which recalled the, to him unforgettable, experience when von Moltke sat on his left enjoying an after dinner cigar at the Kaiserliches Schloss in Berlin and when he spoke about the newly discovered X rays to the Imperial family. The Kaiser had sat on his right

Above, house in Munich where the Röntgens lived from 1900 to 1919; *below,* house where Röntgen lived from 1919 to 1923.

side then. Now there was no Kaiser, nor a monarchy, and nothing but utter despair in Germany. Röntgen read the letter to Bertha's picture which was standing before him, because, as he said, "she would have enjoyed this letter very much. She was so proud of me and yet never induced to take advantage of the fame of her husband, as so many wives do."

He was simply unable to reconcile himself to loneliness, although the girls of his household — Käthe, Marie, and Wally — took care of him as best they could and were thoroughly devoted to him. The Boveris tried to ease his lost feeling by occasional visits that year, but travel was extremely difficult during this tumultuous postwar period. He tried to write more letters than ever, but the number of dear friends had decreased.

He took, as before, great interest in the studies of Margret Boveri, writing to her on December 12:

I am very happy to see that you are still interested in physics. First, because I also like physics very much, but also on your account. The activity of the mind in the study of experimental sciences and especially physics, its not very complicated problems, the probability of reaching a valid solution, and finally the particular method of investigation, the experiment, all of this is so very different from that mental activity which is necessary in studying languages or art, that it is very beneficial in the development of an individual of your talents to learn to know both kinds. Physics is also of great service to you in another way. All living beings, therefore also human beings, and the latter especially in their early years, are given the ability of making observations and of drawing correct conclusions from them. This gift is often withered in youth because of too intense application to too many educational subjects, and it is a great pity, because it is extremely useful and brings great satisfaction. All natural sciences with the exception of those which merely catalog phenomena, are bound to develop this gift. I cannot judge with any certainty which one is most suitable for the purpose, but no doubt experimental physics is not the last in the rank. You will surely have had the experience yourself that it is very agreeable to have a broad knowledge, and it is sometimes useful, but that after all is the only activity that brings real satisfaction.

A year later Röntgen was to write:

I have heard that [Willy] Wien intends to give his lectures in a thoroughly elementary way and that in his first lecture he promised his students not to use any mathematics but to show them great experiments. Apparently he is taking into consideration the well-known and unbelievably meager knowledge of mathematics by the students of medicine. In this procedure I can see only a lowering of the standards of teaching of physics, which will be to the disadvantage of the students of science. What use are such experiments which are made on a large scale for the future teachers who must eventually give their own instructions in a simple manner?

Another time he disagreed with Wien's points in his lecture again,

. . . such as the distinction between experimental and theoretical subjects. To my point of view there are two methods of research, the apparatus and the calculation. Whoever prefers the first method is an experimenter, otherwise he is a mathematical physicist. Both of them set up theories and hypotheses. For this reason I would like to have the usual appellation of "theoretical physicist" replaced by "mathematical physicist." If Wien would be asked in which group he would place Faraday, I believe that his answer would lead him to contradictions.

That year it would be too difficult for Wilhelm Röntgen to go alone at Christmas to Weilheim, and so he agreed to Frau Boveri's suggestion that he visit them at Würzburg. He stayed over New Year's and then returned to the *Jagdhaus* where everything reminded him of his dear Bertha.

When he first arrived and found that all of the flowers and many young shrubs were winter-killed, he became so infuriated that he could not speak for several minutes. It was incomprehensible to him that his Bertha's own garden was allowed to suffer such a fate. But eventually the swollen veins receded, and he calmed down. He went into the house and did not enter the garden again during all that winter. He could not trust himself to see this catastrophe without becoming enraged, and he realized that his blaming the girls for it was quite unreasonable of him.

Wilhelm Röntgen had visibly aged during the past months. He still walked several miles daily, holding himself as erect as before, but something was definitely amiss. The times now were so very different from those he had lived in during all of his life. The many new strange attitudes and the multitude of restrictive regulations confused him terribly. And he could not conduct his experiments with the same energy as previously, for he felt that it was useless to achieve anything in this chaotic existence. He was weighed down by his personal loss and often expressed feelings of deepest melancholy. In the early spring he had a visit from Willy Wien, who had followed him in the Würzburg post, and who promptly reported on his condition to Frau Boveri. She, in turn, wrote to Röntgen, trying to cheer him up and encourage him to remain as active as possible. He replied, describing what he considered a typical day in his life.

First of all I must mention that I was very sorry that Wien told you that he found me suffering and that I worry too much. That is really not so, and to prove to you that I do not even have the necessary time for such things, I will tell you how I have spent today and add that all other days pass along similarly. At eight o'clock I breakfasted, then read your letter and several others and after that went to the *Bayerischen Hypotheken- und Wechselbank* to ask about the savings account (Monday I went for an identical reason to the *Deutschen Bank*). From the bank I went to the institute and made experiments for approximately two and a half hours, so that I returned a little late for the meal, to the utmost displeasure of the concerned Kätchen. However, the experimental work has done me good. After the meal I lay down on the sofa for a short rest and read *Zwischen Himmel und Erde* by Ludwig, which greatly interested me as a study in psychology. Then I had coffee and a piece of cake that Berteli had sent me, and afterward I wrote the results of the morning's work into a manuscript. At about four-thirty I went to the universiy to see Sommerfeld, who had wanted to come to me. Not until seven did I arrive at home, read a few letters that had arrived, ate my evening meal, and then began this letter. Finally, there will probably be a bit of a lecture tonight.

But whenever possible Wilhelm Röntgen went to Weilheim to enjoy the unhurried atmosphere of the country. Instead of walking through the English Garden at Munich, he roamed through the wild nature trails in the forest. Some of the fine hunting grounds nearby had been lost to him when Baron Hirschberg built his new *Schloss* and bought the surrounding forest area. This vexed Röntgen, but he eventually had to accept the curtailment of his range.

From Weilheim, in the fall, he wrote:

The warm, sunny weather has suddenly changed. The entire landscape is heavily covered with snow, now and then some sun, but mostly snowstorms. Despite that I go daily a bit to the Gögerl. The remaining time I utilize to revise the manuscript of my work and to clarify it. In between I read some, either in *Tristram Shandy* or in the *Briefwechsel* [Correspondence] between Goethe and Zelter. Both books interest me very much. These activities help me overcome the otherwise depressing feeling of quietude and solitude. If I did not enjoy so much the Weilheim *Häusli* with all its memories, I would not remain here long. The Munich apartment still seems always very strange to me, although the life in the city affords some mental stimulant, which I do not like to give up.

It was a rather quiet and sedate gathering when Röntgen celebrated his seventy-fifth birthday in the new apartment in Munich on March 27, 1920. Frau Boveri and Margret came to make the day a cheerful one, and it was not as lonely as he had feared. He was most appreciative of their warm friendship, more than mere words could express, and he wrote that it was unfortunate that they lived in Würzburg and could not stay longer than the day or two, but their pleasant visit had taken the great burden of loneliness off his shoulders to a large extent.

The whole nation was in the grip of an appalling postwar crisis when food was the main concern of the surviving people, and when a terrifying inflation wiped out the savings and often the entire property of nearly everyone.

There was but little interest in scientific matters, as Paul Krause, Professor for Internal Medicine of the Bonn University, wrote:

Röntgen celebrated in 1920 his seventy-fifth birthday. The day passed very nearly unnoticed. Only the *Rheinische Röntgen Vereinigung,* founded in 1919, named its great Rheinish compatriot on this day as an honorable member. The daily newspapers have, with few exceptions, no liking and insufficient space to care about personal affairs of our learned men. But despite that it must be said with emphasis: That is needed more today than ever before. Every German should know about the great men whom we have, should have in his lifetime knowledge of their achievements, where they came from, where they live, what they are. Everything that was good and great and beautiful in Germany and in the world can unite us and finally restore us to health, only that can do it — everything else but politics! I am again frightened and depressed when I find how little the Germans, especially doctors and students, know about our great natural scientists and physicians, even about our greatest men. Unquestionably better instruction in this respect is necessary. Already in the schools the beginning should be made. The student attending the Gymnasium should not only learn who and what Goethe and Beethoven were, he should also learn what Robert Koch and Röntgen have achieved and where they came from.

However, several organizations did take notice of Wilhelm Röntgen's seventy-fifth birthday and the coming twenty-fifth anniversary of the discovery of X rays by him on November 8, 1895. The Johann-Wolfgang-Goethe-*Universität* at Frankfurt am Main made him an *Ehrendoktor der Naturwissenschaften,* or Doctor of Natural Sciences, h.c.; and he was made an honorary citizen of the City of Würzburg. He was made an honorary member of the Röntgen *Gesellschaft* of Bonn, the *Frankfurter Röntgengesellschaft,* and the *Gesellschaft für Natur und Heilkunde* of Dresden. The *Preussische Akademie der Wissenschaften* at Berlin and the *Wiener Akademie der Wissenschaften* both elected him nonresident honorary member *(auswärtiges Mitglied),* and the *Strassburger Wissenschaftliche Gesellschaft* of Heidelberg elected him a regular member *(ordentliches Mitglied).* The city of Weilheim named a street of but a few blocks length, the Röntgenstrasse; significantly, the spacious hospital is located on it.

The city council of Lennep named a street the Röntgenstrasse, and Röntgen was sent a copy of an address given by the mayor. A commemorative tablet had been placed on the house of Röntgen's birth, which read:

IN DIESEM HAUSE WURDE AM
27. MÄRZ 1845 DER ENTDECKER
DER RÖNTGENSTRAHLEN
CONRAD RÖNTGEN
GEBOREN. DIE VATERSTADT ER-
NANNTE IHN 1896 ZUM EHREN-
BÜRGER UND WIDMETE IHM ZUM
75. GEBURTSTAGE DIESE TAFEL
LENNEP DEN 27. MÄRZ 1920

Röntgen was, of course, highly pleased at this recognition by the town of his birth. But he was also greatly amused. Earlier, the city council insisted on the erroneous nobility for him; this time it failed to mention his correct first name. Wilhelm Röntgen wrote a lengthy letter of thanks to the mayor, but added, *"Gestatten Sie mir, hochverehrter Herr Bürgermeister . . ."* — Allow me, highly esteemed Mister Mayor . . . — and pointed out that his given name was omitted on the tablet. He suggested that it be included, and that instead of repeating the name "Röntgen," the line *"der nach ihm benannten Strahlen"* — the rays named after him — be used. This was eventually done when the plaque was replaced in 1952! It read then:

> IN DIESEM HAUSE IST
> WILHELM
> CONRAD RÖNTGEN
> DER ENTDECKER DER NACH
> IHM BENANNTEN STRAHLEN
> AM 27. MÄRZ 1845 GEBOREN
> SEINE VATERSTADT HAT IHN
> IM JAHRE 1896
> ZUM EHRENBÜRGER ERNANNT

Wilhelm Conrad Röntgen resigned his position at the institute after his birthday, coinciding with the end of the semester. He had written to the ministry on October 18, 1919, and the representative of the minister of culture, or whomever could be consulted in this postwar turmoil, agreed to the retirement which had been planned long before. Röntgen was placed on the official retirement list as Professor Emeritus to receive the regular pension his position entitled him to. However, he retained his position as Conservator of the Physical-Metronomical Institute, which gave him the use of two small laboratory rooms where he hoped to conclude some of his unfinished experiments. The official post actually made no requirements on his time, and there were no official duties to perform. Ernst Wagner took over Professor Röntgen's work during the summer semester of 1920 *in Vertretung,* as substitute, while during the *Zwischenhalbjahr,* between-half-year, from February 2 to March 31, 1920, Arnold Sommerfeld, assisted by Paul Ewald, took over the work of Röntgen. The official catalog for the 1920–21 semester stated simply, *"Röntgen liest nicht"* — or Röntgen does not read, that is, lecture.

As Röntgen had written to Frau Boveri, he had been to the banks to see about his financial affairs. Since he had a large portfolio of foreign securities (including Denver & Rio Grande 4% bonds), most of which had come from his father's estate, he had prudently contacted his legal adviser regarding the new regulations pertaining to such monetary matters. His lawyer advised him to deposit all of his papers with the *Bayerischen Hypotheken- und Wechselbank* and let them take care of them. He had always been meticulous about these securities, keeping a heavily bound book of copies of the many letters covering such transactions with his Dutch bankers. At the Munich bank he was disagreeably surprised to learn that he must turn in his American, Italian, and Swiss securities to the government, and that the final date for doing so was the fifteenth of the month, only a few days away. Not complying with this order meant a severe fine or even a prison sentence. He was outraged. "I had some little difficulty in convincing the official that I had no intention of defrauding him, that is, of keeping possession of this money secret. And now I am going to receive a great deal of German money, and I do not really know what to do with it."

In fact, when the edict was issued to turn in all foreign exchange, he would have received two million marks (about $500,000), but now it was somewhat less. Through all of these money matters, Röntgen was glad that he had acted honestly, although the entire transaction was most confusing to him.

Käthe Fuchs recalled that as a precautionary measure he took four thousand marks out of the bank, stuffed the bills into a tin can, and buried it behind pine trees in the garden at Weilheim.

Röntgen wrote, "It is all very depressing to hear from many sources that the government actually draws most of its income from the honest people of average wealth, because many of the possessors of real fortunes are said to have found safe ways of keeping their holdings secret." But the whole business had excited him profoundly, and he found some relief in the writing of a long letter on the subject. Yet, he ended the letter with the pleasant observation, "The spring was really beautiful. If my wife could have seen it, she might have hummed her favorite song, *'Mein Herz, mach dich auf, dass die Sonne drein scheint'* — My heart, open up, so the sun can shine in it."

On the day after the birthday of his beloved Bertha — now gone six months — Röntgen wrote to Frau Boveri and Margret:

With a heart full of gratitude I want to write to you while in this sorrowful though calm and almost exalted mood and report to you how I spent the day yesterday. My gratitude is first to you, dear friend, and to dear Margret who with so much kindness and consideration and sympathy have helped me to live and to endure the unavoidable, and who see to it that the last days of my life are not without happiness or lost in the sad realization of absolute loneliness. "God protect you" were the words my wife frequently spoke to me during her last days. You are the instruments in His hands to fulfill this prayer, and He has chosen the best that He alone could give. You take such good care of me that sometimes I ask myself why I deserve this good fortune. Then I like to think that it has been arranged by the dear departed who loved you and me, and it is in this way that the circle of those to whom I am grateful expands.

Before I answer your two letters, let me tell you what happened yesterday. I had told Kätchen to go to Munich on Tuesday to buy some flowers. She did this very well, so on the birthday morning, with blooming plants, roses, cineraria, marigolds, and primroses, we decorated the alcove in the living room where my wife liked to sit in the wicker chair. I should have mentioned first that your lilies of the valley surrounded the photograph on the chair and soon filled the room with their delightful fragrance. Also the picture above the davenport was adorned with flowers. I thought that my wife would have been very happy if she could have seen it all.

After breakfast I looked through some letters that my wife had received a year ago and read a few and was warmed by the thought of the love and veneration which was given to her during her life. I had not yet finished reading these letters when your letter and little package arrived, just at the proper moment to lift my feelings to a still higher level. It is remarkable how much you have been able to keep in your memory to use to make your friends, and especially myself, happy at the proper moment. It was indeed our custom to eat the first asparagus on my wife's birthday, if possible, and I like to keep up these old customs. But this year, on account of the hard times, I would have refrained from keeping it. It is exceedingly good of you to have fulfilled my wish.

Afterward I consulted my wife's diary to see what happened on the twenty-second of April during the last few years, but strangely enough found nothing of importance written on her eightieth birthday. I had made a note in the history of her illness that on that day we found the last violets and I placed them in front of her photograph.

In the afternoon I went over the letters received since 1919. Among them there is a large package from you full of love and friendship. According to my wish, nobody in the house worked during the day. For dinner I had some of the excellent asparagus, and then I reread the letters of condolence which I had received after my wife's death. This was a somewhat sad but still inspiring occupation. For again I saw how many different kinds of people understood my wife and how much love and kindness she had earned, and so I ended the day most peacefully.

On June 8, Röntgen wrote to Ritzmann from Weilheim that he was greatly delinquent in his writing to friends. The birthday congratulations were still unacknowledged, and he asked his friends to pardon him. He was now working on several scientific papers, which he hoped to get ready for publication. So that he would not always be too concerned over her illness, he had promised his wife that he would get the notes on certain observations together and write them up. But this editing work took considerable time and immense effort, and he soon realized he had promised it a bit too freely. It now had become his "reminder of my duty and my promise to help overcome my inertia." His meticulous corrections to achieve painstaking clarity were a bit more exhaustive to him now than a few years before, and he believed that his mental powers for such type of work, which needed sharp concentration, were not as strong as previously. But his time was limited and the work should be completed, he felt. Although he had spent his birthday at Munich, he had come to his beloved house at Weilheim for Bertha's birthday. Here, of course, all of the rooms with the furnishings, and the surrounding garden constantly reminded him of his dear departed. But he found that this gave him a deep feeling of consolation, and he remembered the joyful and later the difficult years. Right now the garden was particularly resplendent with multi-colored flowers, although much of the ground was given over to vegetables for the table. The flowers, the shrubs, the plantings, in fact all growing things, had always been closely supervised by his beloved, and he could never forget how she affected every action ever undertaken there. He enjoyed the forest immensely, still taking long hikes daily, as had been his custom ever since he could remember. That would perhaps never change as long as he could get around, for these long communions with nature always restored him and gave him new strength.

For a few days that July Wilhelm Röntgen visited in Höfen, near Bamberg, invited by Frau Boveri, and from there he wrote a letter to Ritzmann, whose wife had just died. He tried to console his friend in that hour of personal grief. He would like to visit him, but a trip to Zurich is out of the question at this difficult time, still he will not give up entirely on this impossible idea. With the children and grandchildren around him, Ritzmann will perhaps find great joy, and the infirmities of advanced age and the great loss will be somewhat eased, Röntgen hoped. He himself had been working quite steadily from six in the morning until late at night in an effort to finish the manuscripts for publication. Only brief periods were taken out for meals, and with the help of the assistant Joffé, who compiled the tables of calculation, the work was completed just before he departed on this short trip.

Toward the end of the year, Wilhelm Röntgen wrote again to Ernst Ritzmann, asking how he stood the loss of his life's partner. He wrote:

How much the devoted life partner is being missed, I know of my own experience. She is irreplaceable and is often so needed. I could not decide to live with other people for long, and I prefer the loneliness. If only I could get together with my friends occasionally. A change from my steady work habits seems to do me a lot of good, and I believe that such a change would also benefit you greatly. Otherwise I try to live as I imagine my wife would find to be satisfactory.

CHAPTER 21

Alone

SHORTLY AFTER the death of Bertha, while Röntgen was in Munich, the mayor of Weilheim called by telephone to warn him that the newly created *Wohnungskommission,* the housing commission, might force some unwanted renters into his *Jagdhaus.* For one person, even with two or three servants, the house was adjudged to be too large and thus not necessary for the occupancy of but a single citizen. Greatly disturbed and ready to fight for what he believed to be his right as owner of the property, Röntgen hurried to Weilheim, taking with him three boxes with apparatus of little value from the institute.

At the subsequent meeting with the mayor and the city architect as the ranking member of the commission, Röntgen learned that the resident physician of the local hospital was most insistent in forcing strange tenants on him. Röntgen, impromptu, that same afternoon invited the entire commission to inspect his house. Then he went home to carry out the planned alterations. He moved the furniture from his study and from the small adjoining guest room. Then he installed the equipment so that both rooms resembled an austere physics laboratory. On the upper floor, he had the connecting doors removed between two rooms so that they appeared as an interdependent unit. When the commission members came to inspect the facilities, Röntgen showed them his laboratory rooms, his bedroom and the living room, all of which he used almost daily and believed to be essential to his work. The men readily agreed with that point of view. Three other rooms were occupied by the housekeeper and the maids; another room, quite crowded with odds and ends, was used as a storeroom.

The committee members decided right there that the house was adequate only for Röntgen himself and that he did not have a surplus of rooms in it; they suggested diplomatically that from the outside it had indeed looked much roomier than the personal inspection had revealed. In fact, most of the members stated that they had been in favor of the eminent scientist and honored citizen anyway, but since the local physician had forced the issue they just had to make the formal request for additional quarters.

Quite disturbed and considerably excited by all that commotion, Röntgen was nevertheless happy and relieved at the satisfactory outcome of the affair. He could not have tolerated strangers living in the house that now was to him a memorial to his wife. To forestall a similar difficulty in Munich, Röntgen installed a technician from the institute in his Maria-Theresia-Strasse apartment.

But the strict rationing regulations by which the authorities controlled the consumption of scarce food were observed to the letter in the household. Occasionally Bertha had tried to circumvent these annoying regulations, with the conniving of her Kätchen, so that he could get more nourishing meals because of his obviously poor physical condition. But Röntgen would not tolerate any infractions. Usually after such an occasion, he would himself appear in the kitchen for several days afterward, to upset the entire household with his impractical but scientific approach to the problem. With great precision he would weigh out the exact daily allotted quantities of fat, meat, sugar, and flour, on the kitchen scales. He would also inquire about vegetables and fruit which might be obtainable locally, or mushrooms which could be gathered, and which kinds could be preserved as canned goods for future use.

At meals, Bertha had invariably served him the larger pieces of meat, which he then put on her plate, thus beginning often long discussions as to who was the more deserving of the valued morsel. Each had deep personal love for the other and wished to make a sacrifice.

At a usual meager meal, which the Boveris attended at Weilheim, Margret noticed that the girls in the kitchen ate *Rohrnudeln,* a Bavarian style macaroni, instead of the meat and vegetable stew served at the family table. She asked to have some for her meal, and Röntgen became interested in this dish which he had never cared to serve to guests. After tasting the noodles, he liked them so much that he actually consumed several helpings, and the simple dish became a regular staple on the table from then on. Vegetables were not always plentiful, but during the seasons their own garden produced a large amount.

In later years, when substitutes were suggested by the food authorities, Röntgen and Margret went out to gather nettles to be cooked and eaten as spinach. Since gloves were an unavailable luxury during that time, the pickers had inflamed and badly swollen hands from these irritating weeds for several days afterward. And the nettles, cooked as spinach, tasted much more awful than that abused vegetable ever did. The experience was not repeated. However, as a green salad, the smooth leaves of other weeds were preferred, and many other substitutes were acceptable, if hardly palatable, during the later years when food was terribly scarce.

When meat had become impossible to purchase in the butcher shops or the weekly markets in the town, the ingenious Käthe, abetted by the maid Marie, insisted on feeding a pig. They pointed out all of the advantages that such action would bring. But Röntgen did not favor that activity, believing that it actually would constitute an unnecessary luxury. Although the pork would be cheaper than if it could be bought, they all had become strict vegetarians during the past months, when no meat for the table had been available anywhere. Röntgen insisted that now he had no desire to eat meat, although the steady diet of rutabagas, cooked without any fat whatever, was most unpleasant to him. But after the butchering, he reasoned, they would have meat in such abundance that it could not be used thriftily, thus the entire experiment would actually be a rather expensive undertaking of little real satisfaction. "If I should decide to capitulate," he wrote, "in order to preserve their good humor, I shall attempt to sell the fattened pig and use the money to buy fresh meat from time to time."

Wilhelm Röntgen had long abandoned the habit of quoting Latin sayings, because his listeners had accepted him for what he had accomplished. The need to impress upon them that he was quite well schooled in that language — and to satisfy himself in the knowledge that the professors and school authorities were most unfair to discriminate against him for the lack of his formal Abitur — had long since passed into history. Otherwise he might have recalled the observation of Censor Metellus that "Nature has arranged that we can live neither with women nor without them, and that if we could live without them, then we should not have all of this trouble."

The *Schweinegeschichte,* the pig story, or plain *Schweinerei,* became trouble for Röntgen. Perhaps he had never correctly estimated the power of his scheming women. Soon a shoat was purchased and kept in a small fenced-in enclosure near the kitchen. By Christmastime of 1922 he was to write, "Our pig has grown so well that we are considering the entire question of how to dispose of it. I could sell it for almost 80,000 marks (about $20,000), while expenses were about 10,000 marks. I called my three servants together for a consultation and told them that I would consent to our butchering it ourselves only if I might be assured that the provisions of meat would last for several months. On the other hand, I made the suggestion that we sell the animal, deduct the amount of the expenses, buy fifteen pounds of lard from the buyer of the pig, and divide the rest of the money between ourselves. Each would then obtain between 10,000 and 12,000 marks (about $2,500 to 3,000). Of course, Kätchen was the chief spokesman and she vehemently refused to accept this suggestion. I answered that we did not have to come to a definite decision for the time being, and that perhaps the other two girls would feel differently about it."

By this time the money had become so rapidly devaluated that selling anything at all for cash instead of trading for equally valuable goods or services was terribly poor advice. Consequently, the pig was kept and butchered. The experienced butcher, wisely, took his pay for that work in solid meat.

Wilhelm Röntgen had always admired those who could work with simple methods — be it in a scientific laboratory or in the household — and his trusted housekeeper Käthe Fuchs had the ability to improvise cleverly. It was by her resourcefulness and shrewdness that she was able to do the almost impossible task of feeding her employer when ration stamps were absolutely no assurance of getting food. To augment the sparse supply of the household, she would often obtain some vegetables, or even more substantial food products from neighbors and from nearby farmers who knew her and liked her.

Röntgen had written about her once, "She is a person with a fine mind, absolutely honest and very kind, and likes to work. Yet she is not without spirit. I could not put any of my Munich acquaintances on an equal plane with her." And he relied upon her more and more.

During the long winter days, when the weather was too severe for him to go out into the forest to hunt or merely for prolonged hikes with Pascha, his German shepherd, Wilhelm Röntgen worked on putting his private papers in order. He wrote, "Evenings I select, from the still available several hundred letters of the earliest time after my discovery of 1895, several interesting ones for safekeeping. The others serve to heat my room, for which the current winter weather offers a fine opportunity."

Daily now, Röntgen spent several hours at his large ornately carved desk of exquisite wood, with a leather inlaid writing surface, and looked through all of the accumulated material. Stored in large packing boxes, carefully nailed up, were the newspapers dealing with the discovery period. They came first. He usually merely glanced at the articles, then discarded the yellowed papers into a large oval laundry basket at his side. The round leather wastebasket with the embossed stag design had become too small to hold this bulky load.

Occasionally an item would strike his fancy, and after he had read it aloud to Käthe, they would both laugh over it before throwing it into the awaiting basket. One item, for example, was a notice from Vienna, where a public lecture on X rays was being planned for March. The police department had duly been asked for permission to hold that assembly, but the officials did not allow it. "The experiments with X rays cannot take place," they ruled, "until further notice, because no details about it have been learned by this office." Of course not. "Only a handful of scientists knew anything about it, and they knew mighty little," Röntgen added, "and they could not have explained it to the police officials even if they had understood the complexities of the rays."

When the laundry basket was full, Käthe with another girl carried it into the corner to use the papers to heat the *Kachelofen*. This activity was closely supervised by Röntgen, who watched the firing from his desk. He did not even trust the servants to burn the discarded newspapers in the privacy of their kitchen, and he definitely did not wish to have any such papers saved for posterity.

The personal letters that had been kept in a locked wardrobe were also minutely scrutinized by Röntgen. With his round, black horn-rimmed glasses on his nose, held by spiral bows, he reread every one meticulously before making the final decision on its disposal.

Letters on almost any subject had come to Röntgen over the years. In 1906 a woman from Vienna wrote asking advice in a real estate matter. She owned some property covering 10,753 square meters and wondered if she should build twelve houses on it or use it in some other way. Her neighbor had built one house and received 30 percent rental for the summer alone. . . .

But not many unsolicited letters dealt with such trivialities. On March 30, 1915, a naval officer, who often had been driven nearly to desperation by dense fogs at sea, wrote in his own behalf from the coast of England and of his son who traveled on the French coast and in Australian waters. He believed that the discoverer of the so beneficial X rays would find a way also to penetrate the solid fog banks. "Such a utilization of these rays in the great fog dangers would have an immeasurable value for our entire shipping in saving monstrous sacrifices of lives and goods."

The Sunday editor of the *New York World* had telegraphed Röntgen on April 10, 1896, asking if he would write an article of two- to five-thousand words "on the origin and possible development of your great discovery" for a fee of 1,000 marks ($250). He referred Röntgen to the American consul "for our esponsibility [sic]." As with other similar requests, Wilhelm Röntgen did not even answer this query. At least the saved telegram carried no comment in Röntgen's handwriting as to its disposition.

In one letter a locksmith appealed for help for his son who had broken a leg. When healed, it was shorter than the healthy limb and a physician had suggested that it be broken again and set properly. The father wondered if both legs should not be broken so that they could both heal to the same length. "A rather workman-like idea of the locksmith father," Röntgen stated. "A physician would hardly have thought of that remedy."

A rather amazing letter had come to Röntgen from the United States when Dr. E. Carter, professor of physics at Vassar College, wrote to him. Röntgen was astonished at some of the revelations and immediately sent it to Frau Boveri with the following comments (on November 13, 1921):

The enclosed letter from Miss Carter has interested me very much indeed. What tremendous resources are available for physical investigations in America! Just imagine, Millikan is said to have a hundred thousand dollars a year for his researches!! Is this supposed to be the yearly budget, or has this huge sum been granted for only one year? Of course, experiments and observations in optics, which at the present time are done chiefly in America, require much money. Just now we have something like that in Germany, in Berlin, where Einstein has erected a million-mark building to determine whether the lines in the sun's spectrum are shifted toward the red as compared to the spectrum of light from artificial sources, the answer to which question probably will decide the acceptance or rejection of the general relativity theory. Or, rather, from these investigations such a decision is expected. For even if the results are positive, there always will be a question as to whether or not the same result might not have been obtained in some simpler way. The two other *experimenta crucis,* the shift of the perihelion of Mercury and also the deviation of stellar light rays from their straight path as they pass by the sun, still leave doubt as to whether or not these facts might be explained even without the theory of relativity.

I still cannot get it into my head that one should have to use such entirely abstract terms and deductions to explain natural phenomena. However, the youthful mind sometimes has different ideas on the subject, but it is hoped that they do not become entirely lost in remote spheres for there still must be innumerable facts which can and must be disclosed by simpler methods so that we may increase our knowledge of nature. I believe that most of the American physicists still follow this latter course. Several young Americans are working on a subject which was brought out by the investigations of Professor L. Frank of Göttingen, that is, on the excitation of light by electric impact.

Wilhelm Röntgen had always believed that an investigating scientist of ability should have an abundance of ingenuity to be a really successful experimenter; he felt that with the availability of practically unlimited funds for research laboratories, this inherent ingenuity was severely discouraged and even completely deadened. To prove his point, he said that a man should be able to make all necessary things with a pocketknife. He carried a well-worn knife which had served as a file and even a small saw on his outings. In his laboratory he had devised greatly improvised methods for his own experiments and had constructed many a workable apparatus for precise research work. It seemed that he was as proud of some of this equipment as he was of the results of his observations. In fact, he wrote papers on some of his "inventions," describing them in detail for others to copy.

Another point on which Röntgen held a definite and strong opinion was that a person should devote himself to only one certain field of endeavor. To spread himself thin would cause a man to become expert in none. Röntgen's assistant, Rudolph Cohen, was a case in point. After a visit with him, Röntgen remarked to a friend that no outstanding work would ever be accomplished by the able physicist, although he then had a good position at the university.

Cohen played the piano quite well, and in fact, visited the Röntgens quite regularly in their apartment and graciously entertained them with some fine piano recitals. In addition to the mastering of this instrument, Cohen also liked to visit the museums, especially the Museum of Art; with a drawing board, he sketched there for hours on end. With his son he studied medicine; that is, the son actually studied it at the university, but the father was so interested in his son's homework and activities that he had acquired a fair knowledge in that field himself. At his home, Cohen had a cabinet full of data that he had collected on persons who had had contact with Goethe during the poet's life or who had been mentioned by him in his works or letters.

This wide versatility was just too much for Röntgen, and he brusquely suggested that it could result only in an entirely unproductive life. It was not that Röntgen disliked Cohen in any way; he was, in fact, quite fond of the physicist, whose father had been a personal physician of Prince Bismarck. But Röntgen believed that Cohen could have done really remarkable work if he had concentrated on that one subject.

Wilhelm Röntgen got his personal papers in order. He reread most of the many letters he had painstakingly saved, then used them to heat his room by feeding the shiny tile oven, or neatly tied them into separate packages, according to their writers. Those that he decided to keep, he wrapped in brown paper and tied with thin wire. He placed them in the commodious wardrobe for safekeeping, along with this note:

Thousands of communications which relate to the discovery of the X rays — especially those of the earliest years — I have burned as of too little interest.

Enclosed letters represent a part of those received until January 1916 and may be witnesses of that high tide of communications. A second small package contains a hurriedly picked selection of interesting letters. R. 1921.

Some of the smaller bundles he marked, *"Dem Absender zurück senden"* — Return to sender; others were marked *"Nach meinem Tode ungelesen zu verbrennen"* — After my death to be burned, unread.

The letters from Philipp Lenard were all bundled carefully together and marked, *"Briefe von P. Lenard* — of some interest in the judgment of the writer."* These were the letters of which Röntgen wrote to Zehnder, "I was astonished while going over my old letters to find some written by Lenard that show a friendly attitude toward me, which, however, stopped completely about the time Wien succeeded me in Würzburg and I received the Nobel Prize."

On May 7, 1894, Philipp Lenard had answered Wilhelm Röntgen's request for a source of thin aluminum sheets by sending him two sheets from his own supply. On May 21, 1897, Lenard had replied to a letter from Röntgen, *"Verehrter* Herr Kollege Lenard" — Esteemed Colleague — in which he disclaimed knowledge of a newspaper article written by Ludwig Zehnder and critical of Lenard, by writing:

Hochverehrter Herr Professor: Because your great discovery caused such swift attention in the farthest circles, my modest work also came into the limelight, which was of particular luck for me, and I am doubly glad to have had your friendly participation. . . . A short time ago I repeated my former experiments with the cathode rays in the open air to find out whether my former experiments have been disturbed, especially through the presence of the rays discovered by you. However, I have found to my own satisfaction that this is not the case.

Another letter, written from Kiel on June 23, 1899, is also of very friendly nature. The others are dated from Bonn and from Heidelberg, where Lenard was director of the Physical Science Institute. All of the letters were signed, *"Ihr ganz ergebener* [Your totally devoted] P. Lenard."

In his original manuscript of the Preliminary Communication, Wilhelm Röntgen had crossed out the words in the fifth line, *den Lenard Apparat* — the Lenard apparatus, and then substituted *die Röhre* — the tube. Earlier he had written, "If the discharge of a fairly large Ruhmkorff induction coil is allowed to pass through a Hittorf vacuum tube, or a sufficiently evacuated Lenard, Crookes tube, or a similar apparatus . . . ." The sequence of tubes mentioned is believed to be significant.

Wilhelm Röntgen also read again the many citations, addresses, and diplomas he had received during his active lifetime from generous government officials and from scientific organizations the world over. These items were scrupulously kept. Those medals that had not been thrown into the upturned *Stahlhelm* at the time when the government representatives collected gold and silver contributions from the people by dramatically using field gray steel helmets for receptacles, he also placed under lock and key in a drawer of his *Bücherschrank.* "Perhaps they are of historical interest," he said, "but they probably must be gone over and a proper selection be made."

Even while he assembled these mementos, several new honors were bestowed upon Röntgen. The *Gesellschaft von Freunden und Förderern der Friedrich-Wilhelms-Universität zu Bonn* made him an honorary member, as did the *Nordisk Foerening f. med. Radiologi.* The Universität at Bonn also gave him an *Akademisches Ehrenbürgerrecht* (honorary academician right), and the *Physikalische Oekonom Gesellschaft* elected him a corresponding member. The City of Würzburg made him an honorary citizen.

When cities and counties issued their own *Notgeld* in an effort to keep abreast with the rampaging inflation, many bills were printed with the likeness of a local personality.

The city of Lennep used the portrait of Röntgen and the house where he was born on one side of its seventy-five Pfennig note, showing on the other side the memorial tablet which was attached to the birth-house. This valid note was issued on July 15, 1921, but it grew quite valueless within a very short time. The *Bezirksgemeinde* (county) of Weilheim also issued a note, but this was later, in October 1923. It featured a picture of the face of "Professor v. Röntgen" and was in the amount of *Hundert Milliarden Mark,* but this note was nearly as worthless as the unauthorized — and false — use of the title "von" under the likeness of Röntgen. It was merely printed on one side on the cheap paper, for by then the time used for printing both sides, or the material consumed in the process, was more valuable than the face value of the paper money issued. Only a brief time later, the German inflationary monetary system became stabilized, based on the American dollar, with one billion marks equal to 24 cents in United States currency.

Röntgen began the tedious task of listing the many valuable objects in his household, perhaps often of sentimental value only, but held most dear, nevertheless. He had already presented several of his tubes, including the original pear-shaped Hittorf-Crookes tube and his original coil to the authoritative Deutschen Museum in Munich. These historic items of apparatus that Röntgen had used at the time of the discovery were placed on regular exhibition at the museum and attracted many admirers, among whom was Röntgen himself occasionally.

It was June when he wrote detailed instructions for his burial, and he also wrote his *Letztwillige Wünsche,* his last will and testament:

After the administration of the City of Giessen has allowed the burial in the family plot according to the attached paper, I wish that the urn with the ashes of my wife and that of mine be buried there. My testament executors may see to it that the cemetery administration in Giessen is provided to decorate yearly the communal graves with plantings in a simple manner. I would like a simple memorial tablet which carries the names of the deceased and their death dates

    F. C. Röntgen
    C. C. Röntgen, born Frowein, August 8, 1880
    W. C. Röntgen
    B. Röntgen, born Ludwig, October 31, 1919

My bust created by A. Hildebrand I would like best to have made available to the public in the Glyptothek at Munich. Should difficulties arise from the particular authorities, it would probably be best to present the bust to the University at Würzburg for display in their Physical Science Institute.

My diplomas, addresses, medals, etc., which refer to my scientific work, should be presented to the University at Würzburg with the request to preserve them at a suitably appearing place. Perhaps they have some historical interest. At the present time they are kept in a locked portion of a bookcase in my study.

All papers which are kept in the mahogany wardrobe currently standing in the hallway of the Munich residence, should be burned immediately, sight unseen.

As long as my household is not dissolved after my death, I request Frau Geheimrat M. Boveri to undertake the leadership. Consequently all keys are to be turned over to her. I beg Dr. R. Cohen to function eventually as the representative of Frau Geheimrat Boveri, if she approves.

In as far as I myself have not disposed of some objects (check the attached listing) which may be presented in memory of my wife or myself, my executors of this testament may dispose of further objects according to their best judgment for the named purpose.

                      [signed] Dr. W. C. Röntgen
Weilheim (Upper Bavaria), June 28, 1921.

During these years after the death of his wife Wilhelm Röntgen spent occasional week-ends with the Boveris in Würzburg, although train travel was most perplexing, if not impossible. By March 1920 the railroad trains had entirely stopped running into Munich, except for those carrying mail. The unemployed totaled more than fifteen million persons in the whole country, and it was unsafe to be alone in the streets of the city. When it again became possible to make shorter trips, Röntgen made his customary short visits. On these train trips between Munich and Würzburg he made friends easily with fellow travelers by engaging them in conversation. At times he had some difficulty in dialogue because of his deafness, but he nevertheless enjoyed it. Once he had the good fortune to travel

with Oskar von Miller, and for days he enthusiastically told of his interesting conversation with this eminent electrical scientist. Later, when no
luxury compartments at all were carried, and he was forced to share his
Abteil with other travelers, he found many of his companions, while less
educated, also quite stimulating, as this description of one trip illustrated.

Röntgen reported:

The little old woman was very interesting and shortened my trip considerably.
Our discussion soon veered to the realm of religion, which I usually am not
fond of discussing but which this time interested me because the woman, with
great ability and feeling, with appreciable warmth, and motivated by the
sincerest convictions, defended her strictly orthodox views against the doubts
and attacks of her adversaries, who frequently were rather inconsiderate.
Always lively, never stupid or offensive, she presented her point of view in
well-chosen words which were accompanied by lively gestures. She was ready
with an answer to any question. Even though I could not agree with everything
she said, I still had the highest admiration for her and frequently was envious.
I was interested to learn where and how she had been brought up and so
inquired about her circumstances. She told me that she was seventy-two years
old, married to a carpenter who had worked for many years with Hoch in
Würzburg, and that she now lived with her son, who was working at the
Bayernwerk near Munich. Originally she was a Catholic, but later had joined
the Adventists. She reads a great deal and discusses religion and political and
economic questions with her relatives and thinks about things a good deal.
I was surprised to find such ability, intelligence, and kindness in a simple
woman from the working classes and bade her *adieu* very heartily. Judging
from the talk of some time ago with the young man I had mentioned and who
also belonged to the so-called lower middle class, I concluded that interest
and thought on moral and religious questions has increased during the last
years. I hardly believe that before the war I should have found as much interest
under similar circumstances.

Röntgen was pleased occasionally after hearing young people intel-
ligently discuss matters of politics and economics. Usually his travel
companions were salesmen, who kept up a lively discussion of these subjects, but because of his deafness he could not easily follow these exchanges
and only caught phrases of "reasonable statements." A young man, a
student of economics, with whom he traveled at one time, offered "sound
judgment in his well-expressed opinion and defended his views forcefully,
which were full of hope and love for his country. This pleased me so very
much and I was glad that I could tell him so."

Another young student who pleased Röntgen was the grandson of
his deceased friend von Hippel. After attending the Gymnasium, he went
to war full of enthusiasm at the beginning of the conflict and after experi-
encing its horrors, terribly disillusioned at its futile end. The youth was
now attending the university, and Röntgen invited him to his apartment

for coffee on an afternoon. The young man had regained some of his self-esteem and was again full of hope for the future. "Conversation with such people is very comforting," Röntgen wrote, "especially in these unhappy times."

But Wilhelm Röntgen was most indignant when during the annual carnival time people carried on in what seemed to him an unnecessarily boisterous manner. "Of the extravagant — by finery and behavior — and disgusting *Fasching* celebrations here, you have no idea," he wrote. "Four million *more* bottles of champagne were consumed in Germany in 1921 than in 1914. That is about ten-thousand bottles more per day, and so many, many people are suffering from hunger at the same time. It is terribly sad."

The moral responsibilities of the populace had suffered greatly during the difficult postwar years. First, the superhuman war effort, then the following disillusion with its rampant starvation and the utter worthlessness of the saved money, all brought about an irresponsible attitude of most citizens of the land. It was merely another aftermath of a devastating war — almost total moral collapse as well as complete economic bankruptcy.

The seventy-six-year-old Röntgen was not entirely without contact with the law-enforcing agencies. While spending the Christmas holidays with the Boveris in Würzburg, he fell victim to a forester on patrol in the Steinberger Wald.

It was a dark foggy day when he and Margret went into the state-owned forest to pick up a few small pine branches to augment the Christmas decorations in the house. They did not have a tree that year. While looking for appropriate branches, the two separated briefly in the thick forest to better locate some choice pieces of greenery, when suddenly Margret saw a green-coated forester approach. Not being entirely uninitiated in how to act in such situations, she dropped her gathered branches cleverly and quite nonchalantly behind a small tree and walked on as if nothing had happened, right past the official. He stopped to chat briefly with the girl, who was satisfied that she was not doing anything unauthorized in the woods over which he had jurisdiction and care. In fact, Margret opened her cape for him to see that she had no small branches concealed as he had suspected.

As he was about ready to walk away, they saw the approaching shape of Röntgen through the mist. He had not been warned and rather gaily sauntered along with a sizeable pine branch of exquisitely symmetrical shape in his hand to the dismay of the girl and the glee of the forester.

The usual procedure followed. With the meticulous correctness of the minor German official, a summons was written up. Röntgen believed himself to be in a Prussian forest rather than in a Bavarian, where he thought that such offensive officialism of minor government employees did not exist.

The questioning proceeded. The name and profession were easily established, although Röntgen gave his title only as Geheimrat and professor, not mentioning the title of Excellency. Residence: Aeussere Prinzregentenstrasse, but he corrected it to the new Maria-Theresia-Strasse. This aroused the suspicion of the official and he asked the name of the father. Röntgen supplied that, too. But when the forester asked for the name of his mother, Röntgen could not for the life of him recall her first name, and he felt terribly embarrassed by it. After a brief silence, the forester wrote on his paper "Mother unknown."

Sheepishly, Röntgen and Margret walked home. They were quite dejected when they arrived at the apartment without the expected decorations for the holiday. When Röntgen later told the somewhat embroidered story at the dinner table before other friends, including the Hofmeiers, it was quite hilarious, reminiscent of older times when they were all much younger and gayer. Röntgen was summarily congratulated, not for having been caught in the act of thievery, but as a rather unusual person whose mother, instead of whose father, was unknown. None enjoyed the story more than Röntgen himself.

CHAPTER 22

An Eventful Final Year

ALTHOUGH THE OFFICIAL summer semester catalog of 1922 listed Röntgen as a member of the faculty, an *öffentlicher ordentlicher Professor der Philosophischen Fakultät der Universität,* Willy Wien actually had taken over Röntgen's work, with Arnold Sommerfeld and Leo Graetz assisting him. Almost daily Röntgen went to his small laboratory in the institute to do research work on crystals, especially on the effect of rays on crystals. He found that the work was much more difficult than before, and the results were quite unsatisfactory.

Röntgen wrote that he swung between Munich and Weilheim like a pendulum.

At Weilheim he oversaw the planting of the vegetable garden and the sowing of a large patch of wheat to augment the flour shortage. But the weather had generally been awfully bad, and only during the last days of May did they have any pleasant sunshine. Physically he felt quite well. A hike of ten kilometers was his absolute limit, he noted, but he was a fanatic about his daily walking exercise. To walk over six miles daily at the age of seventy-seven was certainly a remarkable feat. But he noticed that "hearing, vision, and memory have been appreciably reduced, and other aging is noticeable, but I have a good appetite."

Usually, when he went to the institute — at times taking a carriage, but mostly walking through the garden — he took his dog with him. Then Pascha would curl up and lie quietly under his master's writing desk. Repeatedly, Röntgen came home alone, the *Schäferhund* forgotten. Kätchen then would be sent to bring the dog home. In time, Pascha showed great fondness for Kätchen, which displeased Röntgen. At Weilheim Pascha annoyed him, too. During their walks the dog often disappeared to chase a rabbit or other game, and Röntgen would return home without his dog. When Pascha came home tired from his excursions, he would get a severe scolding, but soon his master would forgive the outbreak of disobedience.

"Some while back," Röntgen wrote, "while standing on a table to fix something on the ceiling, I fell to the floor, table and all, because I had exceeded the tip-line of the table. Fortunately it did not cause a serious injury." But in a hurt aside, he recalled in jest that he had climbed the Muottas Muragl at Pontresina and that had not even tired him, although that was 8,134 feet high!

One of the girls, Wally, had returned to her home, but his faithful Kätchen and Marie remained with him. "Kätchen is really most trustworthy and takes exceedingly good care of me, looking after me most solicitously, seeing after the garden, and knowing the farmers in the neighborhood, is thus able to secure some produce and other badly needed foodstuffs," he stated.

Wilhelm Röntgen would have liked to give up one of his households, but he did not see just how he could do it. With so many other difficulties and problems facing him he found it impossible to make definite decisions any more. He lived frugally, in fact extremely so; he felt the purposelessness of his life, and the terrifying economic and unruly political situation burdened him. "The solitude presses on me heavily now," he wrote.

Röntgen had written in 1921, when his friend Ernst Wölfflin of Basel had urged him to come to Switzerland for the summer vacation period: "It is especially beneficial for the lonely old man who has lost his life companion and who must live in these sad times to know that there are still persons who remember him in the most intimate way." But Röntgen had steadfastly refused the offered invitation that year. Now, commenting on the rapidly changing and so frightening social and economic situation about him, he recalled nostalgically some amusing and vivid events of his vacation days of the past. He recounted with pleasant memories the many birthdays he had spent with close friends at the Easter vacations at Cadenabbia. The summers in Pontresina in the Engadin, after Lenzerheide, Flims, or Rigi-Scheidegg; and his dear old friends, he recalled with the warmest feelings.

In April 1922 Röntgen sincerely doubted that he would be able to visit the mountains again, "unless a miracle happens. It seems entirely out of the question now." But when the letters and finally a telegram continued to urge him to undertake the trip, he capitulated and decided to spend the summer as a guest of Wölfflin.

Röntgen had met the ophthalmologist Ernst Wölfflin, son of Eduard, first in 1909 when the youngster vacationed with his parents in Rigi-Scheidegg. Wölfflin's mother, also a Züricher, but originally from Winterthur, had been especially close to Bertha Röntgen; the two men also got along fine together.

The desire to see the old familiar places and to relive the joyful days again was high within Röntgen, and he agreed happily to meet his younger friends toward the end of July at Pontresina. Röntgen was deeply moved by the generosity of the invitation and in his responding letter he used the affectionate salutation, *"Lieber guter Freund"* — dear, good friend — instead of the usual formal *"Lieber Herr Doktor."* He wrote on July 15, "Your letter has moved me deeply. Such great goodness and deep feeling speaks in it. Have my warmest thanks for your dear friendship and for the devoted memories of my wife."

The whole trip was one of memories. In Pontresina, where he enjoyed the hospitality of Anna Saratz-Trippi, the granddaughter of his friend Leonhard Enderlin, at tea, he noted that many changes had taken place in the hotel and in the personnel, but the scenery was exactly as he remembered it.

This morning I walked for quite a distance through the forest and along the roaring glacier water in the really beautiful Roseg Valley. From time to time I had glorious views of the glacier in the far distance. I rested on some benches which had supported many a good friend and my dear Bertha. Often I feel as if I were dreaming a happy dream. I still prefer to leave the well-worn paths and to hike over stick and stone. If I ever should be missed, do not look for me on the main road.

While Wölfflin had gone back to Basel briefly, Wilhelm Röntgen hiked alone to the physiological plant station, some 2,100 feet up the Muottas Muragl, to have a discussion with the supervising botanist. When Wölfflin returned, Röntgen undertook an even more ambitious trip. Hiking into the mountains, the seventy-seven-year-old professor leaned a bit more heavily on his spiked cane as they went up the scenic Fextal from Sils Baselgia between the Silvaplaner and the Silser Lakes. He needed a few extra rests, he noted, and sitting on a familiar rock at the grand Marmorei he looked back, once again to enjoy the marvelous view of the two strikingly blue lakes below him, the deeply cut valley to the right leading to St. Moritz, the chain of snow-covered mountains directly before him, the majestic Piz Materdell, Piz Lagrev, and Piz Julier. "This is what I wanted to see once more before I die," he told Wölfflin, with tears in his eyes.

Ernst Wölfflin also recalled that one morning at breakfast Röntgen smiled broadly and announced happily that he had a letter from the president of the *Schweizerischen Röntgenologischen Gesellschaft.* "I was informed," he said, "that a memorial tablet is to be placed on the house where I lived for many years while a student in Zurich. In simple words it is stated, for which one feels a real thankfulness and which communicate a warm heartedness without fancy phrases." The inscription read:

WILHELM CONRAD RÖNTGEN
DER ENTDECKER DER NACH IHM BENANNTEN STRAHLEN
DOKTOR DER UNIVERSITÄT ZÜRICH
WOHNTE HIER 1866-1869 ALS STUDIERENDER AN DER
EIDGENÖSSISCHEN TECHNISCHEN HOCHSCHULE

Soon after his arrival at Sils-Baselgia, Röntgen began suffering from intestinal illness and asthmatic attacks, and on August 13, he and his host Wölfflin left for a lower altitude. Taking again the picturesque *Rhätische Eisenbahn* to Tiefencastel, and from there the yellow *Postautobus,* they went to Lenzerheide to stay at the comfortable Cantiene Gasthaus. Here, some old friends visited with Röntgen briefly. The Zehnders came for a short stay, and so did Ernst Ritzmann. Frau and Margret Boveri also stayed for a few days, during which Margret entertained Röntgen with some musical pieces on the piano, which, Röntgen wrote, "especially charmed me, as did her happy and clever manners. The short, nice visit provided a pleasant interlude."

Röntgen had not seen the Zehnders for several years, and their meeting was most enjoyable, but unfortunately Zehnder and his wife could stay only briefly. "Zehnder has remained the same good and trustworthy man for whom I wished a better fate in life," Röntgen wrote then.

The stay at Lenzerheide proved a most pleasing experience, although Wölfflin had to return home. They said goodby at the depot without many words. A warm handshake conveyed the feelings of both men. When later Ernst Wölfflin called Röntgen by telephone to inquire about his health, Wölfflin believed the guest sounded considerably improved. That evening, Röntgen sat down at the *Kurhaus* to write a long letter to his host at Basel, thanking him again "for his great affectionate interest. I am really fine. The daily short walks in this wonderful weather and the good food of Cantiene's have the effect which you seek, a definite strengthening of my entire physical being." All the people with whom Röntgen came in contact were so very friendly, he observed, and he found the difference between them and those at Munich quite startling. A certain Herr Meisser had presented him with a fine bouquet of flowers from his own garden that very morning, and as he walked past the villa of the Nationalrat Herrn Bossi, the man's small daughter had given Röntgen an especially beautiful carnation, which he happily carried to place into a thin bud vase in his room. In fact, the room was full of colorful flowers, much more attractive, he noted, than the finest floral shop in Munich during these horrible times.

One of the highspots of the days at Lenzerheide was the visit of the Bishop of Chur. Both men discussed, as they had so often and so many years before, all topics exhaustively, including the Tapet question. Over some splendid vintage wine, the hours spent together passed much too quickly, and the bishop left this stimulating meeting most regretfully. Since he had to travel to Berlin and from there to Paris on the following day, he had to return to his residence. Röntgen speculated that it was on a political matter which he could not postpone, and obviously it was an important journey.

A few days after their meeting, the local bookseller delivered a three-volume work to Röntgen, inscribed graciously by the bishop. The extensive work, entitled, *Religion, Christendom, and Church,* was a 1920 paperback edition by Professors Esser and Mausbach, with many other scholars' contributions. Röntgen had already begun reading it with great interest, and he suggested that it would not harm his Protestant friends at all to become more familiar with the Roman Catholic views expressed in these various theses. (However, his interest must have lagged some-what, for only about a third of the pages of the first book of 810 pages were cut apart and looked well read when this author examined the books. A bookmark remained at page 277.) Wilhelm Röntgen concluded the letter, stating that he would not go to Zurich to visit with the Zehnders, as once planned, but would go with the Boveris for two days to Baden in the Aargau before returning with them to Munich. He expressed the hope of going to visit the graves of his parents at Giessen, but that might have to wait until a later time. *Aber vielleicht* — But perhaps.

Röntgen had indeed enjoyed that vacation. It was one of the high-points of his last years. Although he was almost constantly aware of the absence of his beloved Bertha, for every stone, every flower, every path, and every view reminded him of his dear wife, he appeared to be a most happy man to his friends and seemed totally changed from the discouraged old man in Munich.

His meeting with Bishop Schmidt had stimulated Röntgen to more extensive reading of his Bible. He was a believing Protestant — his grand-father having been an Elder of the evangelical community of Lennep — and as a student of natural phenomena and an ardent outdoors enthusiast, Wilhelm Röntgen was well aware of religion and was convinced of an absolutely ordered existence of all things. Creation was not a haphazard or accidental occurrence, but a magnificent process of precise orderliness. Man did not discover anything that did not already exist; each discovery was merely a phenomenon he had failed to recognize earlier. Röntgen had discussed religious beliefs only seldom, but he had a tolerant attitude toward convictions other than his own.

About a month after his return to Munich, Wilhelm Röntgen again wrote a letter to Wölfflin "full of gratitude over his Swiss interlude." With thankful heart he recalled "the many pleasantries encountered and the unbounded joy experienced at revisiting these wonderful memorable spots, which filled him with the most joyful recollections of exhilarating summer experiences."

Throughout that fall Röntgen stayed at his Weilheim place, but his mind was practically all of the time still in the Swiss mountains. He spoke of the trip constantly and mentioned it in every letter he wrote that year. He was especially thankful to Ernst Wölfflin for having made it all possible, and in October he wrote again to him, "recalling with delight the wonderful days in the Engadin. The lovely trip from Tiefencastel to Lenzerheide was a pleasurable fusion of unforgettable past and present reality." Aware of the coming anniversary of his wife's death he recalled their last years together, but again expressed gratefulness that she did not have to live through the terribly confusing and frighteningly unreal postwar instability. "It would have confused her so terribly and saddened her dangerously in her already melancholy terminal illness." The very thought of the tremendous casualties suffered by Germany — over seven million, with nearly two million men killed — would have been too much for her to bear. (Austria-Hungary was estimated to have suffered even greater loss than the 65 percent lost by the German forces. With 90 percent of their mobilized forces of almost eight million men they had suffered greater than any other modern power.)

That October Ludwig Zehnder and his wife visited with Röntgen in Munich. Zehnder later wrote, "Our seeing each other was heartening but also very sad. We found that Röntgen had lost nearly all of his money through large subscriptions of war loans and the rampaging inflation. He lived so frugally that he did not want to eat costly meat anymore. Despite his urgings we remained only less than a day. He accompanied us to the railroad station, and our last farewell there was most painful." Of course, the Zehnders lived in relatively untouched Switzerland and were aghast at the appalling scarcity of everything in a German household.

Shortly after the third anniversary of his wife's death, Wilhelm Röntgen traveled with Frau Boveri to spend three days in Giessen, primarily to make arrangements with the city authorities to have the family graves permanently attended. It was impossible, however, to make such arrangements at that time because of the ever-deteriorating monetary system. Röntgen plucked a sprig of ivy from the grave of his mother, to keep it always with him, as a permanent remembrance of her.

Röntgen did not visit the Institute at Giessen, nor any of the new professors at the university. He had lost contact with it altogether. But on his way he stopped briefly in Friedberg to see Berteli's father-in-law and sister-in-law. Berteli lived with her children in Rostock, and Röntgen had not seen her for over two years.

The trip tired Röntgen considerably, he was not up to such a strenuous journey. The affair at Giessen had exhausted him emotionally, not only because of its character but also because there was no solution at all to the problem of having the graves cared for. Money was worthless. Nobody trusted the valueless certificates ever to regain their former stability, thus contracts based on money values were impossible. Röntgen could not cope with such an unsoluble situation.

Not too tired to maintain his correspondence, he wrote a long letter to his cousin Louise on December 6, 1922:

I have not received an answer to my letter of April 15 of this year, but now Christmas time and the New Year approaches, and that is the time when one likes to get in touch again with those loved ones who are still alive. As usual, I can be rather sure to receive some news from you within the near future, provided of course that you are feeling well and are in the mood for writing. I hope that this is the case, but especially at our age, this is very often uncertain. I frequently ask myself how you are, and then I should like to have an answer.

I am feeling rather well. My hearing and sight have decreased considerably, and other signs of age have appeared, but I am still rather active and have a good appetite. Memory and ability to work are considerably decreased, and loneliness lies heavily upon me.

At my wedding you no doubt met the children of Coo Boddens (my cousin). I still have some correspondence with one of them (Betry). Outside of that I have no connections anymore with Holland.

Since I am a government employee, I receive a pension, which increases somewhat with the rising costs of living. I am thus relatively secure if I live very moderately, but I must continuously practice more and more economy. Just think of it: One pound of bread costs 67 marks; one pound of meat 300 to 400 marks; one pound of butter about 1,400 marks, and a simple suit of clothes about 150,000 to 200,000 marks. For one dollar one can get just over 8,000 marks.

You can imagine that under these circumstances I ordinarily cannot travel in countries that have a high exchange rate, but still I was able this summer to spend three weeks in Switzerland. That was a wonderful time! During this time, I was with people who live under normal conditions. Close to the place where we stayed for some time, there is a famous bathing resort, St. Moritz. In the guest list of one of its greatest hotels I found a "Mr. Ernst Röntgen with governess and maid, U.S.A." Do you know who this apparently wealthy namesake could have been?

And now, my dear Louise, I wish you a Merry Christmas. Begin the New Year in good health and with courage.

On December 12, Röntgen wrote to Zehnder. It was merely a post card, but he filled it solidly in his clear handwriting in extremely small script. Little wonder, though, for this simple card carried ten postage stamps totaling 321 marks! Röntgen sent his heartiest greetings and best wishes for Christmas and New Year and expressed the hope for a longer visit during the coming year. He also wrote that a new physics professor was now at Würzburg, one of his best students, Ernst Wagner. Röntgen asked then, "Have you seen the fine tablet in Zurich which was placed on my old student room on the Seilergraben? I greatly enjoyed the recognition of my work by the Swiss doctors. Perhaps you know the main force behind that affair, Dr. Hermann Suter of Zurich." (Part of a collection at the *Zentralbibliothek* at Zurich, this post card is one of 162 letters and cards from Röntgen to Zehnder.)

For the 1922 Christmas holidays Röntgen again went to Würzburg, and with the Boveris he shared delicacies that had been sent to them from the United States and from Switzerland. They reminisced at that festive time — as did everyone at the traditional *Weihnachtsabend*.

Soon after that (January 5, 1923), Röntgen wrote a very long letter to Wölfflin, describing the Christmas events. He thanked him for the package with the splendid gifts of food. "How over-rich you have been with your generosity." He enumerated the various special items in the *Weihnachtspaket,* all such desirable *Lieblingsleckerbissen* to him, who had not been able to purchase even the basest foods in any quantity to suffice. Such delicacies as his very favorites, *durchgewachsener Speck* — lean bacon — and salami, he had not seen for many years. "You have looked after me so richly that I not only will enjoy the gifts for a long, long time, but also will be able to have the great joy of sharing many things with my dear friends. Again let me express my sincerest, deepest thanks."

He repeated to Wölfflin that it was indeed his good fortune to have such dear caring friends as Frau Boveri and Wölfflin, who were always so concernedly looking after him in these disastrous times. "Words fail me to express this appreciation" — but then he goes on to express his deep gratitude on a whole page of the letter. At the Boveri apartment, Margret had decorated the living room in a very tasteful and artistic manner with three branches, candles, and apples and nuts. They also had been able to secure a small tree, a splendid *Weihnachtsbaum*. They sang songs and watched the candles glow on its branches. Margret had even taken a wreath of pine branches with apples and golden pine cones to his hotel room and hung it on the wall. Their own apartment was too small to accommodate a guest, so he slept at the nearby hotel. Margret also played the piano for them. Röntgen observed that she had considerably gained by the studies at the Würzburg Conservatorium.

From Frau Sulzer-Bühler he had received a most friendly letter, Röntgen wrote, and a box of superb pralines and sugar, and even a whole baked ham! The letter, however, gave away the secret: It had been suggested by Wölfflin, as he had guessed. And he thanked the dear *Anstifter,* the instigator, most heartily.

Röntgen also mentioned to Wölfflin that an experiment was giving him some cause for worry. Apparently he was still conducting some experimental work which actually had been begun several months before. He stated that the walk to the laboratory from his home was so far that he was quite tired out when he got to the institute. Under such adverse conditions he found it nearly impossible to work and to observe the results with any degree of accuracy. His eyesight was failing and seemed not sharp enough to make the necessary correct observations, but he hoped to get back to the task after a short and temporary rest.

In response to another letter, Röntgen wrote to Wölfflin on January 26, 1923, "Dear Friend, I beg you, first of all, to excuse me because I have not written you long ago. Head and heart are so overflowing with the events which are happening here that all private correspondence is suffering strongly because of it."

Wölfflin had suggested to Röntgen that he visit the Italian Lakes region and then remain in Switzerland — perhaps at Wölfflin's own Basel home or at some other place Röntgen loved, like Lenzerheide — where no food problem existed and where living conditions would be so much easier for him. But Röntgen refused to change his residence or even consider a move on a temporary basis. To this proposal he replied:

In both of your last writings you mentioned some plans which visualize a meeting with you this spring, and you name Cadenabbia and Sestri as the possibly best-suited places. I thank you again for your far-reaching caring friendship and your great goodness. But, dear friend, these nice plans will not materialize. First, the fact that you will most probably be extremely occupied this spring because of the taking over of the regular professorship in Basel. Then there are added some difficulties from my side, which I cannot overcome, and which I would like to discuss with you now. No one can tell what the situation will be here in the immediate future. That it will improve appreciably in the coming months appears to me most unlikely. Under this pressure and while thousands of my fellow countrymen suffer the greatest need here, it would be impossible for me to live a regular life in a foreign country. At any event, I would be a most undesirable companion. Although I cannot contribute any active help any more in my home country, I still feel the deep duty to be present at whatever may happen here.

And finally I have to tell you the following: You spoil me by your kindness to such an extent that I now and then worry that I go too far with my acceptance through eventual habit and could by doing so forfeit your friendship, which I wish first of all to keep. To avoid this and to assure my real joy for everything fine that I receive from you, I think it advisable that at least this time I decline your suggestion and turn it down with the warmest thanks. We know each other well enough so that I do not need to fear that you will misinterpret my feelings in this matter.

Not that he could accomplish much in Munich anymore, as he said, but he "could hear what straight-thinking people had to speculate about the dismal future, and get some comfort from the various examples of sincere enthusiasm despite the present chaotic situation." He expressed deep indignation at the occupation of the Rhineland, and speculated on whether Adolf Hitler could become "a second Mussolini."

Another reason Wilhelm Röntgen had refused to live away from his home was his physical condition. At intervals during the past several years he had been ailing with some gastrointestinal distress, and these disturbances returned now in increasing frequency. But this was only a natural result of the war years of deficiencies and the lack of nourishing foods. Diagnosing the trouble himself, he pronounced it to be carcinoma of the intestines, but when he consulted with Friedrich von Müller, director of the Medical Clinic at the university, this eminent medical authority did not concur with that view, and told Dr. Röntgen that there was no cause for alarm and that he did not suffer from cancer.

That winter Röntgen remained mostly at his large apartment in Munich and spent only a few days at Weilheim. When he arrived there, the house was not heated, and he became very angry at Marie for her failure to prepare the place for him. When the maid explained that there was no coal at all and no wood to be had, he quieted down, huddled near the *Kachelofen* in his room, which was quickly warmed with old papers and some pieces of thin branches which Marie had previously gathered in the forest.

His correspondence took most of his time and effort now, but he had a specific item listed on his calendar for his daily attention. Röntgen greatly enjoyed reading occasional lengthy, highly informal letters, dealing with small and inconsequential matters, which Fräulein Hitzig wrote to him. These letters were just another expression of companionship, and they helped to fill the great vacuum of his solitary existence. On January 9, 1923, Röntgen wrote to her, thankful for the *Plauderbriefe* and agreeing with her that "such means are indeed instrumental in bringing tremendous satisfaction and a beneficial comfort in times of mental stress caused by sad personal events."

Although he had lost considerable weight during the last years and now was in failing health, Röntgen still took short walks in the immediate area of his residence, and several times he walked to his laboratory at the institute. In the park, along the Isar river at the waterfall by the dam, he would pause to rest on a bench. "Sometimes I come here alone," he told Frau Boveri who was with him then, "and when I close my eyes the tumult of the falling water sounds to me just like the unforgettable sounds of waterfalls in my beloved mountains in Switzerland."

Wilhelm Röntgen's work tolerance had measurably declined. As he wrote, the experimental work gave him unexpected trouble. His tiredness after a walk to the institute, his failing eyesight and lack of concentration, all of these shortcomings were regular processes of his advanced age. After all, he was about to reach his seventy-eighth birthday in another two months, and he was aware that his long life would soon come to a close.

During his wife's last illness, Röntgen had talked with her about death, and both looked toward that mysterious experience quite calmly. Thus, when he himself felt that his own days were numbered, he was prepared for his "great adventure." He kept a detailed account of his various symptoms of illness, just as he had done in the case of his Bertha. This was merely another typical characteristic of the observing physicist he had been throughout his active life. Often he thought of his many colleagues who had preceded him, especially within the last few years. There was von Hippel, Schönborn, Krönlein, von Kölliker, Stöhr, Hofmeier, and Hitzig, who had gone on, and only younger men were left to staff the university positions. Röntgen felt very much alone.

Not that he gave up entirely being busy. In his diminutive calendar notebook, measuring but 1 by 1½ inches, were listed almost daily reminders of activities to be attended to. The page, beginning with Wednesday, January 17, 1923, carried the notation of some work to be done on Thursday, the 18th; *"Frau Becker"* and *"Weilheim"* on Friday, the 19th; *"Dünkelsbühler"* for Tuesday, the 23rd; *"Wölfflin"* for Monday, the 29th; and *"n.München"* on Tuesday, the 30th. As we have seen, the letter to Ernst Wölfflin was dated the 26th, but Röntgen may well have started writing this exceedingly lengthy missive before his actual schedule to ascertain its completion by that time. He did not like to get behind with his carefully scheduled work, and it may also have taken more than a day to write the several pages to his friend in his meticulous small handwriting. Apparently, Wilhelm Röntgen returned to Munich from Weilheim on the intended Tuesday, although Käthe Fuchs in later years recalled that it was on the 31st. He felt not at all well that day.

To ease his occasional shortness of breath, he had the medical department of the university bring a flask of oxygen with the necessary attachments to the apartment as a precautionary measure. Röntgen felt too tired to go for a short walk, but he did go out of doors for a bit. Mostly he sat around, reading a great deal. When he failed to go out for his daily outing, Kätchen became quite worried about his condition, although he insisted that he was only tired. He complained of severe *Leibschmerzen,* stomach pains.

Some forty-five years later Käthe Fuchs recalled these last days. When she called the family doctor on the morning of February 7, he was too busy to come to the house, having a waiting room crowded with patients at his home office, Jägerstrasse 2. Dr. Quenstedt suggested that Röntgen take some opium drops. When the doctor came at about ten-thirty to see his patient, he found Röntgen looking very bad, and immediately called in Dr. von Müller of the Clinic. They gave their patient some sedatives to make him sleep.

By about four o'clock that afternoon Röntgen awoke without pain and ate a bit of soft food. That night Käthe heard a noise and rushing into his room found him on the floor. Apparently while asleep, he had fallen out of bed; Käthe helped him back in. She insisted then that she be allowed to sleep in the next room with the door left open, but he opposed this strongly. Röntgen, however, was too weak to put up a successful argument, and his housekeeper stayed in that room from then on.

The following day Röntgen was better. Only Dr. Müller came to check on the patient.

On the next day, the 9th, Röntgen felt improved. He insisted that he get up, and was helped out of bed. He washed and combed his beard. Then he sat in an easy chair for some time. But when he tried to hold a newspaper to read, it fell from his hands. He was too weak to hold it. That afternoon at about four o'clock, when he was put back into bed, he had a serious attack of vomiting and hiccups. Very restless now, he insisted on getting up. Röntgen was wrapped in a blanket from head to foot and placed in the chair again, with his feet resting on a stool. Here he slept for about an hour.

In the morning the doctor came again and gave him an injection. Both medical men diagnosed his illness as *Darmverschluss,* a blocked intestine. Röntgen wanted to get up again, but he was then too weak even to sit up in bed. He tried to smile, but seemed exceedingly tired and weak. Käthe Fuchs sat with him, holding his hand. She felt a slight pressure in his feeble grip when he died quietly that morning, February 10, 1923.

The newspapers carried the *Todesanzeige,* the heavily black-bordered death notice, in their advertising pages, as was customary:

Early today, at half past eight o'clock passed away
after a short illness in his seventy-eighth year
His Excellency,   Geheimrat
Professor Dr. Wilhelm Conrad Röntgen
In deepest sorrow,   The relatives and friends,
Munich, February 10, 1923

The Cremation takes place on Tuesday, February 13, 1923,
at 10 o'clock in the morning in the Eastern Cemetery.

"The entire German nation mourns at the bier of its great son," wrote the Minister of Culture in his tribute. A small group of close friends and many prominent scientists and government officials gathered at the Ostfriedhof at Munich at the *Einäscherung* to pay their last respects to the dead benefactor of mankind. His plain coffin was covered with floral tributes from near and far, and huge wreaths with colored bands imprinted with the names of the mourners were placed against the walls of the funeral chapel.

Dr. Glungler officiated at the service. Eulogies followed from Geheimrat Friedrich von Müller, Director of the Medical Clinic, Geheimrat Karl E. von Göbel of the Academy of Sciences, and Geheimrat Emil von Drygalski, Rector and President of the Academic Senate of the Munich University. Professor Willy Wien, Röntgen's successor in the chair of physics at the university, emphasized the significance of the work done and placed wreaths on the coffin in the name of the Philosophical Faculty of the Munich University, the University at Giessen, the German Physical Society, and the Physical Science Institute of the University at Munich.

As rector, Professor Ruland and his colleague, mathematics Professor Rost, spoke for the University at Würzburg. Geheimrat von Miller represented the Deutsches Museum at Munich, where many of the early Röntgen apparatus were exhibited and where Röntgen had spoken at its cornerstone laying ceremonies. Geheimrat Borst spoke for the Munich Society of Physicians, Professor Hermann Rieder for the German Röntgen Society, Professor Rudolf Grashey for the Munich Röntgen Society, Mayor Löffler for the city of Würzburg, and Mayor Weber for the town of Weilheim. A chosen student of mathematics and physics represented the student body of Munich University. A quartet from the National Theater Orchestra played Schubert's *Litanei* and Haydn's *Largo,* as the mortal remains of Seiner Excellenz, Geheimrat Professor Doktor Wilhelm Conrad Röntgen were given over to the flames.

As Röntgen had requested, his ashes were put to rest beside those of his wife and parents in the family plot in the Alten Friedhof at Giessen. A larger crowd than that at Munich attended the memorial services on November 10, 1923, where Professor Walter König recalled the work of his predecessor at the University of Giessen. Professor Laqueur, Rector of the University, and many representatives of the city and the student body spoke at the graveside ceremonies.

Although the many eloquent eulogies spoken at the Munich and the Giessen services expressed and reflected meaningfully the high esteem in which Wilhelm Röntgen was held by his fellow scientists, the true feelings of Röntgen's numerous admirers may perhaps best be found in his very own words, spoken on the occasion of the death of his friend and colleague Theodor Boveri. In that eulogy, Röntgen himself had said:

A great man in the realm of genius has now gone home. . . . He was a truly noble and distinguished man, full of unfathomable goodness of the heart. Kind and strong at the same time. As a friend true as gold. . . . In happiness and sorrow a companion who always entered into the spirit of things and always willing to lend a helping hand . . . and gave of this rich store of gifts with generosity. Yet he was always modest and free of conceit and vanity; always responsive and appreciative, even though he received but little in return. To live with him meant great pleasure and gain. Now he has left us. We stand at his bier, deeply grieved. It will be difficult for many to live without him. But we shall be grateful that we have had him and that his influence upon us was great enough not to cease with his death. On our future pathways we shall often remember him. We thank you, you faithful man, for all you have given us. . . .

Otto Glasser, an outstanding authority on Wilhelm Röntgen, wrote:

The full life that was Röntgen's is to be rejoiced over. His greatest gain was in that he was able to give — to humanity, to science, to his students, and to his friends, and from each he took in proportion — gratitude, fame, respect, and good fellowship.

Margret Boveri, who with her mother, knew Wilhelm Röntgen in his later years perhaps better than anyone, wrote:

His outstanding characteristic was his absolute integrity. Perhaps one can say that Röntgen was in every sense the embodiment of the ideals of the nineteenth century: strong, honest, and powerful, devoted to his science and never doubting its value; in spite of self-criticism and great humor, perhaps endowed with some unconscious pathos; of a really rare faithfulness and sense of sacrifice for people, memories, and ideals. And with all of these characteristics he was not narrow, conceited, or old-fashioned, but open-minded in his acceptance of new ideas if he did not think them to be signs of unproductive spirit or of superficiality.

And housekeeper Käthe Fuchs, who surely knew of his intimate shortcomings and nobility of character better than most anyone, said that "he was a great, honorable man, who had greater weaknesses probably because he had so many really great virtues."

Epilogue

As the *Mittestamentsvollstreckerin,* Frau Boveri saw to it that the terms and wishes of the *Letztwilligen Wünsche* were carried out. The city of Lennep received bonds in the amount of 3,654 "gold" marks for the establishment of a "Professor Doktor Röntgen Stiftung," a foundation to assist deserving pupils in its high school. The town of Weilheim received the sum of 339.927 billion marks to assist its poorer citizens. (The American billion is one-thousand million, but the German billion is one-million million. The *Milliarde* is one-thousand million.) The remainder of the private fortune of Röntgen was given to other charities, but these amounts as well as several other minor monetary gifts were, of course, absolutely worthless within but a very short time afterward. The total collapse of the German mark came toward the end of 1923 when the purchasing power of the paper mark fell to less than one-trillionth of its 1914 (prewar) value. This meant that prices had risen more than a trillion times during this period.

After the devastating inflation following World War I, and another complete devaluation of the mark after the second conflict, a small sum was still realized from the Röntgen legacy. Through the 1960s the University of Würzburg has continued to present an annual prize of about 700 marks (about $175) in books, selected by the faculty, to the most promising student of physics as a special Röntgen Prize.

The diplomas, addresses, and medals were given to the University at Würzburg, and with several valuable apparatus and photographs located in the small laboratory at the Institute at Munich, were placed in a suitable *Röntgen-Gedächtniszimmer,* or memorial room. Opened with a simple ceremony on December 9, 1923, the room contained all the furniture of Röntgen's private study. These furnishings were purchased at the suggestion of Frau Boveri and reassembled with a considerable number of Röntgen's own large collection of special editions and many volumes pertaining to his work, loaned permanently by the library. Professor Ernst Wagner, as head of the institute, took charge of the memorial room; in a special edition of a Röntgenological periodical in 1924 he mentioned nearly all of the items found in that room. The place of honor was given to the original *Mitteilung* in Röntgen's own precise handwriting.

Practically all of these items were later transferred to the former patrician house, which became the Deutsche Röntgen Museum at Lennep in 1932. While many letters and papers of historical interest were destroyed, a vast store of material has remained available.

The correspondence between Ludwig Zehnder and Röntgen during the critical discovery period appears intact, despite published claims by Zehnder that his letters had been "burned, unread" and that he received only very minor ones by the law firm of Helbing long after Röntgen's death. At Lennep this author found Zehnder's letters of February 7, 1895, and of March 25, 1905. For the year 1896, there were letters of January 8, 12, and 18, a telegram of February 2, a post card of February 11, a letter of September 5, and another post card of October 27. (Most of the letters from Röntgen to Zehnder have been placed at the Zentralbibliothek at Zurich.)

The larger portion of Röntgen's letters to the Boveris were published by Margret Boveri in her *"Persöhnliches über W. C. Röntgen"* in 1931.

Later, a brass plaque with a medal-like profile on the top portion was attached by the *Röntgengesellschaft* to the house on Maria-Theresia-Strasse 11, Munich:

Hier wohnte
von 1919–1923
Wilhelm Conrad Röntgen
der Entdecker
der nach Ihm benannten Strahlen
ord. Professor für Experimentalphysik
an der
Universität München
von 1900–1923
† 10.2.1923

It was not until 1955 that a memorial tablet, indicating that its owner had found recreation here, was attached to the house at Weilheim by the Röntgen Society:

Hier suchte von 1904 bis 1928 Erholung
WILHELM CONRAD RÖNTGEN
1845–1923
1905 Deutsche Röntgenges. 1955

This former summer home was eventually sold to a Roman Catholic order as retreat house, then to the town of Weilheim and used after World War II to house refugees. When this author saw it in 1965, it was badly in need of repair, with windows broken, doors ajar, and weeds rampant in what once was Bertha's garden.

At the old cemetery in Giessen, now often used as a quiet park to take children in baby carriages or toddlers to play, with tall trees and green shrubs and wild flowers abundant among the few graves still evident there, there is an ivy-covered *Grabstätte* with a headstone, inscribed:

CONSTANCE CHARLOTTE
RÖNTGEN, GEB. FROWEIN
*28 FEBR. 1806 † 8 AUG. 1880
FRIEDRICH KONRAD
RÖNTGEN
*11 JAN. 1801 † 12 JUNI 1884
BERTA RÖNTGEN
GEB. LUDWIG
*22 APRIL 1839 † 31 OKT. 1919
WILHELM KONRAD
RÖNTGEN
*27 MÄRZ 1845 † 10 FEBR. 1923

The informed visitor, on reading the inscriptions, will notice the misspellings "Konrad" and "Berta" on the headstones, rather than the correct "Conrad" and "Bertha."

Memorial stone at the Röntgen gravesite in Giessen Cemetery.

Chronology

March 27, 1845	Born to Charlotte (Frowein) and Friedrich Conrad Röntgen at 287 Poststrasse in Lennep, Rhine Province.
May 23, 1848	Family moved to Apeldoorn, Holland.
Dec. 27, 1862	Wilhelm entered Utrecht Technical School.
Jan. 18, 1865	Entered University of Utrecht to audit courses on mechanical engineering.
Nov. 16	Moved to Zurich as student of mechanical engineering at the Eidgenössische Technische Hochschule.
1866	Met Anna Bertha Ludwig, born April 22, 1839, in Schwamendingen, Switzerland.
Aug. 6, 1868	Graduated as mechanical engineer from the Polytechnical High School, Zurich.
June 22, 1869	Received Ph.D. degree from University of Zurich and there became assistant to Professor August Kundt.
1870	As assistant to Kundt, went with him to the Julius-Maximilians-Universität at Würzburg.
Jan. 19, 1872	Married in Apeldoorn to Anna Bertha Ludwig.
April 1	As Assistant to Kundt, went with him to the Kaiser-Wilhelm-Universität at Strassburg.
Oct. 3, 1873	Parents moved from Apeldoorn to Strassburg.
March 13, 1874	Röntgen became privat-dozent in physics at the Strassburg University.
April 1, 1875	Became professor of physics and mathematics at the Agricultural Academy of Hohenheim, Württemberg.
Oct. 1, 1876	Returned to University at Strassburg as associate professor of theoretical physics.

April 1, 1879	Became professor of physics at the Hessian Ludwigs-Universität at Giessen.
Aug. 8, 1880	Mother died at Bad Nauheim.
June 12, 1884	Father died at Giessen.
1886	Declined offer of chair of physics at the Friedrich-Schiller-Universität at Jena.
1887	Took Josephine Berta, a 6-year-old niece, and adopted her when she became 21 years of age.
1888	Declined chair of physics at University of Utrecht.
Oct. 1	Became professor of physics at the Julius-Maximilians-Universität at Würzburg.
May 1894	Professor August Kundt died at his summer home near Lübeck.
June	Röntgen began experiments with cathode rays. Became rector of the University at Würzburg.
February, 1895	Declined offer of chair of physics at the Albert-Ludwigs-Universität in Freiburg i.B.
Nov. 8	Discovered strange effects due to a new kind of ray.
Dec. 28	Submitted manuscript, "Preliminary Communication," to the Würzburg Physical-Medical Society for publication in Sitzungsberichte.
Jan. 1, 1896	Sent reprints of his "Preliminary Communication" to colleagues.
Jan. 4	First X ray pictures were exhibited at Berlin Physical Society.
Jan. 5	First newspaper story appeared in *Wiener Presse*.
Jan. 6	Story of discovery of the X ray was cabled all over the world.
Jan. 13	Visited the Kaiser at Berlin and demonstrated newly discovered rays. Received the Prussian Order of the Crown II Class.
Jan. 23	Lectured on his discovery before the Physical-Medical Society, Würzburg, at the Physical Science Institute of the University.
Jan. 30	Declined to lecture before German Reichstag and several scientific societies.
March 3	Received honorary degree of Doctor of Medicine from the University at Würzburg.

March 9	Submitted manuscript of "Second Communication" to the Physical-Medical Society.
April 16	Was made an honorary citizen of Lennep, his birthplace.
April 20	Received Royal Order of Merit of the Bavarian Crown.
March 10, 1897	Submitted the "Third Communication" to the Prussian Academy of Sciences, Berlin.
1899	Declined offer of chair of physics at University of Leipzig. Received title of Royal Geheimrat from Bavarian government.
April 1, 1900	Became professor of physics and director of the Physical Science Institute at the Ludwig-Maximilians-Universität, Munich.
Dec. 10, 1901	Received Nobel Prize in Physics, at Stockholm.
1902	Declined invitation of Carnegie Institute in Washington to use its laboratory for special work.
1904	Declined offer of presidency of Physikalisch-Technische Reichsanstalt, Berlin-Charlottenburg.
March 27, 1905	On Röntgen's sixtieth birthday, a plaque was placed at the Physical Science Institute of the University at Würzburg to commemorate the tenth anniversary of the discovery of X rays.
Dec. 25, 1908	Title of Excellency was bestowed by Prince Regent of Bavaria.
1912	Declined offer of professorship at Prussian Academy of Sciences, Berlin.
March 27, 1915	Spent seventieth birthday with his best friend, Boveri, who was seriously ill, in Oberstdorf.
March 28	Had audience with King Ludwig of Bavaria, in Munich.
1916	Röntgen bust, sculptured by Adolf Hildebrand, was placed in Glyptothek, Munich.
1918	Received honorary degree of Doctor of Engineering, Technical High School, Munich.
Oct. 31, 1919	Bertha, Röntgen's wife, died in Munich.
1920	Retired from University at Munich and became Professor Emeritus.

March 27	Commemorative tablet was placed on house of Röntgen's birthplace in Lennep, at time of his seventy-fifth birthday.
1922	Commemorative tablet was placed on house where Röntgen lived during college years in Zurich.
Feb. 10, 1923	Wilhelm Conrad Röntgen died at Munich.
Nov. 10	Ashes were put to rest in family grave at Giessen.
Dec. 9, 1928	Röntgen memorial room was opened at the Physical Science Institute of the University at Würzburg.
July 27	Röntgen bust, sculptured by Theodor Georgii, was unveiled at University of Munich.
Nov. 30, 1930	Röntgen monument by Arno Breker was unveiled in Lennep.
June 18, 1932	Röntgen museum was opened at Lennep.
1934	Commemorative tablet was placed on Röntgen's favorite lookout mountain spot at Pontresina.
1955	Commemorative tablet was placed on Röntgen's summer home at Weilheim.

Scientific Papers Published by Wilhelm Conrad Röntgen

1. On the Determination of the Ratio of the Specific Heats of Air (1870)
2. Determination of the Ratio of the Specific Heats at Constant Pressure to those for Constant Volume for Some Gases (1873)
3. On Soldering of Platinum-Plated Glasses (1873)
4. On Conducting Discharges of Electricity (1874)
5. On a Variation of the Sénarmont Method for the Determination of the Isothermal Areas in Crystals (1874)
6. On an Application of the Ice Calorimeter for the Determination of the Intensity of Sun Radiation (With Exner, 1874)
7. On the Ratio of Cross Contraction to Longitudinal Dilation of Caoutchouc (1876)
8. A Telephonic Alarm (1877)
9. Communication on a Few Experiments in the Field of Capillarity (1878)
10. On an Aneroid Barometer with a Mirror for Reading the Scale (1878)
11. On a Method for the Production of Isothermals on Crystals (1878)
12. On Discharges of Electricity in Insulators (1878)
13. Proof of the Electromagnetic Rotation of the Plane of Polarization of Light in Vapor of Carbon Disulphide (With Kundt, 1879)
14. Supplement to the Paper on the Rotation of the Plane of Polarization in Carbon Disulphide (With Kundt, 1879)
15. On the Electromagnetic Rotation of the Plane of Polarization of Light in Gases (With Kundt, 1879)
16. On the New Relation between Light and Electricity Found by Mr. Kerr (1880)

17. On the Electromagnetic Rotation of the Plane of Polarization in Gases — Second Communication (With Kundt, 1880)
18. On the Changes in Form and Volume of Dielectric Bodies Caused by Electricity (1880)
19. On Sounds Produced by Intermittent Irradiation of a Gas (1881)
20. Tests of a New Method for the Absorption of Rays by Gases (1881)
21. On the Changes in Double Refraction of Quartz Caused by Electric Forces (1883)
22. Observation on the Communication of Mr. A. Kundt: On the Optical Properties of Quartz in the Electrical Field (1883)
23. On the Thermo-, Actino-, and Piezo-electrical Properties of Quartz (1883)
24. On an Apparatus for the Lecture Demonstration of Poiseuille's Law (1883)
25. On the Influence of Pressure upon the Viscosity of Liquids, Especially of Water (1884)
26. New Experiments on the Absorption of Heat through Water Vapor (1884)
27. Experiments on the Electromagnetic Effect of Dielectric Polarization (1885)
28. On Compressibility and Surface Tension of Liquids (With Schneider, 1886)
29. On the Compressibility of Diluted Salt Solutions and of Sodium Chloride (With Schneider, 1887)
30. On the Electrodynamic Force Produced by Moving a Dielectric in a Homogeneous Electric Field (1888)
31. On the Compressibility of Water (With Schneider, 1888)
32. On the Compressibility of Sylvin, Rock Salt, and Potassium Chloride Solutions (With Schneider, 1888)
33. On the Influence of Pressure upon the Refraction Coefficients of Carbon Disulphide and Water (With Zehnder, 1888)
34. Electrical Properties of Quartz (1889)
35. Description of the Apparatus with which the Experiments on the Electrodynamic Effect of Moving Dielectrics Were Made (1890)
36. Some Lecture Demonstrations (1890)
37. On the Thickness of Coherent Oil Layers on the Surface of Water (1890)
38. On the Compressibility of Carbon Disulphide, Benzol, Ethylic Ether, and Some Alcohols (With Zehnder, 1891)
39. On the Influence of Pressure on the Refractive Index of Water, Carbon Disulphide, Benzol, Ethylic Ether, and Some Alcohols (With Zehnder, 1891)

40. On the Constitution of Liquid Water (1892)
41. Short Communication on Experiments on the Influence of Pressure on Some Physical Phenomena (1892)
42. On the Influence of Compression Heat on the Determination of the Compressibility of Liquids (1892)
43. Method of Producing Pure Surfaces of Water and Mercury (1892)
44. On the Influence of Pressure on the Galvanic Conductivity of Electrolytes (1893)
45. On the History of Physics at the University of Würzburg (1894)
46. Note on the Method for Measuring Differences in Pressure by Means of a Mirror Reading Scale (1894)
47. Communication on Some Experiments with a Right Angle Glass Prism (1894)
48. On the Influence of Pressure upon the Dielectric Constant of Water and Ethyl Alcohol (1894)
49. A New Kind of Ray — Preliminary Communication (1895)
50. A New Kind of Ray — Second Communication (1896)
51. Further Observations on the Properties of the X Rays — Third Communication (1897)
52. Explanation (1904)
53. On the Conductivity of Electricity in Calcium Spar and on the Influence of X Rays on It (1907)
54. Friedrich Kohlrausch (1910)
55. Determinations of the Thermal Linear Coefficient of Expansion of Cuprite and Diamond (1912)
56. On the Conductivity of Electricity in Some Crystals and on the Influence of Irradiation on Them (partly in cooperation with Joffé, 1913)
57. Pyro- and Piezo-electrical Investigations (1914)
58. On the Conductivity of Electricity in Some Crystals and on the Influence of Irradiation on Them (partly in cooperation with Joffé, 1921)

Eine neue Art von Strahlen — A New Kind of Ray
(Vorläufige Mittheilung) — (Preliminary Communication)
von Dr. W. Röntgen

1. If the discharge of a fairly large Ruhmkorff induction coil is allowed to pass through a Hittorf vacuum tube, or a sufficiently evacuated Lenard, Crookes tube, or a similar apparatus, and if one covers the tube with a fairly close-fitting mantle of thin black cardboard, one observes in the completely darkened room that a paper screen painted with barium platinocyanide placed near the apparatus glows brightly or becomes fluorescent with each discharge, regardless of whether the coated surface or the other side is turned toward the discharge tube. This fluorescence is still visible at a distance of two meters from the apparatus.

It is easy to prove that the cause of the fluorescence emanates from the discharge apparatus and not from any other point in the conducting circuit.

2. Observing this phenomenon, one is struck at once by the fact that the black cardboard cover, which stops visible or ultraviolet rays of the sun or the electric arc, transmits an active agent which can produce active fluorescence. One would therefore investigate first whether other materials also possess this same property.

One soon discovers that all materials are transparent to this agent, although differing widely in degree. I present a few examples. Paper is very transparent (*): I observed the fluorescent screen light up brightly behind a bound book of about 1,000 pages; the printer's ink effected no noticeable hindrance. Likewise the fluorescence appeared behind a double pack of playing cards. The eye can hardly notice a single card held between the apparatus and the screen. A single sheet of tinfoil is scarcely per-

---

* "Transparency" of a material I define as the relative brightness of the fluorescent screen placed directly behind the material, to the brightness of the screen under identical conditions, but without interposition of the material.

ceptible. Only after several layers have been placed over one another does one see the shadow distinctly on the screen. Thick blocks of wood are also very transparent, and pine boards two to three centimeters thick absorb only very little. A plate of aluminum about 15 millimeters thick, although reducing the effect considerably, did not cause the fluorescence to disappear entirely. Sheets of hard rubber several centimeters thick also permit the rays to pass through (**). Glass plates of equal thickness react differently, depending upon whether or not they contain lead (flint glass). The former are much less transparent than the latter. If one holds a hand between the discharge apparatus and the screen, one sees the darker shadow of the bones within the slightly fainter shadow image of the hand itself. Water, carbon disulphide, and various other liquids, when examined in mica containers, were found also to be transparent. I have not been able to discover if hydrogen is definitely more transparent than air. The fluorescence may still be clearly detected behind plates of copper, silver, lead, gold, or platinum, but only if the plates are not too thick. Platinum 0.2 millimeters thick is still transparent. Silver and copper plates may be even thicker. Lead 1.5 millimeters thick is practically opaque, and on account of this property it was frequently most useful. A stick of wood having a cross section of 20 by 20 millimeters, and one side painted with white lead paint, reacts differently depending upon how it is held between the apparatus and the screen. While there is practically no effect if the direction of the X rays is parallel to the painted surface, the stick throws a dark shadow when the rays have to pass perpendicularly through the painted surface. In a manner similar to that of the metals themselves, their salts, either in the solid form or in solution, can be arranged according to their transparency.

3. The experimental results cited, as well as others, lead to the conclusion that the transparency of various substances, assumed to be of equal thickness, depends primarily upon their density. No other property is as conspicuous as this one, at least not to the same extent.

That the density, however, is not the only determining factor is proved by the following experiments. I examined the transparency of plates of almost equal thickness made of glass, aluminum, calcite, and quartz. While the density of these substances is approximately the same, it was quite evident that calcite was considerably less transparent than the other materials, which all reacted very much alike. I have not noticed a particularly strong fluorescence of calcite, especially as compared with glass (see No. 6 below).

** For the sake of brevity I should like to use the term "rays," and to distinguish them from others I shall use the name "X rays." (See No. 14)

4. As the thickness increases all materials become less transparent. In order to find a possible relation between transparency and thickness, I made photographs (see No. 6 below) in which the photographic plate was partly covered with layers of tinfoil in a steplike arrangement. Photometric measurements of these will be made when I have a suitable photometer.

5. Platinum, lead, zinc, and aluminum were rolled out in sheets of such thickness that all appeared nearly equally transparent. The following table contains the measured thickness in millimeters, the relative thickness referred to that of the platinum sheet, and their densities:

	Thickness	Relative Thickness	Density
Pt	0.018 mm	1	21.5
Pb	0.05 mm	3	11.3
Zn	0.10 mm	6	7.1
Al	3.5 mm	200	2.6

These values show that by no means is the transparency of different metals equal even when the product of thickness and density is the same. The transparency increases much more rapidly then the product decreases.

6. The fluorescence of barium platinocyanide is not the only detectable effect of X rays. It must be mentioned that other substances also fluoresce, such as, for example, the phosphorescent calcium compounds, uranium glass, ordinary glass, calcite, rock salt, and so on.

Of special significance in many respects is the fact that photographic dry plates are sensitive to X rays. One is thus able to determine more definitely many phenomena, and so avoid deceptions more easily. Whenever possible, as control I have recorded by means of photography every relatively important observation which I made with the eye on the fluorescent screen.

In these experiments, the property of the rays of penetrating almost unhindered thin layers of wood, paper, and tinfoil is very important. In the lighted room one can expose the photographic plate, which is enclosed in a holder or wrapped in paper. On the other hand, as a consequence of this property undeveloped plates should not be left near the discharge apparatus for any length of time if these plates are protected merely by the usual cardboard box and paper.

The question remains whether or not X rays are directly responsible for the chemical reaction upon the silver salts of the photographic plate.

It is possible that this action is due to the fluorescent light which, as noted above, is produced in the glass plate itself or perhaps in the gelatin layer. Films may be used equally as well as glass plates.

I have not yet proved experimentally that X rays are also able to produce a heating action; yet one may well assume that this effect exists, since the observed fluorescent phenomena prove that X rays may be transformed. It is evident that not all of the impinging X rays leave the material unaltered.

The retina of the eye is insensitive to these rays. The eye brought close to the discharge apparatus observes nothing, although, according to experience, the media contained in the eye must be sufficiently transparent to transmit the rays.

7. After I had recognized the transparency of various relatively thick materials, I was anxious to observe how the X rays behaved when passing through a prism, whether or not they were refracted by it. Experiments with water and with carbon disulphide in mica prisms having a refracting angle of approximately 30 degrees showed no refraction either on the fluorescent screen or on the photographic plate. As a control the refraction of light rays was observed under the same conditions; the refracted images fell on the plate about 10 and 20 millimeters distant from the nonrefracted. With hard rubber and aluminum prisms, also of a refracting angle of about 30 degrees, I have obtained images on the photographic plate in which one might possibly detect a small refraction. However, this is very uncertain. And if refraction does exist, it is in any case so small that the refractive index of the X rays in these substances could not be more than 1.05 at the most. Also on the fluorescent screen I was unable to observe any refraction.

Experiments to date with prisms of denser metals have not produced any definite results owing to their feeble transparency and the resultant diminished intensity of the transmitted rays.

Considering these facts on one hand, and on the other the importance of the question whether or not X rays can be refracted when passing from one medium into another, it is most fortunate that this subject can be investigated in a different manner without the aid of prisms. Finely pulverized substances in sufficiently thick layers scatter the impinging light and, because of refraction and reflection, let pass only a small amount of it. So, if the powders are equally as transparent to X rays as the coherent substance is — provided that equal masses of each are used — it follows that neither refraction nor regular reflection takes place to any appreciable degree. Such experiments were carried out with finely pulverized rock salt, with fine electrolytic silver powder, and with zinc dust such as is frequently used in chemical investigations. In all cases no difference could be detected in the transparency between powder and coherent substance, either by observation with the fluorescent screen or with the photographic plate.

From the foregoing it is obvious that one cannot concentrate X rays with lenses. A large hard-rubber lens or a glass lens were ineffective. The shadow picture of a round rod is darker in the center than at the edge, while that of a tube, filled with a substance more transparent than the material of the tube itself, is lighter in the center than at the edge.

8. On the basis of the preceding paragraph the question regarding the reflection of X rays may be considered settled in view that a noticeable regular reflection of the rays from any of the examined substances did not take place. Other experiments, which I shall omit here, lead to the same conclusion.

However, one observation must be mentioned, which at first seems to be contradictory. I exposed to the X rays a photographic plate that was protected from light by black paper with the glass side pointing towards the discharge apparatus. The sensitive layer, with the exception of a small free space, was covered with polished sheets of platinum, lead, zinc, and aluminum in a starlike arrangement. On the developed negative one can clearly perceive that the darkening under the platinum, the lead, and particularly under the zinc is stronger than under the other areas. The aluminum had exerted no effect at all. It seems, therefore, that the three named metals reflect the rays. However, one may conceive of other causes for the stronger darkening, and in the second experiment, in order to be sure, I placed a piece of thin aluminum foil, which is not transparent to ultraviolet rays but is very transparent to X rays, between the sensitive film and the metal plates. Since essentially the same result was again obtained, the reflection of X rays from the aforementioned metals is proved.

If one adds to this fact the observation already mentioned that powders are equally as transparent as coherent materials, and furthermore that materials having rough surfaces have the same effect upon the transmission of X rays as have polished substances, as described in the last experiment, one comes to the conclusion that, as stated before, a regular reflection does not take place, but that materials react to X rays as turbid media do to light.

Since, moreover, I could not detect any refraction when X rays pass from one medium into another, it appears that they move with equal velocity in all materials, and that this speed is the same in the medium which is present everywhere and in which particles of matter are embedded. These particles form an obstacle to the propagation of X rays, which in general is that the greater the effect, the denser the respective substance.

9. Therefore the arrangement of particles within the material may possibly influence its transparency. For instance, a piece of calcite of a given thickness may vary in transparency depending upon whether the rays pass through it in the direction of its axis or at right angles thereto. Experiments with calcite and quartz, however, have given a negative result.

10. It is well known that Lenard, in his beautiful experiments on Hittorf's cathode rays passing through a thin aluminum foil, came to the conclusion that these rays are phenomena of the ether and that they are diffused in all materials. Regarding our rays we can say the same.

In his most recent publication Lenard determined the absorptive power of different materials for cathode rays and, among others, for air of atmospheric pressure; he found it to be 4.10, 3.40, and 3.10, all relative to 1 centimeter, depending upon the rarefaction of the gas in the discharge apparatus. In my experiments, judging from the discharge voltage estimated from the spark gap, I was dealing for the most part with rarefactions of approximately the same order of magnitude and only rarely with higher or lower ones. With L. Weber's photometer — I do not own a better one — I succeeded in comparing in atmospheric air the intensities of the fluorescent light of my screen at two distances from the discharge apparatus — about 100 and 200 millimeters respectively — and I found in three experiments, which were in very good agreement with each other, that they were inversely proportional to the squares of their respective distances between screen and discharge apparatus. Therefore air absorbs a much smaller fraction of X rays than of cathode rays. This result is also in entire agreement with the previously mentioned observation that the fluorescent light may still be observed at a distance of two meters from the discharge apparatus.

In general, other substances have properties similar to air. They are more transparent to X rays than to cathode rays.

11. Another very important difference between the behavior of cathode rays and of X rays lies in the fact that, despite many attempts, I have not succeeded in obtaining a deflection of the X rays by magnet, even in very intensive magnetic fields.

So far, the deflection by a magnet has been considered a property peculiarly characteristic of cathode rays. Although Hertz and Lenard observed that there are different kinds of cathode rays "which can be differentiated from each other by their production of phosphorescence, by the amount of their absorption, and by their deflection by a magnet."

A considerable deflection was found in all their investigations, so that I do not believe that one should give up this characteristic feature without stringent reason.

12. According to experiments made especially for this purpose it is certain that the area on the wall of the discharge apparatus that shows the strongest fluorescence must be considered as the main center from which the X rays radiate in all directions. The X rays proceed from that area where, according to data obtained by several investigators, the cathode rays impinge upon the glass wall. If one deflects the cathode rays within the discharge apparatus by means of a magnet, one observes also that the X rays are emitted from another area, namely from the new terminating point of the cathode rays.

This is another reason why X rays, which cannot be deflected, cannot be simply cathode rays that have been transmitted or reflected without being changed by the glass wall. The greater density of the gas outside the discharge tube certainly cannot, according to Lenard, be made responsible for the great difference in deflection.

I therefore come to the conclusion that the X rays are not identical with the cathode rays, but that they are produced by the cathode rays at the glass wall of the discharge apparatus.

13. This production takes place not only in glass but also in aluminum, as I was able to observe with an apparatus sealed with an aluminum window 2 millimeters thick. Other substances are to be examined later.

14. I find the justification for using the name "rays" for the agent emanating from the wall of the discharge apparatus in the entirely regular formation of shadows which are produced if one brings more or less transparent materials between the apparatus and the fluorescent screen (or the photographic plate).

I have observed and sometimes photographed many such shadow pictures, the production of which is occasionally very attractive. For instance, I have photographs of the shadows of the profile of a door separating rooms, in one of which the discharge apparatus was placed and in the other the photographic plate; of the shadows of the bones of the hand; of the shadows of a covered wire wound on a wooden spool; of a set of weights enclosed in a small box; of a compass in which the magnetic needle is entirely enclosed by metal; of a piece of metal whose inhomogeneity becomes apparent with X rays; and so on.

That X rays are propagated in straight lines is further proved by a pinhole photograph that I was able to make of the discharge apparatus while enclosed in black paper; the picture is weak but unmistakenly correct.

15. I have often tried to detect interference phenomena of X rays

but unfortunately without success, possibly only because of their low intensity.

16. Experiments to determine whether or not electrostatic forces can affect X rays in any way have been started but are not yet finished.

17. If one asks oneself what X rays — which cannot be cathode rays, as we have seen — really are, one might at first perhaps think of ultraviolet light because of their lively fluorescence and chemical effects. But one is immediately confronted with rather serious considerations. For, if X rays were ultraviolet light, this light should have the following properties:

(a) In passing from air into water, carbon disulphide, aluminum, rock salt, glass, zinc, and so on, it suffers no noticeable refraction.

(b) It cannot be regularly reflected to any noticeable extent by these named substances.

(c) It cannot be polarized by any of the ordinary methods.

(d) No other property of the material influences its absorption as much as its density.

In other words, one would have to assume that these ultraviolet rays behave entirely differently from the infra-red, visible, and ultraviolet rays known at present.

I have not been able to arrive at this conclusion and so have sought for another explanation.

Some kind of relation seems to exist between the new rays and light rays. At least this is indicated by the formation of shadows, by fluorescence, and by chemical effects, which are common to both types of rays. Now it has been known for a long time that, besides transversal light vibrations, longitudinal vibrations in the ether can also occur. According to the opinion of several physicists these vibrations must even exist. It is true that their existence has not yet been definitely proved and that therefore their properties have not yet been investigated experimentally.

Should not, therefore, the new rays be due to longitudinal vibrations in the ether?

I must confess that during the course of investigations I have become more and more confident of this thought, and I therefore take the liberty of expressing this theory, although I am perfectly aware that the explanation offered requires further confirmation.

Würzburg, Physikalisches Institut der Universität
Dezember 1895.

Eine neue Art von Strahlen — A New Kind of Ray
(Fortsetzung) — (Continuation)
von Dr. Wilhelm Konrad Röntgen [*sic*]

Since my work must be interrupted for several weeks, I wish to present at this time some new phenomena which I have observed:

18. At the time of my first publication I knew that X rays are able to discharge electrified bodies, and I suspect that in Lenard's experiments it was also the X rays and not the cathode rays, which transmitted unchanged by the aluminum window of his apparatus, that produced the effects described by him upon electrified bodies at a distance. However, I have waited until I could present incontestable results before publishing my experiments.

These can be obtained only if the observations are made in a space that is not only protected completely from the electrostatic forces emanating from the vacuum tube, from the conducting wires, from the induction apparatus, and so on, but is also closed against air which comes from the region of the discharge apparatus.

Accordingly I had a chamber built of zinc plates soldered together, which is large enough to accommodate me and the necessary apparatus and which is completely airtight except for an opening which could be closed by a zinc door. The wall opposite the door is to a large extent covered with lead. At a place near the discharge apparatus, which is set up outside the case, an opening four centimeters wide is cut out of the zinc wall and its lead cover, and this opening is made airtight with a thin sheet of aluminum. Through this window the X rays can enter the observation space.

Now I observed the following phenomena:

(a) Positively or negatively electrified bodies set up in air are discharged if they are irradiated with X rays. The more intense the rays are, the more rapid is the discharge. The intensity of the rays was estimated by their effect upon the fluorescent screen or upon a photographic plate.

Generally it is immaterial whether the electrified bodies are conductors or insulators. So far I have not been able to find a specific difference in the behavior of different bodies with regard to the rate of discharge, nor in the behavior of positive and negative electricity. Yet it is not impossible that small differences may exist.

(b) If an electrified conductor is not surrounded by air but by a solid insulator, e.g., paraffin, the irradiation has the same effect as moving a grounded flame over the insulating cover.

(c) If this insulating cover is surrounded by a tight-fitting grounded conductor, which like the insulator must be transparent to X rays, the radiation exerts upon the inner electrified conductor no effect detectable with the available apparatus.

(d) The observations cited under (a), (b), and (c) indicate that air which is irradiated with X rays has acquired the property of discharging electrified bodies with which it comes in contact.

(e) If this is really the case and, in addition, if the air retains this property for some time after being exposed to X rays, it must be possible to discharge electrified bodies that themselves are not directly irradiated by X rays simply by conducting irradiated air to them.

One can be convinced of the validity of this conclusion in different ways. I should like to describe one experimental method, although it is perhaps not the simplest one.

I used a brass tube 3 centimeters wide and 45 centimeters long. A few centimeters from one end of the tube part of its wall was cut away and replaced with a thin sheet of aluminum. Through the other end a brass sphere, fastened to a metal rod and insulated, was sealed airtight into the tube. Between the sphere and the closed end of the tube there was soldered a little side tube, which could be connected to an exhaust apparatus. When suction was applied, air that passed the aluminum window on its way through the tube flowed around the brass sphere. The distance from window to sphere was over 20 centimeters.

I arranged this tube inside the zinc chamber so that the X rays could enter through the aluminum window of the tube perpendicularly to its axis. The insulated sphere lay in the shadow beyond the range of these rays. The tube and zinc case were connected to each other, and the sphere was connected to a Hankel electroscope.

It was then observed that a charge, either positive or negative, given to the sphere was not influenced by the X rays as long as the air remained at rest in the tube, but that the charge instantly decreased considerably if irradiated air was drawn past the sphere by strong suction. When a constant potential from a storage battery was applied to the sphere, and when irradiated air was continuously drawn through the tube, an electric current was produced just as if the sphere had been connected to the tube wall by a poor conductor.

(f) The question arises in what manner the air can lose the property given to it by X rays. It is still unsettled whether in time it loses the property itself, that is, without coming in contact with other bodies.

However, it is certain that a brief contact with a body that has a large surface, and is not necessarily electrified, may render the air ineffective. If, for example, one placed a sufficiently large stopper of cotton wadding so far into the tube that irradiated air must pass through the cotton before it reaches the electrified sphere, the charge of the sphere remains unchanged, even while suction is applied.

If the stopper is placed in front of the aluminum window, one obtains the same results as without the cotton, proof that dust particles cannot possibly be the cause of the discharge observed.

Wire screens have an action similar to cotton; however, the screen must be very fine, and many layers must be placed on each other if the irradiated air passing through them is to be made ineffective. If these screens are not grounded, as has been assumed so far, but are connected to a source of electricity of a constant potential, the observations have always been what I expected. However, these experiments have not yet been completed.

(g) If the electrified bodies are placed in dry hydrogen instead of air, they are also discharged by the X rays. It seemed to me that the discharge in hydrogen proceeded somewhat slower; however, this is still uncertain because of the difficulties of obtaining equal intensities of the X rays in a series of consecutive experiments.

The method of filling the apparatus with hydrogen precludes the possibility that the layer of air originally present on the surface of the bodies could play an important role in the discharge.

(h) In highly evacuated spaces the discharge of a body struck directly by the X rays proceeds much more slowly — in one case about seventy times more slowly — than in the same vessels when they are filled with air or hydrogen at atmospheric pressure.

(i) Experiments have been started on the behavior of a mixture of chlorine and hydrogen under the influence of X rays.

(j) Finally, I should like to mention that one must often accept with great caution the results of experiments on the discharging effects of X rays in which the influence of the surrounding gas has not been considered.

19. In many cases it is advantageous to insert a Tesla apparatus (condenser and transformer) between the discharge apparatus which furnishes the X rays, and the Ruhmkorff induction coil. This arrangement has the following advantages: first, the discharge tubes are less liable to be punctured and heat up less; secondly, the vacuum, at least so far as my self-constructed apparatus is concerned, keeps for a longer time; and thirdly, many discharge tubes produce more intense rays under these conditions. Some tubes that were evacuated too little or too much to work satisfactorily on the Ruhmkorff coil alone, functioned satisfactorily with the use of the Tesla transformer.

The question arises immediately — and I should like, therefore, to mention it without contributing anything to its solution at present — whether X rays can also be produced by a continuous discharge from a source of constant potential, or whether fluctuations of the potential are essential and necessary to produce the rays.

20. It is stated in paragraph 13 of my first communication that X rays can be produced not only in glass but also in aluminum. In continuing the investigations along these lines, no solid body could be found that was not able to produce X rays under the influence of cathode rays. There is also no reason known to me why liquids and gaseous bodies may not act in the same manner.

However, quantitative differences in the behavior of different bodies have appeared. For example, if one lets cathode rays fall upon a plate, one half of which consists of a 0.3 millimeter platinum sheet and the other half of a 1 millimeter aluminum sheet, one observes on the photograph of this double plate taken with a pinhole camera that the platinum emits considerably more X rays from the front side where it has been struck by the cathode rays than the aluminum emits from the same side. From the rear side, however, hardly any X rays are emitted from the platinum, but relatively many from the aluminum. In the latter, rays have been produced in the front layers of the aluminum and have penetrated through the plate.

One can easily arrive at an explanation of this observation, but it might be advisable to learn first about some other properties of the X rays.

However, it should be mentioned that the observed facts also have a practical significance. According to my experience up to now, platinum is best suited for the production of X rays of highest intensity. For several weeks I have used with good success a discharge tube with a concave mirror of aluminum as cathode and a platinum foil as anode, which has been placed in the focus of the cathode and inclined 45 degrees in relation to the axis of the mirror.

21. In this apparatus X rays are emitted from the anode. From experiments made with apparatus of various shapes I must conclude that, insofar as the intensity of X rays is concerned, it does not matter whether these rays are produced at the anode or not.

A discharge apparatus was built especially for experiments with alternating currents from a Tesla transformer in which both electrodes are concave aluminum mirrors, whose axes form a right angle; in their common focus a platinum plate is placed to receive the cathode rays. A report on the usefulness of this apparatus will appear later.

Würzburg, Physikalisches Institut der Universität
9 März, 1896

Weitere Beobachtungen an den Eigenschaften von X Strahlen —
Further Observations on the Properties of X Rays
(Dritte Mittheilung) — (Third Communication)
von Dr. Wilhelm Conrad Röntgen

1. If one places an opaque plate between a discharge apparatus ([1]) which emits intense X rays and a fluorescent screen in such a position that the shadow of the plate covers the entire screen, one can still detect, despite the plate, a luminosity of the barium platinocyanide. This light can be seen even if the screen lies directly on the plate, and one is at first sight inclined to think that the plate is transparent. However, if one covers the screen lying on the plate with a heavy plate of glass, the fluorescent light becomes much weaker, and it disappears entirely if instead of a glass plate one places the screen in a cylinder of lead foil 0.1 centimeter thick, which is closed at one end with the opaque plate and at the other by the head of the observer.

The phenomenon described may have been produced by diffraction of rays of very long wave length or by the fact that X rays are emitted from substances surrounding the discharge apparatus, notably from the irradiated air.

The latter explanation is the correct one as can be easily demonstrated with the following apparatus, among others. Figure 1 represents a very thick-walled glass bell jar, 20 centimeters high and 10 centimeters wide, which is closed by a heavy zinc plate cemented on. At 1 and 2 are inserted circular segments of lead sheets, which are somewhat larger than half the cross-section of the jar and which prevent the X rays that enter the jar through an opening in the zinc plate, which is covered with a celluloid film, from traveling in a straight line to the space above lead plate 2. On the upper side of this lead plate is fastened a small barium platinocyanide screen, which almost fills the entire cross-section of the jar. This

---

[1] All the discharge tubes mentioned in the following communication are constructed according to the principle given in paragraph 20 of my second communication (Sitzungsberichte der Physikalischen-medizinischen Gesellschaft zu Würzburg, Jahrgang 1895). I obtained a great number of them from the firm of Greiner & Friedrichs in Stützerbach i. Th., whom I wish to thank publicly for putting abundant material at my disposal without expense.

cannot be struck by direct rays nor by those which have undergone a primary diffuse reflection on a solid substance (for example, the glass wall). The jar is filled with dust-free air before each experiment. If one lets X rays enter the jar so that they are all stopped by the lead screen 1, one does not see any fluorescence near 2; only when the jar is tipped so that direct rays can also enter the space between 1 and 2 does the fluorescent screen show an illumination of the half not covered with the lead plate 2. If the jar is then connected to a water aspirator, one notices that the fluorescence becomes gradually weaker as the evacuation progresses; if air is readmitted, the intensity increases again.

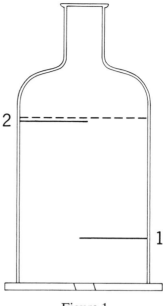

Figure 1

Since now, as I found, mere contact with air which has shortly before been irradiated does not produce any noticeable fluorescence of the barium platinocyanide, one must conclude from the experiment described that air emits X rays in all directions while it is being irradiated.

If our eyes were as sensitive to X rays as they are to light rays, a discharge apparatus in operation would appear to us like a light burning in a room that is moderately filled with tobacco smoke; perhaps the color of the direct irradiation and that coming from the air particles would be different.

I have not yet been able to answer the question as to whether the rays emitted from irradiated substances are of the same kind as those impinging upon them or, in other words, whether a diffuse reflection or a phenomenon similar to fluorescence is the cause of these rays. That the rays coming from the air also are effective photographically can be proved easily. This effect is even noticeable sometimes in a manner disagreeable to the observer. To guard against this action, which is frequently necessary for longer exposure times, the photographic plate must be enclosed in suitable lead containers.

2. For comparing the intensity of the radiation of two discharge tubes and for various other experiments I used an arrangement that is based on the Bouguer photometer, and that I shall also simply call a photometer. A rectangular sheet of lead, 35 centimeters high, 150 centimeters long,

and 0.15 centimeters thick, is placed vertically at the center of a long table and supported by a board frame. On each side of it is placed a discharge tube which can be moved along the table. At one end of the lead strip a fluorescent screen ([2]) is attached in such a way that each half of it receives perpendicularly the rays from only one tube. In these measurements adjustments are made to obtain equal intensity of the fluorescence in both halves.

Some remarks on the use of this instrument may be in order here. First, it must be stated that adjustments are frequently very difficult to make because of the lack of constancy of the source of radiation. The tubes respond to every irregularity in the interruption of the primary current, such as occur with the Deprez and notably with the Foucault interrupter. It is therefore advisable to make repeated adjustments.

Secondly, I should like to enumerate the conditions which influence the brightness of a given fluorescent screen which is bombarded by X rays in such rapid succession that the observing eye can no longer detect the intermittance of the radiation. This brightness depends on (1) the intensity of the radiation emitted from the platinum plate of the discharge tube; (2) very probably the kind of rays that fall upon the screen, since not every type of radiation causes the same degree of fluorescence (see below); (3) the distance of the screen from the point of emission of the rays; (4) the absorption which the rays experience on their way to the barium platinocyanide screen; (5) the number of discharges per second; (6) the duration of each single discharge; (7) the duration and the strength of the afterglow of the barium platinocyanide; and (8) the radiation originating in materials surrounding the discharge tube and falling upon the screen. In order to avoid errors one must always remember that in general these conditions are similar to a comparison of the fluorescent action produced by two intermittent light sources of different colors which are surrounded by an absorbing envelope and placed within a turbid — or fluorescent — medium.

3. According to paragraph 12 of my first communication ([3]) the part of the discharge apparatus that is struck by cathode rays is the point of emission of X rays which spread out "in all directions." Now it becomes interesting to determine how the intensity of the rays varies with the direction.

([2]) In this and in other experiments the Edison fluorescent screen has proved most useful. This consists of a box similar to a stereoscope, which can be held light-tight against the head of the observer and whose cardboard end is covered with barium platinocyanide. Edison uses tungstate of calcium instead of barium platino-cyanide; but I prefer the latter for many reasons.

([3]) Sitzungsberichte der Physikalischen-medizinischen Gesellschaft zu Würzburg, Jahrgang 1895.

For this investigation the sphere-shaped discharge apparatus with smoothly polished plain platinum plates on which the cathode rays fall at an angle of 45 degrees are the most suitable. Even without additional instruments one can recognize from the uniformly bright fluorescence of the hemispherical glass wall surrounding the platinum plate that there are not very great variations in the intensities in different directions. Therefore Lambert's law of emission cannot hold in this case. Nevertheless, this fluorescence might still be produced largely by cathode rays.

To test this more accurately, the intensity of the radiation emitted in different directions from several tubes was examined with the photometer. Furthermore, for the same purpose I have exposed photographic films bent in the shape of a semicircle (radius 25 centimeters), with the platinum plate of the discharge apparatus as its center. In both experiments, however, the variation in thickness of different areas of the tube wall becomes very disturbing, since it causes the X rays proceeding in different directions to be absorbed unequally. However, I succeeded in equalizing the thickness of the glass, through which the rays pass, by interposing thin glass plates.

The result of these experiments is that the radiation through an imaginary hemisphere, with the platinum plate as its center, is practically uniform almost to its very edge. Only when the angle of emission of the X rays reached about 80 degrees could I detect the beginning of a decrease in the radiation. But even this decrease is still relatively very small, so that the main variation in the intensity occurs between 89 and 90 degrees.

I have not been able to detect a difference in the kinds of rays emitted at different angles.

On account of the described distribution of intensity of the X rays, images from the platinum plate — observed either upon the fluorescent screen or upon the photographic plate by means of a pinhole camera, or with a narrow slit — must be more intense the greater the angle is between platinum plate and screen or photographic plate, provided that this angle does not exceed 80 degrees. I was able to confirm this conclusion by means of suitable arrangements which permitted comparisons of images obtained simultaneously at different angles from the same discharge tube.

In optics, in the case of fluorescence we encounter a similar distribution of intensity of emitted radiations. If one adds a few drops of fluorescein solution to water in a rectangular tank and if one illuminates the tank with white or violet light, one observes that the brightest fluorescence proceeds from the edges of the slowly dropping threads of fluorescein, that is, from those parts where the angle of emission of the fluorescent light is the greatest. Herr Stokes, on the occasion of a similar experiment, has explained that this phenomenon is due to the fact that rays which excite fluorescence are absorbed to a much greater extent by the fluorescein solution than is the fluorescent light itself. Now it is remarkable that also cathode rays, which produce the X rays, are absorbed by platinum to a much greater extent than are the X rays, and it is easy to conjecture from this that a relationship exists between the two phenomena — the transformation of ordinary light into fluorescent light and of cathode rays into X rays. However, at the present time no conclusive proof for such an assumption exists.

Also the observations on the intensity distribution of the rays emitted from the platinum plate have a certain significance with respect to the technique of producing shadow pictures with X rays. According to the statements made previously, it is advisable to place the discharge tube in such a position that the rays used to produce the picture leave the platinum at the greatest possible angle, although this should not be much greater than 80 degrees. In this way one obtains the sharpest picture possible; and if the platinum plate is perfectly plane, and if the tube has been constructed so that the oblique rays do not have to pass through a glass wall materially thicker than do the rays which are emitted perpendicular to the platinum plate, then the radiation falling on the object in the described arrangement suffers no loss in intensity.

4. In my first communication I designated "transparency of a material" as the ratio of the brightness of a fluorescent screen placed perpendicular to the rays, closely behind the material to that of the screen, under identical conditions without interposition of the material. "Specific transparency" of a substance will be used to indicate the transparency relative to the unit thickness of the substance; this is equal to the dth root of the transparency, if d is the thickness of the traversed layer, measured in the direction of the rays.

Since my first communication I have used principally the photometer described previously to determine the transparency. A plate of the substance to be investigated — aluminum, tin, glass, and so on — was placed in front of one of two equally bright fluorescent halves of the screen. And the difference in the brightness thus produced was then matched, either by increasing the distance between the discharge apparatus and the uncovered half of the screen or by bringing the other one closer. In both cases the correctly determined ratio of the squares of the distances of the platinum plates of the discharge apparatus from the screen, before and after adjustment of the apparatus, represents the desired value for the transparency of the interposed substance. Both methods led to the same result. After adding a second plate to the first, one finds in the same way the transparency of the second plate to the rays which have already passed through the first.

The described procedure presupposes that the brightness of a fluorescent screen is inversely proportional to the square of the distance from the source of radiation, and this is true if, first, the air does not absorb or emit any X rays and, secondly, if the brightness of the fluorescent light is proportional to the intensity of the radiation of rays of the same kind. Now the first condition certainly is not fulfilled, and it is doubtful whether the second one is. I therefore first convinced myself by experiments, as already described in paragraph 10 of my first communication, that deviations from the law of proportionality mentioned before are so small that they may be neglected in our case. It should also be mentioned that, considering the fact that X rays are also emitted from irradiated substances, first, that no difference could be detected with the photometer in the transparency of an aluminum plate, 0.925 millimeters thick, and of thirty-one aluminum foils, each 0.0299 millimeters thick, stacked on one another (31 times 0.0299 equals 0.927). And, secondly, that the brightness of the fluorescent screen was not noticeably different when the plate was placed directly in front of the screen or placed at a greater distance from it.

The result of these transparency experiments for aluminum is as follows:

Transparency to perpendicularly impinging rays	Tube 2	Tube 3	Tube 4	Tube 2
Of the first 1 mm thick Al plate	0.40	0.45	—	0.68
Of the second 1 mm thick Al plate	0.55	0.68	—	0.73
Of the first 2 mm thick Al plate	—	0.30	0.39	0.50
Of the second 2 mm thick Al plate	—	0.39	0.54	0.63

From these experiments and from similar ones with glass and tin we deduce the following: Assuming that the investigated substances are divided into layers of equal thickness, placed perpendicularly to the parallel rays, each of these layers is more transparent to the transmitted rays than the previous one; in other words, the specific transparency of a substance increases with its thickness.

This result is in complete agreement with what one observes on the photograph of a tinfoil scale, as described in paragraph 4 of my first communication, and also with the fact that occasionally on photographs the shadows of thin layers — such as the paper used to wrap the plates — are sometimes very noticeable.

5. If two plates of different substances are equally transparent, this equality may not persist if the thickness of the two plates, but nothing

else, is changed in the same ratio. This fact may be proved most simply with two scales, one of platinum and one of aluminum, placed side by side. For this purpose I used platinum foil, 0.0026 millimeters thick, and aluminum foil, 0.0299 millimeters thick. When I brought this double scale in front of the fluorescent screen or of a photographic plate and directed rays upon it, I found in one case that a single platinum layer was as transparent as a six-fold aluminum layer. But the transparency of a two-fold platinum layer was not equal to that of a twelve-fold but to a sixteen-fold aluminum layer. With another discharge tube I found that 1 platinum equals 8 aluminum, and 8 platinum equals 90 aluminum. These experiments prove that the ratio of the thickness of platinum and aluminum of equal transparency is smaller in proportion as the respective layers become thicker.

6. The ratio of the thicknesses of two equally transparent plates of different materials depends also upon the thickness and the material of that substance — for instance, the glass wall of the discharge apparatus — which the rays must penetrate before they reach the respective plates.

In order to prove this conclusion — which is not unexpected according to the statements made in paragraphs 4 and 5 — one may use an arrangement which I call a platinum-aluminum window, and which, as we shall see, is also useful for other purposes. This consists of a rectangular piece of platinum foil (4.0 centimeters by 6.5 centimeters), 0.0026 millimeter thick, which is cemented to a thin paper screen and in which are punched 15 round holes, 0.7 centimeter in diameter, arranged in three rows. These little windows are covered with tightly fitting little disks of aluminum foil, 0.0299 millimeter thick, carefully stacked in such a way that there is one little disk in the first window, two in the second, and so on, and finally fifteen disks in the fifteenth window. If one places this arrangement in front of the fluorescent screen, one observes very clearly, particularly if one uses tubes that are not too hard (see below), the number of aluminum disks having a transparency equal to that of the platinum foil. This number will be called the window-number.

In one case, when using direct radiation, I obtained the window-number 5. When a plate 2 millimeters thick made of ordinary soda glass was then interposed, the window-number obtained was 10. Thus, the ratio of the thickness of platinum and aluminum foil of equal transparency was reduced to one-half when I used rays which had passed through a glass plate 2 millimeters thick instead of rays that came directly from the discharge apparatus. Q.E.D. *(quod erat demonstrandum,* which was to be demonstrated).

The following experiment should also be mentioned here. The platinum-aluminum window was laid on a small package containing twelve photographic films and was then exposed. After development the first film lying under the window showed the window-number 10, the twelfth the number 13, and the others, in proper sequence, all the steps from 10 to 13.

7. The experiments described in paragraphs 4, 5, and 6 refer to the changes which the X rays emitted from a discharge tube undergo in passing through different substances. It will now be proved that for one and the same substance, and the same thickness traversed, the transparency may be different for rays emitted from different tubes.

For this purpose the values for the transparency of an aluminum plate 2 millimeters thick for rays produced in different tubes are given in the following table. Some of these values have been taken from the first table in section 4.

Transparency	Tube 1	Tube 2	Tube 3	Tube 4	Tube 2	Tube 5
For rays falling perpendicularly upon an aluminum plate 2 mm thick	0.0044	0.22	0.30	0.39	0.50	0.59

The discharge tubes differ only slightly in construction or in the thickness of the glass wall, but vary mainly in the degree of evacuation of the gas content and in the discharge potential consequent to this; tube 1 requires the lowest, tube 5 the highest, discharge potential; or, as we shall say for the sake of brevity, tube 1 is the "softest," and tube 5 is the "hardest." The same Ruhmkorff coil, directly connected to the tubes, the same interrupter, and the same primary current were used in all cases.

All the many other materials that I investigated behave similarly to aluminum. All of them are more transparent to rays of a harder tube than to rays of a softer tube ([4]). This fact seems to me worthy of special consideration.

The ratio of the thicknesses of two equally transparent plates of different materials is dependent upon the hardness of the discharge tube used. One can recognize this immediately with the platinum-aluminum window (paragraph 5); using a very soft tube one obtains, for example, the window-number 2, while for the very hard but otherwise identical tubes a scale, reading up to number 15, is not even sufficient. This means that the ratio of the thicknesses of platinum and aluminum of equal transparency is smaller in proportion as the tubes are harder which emit the

---

([4])On the behavior of "non-normal" tubes, see section 8.

rays, or — considering the result mentioned above — as the rays are less easily absorbed.

The different behavior of rays produced in tubes of different degrees of hardness is also evident, of course, in the familiar shadow pictures of hands, and so on. Using a very soft tube one obtains dark pictures in which the bones are not very prominent; when a harder tube is used the bones become clearly visible in all details and the soft parts are weak in comparison. And with a very hard tube one obtains only weak shadows, even of the bones. From this observation it follows that the choice of the tube to be used must depend upon the nature of the object to be photo-graphed.

8. It must also be mentioned that the quality of radiation emitted from one and the same tube depends upon different circumstances. As the investigation with the platinum-aluminum window shows, this is influenced: (1) By the manner in which the Deprez or Foucault interrupter ([5]) functions, that is, by the variation of the primary current. Here must be mentioned the frequently observed phenomenon that some of the dis-charges in rapid succession produce X rays which are not only particularly intense but which also are distinguished from others by their absorbability. (2) By a spark gap connected in series in the secondary circuit of the discharge apparatus. (3) By inserting a Telsa transformer in the circuit. (4) By the degree of evacuation of the discharge apparatus (as previously mentioned). (5) By various, not yet sufficiently understood, phenomena in the interior of the discharge tube. Several of these factors deserve to be considered in more detail.

If we take a tube which has not yet been used nor even evacuated and connect it to the mercury pump, we shall reach, after the necessary pumping and heating of the tube, a degree of evacuation in which the first X rays are noticeable by a feeble illumination on a nearby fluorescent screen. A spark gap connected in parallel with the tube registers sparks only a few millimeters in length, the platinum-aluminum window shows very low numbers, and the rays are very absorbable. The tube is very "soft." Now if a spark gap is put in series, or a Tesla transformer is inserted ([6]), more intense and less absorbable rays are produced. I found, for instance, in one case that by increasing the spark gap in series the window-number could gradually be brought up from 2.5 to 10.

(These observations prompted me to wonder whether X rays might

---

([5]) A good Deprez interrupter functions more uniformly than a Foucault ap-paratus; the latter, however, utilizes the primary current better.

([6]) That a spark gap connected in series acts similarly to a Tesla transformer I was able to point out in the French edition of my second communication (Archives des Sciences Physiques, etc., de Genève, 1896); in the German publication this comment was omitted by an oversight.

not be obtainable even at still higher pressures by using a Tesla transformer. This is indeed the case. Using a narrow tube with wire-shaped electrodes I could still observe X rays when the pressure of the enclosed air amounted to 3.1 millimeters of mercury. If hydrogen was used instead of air, the pressure could be even higher. I was not able to determine the lowest pressure at which X rays can still be produced in air, but in many instances it lies below 0.0002 millimeter of mercury, so that the range of pressures within which X rays may altogether be produced is already now a very considerable one.)

As a result of further evacuation of the "very soft" tube — connected directly to the induction coil — the radiation becomes more intense, and a larger percentage of it passes through the irradiated material. A hand held in front of the fluorescent screen is more transparent than before, and higher window-numbers are obtained with the platinum-aluminum window. At the same time the spark gap connected in parallel with the tube must be increased in order to let the discharges pass through the tube. The tube has become "harder." If one evacuates the tube still more, it becomes so "hard" that the spark gap must be increased to beyond 20 centimeters; and now the tube emits rays to which the materials are exceedingly transparent. Heavy iron plates, 4 centimeters thick, when viewed with the fluorescent screen, were still found to be transparent.

The behavior of a tube on the mercury pump connected directly to the induction coil, as described above, is normal, but deviations from this norm, caused by the discharges themselves, occur frequently. Sometimes the behavior of the tubes is altogether unpredictable.

We have supposed that the hardening of a tube is produced by continued evacuation with the pump, but it may also occur in a different way. A fairly hard tube, which is sealed off from the pump, will gradually become harder by itself — unfortunately for the duration of its usefulness — even when it is used correctly for producing X rays, that is, when discharges are passed through it which do not or only faintly cause the platinum to glow. A gradual self-evacuation takes place.

With such a tube which had become very hard in this manner, I obtained a most beautiful photographic shadow picture of the double barrels of a shotgun with cartridges in place, in which all the details of the cartridges, the internal faults of the damask barrels, and so on, could be recognized very distinctly and sharply. The distance between the platinum plate of the discharge tube and the photographic plate was 15 centimeters, the time of exposure 12 minutes — comparatively long because of the small photographic effect of the less absorbable rays (see below). The Deprez interrupter had to be replaced by the Foucault interrupter. It would be of interest to construct tubes permitting the use of still higher discharge potentials than has been possible thus far.

The reason for the hardening of a tube which is sealed off from the pump, was given above as self-evacuation caused by discharges. But this is not the only cause. Changes taking place on the electrodes also have the same effect. What they consist of, I do not know.

A tube which has become too hard can be made softer by admitting air, sometimes also by heating the tube, or by reversing the direction of the current, and finally, by sending very strong discharges through it. In the last case, however, the tube has for the most part acquired other properties than those described above. It sometimes requires, for example, a very high discharge potential and yet emits rays of a relatively low window-number and great absorbability. I need not discuss further the behavior of these "non-normal" tubes. The tubes constructed by Herrn Zehnder, which have an adjustable vacuum, since they contain a small piece of charcoal, have been very serviceable to me.

The observations described in this paragraph and others have led me to the conclusion that the composition of the rays emitted from a discharge tube equipped with a platinum anode depends primarily upon the duration of the discharge current. The degree of evacuation, the hardness, plays a part only because the form of discharge current depends upon it. If one can produce that form of discharge which is necessary for the production of X rays by any form whatever, X rays can also be produced even for relatively high pressures.

Finally it is worth mentioning that the quality of the rays produced by a tube is either not at all or only slightly changed when the strength of the primary current is altered considerably, provided that the interrupter functions the same in all cases. On the contrary, the intensity of the X rays is proportional within certain limits to the strength of the primary current, as is demonstrated by the following experiment. The distances from the discharge apparatus at which, in a certain case, the fluorescence of the barium platinocyanide screen was barely noticeable amounted to 18.1 millimeters, 25.7 millimeters, and 37.5 millimeters, when the strength of the primary current was increased from 8 to 16 to 32 amperes. The squares of those distances are in nearly the same ratio as the corresponding current strengths.

9. The results described in the last five paragraphs were obtained directly from the respective experiments mentioned above. If one surveys the whole of these individual results, one reaches, partly guided by the analogy which exists between the behavior of optical rays and X rays, the following conclusions:

(a) The radiation emitted from a discharge apparatus consists of a mixture of rays of different absorbability and of different intensity.

(b) The composition of this mixture depends essentially upon the time relationship of the discharge current.

(c) The rays which are selectively absorbed by various substances differ for different materials.

(d) Since the X rays are produced by cathode rays and since both have common properties — such as production of fluorescence, photographic and electrical effects, and absorbability, the amount of which depends essentially upon the density of the irradiated material, and so on — the hypothesis is at once suggested that both phenomena are processes of the same nature. Without being willing to adhere unconditionally to this view, I may state that the results in the last paragraphs tend to solve one difficulty which was opposed to that hypothesis. This difficulty arises, first, in the great difference between the absorbability of the cathode rays studied by Lenard and that of the X rays and, secondly, in the fact that the transparency of substances for these cathode rays follows a law in relation to the density of the substance other than that for the transparency of X rays.

With respect to the first difficulty, two facts should be considered. (1) We have seen in paragraph 7 that there are X rays varying greatly in absorbability, and we know from the investigations of Hertz and Lenard that the different cathode rays also differ from each other in their absorbabilities. Thus, if the "softest" tube mentioned in paragraph 7 produced X rays whose absorption does not in any way approach that of the cathode rays investigated by Lenard, there exist without doubt X rays of still greater and, on the other hand, cathode rays of still smaller absorbability. It therefore seems entirely possible that in further experiments rays may be found which, as far as their absorbability is concerned, form a link between the one type of ray and the other. (2) We found in paragraph 4 that the thinner the layer of an irradiated substance is, the smaller in proportion is its specific transparency. Consequently, if we had used in our experiments, plates as thin as those of Lenard, we might have found values for the absorption of the X rays which would have been approximately nearer to those of Lenard.

With reference to the different influences of the density of substances upon their absorption of X rays and of cathode rays, it must be stated that this difference is found to be smaller in proportion as more easily absorbable X rays for this experiment are chosen (paragraphs 7 and 8) and as the irradiated plates are made thinner (paragraph 5). Consequently the possibility must be admitted that this difference in the behavior of the two types of radiation, as well as the one mentioned previously, may be made to disappear by further experimentation.

Nearest in their absorbability are the cathode rays, produced especially in very hard tubes, and the X rays, emitted from the platinum tube, in very soft tubes.

10. In addition to exciting fluorescence, X rays also exert, as is well

known, photographic, electrical, and other effects, and it is of interest to know to what degree these run parallel if the source of radiation is altered. I had to confine myself to a comparison of the two first mentioned effects.

The platinum-aluminum window is also very useful for this purpose. One of these was placed upon a wrapped photographic plate, a second was put in front of the fluorescent screen, and then both of them were placed at equal distances from the discharge apparatus. The X rays had to traverse exactly the same media in order to reach the sensitive layer of the photographic plate and the barium platinocyanide. During the exposure I observed the screen and determined the window-number. After the photographic plate was developed, the window-number was also determined on it, and then both numbers were compared. As a result of such experiments no difference was observed when softer tubes were used (window-numbers 4 to 7). When using harder tubes it seemed to me as if the window-number on the photographic plate was slightly lower, but at most one unit, than that determined with the fluorescent screen. However, this observation, although confirmed repeatedly, is still not entirely incontestable, since the determination of the high window-number on the fluorescent screen is rather uncertain.

Absolutely certain, however, is the following result. If with the photometer described in paragraph 2 one adjusts a hard and a soft tube so as to produce equal brightness on the fluorescent screen and if one then substitutes a photographic plate for the screen, one observes, after the plate is developed, that that half which has been irradiated by the hard tube is considerably less darkened than the other half. The radiations which produce equal intensity of fluorescence have different photographic effects.

In evaluating this result one must not fail to consider that neither the fluorescent screen nor the photographic plate completety utilizes the impinging rays. Both transmit many rays that can again produce fluorescence or photographic effects. The result given, therefore, applies only to the thickness of the sensitive photographic film employed and the layer of barium platinocyanide accompanying it.

How very transparent the sensitive layer of the photographic plate is even for X rays from the tubes of average hardness is proved by an experiment in which 96 films, one laid on top of the other, were placed 25 centimeters away from the source of radiation and exposed for five minutes, the whole being protected against radiation from the air by a lead cover. A photographic effect can be clearly recognized even on the last one of them, while the first is scarcely overexposed. Induced by this and similar observations I asked several manufacturers of photographic plates whether it might not be possible to produce plates that would be more adapted to photography with X rays than the ordinary ones. The samples obtained, however, were not serviceable.

I have had many opportunities, as already mentioned in paragraph 8, to notice that very hard tubes require a longer time of exposure than moderately hard ones, under otherwise identical conditions. This is easily understandable if one remembers the result mentioned in paragraph 9, according to which all examined substances were found to be more transparent to rays emitted by hard tubes than to those emitted by soft tubes. That with very soft tubes a long exposure is again required may be explained by the lessened intensity of the rays emitted by them.

If the intensity of the rays is increased by increasing the primary current (see paragraph 9), the photographic effect is increased in the same degree as the intensity of the fluorescence. In this as well as in the case mentioned previously, where the intensity of the radiation of the fluorescent screen was altered by changing the distance of the screen from the source of radiation, the brightness of the fluorescent screen might be, at least approximately, proportional to the intensity of the radiation. This rule, however, cannot be applied generally.

11. In conclusion may I be permitted to mention the following isolated details. In a properly constructed, not too soft, discharge tube the X rays are emitted principally from a point 1 to 2 millimeters large at which the platinum plate is struck by the cathode rays. However, this is not the only point of emission. The whole plate and a part of the wall of the tube emit rays, although to a very small extent. Cathode rays travel from the cathode in all directions, but their intensity is significant only near the axis of the concave mirror, and therefore the most intense X rays are produced at the point where the axis meets the platinum plate. If the tube is very hard and the platinum thin, a considerable quantity of X rays is also emitted from the rear of the platinum plate and, as the pinhole camera shows, from a point also lying on the mirror axis.

Also in these hardest tubes the maximum intensity of the cathode rays can be deflected from the platinum plate by a magnet. Some experiences with soft tubes led me to investigate once more, and with better instruments, the question of the magnetic deflection of X rays. I hope to be able to report on these experiments soon.

I have continued the experiments mentioned in my first communication on the transparency of equally thick plates cut from a crystal according to different directions. Plates of calcite, quartz, tourmaline, beryl, aragonite, apatite, and barite were examined. Again no influence of the direction upon the transparency could be detected, even with the improved apparatus.

The fact observed by G. Brandes that X rays can produce a light sensation in the retina of the eye, I have confirmed. In my observation journal there is also a note written at the beginning of November 1895, according to which I perceived in a completely darkened room near a wooden door, on the other side of which a Hittorf tube was placed, a feeble sensation of light that spread over the whole field of vision when discharges were sent through the tube. Since I observed this phenomenon only once, I thought it was subjective. The reason that I did not see it repeated is because that later on, other and less evacuated tubes without platinum anodes were used instead of the Hittorf tubes. The Hittorf tube, because of its high evacuation, produces rays of small absorbability and because of its platinum anode, which is struck by the cathode rays, produces very intense rays, a condition which favors the production of the sensation of the light phenomenon as mentioned above. I had to replace the Hittorf tubes with others because all of them were punctured after a very short time.

With the hard tubes now in use the Brandes experiment may be easily repeated. A description of the following experimental procedure is perhaps of some interest. If one holds a vertical metal slit, a few tenths of a millimeter wide, as close as possible to the open or closed eye, and if one then holds the head, completely enveloped in a black cloth, near the discharge apparatus, one observes after some practice a weak and not uniformly bright strip of light, which according to the position of the slit in front of the eye has a different shape — straight, curved, or circular. By a slow motion of the slit in a horizontal direction one can progressively make these forms pass into one another. An explanation of this phenomenon is easily found if one considers that the eyeball is intersected by a laminated beam of X rays, and if one assumes that X rays can produce fluorescence in the retina.

Since the beginning of my work with X rays I have made repeated efforts to obtain diffraction phenomena with these rays. Several times when using narrow slits, and so on, I also obtained phenomena whose appearance recalled diffraction patterns, but when the conditions of the experimental arrangements were altered in order to check the correctness of the explanation of these images as being produced by diffraction, it was refuted in every case, and I could directly prove that the phenomena were produced in a manner quite different from diffraction. I have no experiment to describe from which I could, with sufficient certainty, obtain proof of the existence of diffraction of the X rays.

Würzburg, Physikalisches Institut der Universität
10 März, 1897

Genealogy

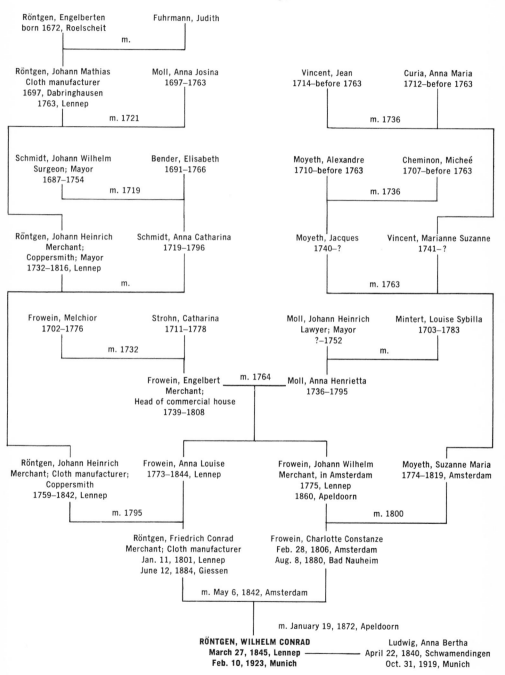

Bibliography

The following abbreviations are used in some of the bibliographic entries to indicate the collection in which a given work is located.

DBF: Deutsche Bibliothek, Frankfurt (copies of all books published in Germany after 1945).

DM: Deutsches Museum Bibliothek, Munich (library of the excellent museum).

DRM: Deutsches Röntgen Museum, Remscheid-Lennep (includes many personal items, thousands of letters, taped reminiscences of acquaintances of Röntgen, private papers and writings pertaining to Röntgen, and a fine technical exhibit of Röntgen-Ray application).

ETH: Eidgenössische Technische Hochschule Bibliothek, Zürich.

GU: Giessen Universität Bibliothek, Giessen.

PI: Physikalisches Institut, Würzburg (private books of Dr. M. Sheer, Director).

RIM: Röntgen Institut, Mainz (at the hospital).

SBF: Senkenbergische Bibliothek of the Stadt- und Universitäts-Bibliothek, Frankfurt (a specialized scientific section).

SM: Staatsbibliothek, Munich (a vast repository of material, not yet wholly restored and assorted after war destruction).

UW: Universität at Würzburg Bibliothek.

ZZ: Zentralbibliothek, Zürich (the Stadt- Kantons- und Universitäts-Bibliothek, with a comprehensive collection of early articles on Röntgen and his discovery).

BOOKS AND PAMPHLETS

Acta des Königlichen Ministeriums für Kirche und Schule (Bavarian State Archives) Hauptstaatsarchiv München, Personalact von Wilhelm Conrad Röntgen (MK 17921). (SM)

Albers-Schönberg, Heinrich Ernst. *Die Röntgentechnik.* Hamburg: Lucas Gräfe & Sillem, 1903. (SM, ZZ)

Baltzer, F. *Theodor Boveri*. Stuttgart: Wissenschaftliche Verlagsanstalt, 1962. (DRM)

Barker, George F. *Röntgen Rays: Memoirs by Röntgen, Stokes, and Thomson*. New York and London: Harper & Brothers, 1899.

Bleich, Alan Ralph. *The Story of X Rays from Röntgen to Isotopes*. New York: Dover Publications, 1960.

Borden, W. C. *The Use of the Roentgen Ray by the Medical Department of the United States Army in the War with Spain*. Washington, D.C.: G.P.O., 1900.

Boveri, Margret. "Wilhelm Conrad Röntgen." In *Die Grossen Deutschen*, Vol. 4. Berlin: Propylaen Verlag, Ullstein, 1957. (GU)

—————. "Persöhnliches über W. C. Röntgen." Chapter in *Wilhelm Conrad Röntgen und die Geschichte der Röntgenstrahlen*, by Otto Glasser. Berlin: Springer Verlag, 1931.

Bruwer, André J., ed. *Classic Descriptions in Diagnostic Roentgenology*. Springfield, Ill.: Charles C Thomas, 1964. (DRM)

Carstensen, R. *Die tödlichen Strahlen*. Kiel: Neumann & Wolff Verlag, 1954.

Dessauer, Friedrich. *Compendium der Röntgenstrahlen*. Leipzig, 1905. (SM)

—————. *Wilhelm C. Röntgen: Die Offenbarung einer Nacht*. Frankfurt a.M.: Josef Knecht Verlag, 1951. (DM, SM)

—————, and B. Wiesner. *Leitfaden des Röntgen-Verfahrens*. Berlin: Vogel & Kreienbrink, 1903. (DM)

Deutsches Röntgen Museum in Remscheid-Lennep. Wuppertal: Kuratorium des Museums, 1952. (ZZ)

Dibner, Bern. *The New Rays of Professor Röntgen*. Norwalk, Connecticut: Burndy Library, 1963. (PI)

Die Universität Giessen von 1607 bis 1907. Giessen: Alfred Töpelmann, 1907. (GU)

Fortschritte der Röntgenforschung in Methode und Anwendung. Die Heidelberger Röntgentagung 1930. Leipzig: Akademische Verlagsgesellschaft, 1931. (DM)

Friedman, Milton; Brucer, Marshall; and Anderson, Elizabeth (eds.). *Roentgens, Rads, and Riddles: A symposium on supervoltage radiation therapy held at the Medical Division, Oak Ridge, Institute of Nuclear Studies, on July 15–18, 1956*. Washington, D.C.: U.S. Atomic Energy Commission, 1959. (ZZ)

Friedrich, Walter; Knipping, Paul; and Laue, Max. *Interferenzerscheinungen bei Röntgenstrahlen*. Leipzig: Johann Ambrosius Barth, 1955. (DM)

Fünfzig Jahre Deutsche Röntgengesellschaft, 1905–1955. Selbstverlag, 1955. (DBF, SM)

Geistiges Deutschland 1902. Berlin-Charlottenburg: Adolf Ecksteins Verlag, 1902. (GU)

Glalitzine, Boris, and von Karnojitzky, Alex. *Ueber die Ausgangspunkte und Polarisation der X-Strahlen*. St. Petersburg, 1896. (ZZ)

Glasser, Otto. "The Human Side of Science." In *The Doctor Writes*, edited by S. O. Waife, New York: Grune & Stratton, 1954.

—————. *Wilhelm Conrad Röntgen und die Geschichte der Röntgenstrahlen* [with a chapter, "Persöhnliches über W. C. Röntgen," by Margret Boveri]. Berlin: Springer Verlag, 1931 (ETH, DM, DRM); 2nd ed., 1959. (DRM)

————. *Wilhelm Conrad Röntgen and the Early History of the Roentgen Rays*. Translation from the German. Springfield, Illinois: Charles C Thomas, 1934.

Grashey, Rudolf, ed. *Fortschritte auf dem Gebiete der Röntgenstrahlen, vereinigt mit Röntgenpraxis* (Holthusen, H.; Haenisch, F.; and Glauner, R., contributors). Deutsche Röntgengesellschaft. Leipzig: Georg Thieme Verlag, 1930; Stuttgart, 1949–1950. (DM)

Hartmann, H. *Wilhelm Conrad Röntgen: Schöpfer des Neuen Weltbildes: Grosse Physiker unserer Zeit*. Bonn: Athenäum Verlag, 1952. (ETH)

Hébert, Alexandre. *La Technique des Rayons X*. Paris: Georges Carré et C. Naud, 1897. (ZZ)

Herold, Gottfried. *Entdeckung neuen Lichtes*. Berlin (East Germany): Rütten & Loening, 1956.

Hjörring, Knut. *Professor Roentgen und die Presse*. Als Manuscript gedruckt (privately printed). (DRM)

Krause, Karl H. *Röntgen, Gedächtnis-Heft*. Jena: Fischer, 1931. (SBF)

Laue, Max von. *Die Interferenzen von Röntgen- und Elektronenstrahlen*. Berlin: Springer Verlag, 1935 (SM)

————. *Röntgenwellenfelder in Kristallen*. Berlin: Akademie Verlag, 1959. (SM)

Lenard, Philipp. *Wissenschaftliche Abhandlungen: Band 3*. Leipzig: S. Hirzel, 1944. (DRM)

Lossen, Heinz. *Wilhelm Conrad Röntgen zum 27. März 1945*. Baden-Baden: Drei-Kreise-Verlag Fritz Knapp, 1948. (DM, SM, RIM)

Miller, John Anderson. *Yankee Scientist, William David Coolidge*. Schenectady, New York: Mohawk Development Service, 1963. (DRM)

Neher, F. L. *Blick ins Unsichtbare*. Reutlingen: Bardtenschlager Verlag, 1956. (DM, SM)

————. *Röntgen, Roman eines Forschers*. Munich: Braun & Schneider, 1936. (ETH, DM)

Nicolle, Jacques. *Wilhelm Conrad Röntgen et l'ere des rayons X*. Paris: 1965 Editions Seghers, 1965. (PI)

Programm der eidgenössischen polytechnischen Schule für das Schuljahr 1865. Zürich: Orell Füssli und Co., 1865–1874. (ZZ)

Referate aus der internationalen Röntgen-Literatur. Hamburg: C. H. F. Müller A. G., 1953. (DM)

Röntgen Atlas der Kriegsverletzungen. Von den leitenden Aerzten des allgemeinen Krankenhauses St. Georg in Hamburg. Hamburg, 1916. (ZZ, RIM)

Röntgenröhren von 1895 bis 1935. Vierzig Jahre Entwicklung. Hamburg: C. H. F. Müller, 1935. (DM, ZZ)

Röntgen, Wilhelm Conrad. *Festrede zur Feier des dreihundert und zwölften Stiftungstages der Julius-Maximilians-Universität, gegeben am 2ten Januar 1894, von Dr. W. C. Röntgen, ö.o. Professor der Physik und zur Zeit Rektor*. Würzburg: Universitätsdruckerei H. Stürtz, 1894. (ZZ)

————. *Grundlegende Abhandlungen über die X-Strahlen*. Medizinische Gesellschaft, Würzburg. Würzburg: Kabitzsch, 1915. (DM, RIM, DBF)

————. *Studien ueber Gase*. (Diss. Phil. Zürich) Zürich, 1896. (ZZ)

Rosenthal, Josef. *Fortschritte in der Anwendung der Röntgenstrahlen*. München: Lehmann, 1906. (DM, SM)

Sagnac, George. *De l'optique des rayons de Röntgen et des rayons second, qui en dérivent.* Paris: Thèse, 1900. (ZZ)

Schimank, Hans. *Nobelpreisträger der Röntgenphysik berichten von ihren Entdeckungen.* Hamburg: C. H. F. Müller A. G., 1951. (DM)

—————. *Wilhelm Conrad Röntgen.* Stuttgart: Mittelbach, 1945. (DM)

Sieper, B. *Der Ruf der Strahlen.* Ein Biographisches Röntgenbildniss. W.-Elberfeld: Hans Putty Verlag, 1946.

Streller, Ernst. *Deutsches Röntgen Museum: Leitfaden durch das Deutsche Röntgen-Museum in Remscheid-Lennep.* Remscheid-Lennep: Selbst-verlag, 1963. (DM)

Unger, Hellmuth. *Wilhelm Conrad Röntgen.* Hamburg: Hoffmann & Campe Verlag, 1949. (DM)

Verzeichnis der Vorlesungen an der königlichen Ludwig-Maximilians-Universität zu München (1895–1910). München: C. Wolf & Sohn, 1895–1910. (SM)

Verzeichnis der Vorlesungen an der Universität Zürich 1865–74. Zürich: Zürcher and Furrer, 1865–74. (ZZ)

Verzeichnisse der Vorlesungen. Ludwig-Maximilians-Universität München (Volumes 1918–1923). München: J. Schön, 1918–1923. (SM)

Walsh, David. *The Röntgen's Rays in Medical Work.* London: Bailliere, Tindall and Cox, 1897. (DRM)

Wölfflin, Ernst. *Meine persöhnlichen Erinnerungen an W. C. Röntgen.* Der Deutschen Röntgengesellschaft zu ihrem 50 jährigen Jubiläum gewidmet. October 16, 1955. (DRM)

Woltereck, Heinz. *Die Welt der Strahlen.* Leipzig: Quelle & Meyer, 1937.

.Wunschmann, E. *Die Röntgen'schen Strahlen.* Berlin: F. Schneider & Co. (H. Klinsmann), 1896: Also Berlin: F. Schmidt & Sohn, 1896. (ZZ, SM)

Würzburger Vorlesungs Verzeichnisse 1881–1900. Würzburg: Thein'sche Druckerei, 1881–1900. (UW)

Zehnder, Ludwig. *Wilhelm Conrad Röntgen's Briefe an L. Zehnder.* Zürich: Rascher & Cie., 1935. (ETH, DM, SM)

—————. *Wilhelm Conrad Röntgen: Lebensläufe aus Franken.* Würzburg, 1930.

—————. *Wilhelm Conrad Röntgen.* Translation of an abstract of *Wilhelm Conrad Röntgen: Lebensläufe aus Franken.* Neuchâtel: Guinchard, 1930. (ETH)

Zeidler, Paul Gerhard. *Wilhelm Conrad Röntgen.* Berlin, 1947 (SM)

Zeuner-Schnorf, Gustav. *Röntgen's Doktorvater in Zürich.* Sonderdruck aus der Technischen Rundschau; Jubiläumsausgabe, Bern, 1958. (ETH)

PERIODICALS

Arnemann, J. L. "Wonder Rays of a Night," *American German Review,* 12 (no. 5, 1951): 17–21. (DM)

Benedikt, Moriz. "Beobachtungen und Betrachtungen aus dem Röntgen-Kabinette," *Wiener medizinische Wochenschrift, 1896 und 1897.* Wien, 1896–97. (ZZ)

Brendler, Wolfgang. "Persöhnliche Erinnerungen an Wilhelm Conrad Röntgen," *Röntgen-Blätter*, 1 (1948): 1–7. (DM)

Bugyi, Balázs. "Zur Geschichte der Röntgenologie in Ungarn, 1896–1916," *Geschichte der Naturwissenschaft*, 1 (no. 3, 1962): 87–114. (DM)

Dam, H. J. W. "The New Marvel in Photography," *McClure's Magazine*, (New York and London) April, 1896.

Debye, Peter. "Röntgen und seine Entdeckung," *Technische Rundschau*, 27 (no. 7, 1935): 21. (DM; SM)

Dessauer, Friedrich. "Erinnerungen aus der Entwicklung der Röntgentechnik," *Röntgen-Blätter*, March, 1956. (DRM)

Donaghey, J. P. "Reminiscences of Röntgen," *Radiography and Clinical Photography*, vol. 10, no. 2, 1934. (SM)

Eiselsberg, A. "Gedächtnisrede auf W. C. Röntgen," *Wiener klinische Wochenschrift*, 36 (1923): 432.

Etter, Lewis E. "Post-war Visit to Röntgen's Laboratory," *American Journal of Roentgenology*, vol. 54, no. 6 (December, 1945). (DRM)

—————. "Some Historical Data Relating to the Discovery of the Roentgen Rays," *American Journal of Roentgenology*, vol. 56, no. 2 (August, 1946). (DRM)

Evers, Gerrit A. "Wilhelm Conrad Röntgen in den Niederlanden," Aus dem Niederländischen übertragen von Dr. Heinz Lossen. P. A. Norstedt & Soner, Stockholm, 1935. *Acta radiologica*, vol. 16, no. 89. (DM)

Färber, Armin. "Das Landhaus Röntgens in Weilheim," *Röntgen-Blätter*, 15 (no. 10, 1962): 338–40. (DM)

Gerlach, Walter. "W. C. Röntgen, der Forscher und sein Werk in der Auswirkung für die Entwicklung der exakten Naturwissenschaften," *Strahlentherapie*, vol. 47, no. 3, 1933. (DM)

Glasser, Otto. "Erinnerungen eines alten Freundes des Deutschen Röntgen-Museums," *Röntgen-Blätter*, 7 (1954): 426.

—————. "Fifty Years of Röntgen Rays," *Radiography and Clinical Photography*, 21 (1945): 58.

—————. "First Observations on the Physiological Effects of Roentgen Rays on the Human Skin," *American Journal of Roentgenology*, 28 (1932): 75.

—————. Röntgen et von Laue; Les Inventeurs Célèbres," *Mazenod*, Paris, 1950.

—————. "Strange Repercussions of Röntgen's Discovery of the X Rays," *Radiology*, 45 (1945): 425.

—————. "The Gift of Wilhelm Conrad Roentgen as Revealed in his Letters," *Scientific Monthly*, 45 (1937): 193.

—————. "The Sixtieth Birthday of the Roentgen Rays," *Bulletin of the Medical Academy of Cleveland*, 9 (1955): 5.

—————. "What Kind of Tube did Röntgen use when he Discovered the X Rays?" *Radiology*, 27 (1936): 138.

—————. "Wilhelm Conrad Röntgen als Physiker," *Röntgen-Blätter*, 5 (1952): 148. (DM)

Günther, P. "Röntgen als Briefschreiber," *Angewandte Chemie*, 50 (1937): 77. (DM)

Henkels, P. "Wilhelm Conrad Röntgen zum Gedenken," *Deutsche Tierärztliche Wochenschrift*, 41 (1933): 81. (DM)

Heuss, Theodor. "Wilhelm Conrad Röntgen," *Physikalische Blätter,* 6 (no. 2, 1950): 49–50. (DM)

Koch, P. P. "Röntgen als Forscher und Mensch," *Zeitschrift der Technischen Physik,* 4 (1923), p. 273.

Köhler, Alban. "Zum Vierteljahrhundert-Jubiläum von Röntgens Entdeckung," *Fortschrift Röntgenstrahlen,* 27 (1921): 654.

Koenig, W. "Gedächtnisrede auf Röntgen," *Fortschrift Röntgenstrahlen,* 32 (1924): 189.

Krause, Paul. "Zum 75. Geburtstage von Wilhelm Conrad Röntgen," *Fortschrift Röntgenstrahlen,* 27 (1920): 448. (DM)

Kuhn, K. "Erinnerungen an die Vorlesungen von W. C. Röntgen und L. Grätz," *Physikalische Blätter,* 18 (no. 7, 1962): 314–16. (DM)

Laue, Max von. "Zum Gedächtnis Wilhelm Conrad Röntgens," *Die Naturwissenschaft,* 33 (no. 1, 1946): 3–7. (DM)

Lenarduzzi, G. "W. C. Röntgen," *Acta Isotopica,* 1 (no. 4, 1962): 331–36. (ETH)

Mosebach, Rudolf. "Wilhelm Conrad Röntgen in Giessen," *Giessener Hochschulblätter der Justus Liebig Universität.* Wilhelm Schmitz Verlag, Giessen, vol. 10, no. 2/4, 1963. (DM, GU)

Pernet, Jean. "Ueber die Röntgen'schen X Strahlen," *Schweizer Bauzeitung,* vol. 27, 1897. (ZZ)

"Personarum Status," *Acta Universitatis Wirceburgensis,* vols. 6-8, 1881–1900. Thein'sche Druckerei, Würzburg. (UW)

Rees, Wilhelm. "Röntgen-Photographien im Jahre 1896," *Röntgen-Blätter,* 2 (1949):174–76. (DM)

Rieder, H. "Glückwünsche und Dankesworte zu Röntgens 70. Geburtstage." *Münchener medizinische Wochenschrift,* 72 (1915): 401.

Rössler, O. "Zur Entdeckung der nach Röntgen benannten Strahlen," *Medizinische Wochenschrift,* München, 16 (1935), 631.

Sarton, G. "The Discovery of X Rays," *Isis,* 26 (1937): 349.

Schimank, Hans. "Die Röntgenstrahlen in der Karikatur," *Rundschau Technischer Arbeit,* 15 (no. 12, 1935): 4. (DM)

Schinz, Hans R. "Röntgen und Zürich," *Acta radiology,* 15 (1934): 562–72. (ETH)

Schmidt, F. "Ueber die von einer Lenard-Fensterroehre mit Platineinsatz ausgehenden Roentgenstrahlen," *Physikalische Zeitschrift,* 36 (1935): 283.

Schoenborn-Remscheid, Siegfried. "Bei Wilhelm Conrad Röntgen daheim und draussen," *Röntgen-Blätter,* 2 (1949): 133–36. (DM)

Schreuss, Hans Th. "Die Stunde der Entdeckung," *Remscheider General-Anzeiger,* October, 1965. (DRM)

————. "W. C. Röntgen, Entdecker neuer Strahlen," Ein kritisches Essay. *Zentralblatt der Sozialversicherung, Sozialhilfe, und Versorgung* (Düsseldorf), 1964. (DBF, DM)

Sommerfeld, Arnold. "Zu Röntgens siebzigstem Geburtstag," *Physikalische Zeitschrift,* 16 (1915): 89. (DM)

Stark, J. "Zur Geschichte der Entdeckung der Röntgenstrahlen," *Physikalische Zeitschrift,* 36 (no. 8, 1935): 280. (DM)

Streller, Ernst. "Beitrag zur Geschichte verschiedener Röntgenbüsten," *Röntgen-Blätter,* 8 (no. 5, 1955): 147–55. (DM)

—————. "Die Schweiz und Wilhelm Conrad Röntgen," *Remscheider General-Anzeiger*, November, 1963. (DRM)

—————. "Hochflut der Zuschriften," *Remscheider General-Anzeiger*, March 1965. (DRM)

—————. "Physikerbriefe in W. C. Röntgens Nachlass," *Röntgen-Blätter*, May, 1965. (SM, DRM)

—————. "Sie würden den blassen Jüngling nicht mehr wiederkennen," *Remscheider General-Anzeiger*, September, 1964. (DRM)

Thurstan-Holland, C. "X Rays in 1896," *Liverpool Medical Chirurgical Journal*, 45 (1937): 61.

Wagner, E. "Röntgen-Gedächtniszimmer in Würzburg," *Fortschrift Röntgenstrahlen*, 31 (1924): 565.

Walther, Kurt. "Ueber die ersten Schritte in Berlin," *Röntgen-Blätter*, October, 1956. (DRM)

Weil, E. "Some Bibliographical Notes on the First Publication of the Roentgen Rays," *Isis*, 29 (1938): 362–65. (DM)

Wien, Max. "Zur Geschichte der Entdeckung der Roentgenstrahlen," *Physikalische Zeitschrift*, 36 (1935): 536.

Wien, Willy. "Röntgen," *Annalen der Physik*, vol. 70, 1923.

Wölfflin, Ernst. "Persönliche Erinnerungen an Wilhelm Conrad Röntgen," *Ciba-Symposium*, 5 (no. 4, 1957): 111–19. (DM)

Zehnder, Ludwig. "Persönliche Erinnerungen an Röntgen," *Acta radiology*, 15 (1934): 557.

—————. "Persönliche Erinnerungen an W. C. Röntgen und über die Entwicklung der Röntgenröhren," *Helvetia Physica acta (Basel)*, 6 (no. 8, 1934): 608–32. (ETH)

—————. "Persönliches über W. C. Röntgen und seine Entdeckung," *Die Umschau*, 39 (no. 13, 1935): 237–41. (DM)

—————. "Röntgen und seine Würzburger Zeit," *Würzburger Universität Almanach*, Vol. 1931–32.

—————. "Ueber Kathoden- und Röntgenstrahlen," *Bericht der Naturforschungsgesellschaft, Freiburg i.B.* (1898).

Zimmern, A. "Röntgen et la decouverte des rayons X," *Presse Medicine*, 22 (1932): 1.

Index